TWILIGHT OF THE SAINTS

COLUMBIA STUDIES IN MIDDLE EAST POLITICS

COLUMBIA STUDIES IN MIDDLE EAST POLITICS

Marc Lynch, Series Editor

Columbia Studies in Middle East Politics presents academically rigorous, well-written, relevant, and accessible books on the rapidly transforming politics of the Middle East for an interested academic and policy audience.

Surviving the Islamic State: Contention, Cooperation, and Neutrality in Wartime Iraq, Austin Knuppe

Mayors in the Middle: Indirect Rule and Local Government in Occupied Palestine, Diana B. Greenwald

Smugglers and States: Negotiating the Maghreb at Its Margins, Max Gallien

The Suspended Disaster: Governing by Crisis in Bouteflika's Algeria, Thomas Serres

Syria Divided: Syria Divided: Patterns of Violence in a Complex Civil War, Ora Szekely

Shouting in a Cage: Political Life After Authoritarian Cooptation in North Africa, Sofia Fenner

Security Politics in the Gulf Monarchies: Continuity Amid Change, David B. Roberts

Classless Politics: Islamist Movements, the Left, and Authoritarian Legacies in Egypt, Hesham Sallam

Lumbering State, Restless Society: Egypt in the Modern Era, Nathan J. Brown, Shimaa Hatab, and Amr Adly

Friend or Foe: Militia Intelligence and Ethnic Violence in the Lebanese Civil War, Nils Hägerdal

Religious Statecraft: The Politics of Islam in Iran, Mohammad Ayatollahi Tabaar

Jordan and the Arab Uprisings: Regime Survival and Politics Beyond the State, Curtis Ryan

Local Politics in Jordan and Morocco: Strategies of Centralization and Decentralization, Janine A. Clark

Protection Amid Chaos: The Creation of Property Rights in Palestinian Refugee Camps, Nadya Hajj

From Resilience to Revolution: How Foreign Interventions Destabilize the Middle East, Sean L. Yom

For a complete list of books in the series, please see the Columbia University Press website.

Twilight of the Saints

THE HISTORY AND POLITICS OF SALAFISM IN
CONTEMPORARY EGYPT

Stéphane Lacroix

Translated by Jeremy Sorkin

Columbia University Press
New York

Columbia University Press
Publishers Since 1893
New York   Chichester, West Sussex

"Le crépuscule des saints" by Stéphane Lacroix © CNRS Éditions, Paris, 2024
Translation © 2025 Columbia University Press
All rights reserved

Library of Congress Cataloging-in-Publication Data
Names: Lacroix, Stéphane, 1978– author.
Title: Twilight of the saints : the history and politics of salafism in contemporary Egypt / Stéphane Lacroix.
Other titles: Crépuscule des saints. English
Description: New York : Columbia University Press, [2025] | Series: Columbia studies in middle east politics | Translation of: Crépuscule des saints. | Includes bibliographical references and index. | Text in English. Translation from French.
Identifiers: LCCN 2024052389 (print) | LCCN 2024052390 (ebook) |
ISBN 9780231215206 (hardback) | ISBN 9780231215213 (trade paperback) |
ISBN 9780231560672 (ebook)
Subjects: LCSH: Salafiyah—Political aspects—Egypt. | Islam and politics—Egypt—History.
Classification: LCC BP195.S18 L3313 2025 (print) | LCC BP195.S18 (ebook) |
DDC 297.2/720962—dc23/eng/20241209

Cover design: Milenda Nan Ok Lee
Cover photo: Sahara Prince/Shutterstock

GPSR Authorized Representative: Easy Access System Europe,
Mustamäe tee 50, 10621 Tallinn, Estonia, gpsr.requests@easproject.com

CONTENTS

ACKNOWLEDGMENTS vii

Introduction: A Grammar Apart 1
1. Battle of the Corpora: The Role of the First Egyptian Salafis 30
2. Egypt After Nasser: A "Salafi Awakening" 65
3. The Salafi Call: Salafism Meets Activism 106
4. Salafism's Ineluctable Ascent Under Mubarak 146
5. Salafism Faces Revolution: The Nour Party and
    Its Rivalry with the Brotherhood 180
6. The Populist Route: Revolutionary Salafism 215
Conclusion: The Fortunes and Misfortunes of Egyptian Salafism 243

NOTES 251
BIBLIOGRAPHY 309
INDEX 327

ACKNOWLEDGMENTS

Social science research is never a solitary endeavor. It would amount to nothing without the goodwill of all those in the field who offer their time: Some give interviews, others share address books or personal libraries, and still others orient (and sometimes even protect) the researcher.

Throughout this journey, I've been able to count on the steadfast support of close friends. I must first give credit where credit is due: to Husam Tammam, whose work in the 2000s brought fresh insight and inspiration to research on political Islam in the Arab world, and who sadly passed away in 2011. *Rahamahu Allah rahmatan wasi'an.* Ahmed Zaghloul, my unwavering, exceptional interlocutor and unrivaled on-the-ground collaborator, also sits at the top of the list. We jointly conducted some of the interviews for this book. The one and only Mahmoud Azab, an illustrious Azhari who taught me at the Institut National des Langues et Civilisations Orientales (INALCO) when I was just twenty, gave me priceless help accessing the inner sanctums of al-Azhar. As a student and a researcher both, I owe him so much. Thanks also to 'Abd al-Rahman Yusuf, Khalid Hamza, 'Abd al-Rahman 'Ayyash, Moaaz Mahmoud, Muhammad Tawfiq, Karim Muhammad, 'Amr 'Izzat, Muhammad 'Affan, 'Amr Magdi, 'Ammar al-Baltagi, Ayman 'Abd al-Rahim, Nawaf al-Qudaymi, and Asmaa el-Ghoul. Without their help and support, this book would never have seen the light of day.

ACKNOWLEDGMENTS

My colleagues and friends from Sciences Po's CERI (Center for International Studies) and beyond—especially from the growing community of scholars of Salafism—broadened my horizons, either at formal seminars or simply over coffee. There are too many to name here, but I want to extend special thanks to Thomas Hegghammer, my longtime intellectual companion, who's been at my side since I first began studying Salafism; to Robin Beaumont, who so carefully reread this manuscript; to Hamit Bozarslan, for all the benevolent support he offered throughout this project; and to Mina, a partner in crime as exacting as she is thought-provoking. Finally, I'd like to honor the memory of Mariam Abou Zahab, a woman to be reckoned with, whom we lost too soon and who—more than anyone else—inspired me to enter this field. This book is for her.

TWILIGHT OF THE SAINTS

INTRODUCTION

A Grammar Apart

> Watching him play, I decide that he's no good at chess. But the game he's playing is checkers.
>
> —CYRIL LEMIEUX, *LE DEVOIR ET LA GRÂCE*

Over just a handful of decades, a movement known as Salafism has thoroughly transformed Sunni Muslim orthodoxy through its burgeoning influence within the Islamic field. The term *Salafism*, often misunderstood, is claimed by movements and individuals with varied (and sometimes contradictory) political orientations. These range from the overt loyalism of ulema who partner with the Saudi monarchy to the bloody jihadism of the Islamic State. All parties, however, agree on several fundamentals: They profess to embody Sunni Islam in its strictest form, excluding both Sufis and followers of the Ash'ari theological school, which pushed for moderate rationalism and remained dominant until the twentieth century. They completely reject non-Sunni schools of Islam, above all Shiism. And they promote social and religious practices that have consolidated into an ultraconservative norm said to be inherited from the earliest Muslims. These fundamentals, corollaries to a normative revolution, have come to distill Sunni faith for a growing number of Muslims—even if the latter don't always apply the principles consistently. In short, Salafism seems to have gained the upper hand in the battle of ideas—a striking turnabout given that, just a few decades back, only a minority of Muslim adherents embraced these interpretations.

Explanations for the rise of Salafism have often wrongly attributed it to a single cause. They tend to foreground the role of Saudi Arabia, which describes its official Islam as Salafi and views itself as the steward of a religious mission. By no means do I intend to deny the influence of Saudi proselytism—especially since the 1970s, when oil profits gave the Saudi Kingdom the means to pursue its goals. But limiting oneself to this explanation would preclude understanding how Salafism, once transplanted, managed to take root, and why it blossomed more in some countries than in others. Emphasizing the transnational character of the Salafi "phenomenon" should not blind us to the very local dynamics that shaped its establishment and success.

First came the local religious entrepreneurs, driven by a genuine ethics of conviction, who played a crucial role in nearly every context.[1] Regimes in the various countries kept shifting strategies, opening a space (though not always by design) for these entrepreneurs. Then, to borrow the words of Pierre Bourdieu, "the logic of the social fields" finished the job by granting religious dynamics a certain degree of autonomy.[2] And this shaped doctrine: Despite claiming to represent an intangible essence, Salafism adapted to the societies where it took root, developing structures of authority tailored to local conditions.

Egypt offers a particularly interesting case study because its political landscape opened up after Hosni Mubarak fell from power, allowing Salafism's appeal (and, more important, its normalization) to be measured at the ballot box. The true surprise of the country's first free elections, held in the fall of 2011, was not the first place won by the Muslim Brotherhood. It was the impressive results of Nour, a Salafi party created just a few months earlier, which took second place with over 25 percent of the votes.

Increasing freedom in the religious field revealed that Salafi devoutness ran deeper than many, especially among the elites, had suspected. And yet they could have understood this just by talking with a sampling of Egyptian Muslims: When I informally surveyed regular Egyptians in 2011 about their views on Sufism and the worship of saints, most respondents said that both violated Islamic principles—while conceding that they sometimes attended a related popular celebration.[3] Asked how women should "ideally" dress, many endorsed the niqab, a full-face veil—while often acknowledging that their wife, sister, or daughter did not wear one.[4] Most of those surveyed did not call themselves Salafi, and a majority did not wear any external symbol of religious observance. But for many, Salafism unconsciously represented the Sunni norm. Had I conducted my survey several decades earlier, these responses would likely have been quite different.

The transformation is all the more noteworthy because Egypt has historically been a bastion of what could be called "traditional Sunni Islam," grounded in the "late Sunni Tradition" (to use Jonathan Brown's term), whose norm became dominant across nearly the entire Sunni world once it crystallized at the turn of the fourteenth century.[5] This "traditional Islam" is the antithesis of all that Salafism aims to promote: It emphasizes Ashʿari theology (and, further east, Maturidi theology, the two being fairly close) as well as the four canonical schools of Islamic law, and it takes a benevolent view of Sufism. In Cairo, this norm was embodied in the prestigious, thousand-year-old mosque-university called al-Azhar, long a center of traditional Islam's worldwide influence—until the institution itself got caught up in the Salafi undercurrents that had begun swirling within (although these never rocked its highest levels).

So how could such a deep religious transformation sweep through Egypt in such a short time? That is the first question this book will tackle, by offering a long-term social history of Egyptian Salafism stretching from its 1920s emergence in Cairo's scholarly circles through to the present era. We will observe how Islamic normativity in Egypt metamorphosed over the twentieth and early twenty-first centuries, examining the individual and collective actors behind the transformation as well as the political and social contexts in which they acted. To this end, I have developed theoretical tools that borrow from several sources: Bourdieu's sociology (because this shift results from a competition, and competitions imply fields—here both political and religious, since the question of orthodoxy ties into both); the theory of social movements, which helps us analyze the collective action of these "normative entrepreneurs" who, with distinct methods specific to their eras, have fought tirelessly since the 1920s to impose their frameworks; and pragmatic sociology, which reminds us that the best way to understand actors is to study their actions and the meaning they ascribe to them. Using these tools, my goal is to explain why (and how) the Salafis have managed—though not without pushback—to impose their understanding of Muslim orthodoxy and orthopraxy, at least at the symbolic level.

Given this project's already ambitious nature, I chose to limit myself to elements at the macro (national) and meso (organizational, group, and community) levels of the transformational process in Egypt. A micro lens that examines how individuals "take in" these changes—participating in and even making them their own through all sorts of everyday actions— would be a welcome complement to my work. That, however, would call for anthropology, a different approach from the one used here. Several such studies already exist, ranging from Saba Mahmood's foundational book *Politics of Piety* to the writings of Samuli Schielke, which focus more specifically on Egyptian Salafism and its ties to Sufism.[6] Also, this project will not study the deeper reasons that might lead a given person—or social group—to Salafism. Nor will I rehash the endless debate on the "socioeconomic roots of Islamism," so often futile because it is framed in terms that deny the very power of ideas.[7] Instead, I have chosen to home in on the ethics of conviction driving those who promote this return to Islam.

A second line of questioning guides this study's narrative: How should we think of the relationship between Salafism—in this case not just a discourse or worldview, but an active movement—and politics? Granted, most Egyptian Salafis maintained a fairly straightforward stance until the 1970s: avoidance of politics that was supplemented, when necessary, with loud declarations of allegiance to whomever was in power at the time. Their position, however, became less clear-cut during that decade, as Salafism began to be influenced by competing Islamic movements. The late 1970s marked a turning point when the first organized, Salafi-identified social movement was formed: the Salafi Call. A little over thirty years later, that same movement would make history by creating the Nour Party, the second-most-powerful political force in Egypt's first democratically elected parliament after the revolution.

Unlike those who would call these shifts doctrinal reversals, this book will try to decrypt the "grammar" of Egyptian Salafism, which is the only way to understand the logic underlying its actors' political choices. This grammatical interpretation will also show how Salafism, once it became virtually hegemonic as a religious norm, could so easily slip through the fingers of those who feel they are its legitimate "grammatical" advocates. The book thus concludes with a look at the "revolutionary Salafism" of Hazim Abu Isma'il, a populist-style Salafi sheikh who, as a political outlier and fleeting presidential candidate in 2012, amassed enormous support and was at one point predicted to win. The chain of events triggered in 2011 has allowed us to gauge the paradoxical effects of Salafism's religious

INTRODUCTION

"success": Having become the standard, it was destined to be appropriated by many actors who disagree on its meaning. This growing competition paralleled its politicization, which itself called into question Salafism's claim to doctrinal purity. All this helps explain the movement's recent decline, however relative, in Egypt.

UNDERSTANDING SALAFISM

Salafism, or *salafiyya*, is a complex subject to study, especially from a long-term perspective. The word refers to both a discourse—the unique Salafi take on a specific corpus of texts—and the movement that championed it, driven by a distinct "grammar of action." In this work I embrace a linguistic metaphor: Salafism is words that form a language, which is in turn brought to life through a grammar. A linguistic metaphor has already been employed by François Burgat, who sees *Islamism* (a term I do not apply here to Salafism) primarily as a form of "Muslim speech" that does not, he clarifies, prescribe a "mode of Muslim action," which depends heavily on context.[8] I would suggest instead that there are various forms of "Muslim speech" that tend to have corresponding "modes of action," although the finer points of these modes are sometimes debated.

As for how it's discussed, we can apply Michel Foucault's concepts to Salafism: It is a "regime of truth" defined by "the types of discourse it harbours and causes to function as true; the mechanisms and instances which enable one to distinguish true from false statements; the way in which each is sanctioned; the techniques and procedures which are valorised for obtaining truth; the status of those who are charged with saying what counts as true."[9] The Salafi regime of truth provides an epistemic norm for thinking about Islam and, more broadly, for "organizing" the world. Having begun as a theological approach, Salafism gradually became an "all-encompassing" discourse during the twentieth century, which its followers tended to view as "scientific" (*'ilmi*) in both the traditional and modern senses of the term. The discourse offered a set of rules and a well-defined corpus as tools for understanding all that exists. And yet what set it apart from other similarly intentioned discourses is that it drew (albeit selectively) from a long history: that of Islam.

A first stumbling block here is that not everyone agrees on what *Salafism* means. In the definition most widely accepted by its contemporary champions, the term refers to the Islam of the Quran and of the sunna as they were understood by *al-salaf al-salih*, the "pious ancestors"—in other words, by the earliest generations of Muslims.[10] According to this interpretation, identifying as Salafi means advocating for a return to Islam's roots—and to the letter of its scriptures. Such an understanding, however, poses two major problems. First, it seems to view "reformism" (or "Islamism") and "Salafism" as synonymous, even though it is crucial to distinguish the religious—and especially theological—corpora from which the various Muslim reform movements drew. The second problem, which Henri Lauzière points out, is a historiographic one centering on the individuals and movements with which Salafism is associated. While references to the *salaf* are common in Muslim religious literature, the terms *salafi* and *salafiyya* are not found in holy texts; their meanings evolved (not without controversy) in parallel with Islamic tradition. As Lauzière demonstrates, while certain medieval ulema who followed Hanbali theology were already referring to themselves as *salafi* and calling their theological stance the "doctrine of the *salaf*" (*madhhab al-salaf*), the concept of *salafiyya* as a movement and established intellectual framework didn't appear until the twentieth century, and its meaning fluctuated at first.[11]

According to some early twentieth-century Islamicists like Louis Massignon—whose theories were extensively cited over the following decades, becoming a true historiographical doxa—a modernization-inspired Salafism took shape in the late nineteenth century. It aimed to facilitate a political resurgence in the Muslim world by reconciling Islam with modern European achievements through a return to its roots. While certain proponents of this synthesis—most important, Muhammad 'Abduh—never adopted the term themselves, others, such as 'Allal al-Fasi of Morocco, did later proclaim themselves followers of the *salafiyya* (likely, Lauzière says, due to an unwitting repetition of Massignon's historiographical error).[12] From the 1960s, usage of the term *salafiyya* to designate a modernization movement has fallen out of practice in the Muslim intellectual world and today is confined to academic circles.[13]

The modernizing "interlude" poses the greatest barrier to categorization, as it represents such a break with the earlier and later meanings of *salafi*.[14] Before and after this period, *salafi* referred to an ideal of religious purity, with an emphasis on theology seen through the lens of a specific religious corpus. During the interlude, the term could also refer to an entirely different undertaking: political revitalization at a time when virtually all the Muslim world was experiencing Western colonization. The push for political revival and the quest for religious purity thus represent two distinct poles of thought and action. Many of those who until the mid-twentieth century called themselves "reformists" (*islahiyyun*: advocates of *islah*, or reform) sat somewhere between the two poles, although each also had its official representatives. In the case of religious purity, the organization Ansar al-Sunna al-Muhammadiyya—to which most of the first chapter will be devoted—played this role in Egypt starting in the late 1920s. And while both poles engaged in the same Kulturkampf,[15] each followed its own logic: For proponents of political revival, religion was above all an identity and a means; for those who championed the ideal of religious purity, it was an end in itself.

In the Egyptian context, this book's focus, I have chosen to reserve *Salafism* for the message of the standard-bearers of religious purity, and for the movement that developed around them beginning in the 1920s. As for the political revivalists, whether they called themselves *Salafis* (during the "modernizing interlude" mentioned earlier) or were referred to as such by certain Islamicists, I will use *modernizing reformism* to describe their school of thought. In so doing, I do not claim to recount the historical truth of Salafism, nor do I wish to imply that it is a rigid category. Quite the opposite: It has evolved and become more complex throughout the twentieth century, as this study will show. But it is possible to sketch out some relatively stable fundamentals that underpinned this evolution.

SALAFISM AS A NORMATIVE DISCOURSE AND IDEAL OF RELIGIOUS PURITY

Our first task, then, must be to examine the discourse that anchors the ideal of religious purity promoted by Salafism in 1920s Egypt, when the movement first took an organized form. This ideal was primarily defined in theological terms and drew from several lines of thinking, each an outgrowth of the Hanbali theological school.[16] It took shape primarily in opposition: Adversaries were denounced for their blameworthy innovations (*bid'a*), which ran counter to the orthodoxy Salafism professed to embody. And Salafi adherents considered themselves the "saved sect" (*al-firqa al-najiyya*)—meaning the only group that is guaranteed salvation (*al-najat*)—in accordance with a hadith where the Prophet Muhammad declares: "My community will split into 73 sects: One will enter Paradise and 72 will enter Hell."

A Question of Orthodoxy: Theological Hanbalism and Its Repercussions

At the heart of Salafism lies the question of creed (*'aqida*), which sparked major debates during the ninth and tenth centuries that sowed conflict between several theological schools. One, the Mu'tazila, encouraged the use of speculative theology (*kalam*), inspired by Greek philosophical concepts, to define the fundamentals of Muslim belief. But the Hanbalis, disciples of Ahmad Ibn Hanbal, called for sticking to the texts—the Quran and the sunna—and nothing else. As they saw it, the lens of reason could only distort the word of God, which should be accepted just as it is. The Mu'tazila-Hanbali disagreement took a political (and violent) turn in the ninth century when various caliphs sided first with the former, then with the latter.

In the tenth century the Ash'ari school appeared, often described as a synthesis of its two predecessors. Named after Abu al-Hasan al-Ash'ari (865–935), its founding thinker, the school's followers believed that—while the understanding of Muslim dogma should be based in the texts alone, without the intervention of reason—theological reasoning remained lawful as long as it did not challenge the fundamentals of the faith. As an example, adherents of the Ash'ari school allowed themselves, within certain limits, to interpret (*ta'wil*) the divine attributes, an idea rejected outright by the Hanbalis.

Bit by bit, the Ash'ari school evolved into the embodiment of Sunni orthodoxy and came to be taught at the most prestigious religious universities, including al-Azhar in Cairo. The great Ash'ari thinker Abu Hamid al-Ghazali (1035–1111), who was dubbed the "Proof of Islam" (*hujjat al-islam*), emerged as the theological reference point. The practice of Sufism expanded, basing its legitimacy in al-Ghazali's writings. With their connection to one of the four canonical schools of Islamic law, Sufism and Ash'arism formed the foundation of what Jonathan Brown calls the "late Sunni tradition."[17] Its variations would spread to nearly all the Sunni world, eventually coming to epitomize Sunni religious normativity until the twentieth century. Mu'tazilism, having been dragged through the mud, declined sharply. Debates about creed became rare.[18]

Although reduced to a minority standing, theological Hanbalism managed to survive in the scholarly circles of cities like Damascus and Baghdad. And indeed in 1263, five years after Baghdad fell to the Mongols, a man was born who would offer the Hanbali theological school its finest expression: Ahmad Taqi al-Din Ibn Taymiyya, who grew up in Damascus. Invoking the wisdom of the pious ancestors (*salaf*) to refute the model of orthodoxy then dominant, he defined the dogma of divine oneness (*tawhid*), central to Muslim faith, as two inseparable elements: the belief in only one God (*tawhid al-rububiyya*) and the conviction that there cannot be any other object of worship than Him (*tawhid al-uluhiyya*).

Four centuries later, this was the tradition to which Muhammad bin 'Abd al-Wahhab (1703–1792)—born to a family of Hanbali legal scholars in the Najd region, in the heart of the Arabian Peninsula—dedicated himself, going so far as to make Ibn Taymiyya his spiritual mentor.[19] Ibn 'Abd al-Wahhab was thus a trailblazer in the rediscovery of Ibn Taymiyya, a trend that would captivate Islamic reformers in the latter half of the nineteenth century. These intellectuals' newfound interest marked a major shift whose significance should not be underestimated. Scorned by "traditional Islam," which had crystallized under the Ottoman Empire, Ibn Taymiyya had been all but forgotten, along with most of his students. Many of his works were lost; any rare mentions in Ottoman-era texts simply mocked him.[20] In late nineteenth-century Ottoman society, "Ibn Taymiyya's name still carried such a stigma that reasonable public discussion of his views was impossible."[21]

Ibn 'Abd al-Wahhab argued that the *tawhid* included the same two inseparable elements as his mentor had, while making explicit a third, already implicit in Ibn Taymiyya's writings: the belief that God was one with His name and His attributes (*tawhid al-asma' wa-l-sifat*), and that these were not open to interpretation.[22]

Let's take a closer look at the significance of these elements. Of the three, *tawhid al-rububiyya* was the most settled. All Muslims agreed that belief in divine oneness was a must. The two other elements—or rather the conclusions drawn from them by Ibn Taymiyya and later Ibn 'Abd al-Wahhab—were more controversial. The *tawhid al-uluhiyya* is understood as follows: Believing in God is not enough to make a person Muslim; one must worship *only* Him. This critique took aim at certain widespread practices in popular, Sufi-inspired Islam, including the adoration of saints and belief in their intercession. The Shia, "guilty" of committing associationism (*shirk*) because they worship the Imams (Ali and his descendants), were also targeted by Ibn Taymiyya, Ibn 'Abd al-Wahhab, and their followers. The latter referred to the Shia as *rafida* (a pejorative meaning "rejectors") because they are accused of rejecting the legitimacy of the first caliphs. Finally, the *tawhid al-asma' wa-l-sifat* is intended as a rebuttal of theological rationalism, an unmistakable distaste for which came across in Ibn Taymiyya's works. Criticism was primarily leveled at the Ash'ari doctrine, which allows for interpreting the divine names and attributes within certain limits.

But the denunciation of Ash'arism didn't stop there: Another major point of disagreement, with significant implications, involved the connection between faith (*al-iman*) and action (*al-a'mal*). Most Ash'aris were open to the general principle that faith and action could differ to a degree, which ensures that "bad actions" cannot invalidate faith and turn those who commit them into unbelievers.[23] But Ibn Taymiyya, like Ibn 'Abd al-Wahhab and his successors, saw faith and action as inextricably linked: A bad action could, in some cases, exclude its perpetrator from the Muslim community.[24] As an example of this distinction, Ash'aris would be much more inclined to consider that Muslims who maintain their faith are still Muslim even if they do not complete their five daily prayers.

Ibn 'Abd al-Wahhab did not just reiterate Ibn Taymiyya's theories; he added his own layer of interpretation, adapted to the specific context in which he produced his work.[25] In 1744 he formed an alliance with Muhammad bin Sa'ud, and the two ended up coleading a military expansion campaign—a jihad—from which the first Saudi state would be born. A logical binary emerged: Ibn 'Abd al-Wahhab deemed "Muslim" those who submitted to his authority and that of Ibn Sa'ud, and "infidel" those who opposed them, with the Ottomans at the top of the list.[26] We see more rigidity and a greater taste for anathema in Ibn 'Abd al-Wahhab's writings than in those of Ibn Taymiyya, where these more often remained abstract.[27]

Ibn 'Abd al-Wahhab felt the society of Najd—where saint worship and "superstitions" abounded, according to Saudi chronicles—had regressed to a state of *jahiliyya*, or pre-Islamic ignorance.[28] Christians and Jews, though, rarely appear in Ibn 'Abd al-Wahhab's writings. He lived prior to European colonialism, and in an area devoid of both. Similarly, shari'a—which would stir up Muslim intellectuals starting in the nineteenth century—was not really a matter of controversy: Ibn 'Abd al-Wahhab, like all his contemporaries, took it for granted, since the intrusion of European positive law had not yet called into question its status as a norm. His battle, centered entirely on creed, was internal to Islam and aimed to restore the religion to his vision of orthodoxy.

The work of Ibn 'Abd al-Wahhab would be carried on by his successors in the Wahhabi school, whose writings followed the vicissitudes of the Saudi state. In 1818, as Egyptian invaders (commissioned by the Ottomans) besieged the Saudi capital al-Dir'iyya, the expression *al-wala' wa-l-bara'* (loyalty and disavowal) came to the fore. Coined by Sulayman bin 'Abdallah, grandson of Ibn 'Abd al-Wahhab, the term systematized the binary already found in his grandfather's writings: Wahhabis, the *only* true Muslims, shared a bond of loyalty, and those who opposed them were infidels. Any resemblance to such unbelievers was to be erased, and in this particular case the "infidels" were to be fought to the death.[29] This principle of loyalty and disavowal became one of the doctrinal trademarks of Wahhabism.

Remember that until the twentieth century—as long as the Sufis and Ash'aris had the upper hand—a vanishingly small minority subscribed to such ideas. Theological Hanbalism admittedly enjoyed a slight upswing in Ibn Taymiyya's time: He formed a small group of students who carried on his work, including Ibn Qayyim al-Jawziyya (also called Ibn al-Qayyim, 1292–1350), Shams al-Din al-Dhahabi (1274–1348) and Ibn Kathir (1300–1373).[30] But their writings, as well as those of Ibn Taymiyya, quickly fell into relative obscurity. The founding in 1744 of the Saudi state, which adopted Ibn 'Abd al-Wahhab's doctrine as its official Islam, inspired just a minor rediscovery of Ibn Taymiyya's theses, at least outside of the Arabian Peninsula; Ottoman Empire propaganda presented the Najdi sheikh as a heretic.[31] Only in the mid-nineteenth century would a massive rekindling of interest in the Damascene scholar spread to the religious circles of Damascus and Baghdad, during a profound crisis in the Muslim world not unlike the one that shook Ibn Taymiyya's era, which was marked by Mongol invasions and the Abbasid Caliphate's demise. While most who read this erudite, prolific writer at the time did not reduce him to his theological Hanbalism, this interpretation did begin to catch on among members of these circles like Syrian scholar Jamal al-Din al-Qasimi or Iraqi scholars Mahmud Shukri and Nu'man Khayr al-Din al-Alusi.[32]

INTRODUCTION

These theological influences—primarily from the schools of Ibn Taymiyya and Ibn ʿAbd al-Wahhab, with their unique nuances—underpinned the movement for religious purification that I refer to as Salafism, which grew in Egypt starting in the 1920s. As in neighboring Saudi Arabia, the Salafis developed a corpus that distinguished them radically from the then-dominant traditional Islam. The body of works grew during the twentieth century, as the unearthing of classic authors allowed the Salafis to "enlist" new sources. Together, these built the bedrock for what Alasdair MacIntyre calls a "tradition," meaning "an argument extended through time in which certain fundamental agreements are defined and redefined in terms of two kinds of conflict: those with critics and enemies external to the tradition who reject all or at least key parts of those fundamental agreements, and those internal, interpretative debates through which the meaning and rationale of the fundamental agreements come to be expressed and by whose progress a tradition is constituted."[33]

The Salafi corpus thus included, first and foremost, the works of Ibn Taymiyya—referred to deferentially as the "Sheikh of Islam" (*Shaykh al-islam*)—and of his students, primarily Ibn Qayyim al-Jawziyya and the exegete and historian Ibn Kathir. Also incorporated were books by medieval Hanbali authors like Ibn Hanbal (780–855) and Ibn al-Jawzi (1116–1201), as well as the work of Yemeni scholar Muhammad al-Shawkani (1759–1839), who was Ibn ʿAbd al-Wahhab's junior by a few decades. And the Saudi Wahhabi authors held a prized place in the corpus from the very beginning; they included Ibn ʿAbd al-Wahhab, ʿAbd al-Rahman bin Hasan Al al-Shaykh, and Sulayman bin Sahman, to name a few. One might even say that this last group carried an outsize influence, as Egyptian Salafis tended to read Ibn Taymiyya and his students as the Wahhabis had, emphasizing the theological questions—even though, as I have noted, there were other possible interpretations of Ibn Taymiyya.[34] For instance, certain modernizing reformists also favored his texts, more entranced by the image of a rebel rising against tradition than by his religious intransigence.[35]

Orthopraxy: A Secondary Matter of Increasing Importance

While the idea of orthodoxy (meaning the right creed) was paramount for Ibn ʿAbd al-Wahhab from the start, orthopraxy—"proper practice" as derived from *fiqh* (Islamic jurisprudence), a discipline seldom emphasized in Ibn ʿAbd al-Wahhab's writings—played an increasingly important role with the rise of the Saudi State.[36] Among non-Saudi Salafis, it still took a back seat to creed during the first half of the twentieth century, at which point this began to change, as we will see in Egypt.

The Salafis' theoretical stance on fiqh—which paralleled that of Ibn Taymiyya and Ibn ʿAbd al-Wahhab—is that any legal opinion must be based only on the Quran, the sunna, and the consensus of the pious ancestors. Accordingly, they do not push one legal school over another (not explicitly, anyway) and even advocate a certain degree of emancipation from the schools' traditionally rigid framework, as the sole authority lies in direct proof (*dalil*) from the Islamic scriptures.[37] Over the second half of the twentieth century, Muhammad Nasir al-Din (known as Nasir al-Din) al-Albani would take this approach to its logical extent, attacking the very principle of adhering to legal schools (*tamadhdhub*).

And yet, with few exceptions, Salafi legal practice either closely aligns to the Hanbali school (as is the case for the Wahhabis) or resembles a neo-Hanbali approach, as in Ibn Taymiyya's case.[38] What distinguishes the approaches is that the Hanbalis stick to the opinions delivered within the eponymous legal school, whereas the neo-Hanbalis allow themselves to contradict the school while still applying Hanbali-like exegetical methods, known for their literalism and accompanying deep suspicion of any rationalizing interpretation. Salafis also routinely apply the legal principle of "blocking the means" (*sadd al-dharaʾiʿ*), which allows for a religiously lawful practice to be forbidden if it can lead to actions that conflict with Islam.[39]

On a day-to-day level, this means that the Salafis openly strive to model their behavior strictly on the traditions of the Prophet Muhammad and the first generations of Muslims, by eschewing the "blameworthy innovations" (*bidʿa*) of their contemporaries. They often draw inspiration from Saudi society, the template for which was institutionalized in the 1920s when ʿAbd al-ʿAziz Al Saʿud began building modern Saudi Arabia. This propagated various practices that gradually became Salafism's external hallmarks. Among other mandates, Ibn ʿAbd al-Wahhab's Saudi disciples require women to wear the niqab; any mingling between the sexes is prohibited; men grow scruffy beards with no mustache, like the Prophet, and their garments never hang below the ankles; and music and images—especially of people—are prohibited.

INTRODUCTION

In Egypt, it was paradoxically a group whose creed differed (at least initially) from the Salafis that first insisted on some aspects of this orthopraxy: the Jam'iyya Shar'iyya, founded in 1912, which I will discuss later in more detail. The Ansar al-Sunna organization, meanwhile, mostly devoted itself to promoting the Salafi creed (after all, creed is the focal point of Salafism), while putting less weight on orthopraxy—even regarding its own members' customs. Only in the 1960s would a synthesis come about between orthodoxy and orthopraxy, partly resulting from the two movements' temporary fusion in 1967; this, too, will be discussed in more detail later. In parallel, the orthopraxy advanced by the Jam'iyya Shar'iyya would increasingly resemble that encouraged by Salafism—for example, on the question of gender mixing, which would no longer be tolerated.

SALAFISM AS A MOVEMENT

Salafism is not just a discourse about imposing norms and ideals. The term also designates the movement that developed to promote this concept of religious purity. While there may be some resemblance to other religious or Islamist movements, its unique grammar of action—which I later describe as purist—puts it in a league of its own.

Salafism and Social Movements

Many studies published over the past three decades have suggested thinking of religious movements as social movements, using the analytical tools developed for the latter. Since the mid-2000s, Islamic activism has often been studied through such a lens. Rather than seeing Islamist movements as the static expression of a "Muslim rage," this meant identifying their organized and strategic dimensions and their adaptiveness to shifting political contexts. According to its proponents, such an analytical approach was better because it "deorientalized" the Islamist movements by "pointing to commonalities shared with other social movements."[40]

In our specific case, the theory of social movements offers other advantages. First, it reminds us (as do Mayer Zald and John McCarthy, among others) that a social movement only develops through the efforts of "entrepreneurs of the cause"—or, in the case of Salafis, what I call "normative entrepreneurs."[41] This term echoes the "rule creators" discussed by Howard

Becker in *Outsiders*, one category of his "moral entrepreneurs." The rule creator, who is clearly distinguished from the "rule enforcer," "is interested in the content of rules," Becker explains. "The existing rules do not satisfy him because there is some evil which profoundly disturbs him. He feels that nothing can be right in the world until rules are made to correct it. He operates with an absolute ethic; what he sees is truly and totally evil with no qualification."[42] Much like the movements Becker studied, the Salafi normative entrepreneurs tend to use categories of "deviance" (*inhiraf*) to discredit their adversaries.

In Egypt, Salafi normative entrepreneurs first appeared in the 1920s when the initial groups of Salafi propagandists took shape. They would eventually pool their resources to build infrastructure that would maximize their impact, as we see in the establishment of Ansar al-Sunna al-Muhammadiyya in 1926 and the Salafi Call in the late 1970s. The agency of these entrepreneurs played a critical role in the movement's rise; understanding this helps us sidestep an illusory structural explanation (specifically, a geopolitical reading of Egyptian Salafism's rise that would see Saudi Arabia at the controls with its supposedly unstoppable proselytism).

It is true that these entrepreneurs were so successful partly because they were able to mobilize resources, both symbolic and material, early on. This is where Saudi Arabia stepped into the picture, offering financial support that was modest at first before increasing in the 1970s. And given its standing as a religious landmark—it is known as the "Land of the Two Holy Mosques"—the country also served as a powerful symbolic resource. With time, however, the Salafis refined their capacity for producing both types of resource locally: They attracted the support of wealthy Egyptians sympathetic to their ideas, and they established themselves as religious authorities independent of the Saudis. Their rhetoric evolved as well, at least partially distinguishing itself from the Saudi version, if only because a discourse must be framed for its target society.[43]

Finally, the theory of social movements encourages studying the "structure of political opportunities" on which the Salafi mobilization relied, which is central to this book's argument:[44] The Salafis managed to prosper from the various regimes' hostility toward their religious competitors and/or the latter's moments of weakness, while themselves dodging the worst repression by the authorities. As counterintuitive as it may seem, we will observe how President Gamal Abdel Nasser's policies of eliminating the

Brotherhood and taming the institutions of official Islam partly helped launch the ineluctable ascent of Salafism, which began as the 1960s drew to a close.

Salafism as Grammar of Action

Around twenty years ago, an emerging research field began to see Salafism as a unique social and religious movement. Until then, the terms *Islamism* or *political Islam* had been used—often undiscerningly—to identify any Islam-inspired conservative reformism, which sometimes obscured the major differences between the movements they were used to describe. These distinctions fall into several categories, starting with the various movements' religious foundations: As we saw earlier, Salafis have their own set of religious references that differ from those of the Muslim Brotherhood; the latter mostly draws from the dominant Sunni tradition.

Even more than their religious vision, Salafis' "grammar of action" sets them apart from other movements often labeled Islamist. Since the 1970s Salafis have used their own term, *manhaj*, to describe what their anglo- and francophone adherents imperfectly translate as "methodology," which mirrors the concept of grammar of action as it is used in this book. I borrow this notion, conceived of "within the realm of the action itself," from pragmatic sociology, where it has been developed by Luc Boltanski, Laurent Thévenot, and, more recently, Cyril Lemieux. "Grammar," explains Lemieux, "refers to the set of rules that the actors tend to respect in their practice."[45] In his book *Le devoir et la grâce*, he judges this concept "likely to improve our ability (which is already surprisingly substantial) to understand human actions that play out in lifestyles very different from our own," allowing researchers—in the spirit of comprehensive sociology, a system of interpretation that brings them as close as possible to the actors—"to better describe what makes a human activity intelligible and relevant for the participants themselves" by focusing on the "positive meaning" that the actors give their action.[46]

Returning to the linguistic metaphor, I suggest that the grammar pulls its praxis from the text—it turns words into actions. This bond between text and grammar should not be oversimplified. It's a construct, but it gains a certain stability over time, beginning when it's internalized by the actors—although even "when their behavior aligns with the rules," Lemieux reminds us not to assume that their "explicit goal at the time is necessarily to follow them."[47] Most important, the connection is constantly reinforced by those who hold authority over the text and consider themselves its guardians. Any self-respecting Salafi sheikh believes that there exists one—and only one—legitimate grammar of action (which he calls *al-manhaj al-salafi*), whose authority comes from the text. And that sheikh would not hesitate, as soon as he saw a fellow self-proclaimed Salafi committing a "grammatical error" (which he would call *al-inhiraf ʿan al-manhaj*), to roundly condemn it. For the researcher, these denunciations of grammatical errors are themselves important heuristic moments because they bring the shared grammar to the surface. They may also engender a grammatical evolution—for example, when the increasing frequency of some "errors" leads to increasing tolerance of them. When the first Salafi sheikhs appeared on television in the late 1990s, fellow Salafis vehemently denounced them because it implied taking part in a medium that broadcasts images of human beings. That was until most Salafi sheikhs started to do the same, understanding the immense potential television offered for preaching. Whatever the Salafis themselves might often say, grammar is thus not an immutable object, and it can simultaneously produce and undergo societal change.

Let's take a moment to clear up any confusion. A grammar of action is *not* a series of well-established rules, forever set in stone within an authoritative text. Rather, it is rules that have taken precedence over time but remain subject to debate, and whose practical implications are often even more controversial. We might find theoretical presentations of such rules in certain texts, but this says nothing about how they are actually applied. I would venture that, rather than clarifying the grammar, the diversity of discourses often helps obscure it—especially because, depending on the audience, the truth is sometimes left unsaid (or left incomplete, or its implications are ignored). A grammar of action, then, is best understood by studying practices—as Lemieux does—and not by dissecting texts.

A grammar, as one will have understood, is not the equivalent of Bourdieu's habitus, particularly because it has a strategic dimension—although a grammar *can* produce a habitus when it stabilizes. Nor is it an imaginary (the collection of images and concepts through which a group defines reality), again because it is action-oriented. Finally, it is not a repertoire of collective action as per Charles Tilly, because this would imply a concrete list of existing practices from which a movement can draw, whereas grammar takes on a more abstract dimension.[48] A grammar can, however, help create a repertoire of action in a given situation.

For observers to understand a grammar foreign to them, Lemieux explains, there are two possible approaches. That of the ethnologist involves "endeavoring to live like the people one is studying.... With this understanding, one can avoid actions that [the subjects] see as wrong—a skill that allows 'their rules' to be stated and described within one's own language games." The historian's method, on the other hand, consists of "studying and comparing the physical traces they left behind, to understand the positive meaning of their various approaches to judging and acting."[49] This book employs both techniques, drawing from my three years of ethnographic field work in Egypt—most of it within Egyptian Salafi milieus—as well as from a detailed analysis of written and oral sources.

Earlier I identified two distinct "poles of thought and of action" among the early twentieth-century Egyptian reformists: those who prioritized political revival, and those who saw religious purification as the only path to renewal. Even though its members were more conservative than some of their mentors (such as Muhammad 'Abduh), the Muslim Brotherhood became the principal heir to the first school of thought starting in the late 1920s. The second school crystallized as the nascent Salafi movement, represented at first by Ansar al-Sunna al-Muhammadiyya, founded two years before the Brotherhood. From the outset, this duality translated into two very distinct grammars of action.

The ultimate goal of Islamist grammar, embodied by the Brotherhood, was to take and exercise power in order to establish the "Islamic State," meaning a state that implements shari'a. Granted, this had to happen—as Hasan al-Banna, founder of the Brotherhood, explained—through reform of the individual, reform of the family, and reform of society, and thus by expanding the organization's sphere of influence.[50] But all these efforts made sense only because they were oriented toward a fundamentally political objective. To this end, the Brotherhood inserted itself into every realm of society: unions, associations, and—starting in the 1940s—institutional politics. In its original plan, this approach was thought of as reformist and peaceful.[51] The Brothers believed that the current societal or governmental reality could be transformed by gradually acting within the existing political system (as long as it allowed them to). They were not revolutionary by nature.

The Brothers mostly saw Islam as an identity, a tool for returning society to its "natural" political and social order. The organization certainly pushed for a degree of conservatism, but it was mostly unconcerned with disputes between theological or even legal schools. Even the Islamic State concept was subjected to relatively little theoretical discussion because detailing it risked sowing discord. Rather than dividing Muslims on religious questions, the idea was to unite them around a shared political objective—which explains why the Brothers long refrained from railing against the Sufis and the Shia. Such denunciation is now more common within the Brotherhood (or at least at its fringes), a reflection of Salafism's later influence.

During the 1950s and 1960s, and at the intellectual impetus of Sayyid Qutb, a revolutionary variation emerged of the Islamist grammar embodied in the Brotherhood. It adopted most of the same fundamentals—particularly the desire to move beyond theological questions in the strict sense, with politics taking precedence—while advocating for a violent overthrow of the government. A small group of Brothers had first forayed into this mode of action (without conceptualizing it) in the late 1940s. Brought together in a "Special Apparatus" (*al-nizam al-khass*), they tried their hands at political violence as tensions were mounting in Egypt. I will refer to this form of Islamist grammar as "jihadi grammar." Starting in the 1990s, the jihadis expanded their list of proclaimed enemies to include the United States and its Western allies. From that point on, the debate would be between those focused on fighting the "near enemy" and those with their sights on the "far enemy."

The Salafi grammar that emerged starting in the 1920s was just the opposite: completely centered on the idea of religious purity. That is why I refer to it as purist in this study and distinguish it clearly from the "Islamist" grammar. Salafis worked to return Islam to its lost authenticity by promoting their religious normative framework via every channel seen as "religiously permissible" (*halal*): publication, teaching, preaching, and so on. On the other hand, they felt that any method that might dilute the purity of the message should be forbidden. As I mentioned earlier, the central issue was creed—even if the question of orthopraxy was garnering new interest, especially in the second half of the twentieth century. While the Brothers saw the debate as primarily political, the Salafis saw it as almost entirely religious.

That said, the Salafis should not be called "quietists" (except, perhaps, for the finite minority that deliberately choose to cut themselves off from the world), as is done in a whole subset of academic literature on the subject.[52] In fact, their actions are far from politically inconsequential, since redefining the religious norm—and the effect of this on social behavior—has a direct impact on the polis. What's more, once they had matured into a social force, the Salafis came to adopt various organizational structures and political postures, even if their approach was in no way limited to these. Finally, none of this should imply that the Salafis—even the most apolitical among them—were not pursuing a long-term political ambition.

In Gramscian terms, though, one could say that the vast majority of them felt the time was right not for a "war of maneuver" but rather for a "war of position," aimed at redefining the religious norm according to the Salafi vision of orthodoxy.[53] Once this was completed, the political project—rarely alluded to, and always put off *sine die*—would fall into place on its own. In short, the Salafis' goal was to attain religious hegemony within Islam. Which explains why—and I will revisit this point—in this struggle their natural adversaries were their religious competitors (including, and sometimes mostly, within political Islam) rather than the political authorities, who were often indifferent to debates within the religious field so long as these did not challenge their standing.

As we will see, the Islamist and purist grammars coexisted in a relatively stable, "ideal-typical" state in Egypt starting in the mid-1920s as they became established within two competing groups, the Muslim Brotherhood and Ansar al-Sunna. There were still reformists at the time who transcended this dichotomy (or wanted to), but their existence does not disprove this divide. Any early crossovers between the groups—for example, some Brothers may have contributed to Ansar al-Sunna's journal, and vice-versa—were rare and grew even more so as the grammars became more defined. This aspect is somewhat overlooked in Henri Lauzière's otherwise remarkable book, *The Making of Salafism*. Because he examines the delimitation of boundaries between Salafis and the rest of the reformist camp, he focuses mostly on borderline cases like Moroccan sheikh Taqi al-Din al-Hilali, the main subject of his study.

Things did get more complicated a few decades later when, for reasons I will analyze, a hybridization took place between these two schools of thought and action. This was particularly apparent starting in the late 1960s as the generation of the *jamaʿat islamiyya* (Islamic groups) came of age and, despite an early Salafi religious socialization, quickly became politicized with Islamist (and often jihadi) views. Things clarified a bit when the jamaʿat islamiyya disintegrated at the tail end of the 1970s, which seemed to reestablish the initial dichotomy: Most departing members joined the Brotherhood, while others split off and created the Salafi Call. But large hybrid pockets remained where, despite the Call sheikhs' best efforts to shore up the original bond between Salafi discourse and purist grammar, there were persistent attempts to chip away at it. Here again, we can understand and analyze these processes of hybridization only once we clearly identify the foundations on which they rest.

Taking a closer look at this melding of grammars and discourses also offers us another way to understand the categories Quintan Wiktorowicz laid out in a canonical article that tries to define the "anatomy of Salafism."[54] He argues that three forms exist: a purist one, which generally corresponds to the way I define Salafism here (again, for historical rather than normative reasons); a political Salafism, whose followers express dissenting political opinions and sometimes even participate in the existing political system; and a jihadi Salafism, which practices politics through violence. Setting aside the debate on the limitations of these categories, which Joas Wagemakers highlights, I see the last two simply as hybrids that borrow as much from Salafi discourse as from Islamist grammar—in the grammar's predominant form for political Salafism, and in its revolutionary variation for jihadi Salafism.[55] In chapter 6 I will add revolutionary Salafism to this discussion of hybrids. It borrows from a new, populist grammar born during the era of political transition that began in 2011.

This grammatical approach to studying Salafism offers many advantages. First, it allows us to take a deep look at actors' practices and motivations, rather than focusing exclusively (as too often happens in studies of political Islam and especially of Salafism) on discourse—or what is sometimes called "ideology," for lack of a better word. It's also a departure from the armchair sociology applied to Egyptian Salafism—in the press, in attack pieces, and sometimes in academic writing—which tends to underestimate the actors' agency.

For example, on the question of hostility between the Nour Party and the Muslim Brotherhood, or that of Nour's support for the July 2013 coup d'état, narratives vary.[56] Some analyses insist on the role of the security apparatus, which supposedly held such sway over the Salafi Call that the sheikhs aided the "counterrevolution" in service of the "deep state."[57] Other assessments emphasize the role of Saudi Arabia, assuming (wrongly, as we'll see) that it maintained close ties with the Salafi Call and that Salafi sheikhs were emulating the country's anti-Morsi stance. Not only are these interpretations factually incorrect; they imply that Nour's political choices were somehow irrational and thus can only be explained by an external intervention. But if one principle is held dear in pragmatic sociology, it's the rationality of actors. And this can be grasped only by trying to put ourselves in the actors' shoes and identifying the grammar guiding their actions.

Another set of analyses points to psychological factors: personal animosity between Salafis and Brothers stretching back to the late 1970s, which would explain the Salafis' singular desire for vengeance on their sworn enemies. Or they suggest strategic maneuvering, portraying Salafis as Machiavellians who would stop at nothing to get their way. Once again, these assessments err by reducing the actors' behavior to reactions. The grammatical analysis helps avoid this fallacy, while still allowing that psychology or personal interest could play a role. In sum, many of the interpretive misunderstandings of Egyptian Salafism come from what Lemieux calls "Frazer's error," featured as this chapter's epigraph: "Watching him play, I decide that he's no good at chess. But the game he's playing is checkers."

This picture is rounded out by two "metarules"—borrowing in part from Lemieux yet again, while changing his intention and wording— that help structure the framework in which the grammars are practiced.[58] The first is "realism," which requires that actors apply their grammar cautiously. Islamic movements of all stripes openly justify this prudence in the name of weighing "benefits and harms" (*al-masalih wa-l-mafasid*), or pros and cons—a guiding principle for Muslim legal scholars in their religious opinions. Prudence, however, is viewed only in terms of each individual's grammar, and there is no objective way of measuring it—particularly, we will see, during periods of political crisis where the shifting context often makes it difficult to calculate.[59]

I call the second metarule "proclaimed solidarity": In Islam's religious sphere, one is expected to show a certain benevolence toward one's fellow believers, in the name of the sacrosanct "unity of the Umma" (Muslim community). Among activists, this sometimes obliges a movement to tamp down (or euphemize) its hostility toward a competing movement, for fear of being accused of *fitna* (sowing suspicion and strife). This metarule offers insight into why public attacks between Brothers and Salafis remained relatively rare—at least until 2011 (and climaxing in 2013)—even when the two groups were at loggerheads and their members thought (and said) as much within their own circles.

Salafism and the Religious Field

Despite all this, Salafism is not exactly a typical social—or even religious—movement. Most of its promoters describe themselves as ulema (whether they were educated at a religious university or are religious autodidacts, as is the case for many), and their often prolific intellectual work touches on religious issues, whether theological or legal. Even when they address subjects that seem secular at first glance, they do so mostly through the lens of creed. With just a few exceptions before the upheaval of 2011, their occupations have been those traditionally held by clerics: publishing, teaching, preaching. Mosques are their natural operations centers. This again sets them apart from the Muslim Brotherhood, whose founders, like most of its leaders to this day, are not clerics but laymen and consider mosques to be one place among many for spreading their ideas. Salafis' preferences stem from what they see as their purpose: Religion is the heart of their mission, and not—as a certain Marxist reading would have it—a cover for something else.

As I have noted, Salafism is characterized by its quest for religious purity, which is expressed in terms relevant to (and developed for) each era, with the goal of redefining Islam's norm. The debate unfolds mostly in the religious field, the Salafis' chosen battleground for confronting the doxa of traditional Islam. This field is relatively autonomous from the political field—not that those in power don't seek to control it (authoritarians, after all, tend to strive for dominion), but because some of its central stakes have no impact on political leaders and are thus not worth their effort. As Pierre Bourdieu writes, "You can't make a philosopher compete for the prizes that interest a geographer."[60] Or with a slight twist, you can't make a politician compete for the prizes that interest a sheikh (and vice versa).

INTRODUCTION

Again, this does not mean that the political context never affects dynamics in the religious field. In fact, we will see how it seems to have even laid some of the groundwork for Salafism's expansion—but not necessarily because the authorities wanted to promote Salafism as a religious discourse. They acted according to their own political logic, the consequences (or as Raymond Boudon says, "perverse effects") of which sometimes happened to help Salafis: same outcome, different reason.[61]

Still, what is striking in the Egyptian case is that the Salafi redefinition of orthodoxy happened away from the halls of power, governmental as well as religious, as this book will show. It came to pass, as it were, through the grass roots, within what Jürgen Habermas calls the "public sphere."[62] To the present day, Salafism has never been validated by official political or religious institutions (at least not in its own right, even though it has sometimes helped reshape their leaders' perspectives—and those of competing movements). In Gramscian terms, one might say that Salafis have achieved something like hegemony, but we will see that this has not translated into anything politically—perhaps because, among other reasons, it isn't quite clear or agreed upon what such a political manifestation should look like.

METHODS, SOURCES, AND STRUCTURE OF THE BOOK

Research for this project began in 2010, one year before the Egyptian revolution. Having examined Saudi Salafism in my previous book, I wanted to look closer at the ties between the Salafisms (and Salafis) on both sides of the Red Sea. I soon realized that the Saudi dimension of Egyptian Salafism, while undeniable, had been overestimated—perhaps because the Egyptian intellectual left, mystified by the movement, wished to believe that it simply came from abroad.

Egyptian Salafism deserved to be studied in its own right. While modern Egyptian Islam and Islamism have inspired dozens of books, these mostly ignored or misidentified Salafism. It seemed we needed nothing less than a revisionist reading of the last hundred years of Egyptian politico-religious history. I had originally planned to write this book with the late Husam Tammam, whose pioneering work had paved the way for others, but fate would have it otherwise.

When I started this project, no scientific literature had yet been published in English or Arabic on Egyptian Salafism, at least not as I use the term here. "Salafism" certainly appeared in some writings on Egypt, but it was most often employed—as a result of Louis Massignon and Henri Laoust—in a broad sense that included all reformists without truly distinguishing between their religious foundations. Henri Lauzière demonstrated why this posed a problem, and a few quality texts have since been published that illuminate certain facets of the subject. Two of these were written by anthropologists: Richard Gauvain's *Salafi Ritual Purity: In the Presence of God* (2011), which looks at purity rituals (*tahara*) and the debates they provoke among a small group of Salafis in the Shubra district of Cairo; and *The Perils of Joy* (2012), by Samuli Schielke, which studies the dispute between Salafis and Sufis over *mawlid*s, popular celebrations at the tombs of saints.

Several other books came from historians. Henri Lauzière's *The Making of Salafism: Islamic Reform in the Twentieth Century* (2016) is an excellent text that retraces the emergence of *Salafi* as a category in intellectual debates from the 1920s through 1950s in Egypt and elsewhere and documents its evolution over the decades that followed. Based on an examination of late 1970s Islamic periodicals, *Practicing Islam in Egypt: Print Media and Islamic Revival* (2018), by Aaron Rock-Singer, analyzes the transformation of Egyptians' religious and social practices during this pivotal decade. More recently, in 2022, Rock-Singer published *In the Shade of the Sunna: Salafi Piety in the Twentieth-Century Middle East*, which provides a fascinating account of the social formation of distinctively Salafi practices throughout the past century. Finally, *Answering the Call: Popular Islamic Activism in Sadat's Egypt* (2014), by Abdullah al-Arian, helps us understand political Islam's renaissance in Egypt during the 1970s but mentions Salafism only indirectly. Pioneering books have also been published in Arabic, most important, those of Ahmed Zaghloul Shalata, including the first monograph on the Salafi Call in Alexandria. In addition, various helpful texts have been published by Egyptian researchers who are themselves close to the Salafi movement, such as Ahmad Salim, 'Amr Basyuni, and Mu'taz Zahir.

Yet all these cover only limited periods or offer partial responses to the questions raised in my research. My study draws heavily on a long stretch of fieldwork in Egypt, from 2010 until a few months after the July 2013 coup d'état. It then became difficult—and even dangerous, as in the tragic example of Giulio Regeni, a young Italian doctoral student brutally assassinated in January 2016 by the Egyptian police—for a researcher to venture into the field when studying movements mistrusted (if not simply deemed "terrorists" and repressed with the ruthlessness that this term claims to justify) by the Egyptian authorities. Starting in late 2013, many actors within the Islamic movement chose exile over prison; I was nonetheless able to continue interviews between 2014 and 2017, mostly in Istanbul.

The period between 2010 and 2013 offered me a special vantage point. A little less than a year before the revolution, I had started spending time with Salafis. This stroke of luck allowed me to observe the movement on almost a daily basis, as events unfolded and it faced new challenges. With the revolution, a whole underground world came to the surface. The Salafi sheikhs, formerly hard to reach, became public figures—even those who belonged to the movement's most subversive factions. I suddenly had unfettered access to their courses and lectures, and some agreed to be interviewed.

In this moment of cognitive liberation, Salafi activists wanted to tell their story, which had been excluded from official narratives despite its major role in restructuring the Egyptian religious field; many of the insights I share in this book came to me during those long conversations. I was also able to speak with leaders and figures in competing movements, whether they belonged to the Muslim Brotherhood or to the jihadi movement, or represented al-Azhar, whose Grand Imam I was able to meet on three occasions.

Rather than simply asking for their opinions on the unfolding events (tempting at such an extraordinary time), I prioritized biographical interviews as much as possible, which meant pushing my interlocutors to dive back into periods that, in 2011, felt so distant. In this moment of reinvention where everyone thought the country's repressive history had been cast off for good, people spoke relatively freely—I say relatively because the characteristic political fluidity of revolutionary periods still required a degree of caution. This constraint, though, paled in comparison to those they had endured until 2011.

The biographical interviews I conducted proved incredibly beneficial. By overlaying various trajectories in order to limit the "biographical illusion" effect, this method helps the researcher piece together events from an unrecorded past—in other words, to gather an oral history—but also, as Howard Becker emphasizes, to reconstruct processes.[63] What's more, such interviews shed light on the present because, as they describe the past, the actors say much about what they have become. The main pitfall was that I mostly interacted with men. Gaining access to female circles was no simple task while studying an ultraconservative movement like Salafism. While women do not appear in the foreground of the movement's story arc, they are nonetheless central to its day-to-day activities. Luckily, some pioneering field studies by young researchers like Naima Bouras have concentrated on their role.[64]

Beyond observation and interviews, this work is based on in-depth documentary research. I first had to gather the hundreds of publications attributable to the Salafi movement since the 1920s: writings of the movement's principal sheikhs through the decades and periodicals published by the various organizations, along with—as much as possible—each organization's internal literature.

Members of the Salafi Call, along with former participants, were kind enough to let me browse their abundant libraries, while others shared some of the handouts used in teaching movement members. Some even helped me decipher these writings, placing them in the context of their publication or explaining the hidden meanings that some conveyed. Furthermore, in the late 2000s, memoirs by Islamist—and Salafi—activists became their own genre in Egypt. Published in book form or as serials in Egyptian newspapers, these yielded priceless material for reconstituting the activist trajectories of those at the heart of my work. Finally, in the moment of revolutionary euphoria that followed Mubarak's fall, the walls of the State Security Investigations Service collapsed (briefly), and hundreds of documents it had produced—some half-burned, in a desperate attempt to destroy them as protestors were bearing down—began to circulate. This gave researchers an unprecedented window into the machinations of Egypt's repression apparatus, especially as relates to Islamist movements and Salafism in particular.

This book is divided into six chapters. The first four address the period before the revolution, showing how in just under a century—from the 1920s through 2011—Salafism came to redefine the Egyptian religious norm. Each chapter addresses a period and/or group that decisively contributed to Salafism's increasing influence. The first chapter concentrates on the crystallization of a well-defined Salafi movement, distinct from competitors like the Muslim Brotherhood, in the Egyptian religious field. Salafism was first embodied in 1926 within Ansar al-Sunna, an organization that promoted its ideas. We will witness the battle waged between competing religious corpora as the Salafis gradually imposed certain texts and authors—in a nascent publishing industry—that aligned with their theological conceptions.

The second chapter looks at the subsequent period, which began when the monarchy fell and the Free Officers seized power. We will see how Salafism managed to continue thriving during this period, becoming the religious bedrock of the Islamic revival that transpired in the late 1960s. After Sadat came to power in 1970, this revival spawned a large number of public and underground groups, the most radical of which would work together to assassinate the president in 1981. The third chapter touches on the Salafi Call, a group that emerged from this defining decade and became the foremost organized Salafi social movement in Egypt. We will study how it functioned and delve into conflicts with critics that the group used to burnish its image as the incarnation of Salafi orthodoxy in the Egyptian religious sphere. The fourth chapter examines the Mubarak era and Salafism's increasing influence at the time, as its normative predominance pushed beyond activist circles to the Islam of the masses.

Then came 2011 and the Egyptian Revolution, which saw the collision between two simultaneous but decidedly distinct processes then reaching their apex: Salafism's religious ascendancy, on the one hand, and a political challenge to the regime by actors who originally had no ties to political Islam, on the other. The last two chapters study how the revolution and subsequent political transition affected Salafism, and vice-versa. The fifth addresses the Nour Party, which was tied to the Salafi Call and became Egypt's second most popular party at the end of 2011. We will see the debates it sparked both within Salafism and without, and its role in the political dynamics that gave rise, in the summer of 2013, to a new authoritarian regime under General el-Sisi. The final chapter looks at revolutionary Salafism, the Salafi-inspired populist movement led by Hazim Abu Isma'il, which took over the Egyptian streets in mid-2011 with a success as dazzling as it was ephemeral. We will conclude with an assessment of the fortunes and misfortunes of Salafism: Even if it has not lost its normative power, today it is in crisis.

NOTES ON ARABIC TRANSLITERATIONS

For transliterations of Arabic, I used a rigorous but simplified version of the system recommended by the American Library Association, while choosing not to notate emphatic consonants and long vowels. Given how many Arabic references are included here, this seemed the best way to avoid overburdening the text. Arabic terms or names that have an established spelling in English were not changed.

Technical terms in Arabic appear in italics. For such terms, I have mostly kept the pronunciation and spelling from literary Arabic rather than those found in the Egyptian dialect. The only exceptions to this rule are proper nouns known by their Egyptian pronunciations.

Chapter One

BATTLE OF THE CORPORA
The Role of the First Egyptian Salafis

> I found nobody around me in this country who takes it upon himself to preach in order to turn the people away from this corruption and purify them of this abomination. At the mosques, I heard imams reveling in sin, goading on their flocks! They set the worst example; the people imitated them, followed in their footsteps. And so the river overflowed its banks. This chaos drove me to speak the truth, and I felt a deep urgency to push for reform.
>
> —ABU AL-WAFA' DARWISH, *THE CRY OF TRUTH*

Egypt should not be confused with Saudi Arabia, where the roots of Salafism run deep. The lineage of Egyptian Islam is completely different: It is Sufi, Ash'ari, tied to the traditional fiqh schools. In the days of yore, these origins were expressed as much through the al-Azhar mosque-university, which promoted and protected them, as in a relatively exuberant popular religiousness. It goes without saying, then, that the first Egyptian Salafis would have had a hostile reception to contend with—at least at first.

Yet in the 1920s, small groups of committed normative entrepreneurs began making it their business to spread the Salafi message across Egypt. They didn't just print their own books; they staked out publishing as their main strategic domain, striving to flood the market with age-old texts that dovetailed with their theological framework. The boosters' limitless zeal, coupled with the resources offered by Saudi Arabia, even if modest at the time, made the operation remarkably effective. This elicited virulent reactions from the Azhari ulema, who understood that Salafis were undermining the rationale behind their authority by questioning—and offering alternatives to—their version of classical Islamic tradition. The end of Egypt's monarchic period, which lasted until 1952, was marked by this "battle of the corpora" in which Salafis scored some significant victories.

But what was the battle's context? This first chapter aims to retrace the trajectories of these normative entrepreneurs—particularly at Ansar al-Sunna, which carried the torch of Egyptian Salafism starting at the association's inception in 1926.

EGYPTIAN ISLAM IN THE EARLY TWENTIETH CENTURY: AL-AZHAR, ASH'ARISM, AND SUFISM

Describing the state of religion in 1930s Egypt, Muhammad Hamid al-Fiqi—one of the pioneers of Egyptian Salafism, discussed further on—painted a dire picture:

> Ninety-nine percent of the Umma lives in ignorance of Islam (*jahiliyya*) regarding religious knowledge, creed, character, judgment and order; ignorance has built an impenetrable wall in their hearts that deprives them of truth and light. An overwhelming majority submit to the dead, bow down to rocks and trees and enslave themselves to idols, temples and tombs of saints. In their creed, their religious practices and everything else, most veer from the guidance and wisdom of God's revelations, and the lion's share also splinter into factions, parties and groups according to their membership in Sufi brotherhoods and traditional schools. They are fulfilled by what these groups offer them, and they trust only their sheikh—no matter how his words contradict revelation and reason—in the belief that, thanks to him, they can access the occult, slip the bonds of fate, and avoid hell![1]

Al-Fiqi gives us the impression that nearly all of his Egyptian contemporaries practiced a popular, deviant form of Islam that had elements of popular Sufism while remaining captive to the traditional schools. Such portrayals abound in the era's Salafi literature, and they are reminiscent of the way Ibn 'Abd al-Wahhab's followers described Najd before the advent of his salvational preaching, thereby echoing Saudi Wahhabism's founding myth.[2] But despite the oversimplification, al-Fiqi's assessment contains a kernel of truth. Academics take a broader view, noting instead a general decline in religious practice during this period—against a backdrop of rising European influence—and pointing specifically to the reduced popularity of Sufi brotherhoods, which until the nineteenth century had constituted the uncontested backbone of Egyptian Islam.[3]

Regardless, al-Fiqi was right to point out that Egyptian religiousness—even while in a decline, however temporary—remained deeply rooted in this model of "traditional" Islam that had developed over the preceding centuries. Thus, while organized Sufism was somewhat diminished, the first half of the twentieth century saw stable attendance at large mawlids, popular gatherings where common believers celebrated the anniversary of a Muslim saint's birth or death with festivities around his mausoleum—a famous example being al-Sayyid al-Badawi, buried at Tanta—in the hopes of receiving his blessings.[4] Incidentally, ministers in the early twentieth century still arranged their meeting schedules so they could attend his mawlid festivities.[5] The Prophet's mawlid also remained immensely popular.

Al-Azhar, the guiding light of Egyptian Islam, was likewise still dominated at the time by those who followed the amalgam embodied in traditional Islam: Theologically speaking, the leading ulema were Ash'ari, and they subscribed to one of the four canonical legal schools (the Hanbali one nonetheless quite underrepresented, as throughout Egypt). And most of them were, if not Sufi, at least inclined to tolerate so-called moderate Sufi practice that wasn't excessively ecstatic, like that promoted by medieval scholar Abu Hamid al-Ghazali. Nor were most opposed to popular practices like mawlid celebrations, sometimes called "good innovations" (*bid'a hasana*)—an expression that would become a flashpoint for Salafis in the 1930s.[6] The Salafis believed that any innovation on the practices of the *salaf* could only be blameworthy.[7]

Traditional Islam was so established in the institution that modernizing reformists like Muhammad 'Abduh, himself a graduate of al-Azhar, would try to avoid unnecessary confrontations by shifting the debate toward political and social issues rather than exclusively religious ones, even though he often derided Sufism for its excesses, which to reformists like him expressed superstitions that contradicted reason.[8] As we shall see, the Muslim Brotherhood later followed a similar blueprint. In contrast, theology would be almost a single-minded focus for early Salafis, whose influence is visible as early as the 1910s and who began to organize in the 1920s.

FIRST ENCOUNTERS WITH SALAFISM

To unearth how Salafi ideas made inroads in Egypt, we must briefly return to the nineteenth century, if only to see how limited their impact had previously been. Egyptians and Wahhabis first made contact during the military campaign Muhammad 'Ali embarked upon in 1811—at the behest of the Ottoman caliph—against the young Saudi state, which had seized the holy cities of Mecca and Medina a few years earlier. The Wahhabis saw the affair as clear-cut: Egyptians and Ottomans were infidels; fighting them meant protecting the true religion. The Egyptians emerged victorious, and Saudi historian 'Uthman Ibn Bishr chronicles their brutal behavior at length. They went so far as to "torture" Sulayman bin 'Abdallah, grandson of Ibn 'Abd al-Wahhab, by playing—horror of horrors for Wahhabis—musical instruments.[9] More concretely, al-Dir'iyya, the capital of "Wahhabi heresy," was razed. However, Egyptian ulema did not unanimously support Muhammad 'Ali's campaign. Wahhabi preaching may have been largely unknown in Egypt, but it was intriguing. The country's celebrated historian 'Abd al-Rahman al-Jabarti even latched onto and defended the religious message of Ibn 'Abd al-Wahhab's disciples.[10]

The Egyptians returned to Cairo with dozens of captives, including all surviving descendants of Muhammad bin 'Abd al-Wahhab (referred to in Saudi Arabia by the honorific "Al al-Shaykh," the "descendants of the Sheikh"). Many of them made the most of their exile by studying at Al-Azhar University, where they discovered a much more sophisticated scholarly world than that of al-Dir'iyya. In the mid-1820s most took advantage of Egypt's eroding control in Najd and returned to the Arabian Peninsula, including Sheikh 'Abd al-Rahman bin Hasan Al al-Shaykh and later his son 'Abd al-Latif bin 'Abd al-Rahman, who would form the backbone of the second Saudi State's religious elite. Others, like 'Abd al-Rahman bin 'Abdallah (1804–1857), chose to settle in Egypt instead. After studying at al-Azhar, he joined the prestigious institution and became the "sheikh of the Hanbalis' portico (*riwaq*)"—its foremost scholar of Hanbalism.[11] According to Saudi historian 'Abdallah al-Bassam, he helped revive the Hanbali school at al-Azhar, where it had all but disappeared. How much these Wahhabis truly influenced Egyptian scholarly circles remains a subject of debate, even if al-Bassam says (without further explanation) he was told that "it is thanks to 'Abd al-Rahman bin 'Abdallah that al-Subki's organization [Jam'iyya Shar'iyya] embraced the Hanbali school and called for *tawhid* in worship practices (*tawhid al-'ibada*)."[12] Regardless, these Wahhabi ulema did not educate any of the central figures in what would become the Egyptian Salafi movement.

It would take the influence of Muhammad Rashid Rida (known as Rashid Rida, 1865–1935) to breathe life into Egypt's Salafi saga. Born in what is now Lebanon, Rida left in 1898 for Cairo to join Muhammad ʿAbduh (1849–1905), whom he viewed as his mentor. ʿAbduh enjoyed considerable recognition at the time as the figurehead for "modernizing reformism." As he saw it, the Muslim world was declining due to his contemporaries' estrangement from authentic Islam, with which he commanded them to reconnect. True Islam, explained ʿAbduh, was that of the pious ancestors, the *salaf.*

The "Salafism" pushed by ʿAbduh (who never actually used the term *salafiyya* to designate his own school of thought) differed greatly, however, from the way the term is understood today.[13] He deeply believed in a rational approach to sacred texts, which he saw as the only way to demonstrate the perfect compatibility between European modernity and Islam's message.[14] Theologically speaking, he avoided opposing the Ashʿari school and seemed to have more unacknowledged affinities with bygone Muʿtazilism than he did with Hanbalism.[15] And while he criticized certain Sufi practices (sometimes rather vehemently), he was less bothered by Sufism's unorthodox character than by incompatibility between the "superstitions" it promoted and modern rationality.[16]

Upon arriving in Cairo, Rida made himself his mentor's spokesman. He created the *al-Manar* journal to disseminate ʿAbduh's views, for example, printing the latter's Quranic exegesis in serial format. After ʿAbduh—the standard-bearer for reformism—died in 1905, Rida inherited his mantle. *Al-Manar* grew considerably in just a few years, its readership now stretching from the Maghreb all the way to Asia. Thanks to the publication, Rida crossed paths with religious intellectuals from across the Muslim world and passionately followed the events unfolding there.

CHAMPIONING THE CREED

During this period, Rida became impassioned with the writings of Ibn Taymiyya and Ibn Qayyim al-Jawziyya. He was not alone: These two authors held a prominent place on the bookshelves of reformist adherents, who interpreted them in various ways. Some emphasized their theological directives, while others stressed their calls for legal interpretation (*ijtihad*) free of the schools' rigid framework—but didn't always abide by the literal interpretational rules that the authors advocated.[17]

The Wahhabi movement's first expansion on the Arabian Peninsula brought the literature of Ibn Taymiyya and his school back into the picture after centuries by the wayside, and there were the first stirrings of a resurgence. The Ahl-e Hadith movement in India, a source of books and manuscripts for the Saudi ulema, also played no small role in this.[18] Syria became one of the epicenters in this surge of rediscovery, as David Commins shows, while in Baghdad Nu'man al-Alusi (1836–1899) was one of the first modern ulema to explicitly echo Ibn Taymiyya's positions, quoting extensively from the latter's works.[19] And it appears that Rashid Rida's exposure to al-Alusi's writings brought him under the influence of Ibn Taymiyya, a figure to whom his mentor 'Abduh paid little heed.[20] Rida gradually replaced 'Abduh's rationalism with a more literal interpretation of creed and a more conservative approach to exegesis.

In the 1920s Rida's interest in the Wahhabi movement grew for reasons both religious and political. On the one hand, he saw it as an extension of Ibn Taymiyya's message, with which he now mostly agreed; on the other, he was fascinated by the Saudis' adventure in endogenous state-building at a time when nearly all Muslims were under colonial dominion. In 1924 'Abd al-'Aziz Al Sa'ud, who would become king eight years later, seized the region of Hejaz, whose capitals were Mecca and Medina. With the Muslim world in turmoil, Saudi Arabia asserted itself as a pivotal player. In *The Wahhabis and Hejaz*, the large essay collection Rida published in 1925, he embraced the Saudi example:

> Sheikh Muhammad bin 'Abd al-Wahhab—may God have mercy upon him—was a renewer of Islam who pulled the inhabitants of Najd from the grasp of associationism and blameworthy innovations. He guided them to the *tawhid* and the *sunna* in the way of Ibn Taymiyya, the Sheikh of Islam, and managed to do so quickly because the Sa'ud clan supported and protected him from his enemies. Despite the clan's status as lesser chieftains in Najd, God supported them because they were on His side. . . . It should be known that the Najdis known as "Wahhabis" are Sunnis who follow the path of the *salaf* in their creed and the Hanbali school's position on law, and they are the most observant (*ashadd ittiba'an*) of the Muslim peoples of our

age, the least tempted by sin and blameworthy innovations, and this is why God has given their Sultan a great victory over the sharif of Mecca.[21]

As we see, the advent of Rida's pro-Saudi stance coincided with his increasingly committed support for the Salafi creed. He did continue to have disagreements with the Saudi ulema—Lauzière suggests that he had hoped to bring the Wahhabis of Najd around to a more moderate stance—but his conversion was sincere.[22] Wahhabi Islam's influence on Rida was also felt in the topics he chose to write about. One clue to this evolution was his position toward Shiism: While he had initially endorsed a possible rapprochement between Sunnis and Shia, allowing like-minded Shia to write in *al-Manar*, he now took a much more uncompromising tone toward those he called—borrowing from the Wahhabi lexicon—"rejectors" (*rafida*).[23] Without completely disavowing its initial eclecticism, *al-Manar* seemed more and more like a mouthpiece for the Salafi creed, leaving behind the modernist position formerly pushed by some of its distinguished contributors.

This change was echoed within a faction of the young intellectuals and ulema marshalled around Rida, who had created the Institute of Preaching and Guidance (Dar al-daʿwa wa-l-irshad) in 1912 to instruct them in his ideas.[24] Courses of study there were financed by scholarships (often obtained through donations from wealthy Gulf individuals, as well as via an Egyptian government subsidy).[25] Muhammad Hamid al-Fiqi, ʿAbd al-Zahir Abu al-Samh, and Muhammad ʿAbd al-Razzaq Hamza all had ties to Rida's institute.[26] Al-Fiqi would in 1926 found the first Egyptian organization of Salafi ulema, Ansar al-Sunna, and the two others would become prominent members.

In the 1920s a handful of sheikhs and Egyptian intellectuals—about whom we know little, and whose direct or indirect ties to the aforementioned circles are difficult to pinpoint—also began to take interest in the Salafi creed. It even seems that similarly inclined individuals may have been active in Egypt as early as the turn of the twentieth century, if we are to believe Sufi sheikh Ibrahim al-Samannudi's controversial book from 1901, which tells of his encounters with several "Wahhabis" whose ideas he strives to deconstruct.[27] Regardless, the 1920s were pivotal because the phenomenon crystallized into a freestanding movement that was increasingly visible in the religious sphere.

One gets a picture of the early 1920s Egyptian Salafi milieu from the memoirs of Moroccan Salafi sheikh Taqi al-Din al-Hilali, who writes that he met "most of the Salafi followers in Egypt" when he lived there from 1921 to 1922.[28] (It should be noted that al-Hilali uses this term in retrospect, employing its latter-day meaning; the Salafis he mentions here are indeed the same discussed in this book.) Besides Rida, whom he describes as the "Imam of the [Salafi] message at that time," he mentions Muhammad al-Rimali, an al-Azhar graduate who in 1921 founded the Group of Those Who Entrust Themselves to the Guidance of Islam (Jama'at al-i'tisam bi-hadi al-islam) in Damietta;[29] 'Abd al-'Aziz al-Khuli (1892–1930), a graduate of the training institute for religious judges who in 1920 published one of the first books on hadith by an Egyptian Salafi;[30] Hasan 'Abd al-Rahman; Muhammad Abi Zaid al-'Adwi; as well as Muhammad 'Abd al-Razzaq Hamza (1893–1972), 'Abd al-Zahir Abu al-Samh, and Muhammad Hamid al-Fiqi, whom I mentioned earlier.

Several more of these early Egyptian Salafis appear in other sources, including Muhammad Mukhaymar, who published a book called *Clear Words on the Religious Opinion on Addressing and Worshipping Prophets, Saints and the Pious (Al-qawl al-mubin fi hukm nida' wa du'a al-anbiya' wa-l-awliya' wa-l-salihin)* (1924).[31] In the Giza governorate, a sheikh named Muhammad 'Abd al-Salam al-Shuqayri and a group of his followers created the Salafi Organization of al-Hawamdiyya (its host city) in the 1920s.[32] A volume he published called *Traditions and Innovations Concerning Invocations and Prayers* made some waves in 1933 (Rida reviewed it in *al-Manar*, and al-Fiqi wrote the preface).[33] The name of Abu al-Wafa' Darwish, quoted in this chapter's epigraph, also surfaces in Sohag,[34] and the memoirs of al-Hilali additionally mention meetings with "proto-Salafi" groups in Upper Egypt, situated in various villages and following a sheikh. They were, however, a tiny minority, and everywhere faced both a hostile Sufi majority and the country's religious authorities, who even sent emissaries to try to set them straight.[35]

A REVOLUTION IN PUBLISHING

Rida's work went beyond defending the Salafi creed. He would above all be a driving force in publishing and promoting works from the Salafi corpus that had theretofore been unfindable or whose distribution had been limited in an Egypt still dominated by traditional Islam, arguably making him the country's first active entrepreneur of the Salafi norm. This became one of the missions at al-Manar, whose publishing division was entirely devoted to the undertaking, which was itself part of a broader movement among reformists of all stripes: rediscovering the *turath* (tradition)—the intellectual output of the classical era—and making it publicly accessible with the goal of helping Arabs and Muslims reconnect with their heritage.[36] The Salafi vision of what qualifies as *turath*, however, was from the outset exclusively religious and particularly restrictive; they defined its limits by selecting titles in line with their beliefs.[37] These books were mainly published as "critical editions," which allowed the editor (*muhaqqiq*) to imprint his own ideology via the introduction or the footnotes.[38] Ahmad Khan writes: "These texts were appropriated, steered and colored with the ideological biases of editors and publishing houses. The presence of the scholar-cum-editor was, in many cases, overwhelming. Editions of classical texts could often contain an excessive amount of editorial intrusions before and throughout the text, and many times a manuscript containing a dozen or so folios would be transformed into a thick volume on the basis of the editor's interventions in the introduction and footnotes."[39]

The Al-Manar Press published two types of texts. First were the works of Ibn Taymiyya, Ibn Qayyim al-Jawziyya, Ibn Kathir, and other paragons of Ibn Taymiyya's school. Most of the texts had already been released in Egypt due to interest among reformists (even modernizing ones) at the close of the nineteenth century. The initial publication of Ibn Taymiyya thus seems to date back to 1888 and was actually two texts grouped together: *The Divine Politics and the Prophetic Verses* (*Al-siyasa al-ilahiyya wa al-ayat al-nabawiyya*) and the famous *Politics According to Religious Law for the Reform of Governors and the Governed* (*Al-siyasa al-shar'iyya fi islah al-ra'i wa-l-ra'iyya*), translated into French by Henri Laoust in 1948 under the title *Le traité de droit public d'Ibn Taymiyya*.[40] Ibn Qayyim wouldn't be published until 1891, with *The Sufficient and the Comforting in Support of the Saved Sect* (*Al-kafiyya al-shafiyya fi-l-intisar li-l-firqa al-najiyya*). Finally, Ibn Kathir's *tafsir* (Quranic exegesis) was published by the Bulaq Press in 1884, not to be reprinted until the 1920s.[41] All these, however, were scholarly editions mostly intended for the ulema. Rida—like his collaborators who later (as we shall see) carried on his legacy—worked to bring these texts to an increasingly educated general public.

Al-Manar also published a second genre: works by Wahhabi authors, until then inaccessible or unknown to Egyptians.[42] Books by Muhammad bin 'Abd al-Wahhab and by Saudi ulema like Sulayman bin Sahman multiplied on the Egyptian market in the 1920s.[43] The impact of these new publications was also enhanced by the social changes then traversing Egypt: With expanded education, the potential readership was no longer limited to ulema and grew exponentially, a process helped along by a drop in publishing costs.[44]

Rida's project coincided with the ambitions of King 'Abd al-'Aziz Al Sa'ud.[45] Amid broad regional maneuvering as the Middle East was redrawn after World War I, the Saudis' growing influence quickly met headwinds from their Egyptian nemesis, whose destruction of the Saudi state in 1818 had not been forgotten. At an already tense moment, the "*mahmal* incident" stirred the hornet's nest: For centuries, every year a caravan called the *mahmal* had traveled from Egypt to replace the veil, or *kiswa*, that covers the Ka'aba in Mecca. In 1926 the delegation was attacked by Wahhabi zealots particularly outraged that the procession was accompanied by musicians, and a bloody fight ensued. The Egyptians responded by breaking off all formal ties with Saudi Arabia.[46] Egypt would not officially recognize the country until 1936.[47]

With regional tensions swirling, it finally dawned on 'Abd al-'Aziz how he could use the soft power that Wahhabi Islam offered him. He began trying to cultivate individuals abroad who seemed receptive to the Saudi interpretation of Islam. They would, he believed, stand up for his country's interests, as well as introduce—and help normalize—a Saudi Islam still widely perceived as extremist or heretical. The Saudi king thus offered his assistance to the most conservative segment of the Arab world's reformists, who saw Saudi Arabia as a potential embodiment of their ideals. Rida and his associates were among the first in Egypt to benefit from this policy, while in Syria the Saudis supported intellectuals like Muhammad Bihjat al-Bitar. In some cases, 'Abd al-'Aziz also sought to employ these reformists more directly, at a moment when the kingdom was sorely lacking capable administrators.[48] Managing the holy cities was particularly challenging, since heightened sensitivities in the Hejaz region precluded an overly visible Najdi presence. Some of these reformists consequently moved to Mecca or Medina to fill one of many religious and administrative roles on a temporary or long-term basis.

Rida's bond with ʿAbd al-ʿAziz quickly deepened, as their prolific correspondence confirms.[49] And on a more practical note, the latter partly subsidized Rida's Al-Manar Press, helping it publish works from the Wahhabi tradition. The press distributed Wahhabi sheikh Sulayman bin Sahman's writings as early as 1921; some of their covers even bore the inscription "Printed on behalf of his Highness King ʿAbd al-ʿAziz bin Saʿud, Imam of Najd and of its dependencies."[50] In 1924 Rida published Ibn Kathir's *tafsir* in a "sumptuous" edition funded by the Saudi monarch.[51] Accused by Egyptian monarchists of taking money from ʿAbd al-ʿAziz, Rida denied any venal intentions in *al-Manar*, explaining that his relationship with the king centered on a "religious and spiritual bond, with God as its sole focus, which financial proceedings neither diminish nor enhance."[52] In a letter to his friend Shakib Arslan, however, he did acknowledge his financial dependence on the Saudi monarch.[53]

Another Syrian living in Egypt, Muhibb al-Din al-Khatib (1886–1969), who settled in Cairo in 1909 and taught for a time at the Institute of Preaching and Guidance, played a Rida-like editorial role, while also enjoying the attention—as well as the financial assistance—of King ʿAbd al-ʿAziz.[54] A journalist active in the political sphere who swung between Pan-Islamism and conservative Arab nationalism, he cofounded, with compatriot ʿAbd al-Fattah Qatlan, the Salafi Bookstore (Al-maktaba al-salafiyya) and the Salafi Press (Al-matbaʿa al-salafiyya), where he published "a selection of rare works from the literature of the *salaf*, and helpful and valuable contemporary literature both written in Arabic and translated."[55] This meant that the Salafi Press offered a large section of religious texts, alongside Arabic novels and translations of European philosophers like Descartes. Some authors belonged to the rationalist tradition, like al-Farabi or Avicenna, while others, like former Grand Mufti Muhammad Bakhit al-Mutiʿi, who was quite hostile to the Salafis, represented the Islam then dominant in Egypt.[56]

The collection also included contrasting works from the Hanbali theological tradition, like those of Ibn Taymiyya and Ibn Qayyim al-Jawziyya, which al-Khatib seems to have brought over from Syria and Iraq through his contacts with reformist circles there. He often published extracts of these imported manuscripts as short, accessible, affordable booklets in order to reach a wider audience.[57] The Salafi Press thus became the first Egyptian publisher to release Ibn Kathir's *tafsir*—viewed by Salafis as the authoritative text on the subject—to the general public.[58] Al-Khatib sometimes received subsidies from the Saudi monarch for these releases. Like Rida, he maintained close ties with Saudi Arabia and defended the country passionately in *al-Fath*, the journal he founded in 1926.[59]

Al-Khatib's story is a fascinating illustration of the polysemy around the term *salafi* in the 1920s. At that time, al-Khatib did believe in reformism, but theologically speaking he doesn't seem to have shared the Salafi creed. His Salafi Bookstore—whose name was reputedly suggested by his earliest mentor, the Syrian reformist Tahir al-Jaza'iri, sometimes called the "Muhammad 'Abduh of Syria"—offered the potpourri of literature just described.[60] Under his leadership, *al-Fath* opened its pages to all the era's reformists—many of them close to (or part of) the Muslim Brotherhood—as well as the known anti-Salafi Yusuf al-Dijwi.[61]

I am primarily concerned here with Al-Khatib's role as a publisher who helped spread Salafism, even though in the 1920s he was far from the Salafi model as I use the term here. With time, though, he did embrace more obvious elements of the Salafi creed. In 1959, for example, while Mahmud Shaltut, the sheikh of al-Azhar, spoke in favor of a possible rapprochement (*taqrib*) between Sunnism and Shiism, al-Khatib published a violently anti-Shia pamphlet entitled *The Key Features of the Founding Principles on Which the Twelver Imamite Shia Religion Is Based*, in which he argued that Shiism and Sunnism are fundamentally irreconcilable because of differences in creed.[62]

The publishing effort was by no means limited to these two figures, but there isn't enough room to list everyone who helped bring works from the Hanbali theological tradition and its followers to Egyptian readers. Like al-Khatib, the majority were more reformist than Salafi and mostly wanted to dig up forgotten fragments of the Islamic tradition, which led them to take interest in the same works the Salafis cherished.[63] I'll mention just one little-known figure here: Muhammad Munir al-Dimashqi, an Azhari reformist who was not (his memoirs imply) "Salafi" in the sense used here.[64] His editorial contribution is made clear in a list, compiled by Aida Nosseir, of the era's Egyptian publications.[65] His Munirian Press (Al-matba'a al-muniriyya) published dozens of works from Ibn Taymiyya's school over the early decades of the twentieth century.

Keep in mind that this campaign extended far beyond Egypt, though Cairo was doubtless its epicenter. From Damascus to Beirut, from Baghdad to distant India, intellectuals whose inclinations overlapped with those of Rida and al-Khatib also struck out to exhume Salafism from within the tradition. Some did so by creating their own publishing houses, while keeping in close contact with Rida and his Egyptian colleagues, then at the vanguard of the Arab publishing world, and supplying them with manuscripts—a crucial collaboration because Damascus and Baghdad had been the last holdouts of theological Hanbalism, so its surviving volumes were more abundant there than elsewhere.[66]

THE JAM'IYYA SHAR'IYYA AND THE PROMOTION OF ORTHOPRAXY

Some of the early promoters of the Salafi creed mentioned earlier, including Muhammad Hamid al-Fiqi, got their start frequenting an organization called the Religious Organization of Cooperation Between Those Who Act According to the Quran and the Sunna (Al-jam'iyya al-shar'iyya li ta'awun al-'amilin bi-l-kitab wa-l-sunna), here called the Jam'iyya Shar'iyya.[67] The group was founded in 1912 by Mahmud Khattab al-Subki (1858–1933), an Azhari sheikh who followed the Maliki school but may have been influenced by 'Abd al-Rahman bin 'Abdallah, one of the Wahhabis exiled to Cairo in the nineteenth century.[68] It was thus sometimes also called "Subkiyya," though mostly by detractors.[69] The group pledged to follow the example of the *salaf* and called for a return to original Islam, as depicted by al-Subki in his monumental *Pure Religion: Guiding People to the Religion of Truth*, an eight-volume work where he wrote that "salvation will come only if we purify the religion of its accumulated superstitions."[70]

In the text, which focused on the rules of worship (*fiqh al-'ibadat*, an issue central to the Jam'iyya Shar'iyya's message), Al-Subki showed great hostility toward what he, like the Salafis, called blameworthy innovations, and he enjoined Muslims to follow the prophetic tradition (sunna) methodically. It should, he said, guide their actions down to the smallest detail, arguing, for example, that beards were a religious obligation and calling it sinful to wear clothes that fell past the ankles (*isbal al-izar*). He also criticized the way in which the Prophet's mawlid was celebrated, and without rejecting Sufi Islam wholesale, he warned against the practice of intercession (*tawassul*) that was fundamental to popular Egyptian Islam.[71]

On these questions of ritual—as well as social—practice (the two cannot be kept entirely separate), al-Subki's views resonated with the Salafi project as it simultaneously unfolded in Saudi Arabia, which explains why some literature refers to his organization as "Salafi." His positions of course made him few friends in the Sufi brotherhoods (his followers sometimes came to blows with their members) or at al-Azhar, where traditional Islam—whose practices he was combatting—still reigned.[72]

In reality, the orthopraxy pushed for by the Jam'iyya Shar'iyya shared many common points with Saudi-inspired Salafism's puritanical vision. But on creed—which was, after all, the key issue for Salafis—al-Subki stayed rather mum, as his priority was to correct the popular practices that he saw as deviant "without getting into quarrels about speculative theology [*mushaghabat kalamiyya*] and rational reasoning that the common man would have a hard time understanding."[73] And when he did touch on the issue, as in the introduction to *Pure Religion*, he generally limited himself to reaffirming the validity of the then-dominant Ash'ari doctrine.[74]

One oft-debated question seems anecdotal, but it demonstrates al-Subki's deep theological divergences from the Salafis. The Ash'aris (and thus al-Subki) preached that the divine action in the "Most Gracious is firmly established on the throne" (Quran 20:5) could be interpreted metaphorically, which the Salafis roundly rejected. The controversy grew, prompting al-Subki to publish an entire book in 1931 that responded to his critics and denied them the "Salafi" label he claimed for himself. Picking at an old sore point between Ash'aris and followers of theological Hanbalism, he specifically accused his critics of being "anthropomorphs" (*mujassimun*).[75] But beyond this scholarly debate and the true distinctions that al-Subki brought to light (they at least felt true to those involved), what really made Ansar al-Sunna and the Jam'iyya Shar'iyya incompatible was the clash between the former's profoundly elitist nature and the latter's "mainstream" quintessence—in short, a scholarly Salafism versus a popular proto-Salafism.

The Jam'iyya Shar'iyya's theological identity, at first exclusively Ash'ari, broadened slightly with time, although to this day the council of ulema at its helm is composed of Azharis who follow the Ash'ari tradition. When its founder died in 1933, he was replaced by his son Amin Khattab, who had a better relationship with nascent Salafism; this leadership change contributed significantly to the organization's evolution.[76] Khattab would also further expand the worship-related orthopraxy pushed by his father to include more social aspects. In so doing, he assumed stances closer to those advocated by the Saudi Salafis, at a moment when their Egyptian counterparts were also increasingly focused on such questions. One example is the prohibition on gender mixing: Aaron Rock-Singer writes that Khattab added a long footnote on the subject in his updated edition of *Pure Religion*, as his father hadn't addressed it in the original book.[77]

Another reason for this relative ideological plasticity was that, early on, the Jam'iyya Shar'iyya focused on running mosques and acting as a service organization (*jama'a khadamiyya*) that was quite involved in social work—through a number of member-funded charitable projects—but separate, on the whole, from intellectual debate. Its various divisions took great care to avoid any explicit politicization by focusing their discourse on socioreligious questions. The association would experience a meteoric rise over the following decades: By 1981 it oversaw around 2,200 mosques, a number that soared to nearly 6,000 after the turn of the century, at which point it also operated twenty-six preacher training institutes (*ma'had i'dad al-du'at*) throughout the country and supervised some twenty social projects, including its flagship effort aiding orphaned children (almost 500,000 of them, according to its president).[78]

The Jam'iyya Shar'iyya would contribute doubly to Salafism's rise. First, its promotion of orthopraxy resonated with a plank of the Salafi project in its latter twentieth-century form. The nickname *sunniyyun* (Sunnis), first given to its members, would be adopted by ordinary Egyptians in the 2000s to describe those who were increasingly wearing visible symbols of Salafi observance.[79] Moreover, despite the Ash'ari leanings of its leadership, the Jam'iyya Shar'iyya showed increasing tolerance toward Salafism. The association's decentralized structure afforded its five hundred branches (during the 2000s) considerable autonomy, providing many Salafis a place and the means to spread their message.[80] Case in point: The al-Istiqama mosque in Giza, one of Cairo's largest Salafi mosques at the time, was in fact an official Jam'iyya Shar'iyya outpost.

THE FOLLOWERS OF THE PROPHETIC TRADITION CONFRONT A HOSTILE WORLD

Back in the 1920s, however, al-Subki's overt Ash'arism pushed some adherents of the Salafi creed to strike out on their own. They founded Ansar al-Sunna al-Muhammadiyya (Followers of the Prophetic Tradition), the first true Salafi organization in contemporary Egypt, in 1926, with a simple mission: to support and spread the Salafi creed, establishing it as the heart of the Islamic norm. The issue of orthopraxy—so dear to al-Subki—initially seemed relegated to the back burner. While a few of the association's publications denounced music or the wearing of short pants, these issues remained secondary.[81] And many members followed renowned figure Ahmad Shakir in dressing like their Egyptian compatriots, hoping "not to stand out from the rest of society"; some didn't even grow beards.[82] This question, though—and the way members applied it to themselves—gained prominence over the years, especially post-Nasser.[83]

Histories of Ansar al-Sunna universally portray it as the brainchild of Muhammad Hamid al-Fiqi (1892–1959), a normative entrepreneur who would become its first president. Al-Fiqi had studied with Rida—notably attending the Institute of Preaching and Guidance and working at the Al-Manar Press—but was also close with al-Khatib, whom he even seems to have assisted for a time at the Salafi Bookstore.[84] Most important, al-Fiqi (unlike Rida) was among the rare 1920s Egyptian Salafis—and, moreover, one of the first—to have studied at al-Azhar. His degree, obtained in 1917, automatically gave him authority over the growing movement.

The creation of Ansar al-Sunna is often depicted as a response to the "persecution" Salafis then faced.[85] Al-Fiqi, for example—who upon graduating from al-Azhar was named imam of the al-Hidara mosque in Cairo's Abdeen area (a stone's throw from the royal palace)—was expelled from his mosque at the request of neighbors who disliked his sermons' contents.[86] One biography even recounts that "the palace's senior officials were perpetually trying to prevent the people from meeting him and hearing him speak."[87] In Alexandria, 'Abd al-Zahir Abu al-Samh endured similar harassment, as Taqi al-Din al-Hilali describes in his memoirs.[88] Al-Fiqi and his colleagues thus often preached in cafés, the only venues that would have them.[89]

The Salafis hoped to protect themselves by forming a legal structure, which would allow them to spread their message more effectively in a still-hostile society. Creating an association also allowed them to gather the disparate groups of the movement's base. Most "first wave" Salafi preachers, who had operated until then as lone agents, quickly flocked to Ansar al-Sunna. Existing local associations like the Salafi Association of al-Hawamdiyya or the Group of Those Who Entrust Themselves to the

Guidance of Islam became branches of Ansar al-Sunna, which established its headquarters in the heart of Cairo—in a house right next to al-Fiqi's mosque.[90]

Three young Saudis also played a key early role in Ansar al-Sunna: 'Abdallah bin Yabis, 'Abd al-'Aziz bin Rashid, and—last but certainly not least—'Abdallah al-Qasimi, by far the most active of the bunch during Egyptian Salafism's emergent period. Born in 1907 in Burayda, a city in the Qasim region, al-Qasimi came to Cairo with his two friends in 1927 to study at al-Azhar on the Saudi government's dime. Despite his youth, al-Qasimi quickly made a name for himself at the university by openly criticizing his professors' understanding of Islam, which he contrasted with authentic (or "Wahhabi," a term he used freely) Islam. He grew closer to al-Fiqi and began getting involved with Ansar al-Sunna. In 1931, at just twenty-four years old, he published his first book, which lambasted one of the university's most eminent sheikhs, Yusuf al-Dijwi (1870–1946), a member of al-Azhar's Committee of Grand Ulama (Jama'at kibar al-'ulama'). Entitled *Najdi Lightning to Sweep Away al-Dijwi's Darkness* and possibly cowritten with al-Fiqi, it was published by Al-Manar Press under Rashid Rida.[91] Rida gave it positive coverage in his journal: "Al-Qasimi outshined the ulema with his vast knowledge, and he embarrassed them.... The battle he began with al-Azhar's ulema has earned him great popularity among followers of the Islamic revivalist movements."[92]

Such virulence from a mere third-year student elicited consternation and anger within al-Azhar. Brought before a disciplinary hearing, al-Qasimi was expelled.[93] But he remained in Egypt, and the following year he published a sequel titled *Al-Azhar Sheikhs and Their Additions to Islam*, in which he bluntly criticized the discourse of al-Azhar's ulema. This was followed by two pro-Wahhabi works, *The Decisive Difference Between Wahhabis and Their Critics* and *The Wahhabi Revolution*; an anti-Shia text, *The Battle Between Islam and Polytheism*; and, in 1940, the last book of his Salafi period, *How Muslims Lost Their Way*.[94] Most of these were published by Al-Manar Press, the Salafi Press, or that of Ansar al-Sunna, and several were financed by Fawzan bin Sabiq al-Fawzan, the Saudi ambassador to Cairo.[95]

Al-Qasimi's nerve and panache earned him significant recognition; his biographer Jürgen Wasella calls him "the champion of Wahhabism in [1930s] Egypt."[96] But the following decade, in a stunning reversal, al-Qasimi distanced himself not just from Wahhabi Islam but from Islam as a whole, even questioning the existence of God. This naturally drew the ire of those who had embraced him until then—especially Ansar al-Sunna, which quite literally erased him from its official history.[97] He would spend the next fifty years laying out the basis for an Arab atheism, before passing away in 1996.

But let's get back to Ansar al-Sunna. Still in its infancy, the group went into hibernation when founder Muhammad Hamid al-Fiqi left for Saudi Arabia's Hejaz region in 1928, following in the footsteps of two principal collaborators, 'Abd al-Zahir Abu al-Samh and Muhammad 'Abd al-Razzaq Hamza. He would remain there until 1931, during which time King 'Abd al-'Aziz put him in charge of *al-Islah*, the first Saudi religious journal. Abu al-Samh and Hamza, both appointed as imams at the Great Mosque of Mecca, stayed on permanently.[98]

Upon al-Fiqi's return, the association came back to life and created supervisory structures, including an elected general assembly (*al-jam'iyya al-'umumiyya*), an administrative committee, and an executive board.[99] 'Abd al-Razzaq 'Afifi, one of a handful of Azhari members, became second-in-command. The association's branches multiplied across the country, each with its own elected general assembly. In 1936 a ten-person religious committee (*hay'a shar'iyya 'ilmiyya*) was formed, in which the group's handful of Azhari members once again played an outsize role.[100] It was headed by Muhammad al-Rimali, mentioned earlier, along with Ahmad Shakir (1892–1958), a respected judge and religious intellectual, who despite his membership in the association would remain a lifelong independent spirit.

Unlike the Jam'iyya Shar'iyya, Ansar al-Sunna at first furnished few services (it would eventually increase its involvement somewhat, especially starting in the 1970s). Ansar al-Sunna saw itself above all as a league of ulema committed to spreading the good (Salafi) word. One of its former presidents, Safwat Nur al-Din, put it well: "We are not a humanitarian association, a charity. We are a preaching organization, and that is what matters to us. So, even when we do charity work, it is always with the goal of spreading our message."[101] The organization's main social involvement came through its oversight of mosques (duly registered with the authorities) where its sheikhs officiated, and later through the creation of Quran learning centers (*marakiz tahfiz al-qur'an*) and training institutes for preachers, where it prepared future leaders.[102] In 1936 Ansar al-Sunna passed the thousand-member milestone.[103] By the 1990s the organization oversaw more than a thousand mosques, according to its former president Safwat Nur al-Din.[104] It boasted 144 branches in 1997, and a specialist from the Salafi movement estimated its membership at around ten thousand in the early 2000s.[105]

More than anywhere else, the association focused its activity on the intellectual sphere. Members dedicated themselves to publishing critical editions (*tahqiq*) of ancient manuscripts that aligned with their vision of Islam, carrying on the initiative begun by Rida and al-Khatib to make accessible a whole body of literature then absent from Egyptian libraries. Often, this undertaking was paired with a verification and detailed authentication of the hadiths contained in each book (*takhrij al-ahadith*); this gave the collection an extra badge of religious credibility.

Among Ansar al-Sunna's publications, we find works by Ibn Taymiyya, Ibn Qayyim, Muhammad bin 'Abd al-Wahhab, and other Saudi ulema like 'Abd al-Rahman bin Hasan Al al-Shaykh, as well as authors from the first centuries of Islam.[106] Ahmad Shakir, also an eminent specialist of hadith (*muhaddith*), became one of the most active critical editors (*muhaqqiqun*) at Ansar al-Sunna. His biography lists dozens of ancient texts he helped publish, including certain works of Ibn Hanbal, Ibn Taymiyya, and Ibn 'Abd al-Wahhab.[107] What's more, Shakir published an abridged version (*mukhtasar*) of Ibn Kathir's *tafsir*, thereby demystifying it for a much wider audience; to this day it remains a staple of Egyptian religious libraries. Ansar al-Sunna set up its own Prophetic Tradition Press (Matba'at al-sunna al-muhammadiyya) in 1936, allowing it to directly publish its preferred texts without dealing with intermediaries.

Beyond publishing books, Ansar al-Sunna wished to actively participate in the debates that rocked Egypt during the interwar period. To this end, it created a bimonthly journal in 1936, *al-Hadi al-Nabawi* (Prophetic guidance) that printed contributions from members and sympathizers of the association. Why foray into public debate? By sharing the perspectives of the association's ulema, the idea was to realign the conversation according to Ansar al-Sunna's priorities. The journal analyzed all political or social issues through its lens of choice: creed.

But another question kept Muslim reformists up at night. What posture should be taken toward Europe and its influence? Ansar al-Sunna's discourse did address the issue, often in unequivocal terms: All that comes from Europe is bad to the core; there can be no source of inspiration besides Islam. Atheists, secularists, communists, and others, all denounced as agents of European (meaning Christian) influence, were similarly vilified. Such critique of "modern ideologies" was nonetheless a new undertaking for Salafism, whose ulema (particularly those in Saudi Arabia) were more accustomed to debating ancient manuscripts or excoriating Muslim schismatics. Ansar al-Sunna was in a class of its own because its members were more than Salafis: They were modern Egyptians stirred by a plethora of questions that their Saudi counterparts were not raising. This effort foreshadowed the formalization of Salafi thinking into more of an ideology, something that wouldn't truly come to pass until the 1970s.

Their principled stance also favored implementing shari'a, or God's law, a premise sometimes outlined in uncompromising terms. In his critical edition of a book by an eminent nineteenth-century Wahhabi scholar, al-Fiqi included the following annotation:

> An idol (*taghut*) is anything that diverts man from the worship of God, faithfulness to His religion, and obedience to Him and His prophet.... This category includes, without the slightest doubt, any governance according to rules foreign to God and to His laws, as well as all that man has conceived of to regulate the body, property, and private parts in order to suspend the divine rules regarding Quranic punishments, the prohibitions on usury (*riba*) and wine, et cetera.... These laws are idols, and those who follow and promote them are idols.[108]

This acrimonious outlook, however, remained overwhelmingly theoretical. Ansar al-Sunna members were, at most, expected to convince their contemporaries of these "truths" through preaching (*da'wa*). Unlike the Muslim Brotherhood's approach, Ansar al-Sunna refused to participate in any political activism, opting instead to show boundless loyalism to the powers that be. This attitude was a natural outgrowth of the traditional political conformity among Sunni ulema; it was also considered the best way to protect the association's mission to preach.

No surprise, then, that in 1936 al-Fiqi assured the "ever wise" King Farouk—freshly installed on the throne—of Ansar al-Sunna's complete loyalty. One article describes how the members of Ansar al-Sunna "celebrated this important event" (the coronation) by gathering at the association's headquarters to "ask God to bless his highness Farouk." But just two weeks after the revolution of July 23, 1952, its leaders didn't bat an eye when they sent a delegation to meet Muhammad Naguib, commander in chief of the armed forces, congratulating "the heroes God has sent us to save the country from despotic tyrants (*al-bughat al-zalimun*) and rid it of the corrupt and their corruption." Each flourish of allegiance may have been paired with "advice" (*nasa'ih*) demanding that the authorities make Islam more central, but Ansar al-Sunna never endangered itself by being overtly critical; it presented its role as simply "helping the state teach the true religion to the people."[109]

The organization indeed put little emphasis on political concerns, saying that "politics are nothing more than corruption and division."[110] For Ansar al-Sunna, the core issue lay elsewhere. It was waging battle—for the very heart of Islam—against an array of deviant beliefs and behaviors that, in its view, had corrupted the dogma of divine oneness. Political renewal, so dear to Muslim reformists, would not come to pass until this purification was complete. With this in mind, Al-Fiqi said he had refused to participate in the 1919 revolution, which led to the country's independence three years later, because he believed that "we will not end occupation with demonstrations where bare-skinned women march alongside men" but through "the return to the Prophet's sunna and the abandonment and rejection of blameworthy innovations."[111] Openly defending his abstention was particularly bold, given that al-Azhar proudly advertised its involvement in the 1919 revolution; this represented a "galvanizing myth" for the institution.[112]

For Ansar al-Sunna, enemy number one lay elsewhere: Sufism, the true basis for Egyptian popular Islam. The organization thus trained the brunt of its intellectual output on Sufi practice, in a style whose virulence owes more to the Wahhabi spirit than to that of Ibn Taymiyya and Ibn Qayyim, who were a bit more measured in their anti-Sufi views. This was a recurring theme in *al-Hadi al-Nabawi*. In the first and second issues of the journal's sixth year (sold as a pair in January 1942), one article is devoted to refuting Sufi thinker Ibn 'Arabi's theories on the unity of existence (*wahdat al-wujud*); another compares Islam's present and past and frames the rise of associationism (*shirk*), brought to life in the form of Sufism and the "Islam of the saints," as the primary cause of Islam's decline. Further on, a feature entitled "Superstitions and the Cult of Idols" demands that al-Azhar's leading sheikh purge his university's curriculum of Sufi content; this is followed by an anti-Sufi poem.[113] Other issues of *al-Hadi al-Nabawi* contain explicit calls for the authorities to bar mawlids, or even brotherhoods themselves.[114]

'Abd al-Rahman al-Wakil (1913–1970) would become Ansar al-Sunna's president in 1960, having established himself as one of the organization's most biting polemicists and after a long stint as chief editor of *al-Hadi al-Nabawi*. The "destroyer of idols" (*hadim al-tawaghit*), as Ansar al-Sunna members called him, lays out the group's grievances with Sufism in a 1955 book wherein Sufism (which he dubs "the sworn enemy of Islam") is portrayed as a doctrine wholly unrelated to Islam, mixed with beliefs from paganism or from other religions.[115] He paints a picture of cynical, power-hungry Sufi sheikhs exploiting the commoner's ignorance for personal gain, and presents various examples of what he sees as Sufism's moral failings; what's more, he charges that it sanctions theft and incest. The ecumenicism of certain Sufis is also framed as a mortal threat to Islam. The book closes with a plea enjoining followers of Sufism to leave behind "the darkness of the caverns" and embrace "the truth."[116] The mystics Ibn 'Arabi and Ibn Farid are among the writers most frequently taken to task. But even Abu Hamid al-Ghazali, who had until then been considered one of Sunnism's primary reference points, does not escape al-Wakil's wrath.[117]

This is because, beyond Sufism, it was indeed Ash'arism (which was still the dominant Sunni theology) that the ulema of Ansar al-Sunna had in their sights. The critique of al-Ghazali should mostly be understood with this in mind. In addition to being the medieval scholar who gave Sufism—or at least a specific brand of it—the trappings of orthodoxy with his famous volume *Deliverance from Error* (*Al-munqidh min al-dalal*), he was indeed considered one of the fathers of Ash'ari theology. His best-known book, *Revival of the Religious Sciences* (*Ihya' 'ulum al-din*), was one of the most widely taught texts in the Sunni world—especially at al-Azhar University, which complicated any direct theological attack and explains the choice to lay into al-Ghazali by excoriating his Sufism.

Despite this indirect approach, al-Wakil would be forced to explain himself in the pages of *al-Hadi al-Nabawi* when his attacks on the man many Sunnis still considered the "Proof of Islam" (*Hujjat al-islam*) incited a violent outpouring.[118] (The affair even saw him dragged to court by Sufi sheikhs.)[119] Al-Wakil then shifted strategy: Rather than attacking Ash'arism in its entirety and thus antagonizing most of the Egyptian Islamic establishment, he tried to demonstrate that there were "good" and "bad" Ash'aris—the former being those who espoused Salafi theories.[120] Above all, he did his best to show that al-Ash'ari himself, in his final writings, had renounced his early prudent rationalism in favor of a quasi-Salafi theology. In a nutshell, he was saying: If you really want to be good Ash'aris, become Salafis!

Ansar al-Sunna attacked Islam's non-Sunni branches with the same vitriol. Since nearly all of Egypt's Muslims were Sunni, the other followings had initially seemed like a nonissue and were thus seldom discussed. But the question became more central during the 1950s, when a potential rapprochement between Sunnism and Shiism was gaining traction—with the support of some in the al-Azhar establishment. Meanwhile the Baha'is, a small minority in Egypt, would also endure the association's zeal.[121] But Ansar al-Sunna still saw Sufism as the cornerstone of the structure it wished to demolish. In attacking Shiism, it underscored that "the mawlid is Shiism's path to infiltrating Egypt."[122] Its rebuke of communism argued that the movement was cut from the same cloth as Shiism.[123]

A SAUDI-WAHHABI SATELLITE

I mentioned earlier the close ties that Rida and al-Khatib maintained with Saudi Arabia; Ansar al-Sunna's bond was even tighter. Rida was seen as sympathetic to Wahhabism, but he remained an independent spirit. Ansar al-Sunna's founders, though, seemed to embrace a literal Wahhabism; on his visit to Cairo in April 1954, young Prince Nayif bin 'Abd al-'Aziz described them as Saudi Arabia's "religious ambassadors" to Egypt.[124] When King 'Abd al-'Aziz had passed through the city in 1931, he had prayed with al-Fiqi at the mosque adjacent to Ansar al-Sunna's headquarters.[125] And each time a Saudi official stopped in Cairo, *al-Hadi al-Nabawi* related how the organization welcomed him with the honors an embassy reserves for its head of state. It was only natural, then, that Muhammad bin Ibrahim Al al-Shaykh—the "sheikh of the ulema of Najd" and future Grand Mufti of Saudi Arabia—enjoyed the organization's royal treatment in 1951 when he came to town for medical reasons.[126]

Ansar al-Sunna openly embraced Saudi Arabia as a model country and often pushed the Egyptian king to take a cue from his Gulf neighbor's policies.[127] Al-Fiqi and Muhammad Khalil Harras, another sheikh from the association, in fact published texts that celebrated, in equal measure, Wahhabism and the achievements of King 'Abd al-'Aziz.[128] Al-Fiqi even penned a whole book lauding the Saudi sovereign, evocatively titled *Flowers from the Gardens: Biography of the Just Imam 'Abd al-'Aziz bin 'Abdallah al-Faysal Al Sa'ud*.[129] (*Riyadh* means "gardens" in Arabic.) And Ahmad Shakir drew up a secret report for King 'Abd al-'Aziz in 1949 on the reform of the Saudi judicial system.[130]

Al-Fiqi's relationship with the Saudi government seems particularly enduring. He recounts that in 1910 he met Fawzan bin Sabiq al-Fawzan, the ambassador sent to Cairo by King 'Abd al-'Aziz, who lavished him with books and opened doors for him in Saudi government circles.[131] But that's not all: Al-Fawzan may have encouraged the creation of Ansar al-Sunna. Al-Fiqi writes: "It was through him and by his hand that the seeds of Ansar al-Sunna were sown; through him and by his hand that the organization grew, becoming, by the day he departed—may God's mercy be upon him—a smile on his lips."[132] It is nonetheless difficult to determine if al-Fiqi is simply singing the praises of an unfailing supporter or if he's describing concrete authority al-Fawzan had over the project. The connections made by Rida, who was much better known at the time than al-Fiqi, undoubtedly played a role as well.[133]

These networks allowed al-Fiqi to strike out for Saudi Arabia in 1928, where he used his time to build close relationships with the country's political and religious elites. One example of his proximity to power was that King 'Abd al-'Aziz appointed him director of the printing and publishing bureau in Mecca after his time directing the journal *al-Islah*.[134] Over the course of his stay, he became close with Muhammad Nasif (1885–1971), descendant of an important Hejaz family—early loyalists of 'Abd al-'Aziz who had adopted Wahhabi Islam. Nasif, who had also met Rashid Rida when the latter visited Hejaz in 1916, was a passionate collector of manuscripts from the Salafi tradition, building what some described as the largest archive in the Middle East.[135] He would furnish many of the manuscripts that served as the basis for critical editions published by Rida and later Ansar al-Sunna, while serving as a crucial intermediary in obtaining residency permits for association members who settled in Saudi Arabia.[136]

The fact that 'Abd al-Zahir Abu al-Samh and Muhammad 'Abd al-Razzaq Hamza stayed on in Saudi Arabia after al-Fiqi's 1931 return to Egypt allowed him to maintain his connection. Like Hamza and Abu al-Samh, other Ansar al-Sunna members—including two association presidents, 'Abd al-Razzaq 'Afifi and 'Abd al-Rahman al-Wakil—would come to hold prestigious positions within the kingdom. 'Afifi, who left to teach in Saudi Arabia in 1949, would go on to help establish the country's religious institutes (*ma'ahid 'ilmiyya*) based on his experience at al-Azhar.[137] He took the reins at the Higher Judicial Institute in 1965 and was called in 1971 to sit on the prestigious Council of Senior Ulema, the highest body in the Saudi religious field. Al-Wakil was made a professor of creed at Mecca's faculty of shari'a in 1969. Their contribution was especially important to the Saudis because they came from a pluralist society where conservatives and "progressives" of all kinds coexisted; what's more, they commanded a modern vocabulary then unfamiliar to the kingdom's ulema—all the better to denounce the manifestations of modern society. And during the Arab cold war, which pitted Saudi Arabia against its Arab nationalist neighbors, their discursive skills became more prized than ever.

The Wahhabi authorities' special treatment of Ansar al-Sunna also reflected their unique outlook on the organization. In the 1950s the kingdom had begun hosting Islamist ulema and intellectuals of all stripes and nationalities, and many built their careers in the Saudi system. These foreigners held many positions but were generally kept at arm's length from Saudi Islam's higher bodies, especially the Council of Senior Ulema. Ansar al-Sunna's ulema were among the few outsiders welcomed into such circles, proof that the Saudi Wahhabis saw them as part of the family.[138]

On a more practical level, the Saudis helped finance Ansar al-Sunna's development. King 'Abd al-'Aziz, for example, partly financed what would become the association's headquarters.[139] During Prince Nayif's visit to Cairo in 1954, he announced that he would personally donate two hundred pounds a year to the group.[140] And Muhammad Nasif underwrote a portion of Ansar al-Sunna's publications, as evidenced in various letters published by historian (and sympathizer) Ahmad al-Tahir.[141] With time, benefactors based in other Gulf countries would add to the initial Saudi support. These contributions—especially from Qatar's 'Id Al Thani Foundation and from Kuwait's foremost Salafi organization, the Society for the Revival of Islamic Heritage (Jam'iyyat ihya' al-turath al-islami), both close to the Saudi religious establishment—actually seem to have represented the bulk of Ansar al-Sunna's external sponsorship in the 2000s, after the September 11 attacks put Saudi organizations under scrutiny and gave them pause about giving (of course, there were also likely unofficial, untraceable contributions).[142] While Ansar al-Sunna tends to emphasize that its funding—which comes mostly from donations—is by and large Egyptian,[143] it seems the flow from the Gulf remained significant until at least 2011. A judicial investigation at the time into foreign financing of Egyptian organizations suggested it amounted to hundreds of millions of Egyptian pounds.[144]

AL-AZHAR AND SALAFISM: AMBIVALENCE IN A TROUBLED RELATIONSHIP

The relationship between al-Azhar and the young Salafi movement (most visibly embodied in Ansar al-Sunna) was profoundly ambiguous. On one hand, books by association sympathizers try to show that Ansar al-Sunna has always been on good terms with the prestigious university.[145] On the other hand, authors more critical of Salafism underscore the fundamental theological antagonism between the two institutions and their strained relationship.[146]

Ansar al-Sunna maintained an ambivalent stance. It frequently sang al-Azhar's praises, both because the mosque-university was an unassailable symbol of Sunni Islam and because an overly explicit critique could be seen as political (al-Azhar also represented the Islam of the state). Al-Fiqi, like 'Abd al-Razzaq 'Afifi and 'Abd al-Rahman al-Wakil, who would succeed him as leaders of Ansar al-Sunna, never missed an opportunity to proudly flaunt his al-Azhar affiliation.[147] One might even say that such ties were long a prerequisite (if an unspoken one) for Ansar al-Sunna presidents, even though Azharis then, as now, represented a minority within the organization—a symbolic way of riding on al-Azhar's coattails. But in almost the same breath, the mosque-university would be accused (always indirectly) of teaching a corrupted form of Islam that directly contradicted the vision of the *salaf*. Obliquely alluding to his time at al-Azhar, al-Fiqi recounted: "In my early life I followed the masses and emulated their superstitions, advocating for blameworthy innovations and *jahiliyya*. But God guided me. He pulled the blinding veil of ignorance from my eyes and showed me the light of truth. He saved me from dying as a pagan."[148]

Indeed, al-Azhar remained a bastion of traditional Ash'ari and Sufi Islam—the very same Islam targeted by Salafi critics time and again. Many Azhari ulema returned fire, attacking these newcomers to the country's religious landscape. Of the sheikhs who oversaw the institution, Abu al-Fadl al-Jizawi (1917–1927) and al-Ahmadi al-Zawahiri (1930–1935) fought hardest to put the brakes on Salafism's emergence. In the wake of al-Fiqi's publication in 1921 of *Gather the Muslim Armies to Combat the Mu'attila and the Jahmiyya* (*Ijtima' al-juyush al-islamiyya 'ala ghazu al-mu'attila wa-l-jahmiyya*), a controversial anti-Ash'ari text by Ibn Qayyim al-Jawziyya, al-Jizawi issued a fatwa denouncing the book's ideas and their threat to the Muslim faith.[149]

That same year, al-Azhar launched an investigation into Muhammad al-Rimali, its own graduate and a future founding member of Ansar al-Sunna, due to his hostile stance toward mawlids, saintly intercession, and anything remotely related to Sufism. When the inquiry wrapped up, al-Rimali was threatened with having his Azhari status suspended, but he appealed and got off with an official reprimand. Al-Zawahiri would continue al-Jizawi's approach, transferring pro-Salafi professors away from their Azhari institutes; he was also the president who expelled 'Abdallah al-Qasimi. Al-Zawahiri even wrote an anti-Salafi book whose title wasn't exactly subtle: *Those Are Jews, Not Hanbalis* (*Yahudan la hanabila*). During the same period, former Egyptian Grand Muftis Muhammad Bakhit al-Muti'i (1914–1920) and 'Abd al-Rahman Qarra'a (1921–1928) pushed similar postures, sounding the alarm about errors and discord-sowing (*fitan*) in Salafi-published books.[150]

Other sheikhs from the institution threw themselves headlong into the fray. Starting in the 1920s, Sheikh Yusuf al-Dijwi, a popular figure and member of al-Azhar's Committee of Grand Ulema, became fixated on refuting, across thirty-some articles in al-Azhar's journal and in the newspaper *al-Ahram*, the Salafi critiques of Sufism and specifically of saintly intercession.[151] These writings would provoke al-Qasimi's angry response to "al-Dijwi's darkness," mentioned earlier, as well as criticism from Rida. Al-Dijwi, anything but discouraged, would go on to publish several works assailing those he labeled "the Wahhabis," exhorting his readers: "Do not pay them heed; fight them to protect the beliefs of the commonfolk, the populace, among whom this movement's impact is being felt and will be difficult to erase."[152]

Al-Dijwi also showed great hostility toward al-Fiqi's publication of ancient authors with Salafi-compatible ideas, arguing that this fueled the discord. A large controversy did erupt when in 1939 al-Fiqi issued a critical edition of *Al-Darimi's Response to Bishr al-Marisi*, a ninth-century book by one of Ibn Hanbal's students that defends doctrinal viewpoints shared by the modern era's Salafis.[153] Al-Dijwi added to the outcry, denouncing "a bad book that people should have no right to publish, printed by Ansar al-Sunna—which has nothing better to do than adulterating the beliefs of the common man."[154]

Al-Azhar investigated al-Fiqi and discussed stripping him of his affiliation—as had been done ten years before to 'Ali 'Abd al-Raziq, the modernist author of *Islam and the Foundations of Governance*—but al-Fiqi would be saved at the eleventh hour.[155] Another Azhari sheikh, 'Abdallah al-Ghumari, devoted ten or so volumes to attacking Wahhabism, including one that offered a biting response to 'Abdallah al-Qasimi's book attacking al-Dijwi.[156] Like al-Dijwi, al-Ghumari accused Ansar al-Sunna of calling Sufis and Azharis nonbelievers, thereby excommunicating them (committing *takfir*). Other al-Azhar ulema, like Ibrahim Ahmad Shahata and Hasan Khazbik, took part in this offensive.[157]

Most Azharis were thus hostile to the Salafis, as 'Abdallah al-Qasimi implies in his unsparing book *Al-Azhar Sheikhs and Their Additions to Islam*. Ansar al-Sunna nonetheless enjoyed a few allies of convenience within the university, some of them powerful, who fell into two categories: One group consisted of explicit Salafi sympathizers, of which there were vanishingly few in the first half of the twentieth century—at its founding, Ansar al-Sunna included just a smattering of al-Azhar graduates, most members being professionals or self-taught ulema. More important, some holdouts of late nineteenth-century modernizing reformism remained an active minority at al-Azhar after Muhammad 'Abduh's death in 1905. Though they did not follow Ansar-al-Sunna's literalist ideal, many shared both the association's desire for reform of Islam and its hostility toward Sufism and its practices—often because they saw these as superstitions that defied reason rather than innovations incompatible with religion.

In the decades following Ansar al-Sunna's creation, some of al-Azhar's Grand Imams would fall into this second category, including Muhammad Mustafa al-Maraghi (1928–1930, 1935–1945), 'Abd al-Majid Salim (1950–1951, 1952), Muhammad al-Khadar Husayn (1952–1954), and even Mahmud Shaltut (1958–1963).[158] Shaltut's story is interesting because it illustrates the limits of the modernizing reformists' relationship with Salafis. He had friendly ties with Ansar al-Sunna in the 1940s and 1950s, even writing in *al-Hadi al-Nabawi*.[159] But after taking the helm at al-Azhar, he began to orchestrate a new movement for rapprochement between Sunnism and Shiism, going so far as to issue a fatwa in 1959 that the twelver Shia (or Ja'fari) legal school could be considered Islam's fifth. This of course dismayed those Salafis who had until then seen him as an associate.[160]

Allies of convenience such as Shaltut nonetheless played a key role in protecting the association at moments when its existence was threatened. A good example is the affair surrounding the investigation of al-Fiqi in 1939 after he published *Al-Darimi's Response to Bishr al-Marisi*. First, several figures hostile to Salafism issued reports, including al-Ghumari and 'Abd al-Majid al-Labban, who oversaw the faculty of principles of the faith (*usul al-din*) at al-Azhar.[161] A committee of ulema was named to examine the question and for a time considered dispossessing al-Fiqi of his al-Azhar degree and thus his affiliation with the institution. Al-Maraghi then intervened, asking Mahmud Shaltut to write an assessment of the book. Shaltut took a much more generous view of al-Fiqi, suggesting that a few "trigger warnings" should perhaps have been added to the most controversial sections, but that because the book was already on the shelves, the urgency had passed; no action was necessary.[162] Al-Fiqi thus dodged—in extremis—the humiliation dealt a decade earlier to modernist 'Ali 'Abd al-Raziq, which would have been a damaging blow given Egyptians' abiding esteem for al-Azhar.[163]

The ambiguity described here was found, to varying degrees, in Ansar al-Sunna's relationships with most influential Egyptian political actors from the 1920s through the late 1940s; as with al-Azhar, this would ultimately serve the organization. For instance, the liberal Wafd Party, which dominated Egyptian politics during those decades, had little sympathy for Salafi theses but looked kindly on the critique of popular superstitions.[164] The king himself, despite having every reason to distrust a group that so openly flaunted its ties to a foreign country—and a rival one, at that—could only take comfort in Ansar al-Sunna's constant and conspicuous demonstrations of loyalty to him. Finally, despite deep differences with the Muslim Brotherhood, the fact that each hoped to rally the other to its cause would inspire a minimally cordial relationship—at first.

MUSLIM BROTHERS AND SALAFIS: UNITY VERSUS PURITY

The Society of the Muslim Brothers—commonly called the Muslim Brotherhood—was founded in 1928 by another of Rashid Rida's students, schoolteacher Hasan al-Banna (1906–1949). Unlike for al-Fiqi, what resonated most with him were Rida's calls for building an Islam-inspired system that would allow the Muslim world to catch up with the West, which became more urgent when the Ottoman Caliphate was abolished in 1924. Conversely, al-Banna was rather uninterested in the finer points of theological questions.

If al-Fiqi's project was inherently religious, al-Banna's was fundamentally political. The latter, following in the footsteps of the first reformists, felt dwelling on theological and religious differences posed a stumbling block to unity of the Umma, without which any political rebuilding would be impossible. The Brothers' framework was thus inherently identity-based.[165] It consisted of Islamizing the individual, society, and eventually the state without getting into an endless debate about the details of authentic Islam. One might say that from the beginning, the Brotherhood saw Islam both as a "total" (*shumuliyya*) ideology[166]—in the modern sense of the term—and as a religion.

This meant al-Banna was not inclined to attack Sufism, which Ansar al-Sunna considered "Islam's sworn enemy." For example, he saw seeking intercession (*tawassul*), especially from the Prophet, as just a form of worship. He acknowledged that jurists had diverging views on the practice, but felt it was acceptable since it had no impact on faith.[167] Al-Banna saw visits to saints' tombs as lawful and even encouraged his disciples to celebrate the Prophet's mawlid together.[168] He went no further than criticizing the "excesses" of some Sufis, as the al-Azhar sheikhs were also wont to do, while lamenting—for reasons more political than religious—the factionalism and political apathy that he felt brotherhoods fostered.[169]

Like many of his Egyptian contemporaries, al-Banna first experienced religion within a Sufi brotherhood, the Hasafiyya, an experience that may have rubbed off on his younger self. As Husam Tammam notes, he borrowed some elements from such brotherhoods when he created his own. For example, the Muslim Brotherhood's Supreme Guide is appointed for life and deeply revered, recalling the way Sufi disciples (*murid*) cherish their *shaykh*. More enlightening still: Brotherhood members at the time had to follow a curriculum that included texts fundamental to Sufi thought, like *The Revival of the Religious Sciences* by Abu Hamid al-Ghazali, and they practiced collective recitations (*awrad*) that echoed Sufi ones.[170] Al-Banna did not show much hostility toward Shiism either. He even participated in the early rapprochement initiative instigated in the 1940s by some al-Azhar ulema and Iranian mullahs.[171] Several decades later, the Brothers would again take the same approach when, eager to build a strong relationship with the nascent Islamic Republic of Iran, they hurried to Tehran to congratulate Ayatollah Khomeini after the revolution that carried him to power.[172]

The former schoolteacher cared little about debates on creed. A de facto Ash'ari because that current then predominated in Egypt, his priorities lay elsewhere. Al-Banna certainly had no desire to defend or spread Ash'arism or Sufism at the expense of other doctrines. He wanted to build a Muslim society as the basis for an Islamic State; from his standpoint, the main ingredient, Islam, was already at hand. In contrast, Ansar al-Sunna saw Islam as a lost essence to which the people had to return.

As long as they agreed with the project, all well-intentioned Muslims were welcome in the Brotherhood. "Let us cooperate in those things on which we can agree and be lenient with each other in those on which we cannot" (*nata'awun fima ittafaqna 'alayhi wa ya'dhir ba'duna ba'dan fima ikhtalafna fihi*), al-Banna is said to have remarked.[173] He pulled off the masterstroke of using "Salafi" and "Sufi" in the same sentence when he defined the Brotherhood, signaling his desire to transcend the antagonism then tearing them apart: "a *salafiyya* message, a Sunni way, a Sufi truth, a political organization, an athletic group, a cultural-educational union, an economic company and a social idea."[174] (Bear in mind that the word *salafiyya* clearly meant something quite different to him than it did to Ansar al-Sunna—yet another example of the word's initial polysemy.)

Al-Banna was also relatively liberal in his approach to Islamic practice. Regarding female attire, for example, the Brothers of his era did advocate a certain conservatism, but a simple veil covering the hair was good enough;

this meant that the women of the Brotherhood did not look much different in that regard from many of Egypt's working-class women.[175] Many men, including al-Banna, dressed like members of the effendi class, and a good percentage were clean shaven (al-Banna sometimes requested this explicitly, fearing that beards would be off-putting to the rest of the population).[176] The attitude toward non-Muslims was also relatively inclusive: While al-Banna strongly condemned Christian missionaries' proselytism, he emphasized the "human fraternity" in his relationship with Egyptian Copts.[177]

Faced with the proliferation of Egyptian Islamic associations and groups in the first half of the twentieth century, Hassan al-Banna hoped his welcoming approach would draw them into his brotherhood. He thus forbade instigating controversy on religious issues and kept critiques of both Sufis and Salafis to a minimum.[178] But when it came to al-Fiqi, each of al-Banna's offers of cooperation hit a wall.[179] Given the Brothers' overt "ecumenicism," Ansar al-Sunna's leader could only respond with hostility, even if he at first ignored the Brothers more than he criticized them—perhaps similarly convinced that he could bring them around to Salafism.

The relationship between the two organizations was likely also complicated by personal animosity between al-Fiqi and al-Banna, who had both studied with Rida and then laid claim to his legacy. In the end it was al-Banna who inherited the *al-Manar* journal upon Rida's death, which he would publish until 1940; al-Fiqi was left to found his own journal, *al-Hadi al-Nabawi*. It was al-Fiqi, however, who would complete the Quranic commentary begun in *al-Manar*. This seems like a logical allocation of their mentor's heritage: The religious parts fell to al-Fiqi while al-Banna took the political.

Only after World War II did Ansar al-Sunna decide to go after al-Banna's disciples directly. The timing was no coincidence: Ansar al-Sunna was now well established. What's more, after years as the monarchy's ally of convenience against the Wafd Party, the Brotherhood's ties with the palace were fraying—so much so that the organization would be disbanded (for the first time) in 1948.

By attacking the Brotherhood, Ansar al-Sunna could strengthen its own bond with the regime. In April 1946 al-Fiqi published a long article criticizing the Brothers because "in recent times they have strayed from the path they laid out for themselves." He complained about close collaboration on the upcoming election between the organization and some members of the Coptic community: "What remains of the Muslim Brotherhood if it is now possible for absolutely anyone—no matter their religion—to become their brother?"[180] Al-Fiqi then criticized the Brothers for staging a theatrical production in honor of Fatimid caliph al-Muʻizz li-din Allah, who founded Cairo and built al-Azhar, depicting it as "a direct attack on both dogma and morality" (not just because the protagonist was an Ismaili Shia, but because it was theater).[181]

Shortly thereafter, ʻAbd al-Rahman al-Wakil attacked al-Banna's tolerance of Sufism, accusing him of compromising on creed in order to draw in ever more disciples: "You want them by the thousand, even by the million... but do you want believers who build... or do you want them to come as they are, destroying the last relics of Islam's ruins with their own hands?"[182] In the wake of Prime Minister al-Nuqrashi's assassination in 1948, Ahmad Shakir would even accuse the Brothers of being Kharijites, a sect from Islam's early days denounced in Muslim histories for its extremism.[183] Al-Fiqi was equally ruthless: According to Salafi sheikh Nasir al-Din al-Albani, who met him during the pilgrimage to Mecca in 1948, he referred to the organization as the "Muslim Traitorhood" (Al-khawwan al-muslimun).[184]

This first chapter retraced the intertwined emergence of two Egyptian schools of thought that grew out of Muslim reformism in the latter half of the 1920s. In a sense, they represented its competing currents, which in quick succession (1926, then 1928) transformed into two movements: Ansar al-Sunna and the Muslim Brotherhood, distinguished as much by their religious concepts as by what I call their "grammar of action."

The Muslim Brotherhood—and the "Islamist" school of thought it represents—prioritized reviving the Umma politically by creating an "Islamic State." Strictly religious issues were thus secondary: The movement's mission was not to spark debate within Islam but rather to unify conservative Muslims, no matter their differences, around a shared political project. To get there, the Brothers participated in all available spheres. Starting in the 1940s, they ventured into institutional politics, running in parliamentary elections for the first time.

Ansar al-Sunna, on the other hand, embodied the Salafi movement. Named for the Muslim creed it follows, the group practiced a purist grammar of action. Its single-minded focus was on ridding Islam—starting with its creed—of "innovations" that had accrued over the centuries, in order to restore the religion to its authentic form, according to the ideals of the Hanbali theological tradition and its Wahhabi offshoot. The Salafi movement maintained close ties with Saudi Arabia, though these alone do not (as we'll see) explain Salafism's rise. Salafis steered clear of political debate, however, most often defaulting to fervent support for whichever regime was in power. They did not believe that change could come "from above" until they had radically transformed society. Although the term *salafi* remained somewhat polysemic until the 1950s, the Salafis discussed here would become its sole heir.

These Salafi circles gave rise to a new class of ulema radically opposed to the traditional Islam that predominated at the time. But they did all they could to avoid direct conflict with its representatives—if we exclude the unique case of 'Abdallah al-Qasimi, a true zealot as prolific as he was uncontrollable. Salafi writings glorified al-Azhar even as they cast doubt on the doctrines taught there. Some Azharis were able to read between the lines, however, and intensified their attacks on Salafis, who were ultimately (and perhaps paradoxically) protected by the institution's reformists.

The movement's skill at harnessing the religious field's dynamics should not go unnoticed. One could almost say—again, paradoxically—that Ansar al-Sunna leaders acted as shrewd politicians: The movement's hostility toward Sufism earned it the good will of both reformist ulema and Wafd modernizers.[185] Its early nonaggression pact with the Muslim Brotherhood kept it on the good side of what would become the most powerful Islamic organization in Egypt, and its overt loyalism bought the authorities' benevolence—no matter who was in power.

This generation of normative entrepreneurs fought most battles using books. Rediscovery of tradition (*turath*) was in the air, so the Salafis got busy promoting authors that aligned with their theological perspectives, advancing those interpretations by adding carefully crafted critical commentary to the books they published. Some followers of traditional Islam may have tried to follow suit, but the Salafis were better organized, more agile, and above all more "enterprising," to quote Ahmad Khan—and so had greater success.[186] Within a few decades, the Salafi corpus of formerly marginal authors would gain an increasingly central place in the Sunni one. Walid Saleh demonstrates this well in the case of Quranic exegesis: While the works of al-Razi, al-Baydawi, and al-Zamakhshari (representing a mix of classical Ash'arism with some Mu'tazili influence) had been the authoritative texts on the subject, Ibn Kathir's *tafsir* (the one most favored by the Salafis) gradually eclipsed its competitors—despite formerly seeming so peripheral that it didn't even warrant a mention in Islamicist Ignaz Goldziher's canonical 1920 history of Quranic exegesis.[187] As for Ibn Taymiyya, who was largely unknown in Egypt at the turn of the twentieth century, 130 of his books were published over the fifty following years.[188]

This radical transformation of the authoritative Sunni corpus would profoundly affect the religious field, setting the stage for the normalization of Salafism. Even if not everyone shared the Salafis' interpretation of Ibn Taymiyya or Ibn Kathir, the canonization of these works undoubtedly helped legitimize their (self-appointed) official interpreters and grant them an edge over competitors. Having won the battle of words, promoting their grammar would only get easier with time.[189] In an unlikely turn of events, this normalization of Salafism reached its apex during the Nasser period, which explains why the "Islamic awakening" of the 1970s would largely be a "Salafi awakening." We will explore this in the following chapter.

Chapter Two

EGYPT AFTER NASSER

A "Salafi Awakening"

> At the Istiqbal Tura prison, everybody was together. At that time there were only *jama'at islamiyya* at the universities in Egypt, and those were 100% Salafi—the universities were entirely Salafi. Cairo University had a journal called *The Voice of Truth*; Alexandria had *The Salafis Speak*. Under these imprints they would publish the books of Ibn Qayyim, Ibn Taymiyya, and others. The whole prison embodied a single movement!
>
> —ABU ISHAQ AL-HUWAYNI ON HIS IMPRISONMENT IN SEPTEMBER 1981

Most scholars agree that 1967 was a pivotal year for Egypt. The country's humiliating defeat in the Six-Day War against Israel led to the delegitimization of Arab nationalism and set off a vast religious revival that its followers called an "Islamic awakening" (*al-sahwa al-islamiyya*). Under Anwar Sadat, who succeeded Gamal Abdel Nasser, movements claiming to act in the name of Islam flourished in the 1970s; a violent fringe would eventually assassinate Sadat himself.

Examinations of this period, however, tend to be problematic. They concentrate almost exclusively on the role of Sayyid Qutb's ideas and thus fail to identify the underlying forces that inspired this return to religion.[1] Authors usually depict the Nasser period (1952–1970) as a sort of tabula rasa, implying that the Islamic awakening could have come only from the dark side of Nasserism: its prisons, where Qutb languished. This chapter aims to provide a more complex version of events, beginning with the Nasser era, which I see as a period of abeyance for the religious field as a whole—a net positive for Salafism, whose grammar of action made it seem benign to the ruling government.

The chapter develops a two-part hypothesis. Building on the previous chapter, we will first observe the extent of Salafism's impact on the Sunni norm, as it was expressed in activist religious circles at the end of Nasser's reign. The post-1967 religious revival launched from an essentially Salafi springboard. Emmanuel Sivan is among the few authors who portray Ibn Taymiyya, rather than Sayyid Qutb, as the star of the moment (on this point at least, he is surely closer to the truth than Gilles Kepel).[2] While we can't ignore Qutb's significant influence on the "1970s generation," this was felt later than is often asserted and cannot truly be understood without considering the generation's prior religious exposure. The 1970s revival was not simply Islamic: It was a "Salafi awakening." What's more, this was already in motion when the decade-defining, oil-fueled Saudi proselytism started to affect Egypt's religious domain—which proves that, despite all appearances, this awakening was not simply a consequence of foreign intervention (although we did see Saudi Arabia's crucial, if more modest, role during the royal era).

The 1970s political and religious context also inspired Salafism to profoundly reinvent itself. It took on more of an activist dimension, veering somewhat from the grammatical vision of its earliest champions. This transformation isn't altogether surprising: Already nearly ubiquitous in activist circles, Salafism was destined to be appropriated by new actors with new agendas. The Salafi corpus and lexicon would be revisited by a radical movement that, as the echoes of Nasser's brutal repression remained, would unearth justifications—through reinterpretations of inherently ambiguous texts—for a grammar of action foreign to the Salafis of prior decades.

THE PARADOXICAL LEGACY OF THE NASSER ERA

The revolution in 1952, which brought the Free Officers—and subsequently Gamal Abdel Nasser—to power, precipitated deep restructuring within the Islamic field that largely benefited the Salafis. For a regime that embraced secular nationalism, such an outcome might seem surprising. Make no mistake, though: However secular Nasser's ambitions may have been, he never shied away from mining Islam as a resource, whether domestically or in foreign policy.

Brothers and Free Officers got on well at first, with the former supporting the new regime and even playing an early role in the government. Then, in November 1954, Nasser—who had prevailed over the other officers—broke the alliance. The Muslim Brotherhood's influence and growing ambitions now felt like a threat to a regime that had modernist and secularist inclinations; using an attempt on his life as pretext, Nasser declared the Brotherhood an enemy of the state.[3] Apart from a small minority who left the organization to support the regime, its leadership was imprisoned or went into exile, especially in Saudi Arabia. Many books already describe this "ordeal" (*mihna*, as the Brotherhood calls it), so there is no need to repeat the story here.[4] Suffice it to say that this political upset nearly erased what had been the country's foremost Islamic organization.

While it was busy liquidating the Brotherhood, the new government was also angling for better control of the religious field. In 1953 charitable awqaf (*awqaf khayriyya*)—mortmain religious properties supporting endowments that financed mosques and more—were nationalized under the Ministry of Awqaf (Wizarat al-awqaf),[5] which was expressly created to oversee them. This cost the ulema the cornerstone of their economic independence. Religious courts were abolished in 1955, stripping ulema of a powerful (if symbolic) role in society and cutting off a career path for religious scholars. A law in 1960 (only partially implemented, as I will explain later) decreed that within ten years, all mosques would be overseen by the Ministry of Awqaf.[6] But 1961 brought the centerpiece of the regime's religious takeover: the Law on the Development of al-Azhar (*Qanun tatwir al-azhar*), which entirely restructured the university on the blueprint of Egypt's other universities, creating schools of secular sciences and burying religion among a plethora of other disciplines. Moreover, the university itself was nationalized. Its clerics became civil servants, and the sheikh of al-Azhar (soon officially retitled its Grand Imam)—along with the university president and the members of the Islamic Research Academy (which replaced the Committee of Grand Ulema)—was now directly named by the head of state.[7]

All figured into Nasser's plan to weaponize Islam for his propaganda war against regional enemies, particularly Saudi Arabia. He hoped to make al-Azhar the religious standard-bearer for Nasserism—and he would be surprisingly successful. The annexation of the institution did stir strong pushback, but most of its leaders played ball in the end; holdouts were quickly replaced by more subservient ulema.[8] Some even argued that socialism was inherently Islamic.[9] Going forward, however, al-Azhar ulema would be much less visible in public debate than they had been before the revolution.

Nasser's conquest of the religious field extended to the Sufi brotherhoods. Cairo's governor now served as president of the Sufi High Council, which was founded in 1905 and represented all officially recognized brotherhoods; elections of its general assembly were now held at the offices of the governorate.[10] And the highest Sufi authority in Egypt, the Supreme Sheikh of the Sufi Orders (Shaykh mashayikh al-turuq al-sufiyya), a position that had existed since Ottoman times, was now appointed by the regime—just like al-Azhar's sheikh.[11] He was assisted by a "general supervisor of Sufi orders" (al-mushrif al-'amm 'ala al-turuq al-sufiyya), none other than Field Marshal 'Abd al-Hakim 'Amir. Lastly, Sufis were appointed to the Arab Socialist Union (the sole political party allowed under the regime) and to other state institutions, and a representative of the security apparatus was designated to oversee the mausoleum (khalifat al-maqam) of al-Sayyid al-Badawi, which was the nerve center of Egyptian Sufism.[12] This guaranteed the extreme loyalty of Sufi organizations; in the wake of Egypt's defeat in 1967, for example, they held a huge procession in support of the president, despite the heavy criticism he was facing.[13]

By making traditional Islam an arm of the regime, Nasser's policy weakened its grasp on society, which—with Brotherhood Islam eliminated as well—left a vacuum in the religious field. This would be filled by the few independent religious actors left standing, especially Ansar al-Sunna and the Jam'iyya Shar'iyya. The two had weathered the president's takeover and retained their respective journals, *al-Hadi al-Nabawi* and *al-I'tisam*, as well as their mosques. Ansar al-Sunna issued critical editions at a brisk pace, helped by figures like al-Azhar's Muhammad Muhyi al-Din 'Abd al-Hamid, along with Ahmad Shakir and his brother Mahmud.[14] Book distribution (whether published by Ansar al-Sunna's Prophetic Tradition Press or by the Salafi Press, which were still in operation) continued relatively unhindered, even as anything remotely Brotherhood-related was closely surveilled and often strictly forbidden. The availability of the Salafi corpus elevated its standing among Islamic literature.

Salafi associations' open refusal to be politicized—in the sense of participating in political opposition—explains why they seemed so inoffensive to the regime. After the repression of 1954, Ansar al-Sunna took care to unequivocally dissociate itself from the Brotherhood. It would reaffirm this stance when Brotherhood-inspired activism resurfaced with the Organization of 1965—a brief regrouping of Brothers who had avoided arrest or been freed from prison—which was dismantled and accused of plotting to overthrow the regime. True to form, Ansar al-Sunna extolled Nasser's virtues in almost lyrical terms, celebrating in *al-Hadi al-Nabawi* "the man of the revolution, hero of the Arabs, emancipator of slaves, destroyer of colonialism, who inspired the spirit of revolution in Algeria, who helped spread peace around the world."[15]

Nasser, facing what amounted to a cold war with Saudi Arabia, was no doubt thrilled to receive such apparently enthusiastic support from a movement that, like Riyadh, identified with Salafi Islam. What's more, both Ansar al-Sunna and the Jam'iyya Shar'iyya were duly registered (in compliance with the law governing associations) and still modestly sized as compared with the Brotherhood's peak membership in the late 1940s.[16] For all these reasons, they seemed innocuous to Nasser who, wanting to be seen as a modernizer, likely didn't mind critiques of Sufi "superstitions."[17] In official Islamic institutions, the regime favored the last holdouts of modernizing reformism (the docile ones, anyway), including 'Abd al-Majid Salim and Mahmud Shaltut—the individuals mentioned earlier who, despite deep differences, remained close with the early Salafi movement.

All those searching for alternatives to official Islam and its outgrowths thus had few options beyond one explicitly Salafi association and another pushing an orthopraxy that happened to overlap with the Salafi *Weltanschauung*. Some differences between the two groups had faded over time: With the death of Mahmud al-Subki in 1933, the Jam'iyya Shar'iyya had already lost some of its Ash'ari character, and Mahmud 'Abd al-Wahhab al-Fayid, editor-in-chief of *al-I'tisam* in the 1960s, was even described as "Salafi-leaning."[18] Things culminated when, for reasons beyond their control, the two organizations officially merged toward the end of Nasser's reign.

A ministerial decree in 1967 ordered that Ansar al-Sunna be folded into the Jam'iyya Shar'iyya.[19] The relationship between Nasser and King Faisal of Saudi Arabia had grown tempestuous, and it seems the authorities were finally fed up with Ansar al-Sunna's ongoing Saudi ties.[20] Sarah Ben Nefissa hypothesizes that this takeover also had something to do with the post-1967 return of visible religious observance, which was starting to make the regime uneasy—in addition to the fact that, among those who had been detained in 1965 during Nasser's last major wave of arrests, some frequented the two associations.[21] The government now seemed more intent on controlling them than it had in prior years: In 1968, it dissolved the board of directors of the Jam'iyya Shar'iyya (which now included Ansar al-Sunna) and created a new one headed by a military officer, 'Abd al-Rahman Amin.[22] Only in October 1972, two years after Nasser's death, would each association regain its legal identity; several months then passed before the separation took effect and Ansar al-Sunna's property was returned.[23]

The merger in 1967 initially seemed like a gut punch to Ansar al-Sunna, according to Safwat Nur al-Din, a prominent member who became its leader in 1992: "Ansar al-Sunna's preachers found themselves jobless at first. In their mosques, they had been replaced by Jam'iyya Shar'iyya members." But "little by little, Ansar al-Sunna members started mingling with those of the Jam'iyya Shar'iyya; they got together, talked, wrote and debated." The result was clear: "In 1971, the Jam'iyya Shar'iyya, entirely Ash'ari until then, became majority Salafi after the merger, which had initially seemed like it would destroy all our hard work. But it allowed Salafism to spread beyond Ansar al-Sunna's mosques."[24]

Despite these transformations, leadership at the Jam'iyya Shar'iyya has remained unchanged. To this day, and despite the fact that some past presidents—like 'Abd al-Latif al-Mushtahari (1976–1995)—were more supportive of Salafism, the board of directors is still predominantly composed of Azharis who follow the Ash'ari school.[25] Those most "Salafized" were imams and rank-and-file members. The merger influenced Ansar al-Sunna as well: The question of orthopraxy, which had been secondary, now figured prominently in its discourse, a shift evident in *al-Tawhid*, the journal it published starting in 1973 as a replacement for *al-Hadi al-Nabawi*.[26]

The period of fusion gave rise to further initiatives. In fact, according to Safwat Nur al-Din, "when Ansar al-Sunna was incorporated into the Jam'iyya Shar'iyya and lost its platforms, some of its former preachers began founding Salafi mosques that belonged to neither Ansar al-Sunna nor the Jam'iyya Shar'iyya."[27] This brings to mind the influential Muhammad Jamil Ghazi (1936–1988)—member and later vice president of Ansar al-Sunna, Ministry of Culture employee, sometime critical editor (*muhaqqiq*), and tireless detractor of Sufism—who was acclaimed in Salafi circles for a legendary disputation (*munazara*) with thirteen Sudanese

Christian preachers, at the end of which all are said to have converted to Islam.[28] In 1968, in Cairo's Zeitoun neighborhood and not far from a Coptic church where the Virgin Mary was said to have appeared that year, he founded the Islamic Public Center for Missionaries of the Tawhid and the Sunna (Al-markaz al-islami al-'amm li du'at al-tawhid wa-l-sunna) and the al-'Aziz billah Mosque. The latter (which would, down the line, become officially affiliated with Ansar al-Sunna) was Cairo's main Salafi house of worship in the 2000s, known for hosting all the movement's "stars." It included an Islamic hospital and a highly sought-after training institute for preachers. Around the mosque a small Salafi neighborhood even sprang up with bookstores, clothing boutiques, and incense shops.[29]

Institutions aside, the 1950s and 1960s also saw a spate of intellectuals enthralled by the person and the ideas of Ibn Taymiyya, whom the Nasser regime unabashedly honored with an official celebration in 1961.[30] Through publishing, writing, or teaching, scholars continued to build the Salafi movement's momentum, using Ibn Taymiyya as a battering ram against Abu Hamid al-Ghazali, the guardian figure of Ash'arism, in an effort to topple him.[31] One Egyptian author, a secular leftist, lamented that sales of these scholars' texts continued unchecked under Nasser, describing a boom in "Islamic newspapers and journals, books on obsolete Islamic tradition that were edited and published, and a flood of books filled with obscurantist and retrograde ideas that were dumped on the market at piddling prices."[32]

These Ibn Taymiyya–focused intellectuals included academics like Muhammad Rashad Salim (1926–1986), who earned his PhD degree in 1959 from Cambridge University in England with a dissertation on "The Concordance Between Reason and Divine Law in Ibn Taymiyya's Writings."[33] Known for his many critical editions of Ibn Taymiyya's books, Salim taught at 'Ayn Shams University throughout the 1960s before departing for Saudi Arabia in 1971.[34] Another was Mustafa Hilmi (b. 1932), who in 1971 completed a doctoral dissertation at Alexandria University on "The Salafi School's Position Toward Sufism, from Early Times to Today." A prolific writer, Hilmi was defined as much by his intellectualization of Salafism as by his independence from all Salafi currents (which unanimously revered him), a remarkable fact given his past proximity with the Muslim Brotherhood—which he helped Salafize.[35] We will revisit Hilmi later.

More surprising still is the story of Muhammad Rashad Ghanim (1916–1992), who, according to a fascinating portrait by the late Husam Tammam, seems to have played a major role establishing Salafism in 1950s and 1960s Alexandria.[36] Ghanim had no intellectual or religious education; he started out as a merchant of silver and antiques. Deeply pious and fascinated by the writings and character of Rashid Rida, he became well-versed in Islamic culture, steeping himself above all in the writings of Salafi thinkers. He decided to assemble a library of ancient manuscripts, gathering them via the networks and resources of a lifetime in business. He brought over huge numbers of texts from India and elsewhere, and he paid considerable sums for rare works. In the 1960s he held one of only three existing copies in Egypt of Ibn Taymiyya's complete fatwas (in thirty-six volumes!). He was happy to share his finds with all who could use them, be they ulema or students. It was in his archive, for example, that Mustafa Hilmi gathered the building blocks for his thesis. His repository soon became a favorite haunt for Alexandrian Salafis. Celebrated preacher Ahmad al-Mahallawi and Ansar al-Sunna ulema such as 'Abd al-Rahman al-Wakil were among those who flocked to the salon he hosted; foreign sheikhs even stopped by, including Nasir al-Din al-Albani in 1976. Muhammad Rashad Ghanim had become an institution in his own right—and the authorities left him alone, especially because he advocated total apoliticism.

Finally, I should mention the influence of the Tabligh (*jama'at al-tabligh wa-l-da'wa*) movement, of Indian-Pakistani origin, that began taking root in Cairo during the late 1950s and grew under the guidance of Sheikh Farid al-'Iraqi.[37] In 1963 Ibrahim 'Izzat (1939–1983), a former Brotherhood member and young religious-programming host on Egyptian television, joined the movement; he would become its public face and most popular preacher.[38] Other Brotherhood members, disenchanted with politics, followed in his footsteps.[39]

The Tabligh movement was known for advocating individual reform and encouraging followers to practice the sunna in their daily lives, down to the smallest detail—an orthopraxy that, for example, required men to grow beards and encouraged all women to wear a niqab.[40] Members organized outings (*khuruj*)—preaching trips, really—to bring the good word to fellow Muslims. On the Indian subcontinent, their injunctions coexisted with both an acceptance of Sufism and a doctrinal posture known as Maturidism (a cousin of Ash'arism).[41] In Egypt, and in Saudi Arabia for that matter, the movement was much closer to Salafism in terms of creed.[42] Its lack of interest in politics allowed it to grow under Nasser, but Tabligh leaders were repressed nonetheless; al-'Iraqi and 'Izzat went to prison in 1965.[43] The movement began a period of exponential growth in the 1970s and set up its headquarters in one of the Giza governorate's enormous buildings, from which it operated legally for decades.[44] In the early 2000s, Tabligh represented one of the largest strains of Egyptian Islam and still functioned with little governmental interference.[45]

The paradox of Nasser's reign, then, was that while traditional Islam was weakened and the Brotherhood's Islam besieged, Salafi-inclined religion enjoyed rather bountiful success. Of all varieties then on offer, Salafism functioned with the least governmental interference—even if that freedom was still circumscribed by the Nasserist atmosphere. The movement thus naturally became a seedbed for the new Islamic activism that flourished in Egypt in the late 1960s.

A FIRST SALAFIZATION OF THE BROTHERHOOD FALLS SHORT

In truth, the effects of Salafization could already be felt in the Muslim Brotherhood during the Nasser era. That was when the distinction began to blur (at least at the edges) between the two ideal types, "Islamist" and "Salafi," while remaining applicable for the most part. Finding themselves the targets of oppression, Brotherhood members or sympathizers by and large retreated into Ansar al-Sunna and the Jam'iyya Shar'iyya, which, as Muhammad al-Sarwi (a Brother) writes in his memoirs, offered "a convenient loophole that allowed them to live in an Islamic environment until things improved."[46] So many were joining, in fact, that Ansar al-Sunna's journal warned its readers in late 1955 against an "infiltration by members and preachers from dissolved groups and committees."[47] The presence of Brothers in the two associations would lay the groundwork for a "Salafization" of the Brotherhood that has continued—nonlinearly, ebbing at times—to the present day.[48]

'Abbas al-Sisi, a Brotherhood leader, had described the impact of the first (pre-Nasser) anti-Brotherhood measures in similar terms:

> When a decision was made in 1948 to dissolve the Muslim Brotherhood—when they were repressed and their activities quashed—the young Brothers

headed to Ansar al-Sunna's mosques to continue their preaching. Ansar al-Sunna had not been dissolved, because it complied with its legal obligation to stay out of politics and because its preaching style differed so from the Brothers, who emphasized the all-encompassing nature of their message. When the decision to shut down the Brotherhood was reversed, some Brothers came back influenced by Ansar al-Sunna's preaching style. They tirelessly endeavored to forbid imagery, visiting tombs, men from wearing gold jewelry. Their speeches and conversations touched on little else, which caused controversies and disputes in the Brotherhood that sapped all our energy.... It got to where the Brothers had to confront them with an ultimatum: This here is the Muslim Brotherhood, and our objectives, our techniques, our teachings, and the all-encompassing nature of our ideas are not open to discussion. Anyone who shares our beliefs is one of us, and anyone who believes otherwise can go look for an environment better suited to his ideas.[49]

Mahmud Jami,' a Brotherhood member from the same period, relates how, after Hasan al-Banna died in 1949, a "group of young Muslims" (*jama'at al-shabab al-muslim*) formed within the organization. Its participants had grown close to prominent Salafi sheikh Muhammad Shakir, whom they had taken as their mentor. They believed that "the youth should focus exclusively on religious education (*tarbiya islamiyya*), deepening their knowledge and studying the *shari'a* and *sunna*, and that the duties of *jihad* or political opposition shouldn't be their objective."[50] This group of young Muslims even managed to open a bookstore across from Brotherhood headquarters that sold books on "ancient Islamic heritage," a provocation that fed conflicts with the remaining Brothers.[51] While these episodes stayed parenthetical during the royal era, the process repeated itself on a larger scale in the decades that followed, with similar consequences.

Under Nasser, this resulted in changes (minor at first) to the religious literature used by the Brothers. Muhammad al-Sarwi emphasizes the centrality of Ibn Kathir's *tafsir*—and its synopsis by Ahmad Shakir, a member of Ansar al-Sunna—among the books read by the first circle of Brothers that regrouped outside of prison between 1957 and 1962.[52] After 1964, two of Ibn Taymiyya's works—*The Book on Faith (Kitab al-iman)* and *The Book on Servitude (Kitab al-'ubudiyya)*—along with *Provisions for the*

Hereafter by Adopting the Ways of the Prophet (*Zad al-maʿad fi hadi khayr al-ʿibad*), by Ibn Qayyim, and *The Pathways of Peace* (*Subul al-salam*), by Muhammad al-Sanʿani, were added to the reading list of what would become the Organization of 1965 (which the authorities dismantled before it could act).[53] In the 1960s the religious texts that penetrated the gates of Brother-populated prisons often came from the Salafi corpus, likely because guards censored such content less harshly: *al-Mughni*, a treatise on comparative fiqh by Hanbali scholar Ibn Qudama al-Maqdisi; Ibn Qayyim's *Provisions for the Hereafter*, already mentioned, and *The Ascents to Divine Acceptance* (*Maʿarij al-qabul*), a book on creed by Saudi Sheikh Hafiz al-Hakami (1924–1958). By dint of their availability, such texts were what imprisoned Brothers read.[54] This initial Salafi influence on the Brothers resonates in the writings of two authors from the period.

The first is Sayyid Sabiq, a famous Brotherhood sheikh born in 1915, whose conciliatory approach to Nasser's regime saved him from prison in 1954. Between 1945 and 1965, he wrote his bestselling textbook, *The Fiqh of the Sunna* (*Fiqh al-sunna*), which did not preach the Salafi creed as such—this was not its objective—but its approach to fiqh was unmistakable. True to Salafi form, it aspired to transcend the legal schools with a unified interpretation of the law, basing its judgments only on the Quran and the sunna, taking inspiration from Ibn Taymiyya at several points, and aligning with the Salafi outlook on many questions—for example, the prohibition on gender mixing.[55] Until then, the Brotherhood's orthopraxy had been much less restrictive than the version he advanced. To this day, the book is still portrayed positively by Salafis, including Sheikh Yasir Burhami, who feels it was crucial in helping the Salafi approach to religious texts catch on with a pious Egyptian audience. He even acknowledges its role in his own path to Salafism.[56]

The second author is Sayyid Qutb, an ideologue and—to use Olivier Carré's term—"radical Muslim Brother."[57] Born in 1906, Qutb studied at the Dar al-ʿulum school before becoming a journalist and literary critic. He had ties to Islamic modernism for a time but grew closer to the Islamist movement in the mid-1940s—specifically that of the Muslim Brotherhood, which he would formally join only in 1953. Having quickly become one of the Brotherhood's core intellectuals, he was arrested when the organization began facing repression in 1954. In prison he wrote his most celebrated work, *In the Shade of the Quran*, a long Quranic exegesis from which he would draw some of the material for his widely read (and much shorter) book *Milestones*.

Nowadays, Qutb is mostly known for radicalizing Hasan al-Banna's theses, via a conceptual framework theretofore unseen in Arabic writing—borrowed, in fact, from the Indo-Pakistani Islamist Abul A'la Maududi. Qutb envisaged *hakimiyya*, or sovereignty, as the fundamental attribute of the divine in Islam.[58] God's sovereignty, however, could only be manifested by implementing His law, the shari'a, completely and absolutely; any infringement was unacceptable. This state of divine sovereignty was diametrically opposed to *jahiliyya*, or "ignorance of Islam," a term classical authors had used to describe the "ignorant" era before the prophetic revelation. But Qutb felt this phenomenon had never fully disappeared. The contemporary Muslim world, he explained, had fallen back into *jahiliyya* because it did not recognize God's sovereignty. Only a "vanguard" (*tali'a*), modeled on "the unique Quranic generation" (*al-jil al-qur'ani al-farid*), would be able to reverse course—through action (*haraka*) instead of rhetoric (*bayan*) alone—and establish the Islamic State.[59]

Qutb's logic had major implications. A society or state was only Islamic—and could only claim to be so—if it matched his utopian model of "divine sovereignty." This allowed for no gray area between Islamic and non-Islamic, as the Muslim Brotherhood's views had in the first half of the twentieth century. Al-Banna had felt the Islamic State should be worked toward through gradual reform of the existing system—a system thus judged "fixable." For Qutb, however, any reform was impossible: How could impiety be "reformed"?

This meant there was only one solution: revolution in the name of a jihad. But rather than countering the external enemy—the classic Islamic understanding of the term—this jihad would take on the existing authorities. Qutb's thinking was revolutionary; it was also eminently theoretical. Tariq al-Bishri may have been wrong, then, to consider *Milestones* the *What Is to Be Done?* of the Islamist movement.[60] A more fitting moniker might be "What Is to Be Thought?" since practical next steps were left to the reader's imagination. Regardless, Qutb's ideas helped bring about a revolutionary variation on the Brotherhood's Islamist grammar. I will refer to this as "jihadi grammar."

Qutb had shown an inclination (entirely theoretical at the time) toward Salafism as early as 1952, which was apparent in his defense of Saudi

Wahhabism: "We have allowed whole generations to believe that Muhammad 'Ali's destruction of the Wahhabi movement on the Arabian Peninsula was a heroic act, when it was in reality a historic crime against the Islamic revival that could have come to pass a century sooner—had we let this movement follow its course and achieve its aims."[61] The texts Qutb wrote in prison are undeniably influenced by the Salafi corpus, even if he interpreted it in an original way. Incidentally, we know that when he was briefly freed in 1964, he recommended several books to the young Brothers who were regrouping at the time, including three mentioned earlier: the treatises on faith and on servitude by Ibn Taymiyya, along with Ibn Qayyim's *Provisions for the Hereafter*.[62] Qutb's commentary on the Quran may not refer to Ibn Taymiyya (perhaps unsurprising, because Ibn Taymiyya never wrote a *tafsir*), but it does mention Ibn Qayyim three times—and alludes to Ibn Kathir's *tafsir* on some twenty occasions.

More important, his whole framework is infused with Salafism. Qutb's true innovation on the Brotherhood's approach was putting creed (*'aqida*, or more specifically the *tawhid*, a central Salafi preoccupation) at the heart of his message, while al-Banna had mostly focused on shari'a—this according to his friend Ahmad 'Abd al-Majid, a member of the Organization of 1965 who was imprisoned with him after the group's dissolution.[63] And, as Daniel Lav shows, Qutb's conception of creed was unmistakably Salafi. It questioned the idea that professing faith in Islam (*shahada*) was enough to make a person Muslim: A pious society without *hakimiyya* was destined for *jahiliyya*. According to Lav, this was likely due to Qutb's reading of Ibn Taymiyya's *Book on Faith*, which is entirely devoted to demonstrating that faith is not enough.[64] And Emmanuel Sivan suggests that "he was actually trying to work [Maududi's] ideas into Ibn Taymiyya's framework."[65] Ansar al-Sunna Salafis may have brought Ibn Taymiyya's puritanism to the fore, but Qutb unearthed the revolutionary potential in his ideas.

At the same time, Qutb was anything but Salafi in the term's canonical sense, because his effort was ultimately more political than religious, and he remained an intellectual rather than a cleric. He rarely engaged in theological debates as such. What's more, the questions that obsessed the Salafis were so far outside his intellectual outlook that they just didn't seem to interest him. On Sufism, for instance, he never weighed in.[66] Olivier Carré and others have actually argued that his approach was "mystical."[67]

Qutb's writings ignored the debate between Ash'aris and Salafis, and in certain passages of his Quranic commentary, he even insisted that God was in everything, an assertion that brings to mind the approach of the medieval Sufi scholar Ibn 'Arabi—a resemblance incessantly excoriated by his modern-day Salafi detractors.[68] What about blameworthy innovations (*bida'*), a question so central to Salafism? Barely a mention. Finally, Qutb, a clean-shaven man in a suit, looked nothing like a Salafi.[69] In this sense, while he drew from aspects of the Salafi corpus, Qutb fundamentally rejected its grammar.

In the wake of Qutb's execution in 1966, it would take the full force of the Brotherhood's Supreme Guide, Hasan al-Hudaybi, to stamp out Qutb's ideological transformation of the organization.[70] In 1969 al-Hudaybi, while still in prison, completed a book called *Preachers, Not Judges* (*Du'at la qudat*) in which he distanced himself from Qutb's ideas (without explicitly naming their author, attributing the concepts to Maududi instead).[71] The book reaffirmed that anyone who says the *shahada* is Muslim, returning to the Brotherhood's original, Ash'ari stance.[72] Although al-Hudaybi also quoted Ibn Taymiyya, he reminded his readers that there were various ways to interpret the medieval theologian. Various al-Azhar ulema followed with their own refutations of Qutb, all of them agreeing that he had "misunderstood" Ibn Taymiyya without attacking the theologian himself.[73] This was a far cry from the controversies of the 1920s when, to denounce the nascent Salafi movement, some Azharis openly lambasted its emblematic figure. Ibn Taymiyya had unquestionably become central to the Islamic canon.

'Umar al-Tilmisani, who replaced al-Hudaybi as Supreme Guide when the latter died in 1973, had been close with his predecessor and carried on his approach. He managed, albeit with difficulty, to swing the Brotherhood around to its original theological position—despite, as we shall see, opposition as much from within as from without. Inside the organization, undercurrents remained that were equally inspired by Qutb's ideas and by the Salafi discourse on which they were based, but the impact of his concepts would be most visible outside of the Brotherhood, after Nasser's death.

A SALAFI GENERATION EMERGES

Egypt's defeat in 1967 brought a semblance of calm to Nasser's repression, making room for a new activist "political generation."[74] Since state-controlled

Islam lacked credibility and attractiveness, "the only mosques available to youth at the time were those of Ansar al-Sunna and the Jam'iyya Shar'iyya" or the Tabligh movement.[75] As a result, many of these activists first experienced religion through one of the three groups. Meanwhile, the ranks of this pious generation were swelling because the 1967 loss, often seen as Arab nationalism's last stand, had stirred up extraordinary demand for religion.

Circumstances would soon smile on this "awakening." In 1970 Nasser's death led to a paradigm shift at the impetus of Anwar Sadat, the new president. Sadat was eager to distinguish himself wherever possible from Nasser, his rhetoric, and his alliances. He more explicitly pushed religion to the forefront, announcing his desire to build "a state of science and faith" (*dawlat al-'ilm wa-l-iman*) and adopting a new constitution whose second article now defined shari'a as a "primary source of legislation."[76] While Sadat continued to support Sufi organizations, he regarded the Islamist movement as a useful ally for countering the "centers of power" inherited from the Nasser period and their supporters in society.[77] This high-level turnabout made it much easier to express piety in public. Restrictions were also lifted on building "private mosques" (*masajid ahliyya*), which multiplied with little state oversight.[78]

Salafism's influence on the new activists manifested most obviously in their insistence on *al-hadi al-zahir*, or "conspicuous piety." The term refers to wearing external signs of observance prescribed by the Prophet's sunna. The Jam'iyya Shar'iyya had preached this practice since the beginning, but it now saw an unprecedented implementation and spread, sometimes taking a more conservative form than al-Subki had envisioned.[79] The term *al-hadi al-zahir* was itself borrowed from Ibn Taymiyya, who felt the obligation would differentiate Muslim from unbeliever.[80] Men did as the Prophet had prescribed, shaving their moustaches and leaving their beards untrimmed; they also wore various types of traditional attire and avoided anything Western. The 1970s likewise saw more women wearing a loose-fitting tunic and a niqab. And these activists applied a Salafi lens that saw gender mixing as a clear violation of the shari'a. Regarding creed, the doctrine of the *salaf* surfaced in several areas, including in activist circles' increasingly critical tone toward Sufism. Most of all, Salafism's binary worldview took hold: It was Islam or impiety (*kufr*), without the gray area that Ash'arism allowed.

This was a significant departure for Egypt and its Islam. A man of his time, al-Banna had worn European garb with a tarboosh and trimmed beard. We saw how he avoided attacking Sufism and tried to redirect the debate away from religion in the strict sense—Islam versus impiety—and toward political and social issues. Until the Nasser era, the Brotherhood had followed his example.

As Qutb's ideas rippled outward, many from this new generation of activists brought to life a spontaneous, intuitive synthesis whose theoretical details would be hashed out only later. It merged the purist grammar from their religious background, centered on issues of orthodoxy and orthopraxy, with the Islamist—or jihadi—grammar offered by Qutbist thought. This fusion was facilitated by common points between the two aforementioned discourses: Qutb placed creed at the core of his message, which resonated with the Salafi mindset, and his writings, like those of Ibn Taymiyya or Ibn 'Abd al-Wahhab, presented the same diametrical (and irreconcilable) opposition between Islam and impiety. This initial hybridization highlights one of the unique aspects of 1970s Egyptian Salafism: It was political, or even jihadi, almost from the outset. Only later, as the decade wound down and the next began, would some of this generation's activists slowly return to a purist grammar free of Qutbist influences.

At the dawn of the 1970s there was a proliferation of highly visible groups with the same amorphous mix of Salafism and Qutbism, the same medley of references to Ibn Taymiyya's ancient school and Qutb's modern one—even if the actors had diverging interpretations of each—and the same insistence on differentiation in public by wearing clothing intended to embody the prophetic sunna. I will touch on a few of these groups.

ACTIVISM TAKES FLIGHT

Groups that appeared at the turn of the 1970s were usually headed by a charismatic religious leader to whom their members pledged allegiance (bay'a).[81] Such figures filled a void; former activist Muntasir al-Zayyat explains that the youth were not finding the sheikhs they sought. The Brothers were still in prison and, since Qutb's death, no longer had any easily identified public figures; official Islam had been discredited; and the sheikhs of Ansar al-Sunna and the Jam'iyya Shar'iyya were out of phase with the Salafi-Qutbist model then taking root among the younger generation. Asked about his group's success, 'Abdallah al-Samawi, one of the trailblazers of this new Islamic activism, offered a candid response: "The people couldn't find anyone besides me; there really wasn't anybody but me at the time."[82]

The first sheikhs to make headway were those who could boast of having been imprisoned in 1965 with Sayyid Qutb, which gave them unrivaled prestige. The group Shukri Mustafa founded, known as the Society of Muslims (Jama'at al-muslimin), would have the most enduring reputation. It was in prison that Mustafa, arrested in 1965 on presumption of contact with the Muslim Brotherhood (to which he apparently never belonged, actually being closer to the circles of the Jam'iyya Shar'iyya), discovered the ideas of Sayyid Qutb through fellow inmate Muhammad, Qutb's brother.[83] Upon his release in 1971 after several years of torture and ill treatment, he spread a particularly radical reading of Qutb that took the *jahiliyya* quite literally; he came to see the society of his era as impious and to promote physical separation from it. This earned his group the pejorative moniker *al-takfir wa-l-hijra* (excommunication and emigration) in the Egyptian media. And yet it was surprisingly successful among a population hungry for religious guidance, soon counting hundreds, then thousands, of followers.

The inspiration for Mustafa's movement reflected the 1970s Salafi zeitgeist: He championed a return to the earliest Islam, which for him meant the first three centuries after the Prophet Muhammad's Hijra (exile), and argued that any religious judgment must be based on a direct proof (*dalil*) from the Quran and the sunna, with no intermediary.[84] This meant tossing out "consensus" and "analogy," principles of legal interpretation, in favor of an uncompromising literalism, and rejecting any imitation (*taqlid*)—especially of the four canonical legal schools.[85] Mustafa additionally advocated a Salafi-like orthopraxy, encouraging his disciples to wear tunics, grow beards, and, if possible, keep their hair long in the image of the Prophet.[86] Moreover, he opposed films and music, and his group's first violent actions targeted a cinema and the institute of Arabic music.[87]

Mustafa's "Salafism," however, was anything but orthodox: He condemned nearly all classical ulema, suggesting that "closing the doors of *itjihad*" in the tenth century had been their plot to hang onto power.[88] Even the revered ulema of the Salafi tradition were not spared this methodical attack, which culminated in some cases with excommunication. Famed exegete Ibn Kathir—whose name translates to "son of plenty"—was tagged with the derisive sobriquet "Ibn Qalil," Arabic for "son of little."[89] Mustafa's disciples were forbidden from studying Ibn Kathir's books or those of his peers. Their only approved reading, in fact, was written by Mustafa himself, starting with his *Book of the Caliphate (Kitab al-khilafa)*.[90] Other stances raised eyebrows, including his opposition to holding Friday prayers—he felt such worship didn't belong in a society of *jahiliyya* where the "Society of Muslims" was not firmly implanted (*mutamakkin*). Among his peculiar choices, Mustafa also proscribed learning to write except when it was needed for practical purposes.[91]

His group's early momentum was soon repaid with criticism from across the religious field. The Ministry of Awqaf predictably took the lead in this ideological counteroffensive, but Mustafa's competitors among the new activists did their share, too. Some, like Khalid al-Za'farani, who had at one point rubbed shoulders with the Society of Muslims, actually say this confrontation deepened their exposure to Salafi religious literature—collateral education as they scoured Salafi tomes for arguments against Mustafa, whom they denounced as the leader of a "Kharijite sect."[92] But his opponents were playing with fire: Hasan al-Halawi, of Giza's Salafi circle (more on this later), was beaten nearly to death by members of the Society of Muslims after a recording circulated in activist milieus of a twelve-hour-long religious disputation (*munazara*) in which he faced Mustafa.[93] The latter's thirst for revenge against critics, however, would eventually be his downfall: In 1977 the society kidnapped Sheikh Muhammad al-Dhahabi, a former minister of awqaf, whom it accused of disparaging Mustafa. The operation spun out of control and the sheikh was killed, unleashing a broad police offensive against Mustafa and his followers that led to his arrest and execution.[94]

A similar but less sectarian group was led by 'Abdallah al-Samawi (1946–2009), born Taha al-Samawi in Egypt's Assiut governorate, who, like Shukri Mustafa, was imprisoned in 1966 at the same institution that held Qutb and his disciples.[95] At first inspired by Mustafa, he then distanced himself and founded a separate group that disavowed his mentor's most controversial positions.[96] Al-Samawi did condemn the *jahiliyya*, as

Mustafa had, but he reserved the term for governing authorities and specific social behaviors—not society as a whole.[97] And unlike his mentor, he presented his movement as "*a* group" rather than "*the* group" (or society) of Muslims. He suggested that his disciples read Sayyid Qutb, but alongside authors like Ibn Kathir and al-Shawkani, who were associated with the Salafi corpus.[98] Only one of the group's publications survives—an epistle called *Some Fundamentals of Our Message* (*Min maʿalim daʿwatina*)—but its Salafi overtones are unmistakable. In the text, al-Samawi suggests that he is adopting "the creed of the pious ancestors [*al-salaf al-salih*] and the saved sect [*al-firqa al-najiyya*]."[99]

Like Mustafa, however, al-Samawi encouraged his followers to abandon their studies (school and university teachings were "detrimental") and advocated splitting off from society by building isolated, self-contained communities.[100] A tireless preacher, he crisscrossed Egypt constantly in search of new members.[101] According to Muntasir al-Zayyat, a participant, al-Samawi's group counted several dozen members in 1974 and several thousand in 1978, by some accounts making his movement the largest of the era. Although the group had a presence in Cairo, the bulk of its followers resided in Upper Egypt. As a side note, al-Zayyat recounts that his superior in the group was none other than Usama al-Qawsi, discussed later, who in the early 2000s became one of the figureheads of loyalist Salafism.[102] Al-Samawi's flock also included, at least briefly, most of those who would form the group behind Sadat's assassination in 1981.[103]

While al-Samawi's movement would eventually crumble on its own, several of its successors are worth mentioning here. Their legacy illustrates that many of the era's activists cared more about orthodoxy and orthopraxy than about political questions. A first group derived from that of al-Samawi was arrested in the late 1970s as its members prepared to torch al-Sayyid al-Badawi's mausoleum in Tanta, a gathering place for Egyptian Sufis, after having attacked other mosques that contained tombs and mausoleums.[104] Other disciples of his would cause a fuss in the 1980s when they incinerated video stores and cinemas, pushing al-Samawi to formally distance himself.[105]

Finally, we should not overlook the role of independent sheikhs in Salafism's 1970s Egyptian expansion. Unlike the leaders just mentioned, these sheikhs may not have languished for long years in Nasser's penitentiaries alongside Qutb's disciples, but other qualities lent them undeniable authority. Along with 'Abd al-Hamid Kishk (a more "Brotherhood-compatible" sheikh) and the unclassifiable independent Sheikh Ahmad al-Mahallawi, they came to symbolize religious dissent.[106]

The first of these independents was named Hafiz Salama.[107] A religious autodidact born in 1925, he had at one point participated in Youth of our Lord Muhammad (Shabab sayyidina Muhammad), a small, radical (and in some ways proto-Salafi) splinter group of the Muslim Brotherhood.[108] Salama gravitated early on toward an interpretation of Islam that was simultaneously Qutbist and Salafi. After a stint in prison, he was freed by Nasser in 1967 and made a name for himself in his hometown of Suez as the leader of and inspiration for the "popular resistance" against the "Israeli enemy." This brought him considerable renown across Egypt, and he used this fame to spread his religious message. At the same time, Salama founded the Islamic Guidance Society (Jam'iyyat al-hidaya al-islamiyya), which allowed him to construct mosques and Islamic centers throughout the country by fundraising at home and abroad (most likely in the Gulf). His most popular project, built across from the Coptic cathedral on Cairo's Abbassia Square—an intentional provocation—was the immense al-Nour Mosque, which Salama called the "grand fortress of Islam."[109] It became a stronghold of political Islam (with a strong Salafi overtone) until it was forcibly repossessed by the Ministry of Awqaf—on orders from the highest levels—in 1986.[110]

Sheikh 'Umar 'Abd al-Rahman, born in 1938, was another of Egypt's rebellious Islamic figures during the 1970s.[111] But in contrast to Salama, 'Abd al-Rahman was Azhari, an affiliation he flaunted at every opportunity. From the late 1960s on, his virulent criticism of Nasser's regime—following the execution of Qutb, whom he admired—and then of Sadat earned him constant state surveillance.[112] (When Nasser died in 1970, 'Abd al-Rahman refused to pray for the president, whom he considered an apostate, and spent eight months in prison as a result.)[113] Despite his Azhari roots, he was drawn to the Salafi corpus, as evidenced by the books he cited when he described his education in his polemic *Speaking the Truth* (*Kalimat haqq*, which was actually the transcript of his defense in the trial of Sadat's assassins). On creed, for instance, he mentions only the writings of Ibn Taymiyya and *The Ascents to Divine Acceptance* by the Saudi sheikh Hafiz al-Hakami, before discussing his prolific reading on deviant groups (*firaq*): "Shia, Murji'ites,

Muʿtazilites, Jabriyah, Ashʿaris, Kharijites…"—terminology that again reflects his Salafi inclinations.[114] In 1977 he left for a three-year teaching job in Saudi Arabia, a stay that further familiarized him with Salafism. Upon returning in 1980, he frequently preached at the al-ʿAziz bi-llah Mosque, founded by Muhammad Jamil Ghazi in 1968, and was among the most consequential voices for young radicals.[115]

THE PIONEERS OF JIHAD

The groups and figures discussed thus far acted in the public arena, mostly unconcerned with discretion. Meanwhile, in the shadows, many smaller cells were also forming that advocated—and planned—violent action against the regime.

Some of the big names in 1970s jihadism first forayed into activism during the late 1960s, while Nasser was still in power. Here, too, their composite Salafi and Qutbist backgrounds led to both a deeply politicized Qutbist take on Salafism and a Salafi reframing of Qutb's philosophy and ideas in purely theological terms. In the shadows of the repressive climate, the jihadis secretly debated how best to overthrow an "impious" regime. They sketched out what Egyptian media called the "Jihad Organization" (Tanzim al-jihad), which never actually existed under that name and was more an aggregate of overlapping circles. These pioneers formed two pockets, one in Alexandria and the other in Cairo, the latter composed of several circles with mutual acquaintances. The Alexandrian coterie spawned the group that attacked a Cairo military college in 1974, while most of those behind Sadat's assassination emerged from the one in Cairo.

The first to expand to a respectable size was the Alexandrian circle. Talal al-Ansari, who was sentenced to death (then pardoned) for his role in the 1974 attack, says that it all started in the winter of 1968 when "five friends gathered for a course (*halaqat dars*) being taught at one of Ansar al-Sunna's mosques."[116] Those present included Muhammad Basyuni—an Ansar al-Sunna sheikh in his thirties who would be expelled from the organization in 1970—and several secondary school students: Talal al-Ansari, Yahya Hashim, and Hamid al-Difraoui, as well as Rifaʿi Surur, who would become one of the most influential theorists of Egyptian jihadism.[117] Most—like Rifaʿi Surur, who was born in 1946—had frequented

Anar al-Sunna's mosques for a number of years. Journalist 'Ali 'Abd al-'Al wrote of Surur:

> His time with Ansar al-Sunna was a turning point; it was where he developed his religious awareness of right and wrong, or what Islam authorizes and forbids, but also a transitional moment because he began to reflect—above all, about Ansar al-Sunna's intellectual outlook and approach. His questions and criticisms revolved around the organization's methods and message, which reduced all religious issues to that of associationism (*shirk*) at mausoleums and tombs, and supported Nasser as he arrested the Brothers. The organization stood up to the president—printing its journal under the headline "No, Mr. President"—only when he visited the mausoleum of al-Husayn.... "We were asking ourselves," explained Surur, "why are we not promoting virtue? Why are we not trying to enforce the Quranic punishments?"[118]

Surur and his comrades responded by organizing on their own. Talal al-Ansari asserts that theirs was "the only Islamist group in Egypt" at the time.[119] They expanded quickly by recruiting at Alexandria's two main high schools. Several notable people joined either the group or one of the cells that were associated with it directly or indirectly. Among them were Wagdi Ghunaym, today a figure in the Salafi wing of the Muslim Brotherhood, who frequently appeared on Salafi satellite television channels in the 2000s; Muhammad Isma'il al-Muqaddim, future cofounder of the Salafi Call in Alexandria; and Khalid Dawud, who in the 2000s became prominent in the Brotherhood's reformist wing. These youth "found a second home in the mosques of Ansar al-Sunna and in its many small prayer rooms in working-class areas."[120] Communal meals were hosted, and weekly lessons were given in the association's mosques or at members' homes. There, in a fusion characteristic of the era, texts by Sayyid Qutb, Muhammad Qutb, and Abul A'la Maududi were read and discussed alongside *Provisions for the Hereafter* by Ibn Qayyim al-Jawziyya and the writings of Muhammad bin 'Abd al-Wahhab.[121] It does seem, however, that for at least some members, Qutb's influence arrived relatively late, as Khalid Dawud explained: "For us, Salafi culture came first. We didn't read Sayyid Qutb; we said he was Ash'ari. Qutb's influence in Alexandria was initially very minimal. I only read *Milestones* some time later."[122] Young members also participated in sports, especially running. Word spread quickly within Alexandria's religious circles about the group and its activities.

The initial group birthed several cells. One started out by targeting Sufi mausoleums. According to their contemporary Mukhtar Nuh, its members were even on the verge of burning down the famous mausoleum of al-Mursi Abu al-'Abbas, one of the centers of Alexandrian Sufism. "But in the end," he writes, "'the operation,' as they liked to call it, didn't happen, even though they had gathered the necessary materials—gasoline and empty bottles. They decided to focus on other similar actions instead."[123]

Others in the group were taking a more political approach. Their objective was to overthrow the "impious" regime and found an Islamic State, which led them to build connections with the few leaders of the Muslim Brotherhood not in prison. Talal al-Ansari tells how he and his comrades aligned behind 'Ali Isma'il, a recently freed Brotherhood member and the biological brother of 'Abd al-Fattah Isma'il (a friend of Sayyid Qutb who was executed with him in 1966).[124] Through Isma'il, they met Zaynab al-Ghazali, an ardent female supporter of the Islamist movement who over a long period had been close with Qutb.

Here is where the accounts diverge. Talal al-Ansari says that al-Ghazali introduced them to the Brotherhood's Supreme Guide, Hasan al-Hudaybi, to whom they swore allegiance in 1972.[125] Other members beg to differ: Some doubt this ever happened, while others question whether, if such a pledge was indeed proffered, the Guide accepted it.[126] They are right to be skeptical. For one thing, it would be strange for Hasan al-Hudaybi, the earliest challenger of Qutbist thinking, to court disaster when the Brotherhood had already been nearly obliterated. What's more, in an Egypt where the "Brotherhood question" was so heavily politicized, one can imagine that al-Ansari—who had repented and just barely dodged the death penalty, and whose memoirs were written at the end of Mubarak's reign—would be motivated to offer a scenario that tied the Brothers to violence.

Regardless, the Brotherhood's tattered network did connect the young activists with the man who would become their leader: Salih Sirriyeh, whom Zaynab al-Ghazali introduced to the group. Once al-Ghazali's introduction had greased the wheels, Sirriyeh easily assumed leadership thanks to his apparently exceptional charisma, which was especially effective on the young, inexperienced members. Sirriyeh was long a murky figure in jihadi history, sometimes said to have participated in the Islamist

Hizb al-Tahrir Party at one time.[127] Born in Palestine in 1934, he moved with his family to Iraq after 1948. There, he obtained a degree in education sciences at the University of Baghdad while pursuing a career as an army officer. In parallel, he studied Islam, specifically hadith, and al-Ansari says Sirriyeh became close for a spell with the Salafi Sheikh Nasir al-Din al-Albani. While still a member of the Palestinian National Council, where he rubbed shoulders with Yasser Arafat and Ahmad al-Shuqayri, he joined the Iraqi branch of the Muslim Brotherhood. There, again according to al-Ansari, he held an important role. Sirriyeh fled Iraq after the Baathist Ahmad Hasan al-Bakr took over the country in 1968, eventually landing in the Egyptian capital, where he taught at ʿAyn Shams University after earning his doctorate there.[128] He additionally became a civil servant in the Cairo-based Arab League.

Starting with his time in the Iraqi Brotherhood, Sirriyeh's push for revolutionary action set him apart from movement leadership. Once in Egypt, he laid out his views in a text called *Epistle on Faith* (*Risalat al-iman*) (1973), where he took up the Qutbist refrain: Modern Arab societies were nothing but *jahiliyya*, the authorities were impious and jihad was the only path.[129] But the theological approach he embraced was quite explicitly Salafi. According to his account of Islamic theological history, orthodoxy had been replaced by a dominant "false" tradition—defended by ulema who were in the pockets of the authorities—that separated actions from faith. He explicitly attacked Ashʿari theologians like the prominent Abu Hamid al-Ghazali.[130] To return to a more "accurate" approach to the Quran, Sirriyeh recommended reading exegetic treatises by Ibn Kathir and Sayyid Qutb.

In the group of youth to which al-Ansari belonged, Sirriyeh found the troops he needed to bring his revolutionary plan to fruition. According to al-Ansari, he eventually found them too enthusiastic: While Sirriyeh had envisioned a military coup d'état requiring two years of preparation, the youth were determined to act immediately.[131] The most impatient members left the group after this disagreement, many for a second group then forming in Alexandria around Yahya Hashim, a deputy public prosecutor by day who moonlighted as an advocate of urban guerilla warfare. Among those who joined this group was Rifaʿi Surur, whom Hashim had contacted after discovering Surur's first book, *People of the Ditch*.[132] The title came from a hadith that he took as a call for advocates of Islamic rule to take action and to persevere. Hashim's group grew slowly because, to stay below the radar, he required that his followers abandon any external signs of religious observance; he felt conspicuous piety was only obligatory in an established Islamic State. A large faction of the young recruits refused to relinquish this practice, saying that it was nonnegotiable for Muslims.[133]

While the first large post-1967 Islamist group did form in Alexandria, Cairo was not completely left behind. One activist circle had formed in the mid-1960s in Maadi, a well-to-do suburb of the capital.[134] Among the group's members were Isma'il Tantawi and 'Alawi Mustafa, both high school students who later studied engineering; so was Nabil al-Bar'i, who recounts how an Ibn Taymiyya book he stumbled on catalyzed his transformation. Determined to make moves, al-Bar'i rejected any collaboration with the Brotherhood, both because he found its approach to action too "moderate" and because the Brother he had met with wore Western clothing and had no beard.[135] The group was soon joined by Ayman al-Zawahiri, who was a high school student, and then by military officers including 'Isam al-Qamari.[136] Once again, almost all members were regulars at Ansar al-Sunna mosques, which served as their most frequent gathering places.[137] They were especially moved by one of the association's foremost figures at the time, the Azhari Muhammad Khalil Harras, whose classes they took at Ansar al-Sunna's headquarters in the Abdeen neighborhood.[138] Participants often acquired classics, especially by Ibn Taymiyya, at the Salafi Bookstore, founded long before by Muhib al-Din al-Khatib.[139]

Differences with Ansar al-Sunna's Salafism soon became apparent; 'Alawi Mustafa even wrote a small book about them.[140] But the group seemed to maintain allies in the organization, according to al-Zawahiri, who says that he continued to see Harras. During a private meeting several years later at his home in Tanta, Harras even supposedly stated that "the Egyptian regime is apostate, and anyone capable of overthrowing it is duty-bound to do so," after having endorsed al-Zawahiri's understanding "of the words of Imam al-Shafi'i, sheikh of Islam Ibn Taymiyya, and Sheikh Muhammad bin 'Abd al-Wahhab."[141] Kamal Habib, who had been close to the group, explains that its "members laid the groundwork for what we now call 'jihadi Salafism'—they took inspiration from the Salafi sources they were then reading at Ansar al-Sunna, and developed an intellectual synthesis between those sources and what they had read by Sayyid Qutb." According to Habib, however, their interpretations of his texts were only later integrated into the primary Salafi framework.[142]

A second circle developed in Giza, another Cairo suburb, around Hasan al-Halawi, Mustafa Yusri, and 'Abd al-Fattah al-Zayni, and maintained contact with the first circle (but never joined). In this case as well, Salafi thinking, much more than that of the Brotherhood or even Qutb, informed its leaders' intellectual development. Hasan al-Halawi, who describes "studying under the sheikhs of the Jam'iyya Shar'iyya and Ansar al-Sunna at a time when the Brothers were in Nasser's prisons," says: "In the group I belonged to in Cairo, we hadn't read any of the books on the Brotherhood's ideas; we were among the Egyptian pioneers of the Salafi current that was centered on religious authentication (*al-ta'sil al-'ilmi*). We based our outlook on books by Salafi sheikhs like Nasir al-Din al-Albani, and we focused on verifying and authenticating hadiths (*takhrij al-ahadith*), as well as on the exegetic sciences (*'ulum al-tafsir*)."[143] As a side note, 'Abd al-Fattah al-Zayni was the first Egyptian to have the "complete fatwas of Sheikh of Islam Ibn Taymiyya" printed; he also founded the Ibn Taymiyya Salafi bookstore.[144]

Bridges were finally built between the groups in Alexandria and Cairo. The two shared a desire to act to bring about the Islamic State, and both believed a military coup d'état was necessary. Al-Ansari describes an attempted merger with Isma'il Tantawi's group, which he says fell through because the Alexandrian activists were more revolutionary at the time than those in Cairo.[145] Former jihadi 'Abd al-Mun'im Munib offers another explanation for the failed fusion: Tantawi's attachment to Salafi orthopraxy. Wanting to expand his circle of followers at any cost, Sirriyeh—perhaps echoing the Brotherhood grammar of his youth—decided it preferable to forestall debate on questions of religious practice until after the Islamic State was established, while Tantawi insisted that it was paramount to adhere to the ways of the pious ancestors and exclude any transgressors.[146] Former activist Muntasir al-Zayyat states, for example, that Sirriyeh counseled his disciples to remain cleanshaven, noting that "as a Salafi current ... we criticized Salih Sirriyeh for going too far in camouflaging his convictions."[147] Some members of Cairo's second circle, in Giza, nonetheless enlisted in Sirriyeh's organization, but they did so on their own.

In April 1974 his group, with the help of those who had joined in Cairo, decided to act. They would attack Cairo's military technical college (Al-kulliya al-fanniyya al-'askariyya), where they had some followers, to seize weapons for a coup d'état. The operation was a total fiasco: seventeen died, and most members were arrested. Even the "dissidents" who had split off to follow Yahya Hashim got caught up in the ensuing investigation. Their group was dissolved, and Hashim died fighting. Former jihadi Muhammad Muru notes that the imprisonment of all these activists had an unexpected consequence: Having landed in the Liman Tura prison, where Sayyid Qutb's last living comrades were rotting away, these militants—who had essentially grown up around Salafi ideas—became more familiar with those of Qutb.[148]

The relics of Sirriyeh's organization stumbled on. Members who had avoided arrest or been acquitted began regrouping and recruiting replacements. After a new round of arrests in 1977, a fresh attempt to organize the activists sputtered and brought yet more arrests in 1979. The group then splintered into smaller cells, with one of them again directed by a Palestinian, Muhammad Salim al-Rahhal.[149] An aficionado of Salafi literature, he was the first to compare Sadat to the Mongols, advocating jihad on the basis of Ibn Taymiyya's fatwa that justified revolting against the ruling Mongols because they were insincere Muslims.[150]

Then, in the summer of 1980, 'Abd al-Salam Faraj appeared on the scene. An electrical engineer by trade, Faraj first made his name as the imam of a small Cairo mosque, where he taught Qutb's books—*Milestones*, for example—as well as works from the Salafi tradition like *Jihad for the Sake of Islam* (*Al-jihad fi sabil al-islam*), by the eminent Muhammad al-Shawkani.[151] His main contribution to jihadi thought was a book called *The Neglected Duty* (*Al-farida al-gha'iba*), which, referring to Ibn Taymiyya's aforementioned fatwa, declared Sadat an apostate who deserved to die. In addition to Ibn Taymiyya and Ibn Qayyim, he introduced the group's members to works by Abul A'la Maududi and, somewhat surprisingly, to one of the epistles of Juhayman al-'Utaybi, a Saudi Salafi "rebel" responsible for the November 1979 attack on Mecca's Great Mosque.[152] Faraj managed to unite the various existing groups under his command and even, as we will see, to augment his flock with student activists from Upper Egypt. The resulting organization would be behind Anwar al-Sadat's assassination on October 6, 1981.

THE STUDENT MOVEMENT

The 1970s Islamic awakening swept across society as a whole, but universities played an outsized role because—as is often the case—students were at the forefront of the social movement. This phenomenon took hold during a rapid upswing in student activism in the late Nasser years, with campus protests beginning as early as February 1968.[153] Repression relaxed somewhat after the president's passing, and the movement grew accordingly. Besides, access to higher education had recently expanded, landing hundreds of thousands of young Egyptians, many from rural areas, at overcrowded universities without much prospect of getting good jobs.[154] As the activist movement gained steam, left-wing groups initially seemed to dominate, but in just a few years' time Islam would eclipse their ideals as the new unifying value.

In the wake of Nasser's death, most university faculties began offering a "religious group" (*jama'a diniyya*), sometimes called an "Islamic study group" or "religious awareness committee" (*lajnat al-taw'iya al-diniyya*), a sort of club where the religious students got together, just as others might do for theater or sports.[155] The Islam promoted there was essentially the official brand, meaning traditional and Sufi-inspired. But these groups were quickly flooded with the new devout generation that emerged at the turn of the 1970s. Like the youth discussed earlier, most were educated in Ansar al-Sunna, the Jam'iyya Shar'iyya, or at Tabligh mosques and read Ibn Taymiyya, Ibn Qayyim, and Muhammad bin 'Abd al-Wahhab.[156] And many were also familiar with (or would soon be introduced to) the ideas of Maududi and Qutb.

Their religious culture, then, was a world apart from that of their elders, prompting a radical transformation within the universities' religious "clubs" or groups: The new students demanded action, and what had begun as an administrative structure soon morphed into an activist one. In a further departure, the Islam preached there now took on Salafi overtones; Salah Hashim, one of the period's principal actors in Assiut, describes the drastic rebranding that followed.[157] One after another, the existing groups adopted new names to signify this shift: *jama'a islamiyya* ("Islamic group," pl. *jama'at islamiyya*), which also refers to the organization Maududi founded in India in 1941 (*jama'at-e islami*, in Urdu).[158] Whereas the group had formerly been led by a president (*ra'is*), he was now given the religious title of emir (*amir*) and assisted by an advisory committee (*majlis al-shura*).[159] These groups amassed power, especially—and this was no accident—after 1973, when Egypt's "victory" in the name of Islam over the Israeli Army (as government propaganda would have it) boosted the cachet of everything Muslim.[160]

Expanded coordination between the groups in various faculties and then universities soon led to the unification of the various jama'at islamiyya under one national structure: the "jama'a islamiyya of Egypt," founded in 1977, led by an elected "emir of emirs" (amir al-umara'), Hilmi al-Gazzar. What's more, the groups participated in student union elections and secured surprising victories. In 1975, for example, the jama'a islamiyya of Cairo managed to elect one of its own, 'Abd al-Mun'im Abu al-Futuh, as the head of Cairo University's student union, which until then had been the exclusive domain of the left. This phenomenon repeated itself across most Egyptian universities, bringing a bumper crop of resources for the activists who now stewarded the official unions' budgets.[161]

There was some overlap between the jama'at islamiyya and the jihadi cells mentioned earlier, both because of true intellectual proximity and their shared theoretical acceptance of "using violence as a tool for change," and because some young jihadis went to university and participated in the student activism.[162] Differences in the actors' approaches and objectives, however, limited this covalence. Plus, as underground entities, the jihadi groups tended to keep their plans on a need-to-know basis. Regarding the military college attack in 1974, 'Abd al-Mun'im Abu al-Futuh relates that "we only learned about the military college group after the mission failed; we were surprised to learn that they had managed to recruit two participants from the jama'a islamiyya at the Qasr El Eyni Faculty of Medicine."[163] The ties between student activism and underground groups nonetheless solidified in the late 1970s, especially in Upper Egypt.[164]

The jama'at islamiyya also thrived thanks in part to an indulgent regime eager to Islamicize its image and willing to do anything necessary to neutralize campus communists and Nasserists. Early on, there were many conflicts with left-wing activists—in Cairo, the jama'at islamiyya tore down adversaries' wall magazines, while students in Upper Egypt often came to blows—but these subsided as proponents of Islam became dominant at universities.[165] Some were certain a formal agreement had been struck between the young activists and the regime, but this was likely not the case; it's probable that the authorities had simply intuited the strategic advantage in the Islamic activists' omnipresence.[166]

Several studies mention the initiatives of the jama'at islamiyya.[167] Some of these made the jama'at quite popular because they improved students' daily lives, for example, by establishing a bus service reserved for female students or offering their members course readings at cut-rate prices. Participants also fought passionately against gender mixing; one notable victory at Cairo University separated young men and women in the crowded lecture halls. The groups campaigned against showing certain films, performing specific plays, or hosting concerts. Abu al-Futuh sees this as a consequence of their Salafi socialization, noting that these youth were primarily obsessed with societal mores—which they transformed, as he recounts: "Some female students began following our edicts on behavior, on the obligation to wear long veils (*jilbab*) or fuller coverings (*khimar musdal*) that showed only the face and hands. We then became more uncompromising; we required them to wear the niqab and show nothing at all. The *niqab* caught on widely starting in 1975."[168]

Other activities focused on spreading the message. The jama'at frequently held lectures and, during school breaks, "Islamic camps" (*mu'askarat islamiyya*) where, as Gilles Kepel writes, "the participants did not spend all their time contemplating the Quran ... but also trained in various group sports and self-defense, prayed collectively, and, at dusk, listened to preachers expound Islamicist solutions to the bitter disappointments of contemporary Egyptian society. The camps were microcosmic experiments in Islamicist utopia, past and future."[169]

The students' hybrid religious culture was reflected in the array of invited sheikhs and preachers. Some guests were members of (or close to) the Muslim Brotherhood, like Muhammad al-Ghazali, Mustafa Mashhur, Sayyid Sabiq, 'Umar al-Tilmisani, 'Abdallah 'Azzam of Palestine, and Yusuf al-'Azm of Jordan; other participants included the few official or semiofficial ulema still popular with the masses, like Sheikh Muhammad Mitwalli al-Sha'rawi.[170] According to Husam Tammam, however, most invitees were Salafi-leaning ulema: sometimes Ansar al-Sunna members or those with ties to the association, like Muhammad Jamil Ghazi; sometimes Tabligh figures like Ibrahim 'Izzat; sometimes independents like Hafiz Salama and Ahmad al-Mahallawi; and sometimes, like Abu Bakr al-Jaza'iri, people brought over from Saudi Arabia for the occasion.[171] Other figures from the aforementioned preaching groups were also invited, including 'Abdallah al-Samawi. The presence of these Salafi-leaning figures at the camps of the jama'at islamiyya should come as no surprise. In Alexandria, for instance, the program was established by Muhammad Isma'il al-Muqaddim, a participant in the city's first Salafi group in the late 1960s who was briefly imprisoned in 1974 and later cofounded the Salafi Call.[172] And Cairo's "emir of summer camps" was none other than Usama 'Abd al-'Azim, one of the future leaders of independent Salafism in the capital.[173]

The jama'at islamiyya also published books, representing a hodgepodge of Brotherhood and Salafi references, that reflected their religious beliefs. This undertaking was made easier by the fact that the jama'at islamiyya had taken over the information and publishing committee of the national student union organization in 1975, allowing the jama'a islamiyya at Cairo University to put out a monthly book series called *The Voice of Truth* (*Sawt al-haqq*) under the student union's imprint, overseen by Mahmud Ghuzlan.[174] (In the 2000s Ghuzlan became a mainstay of the conservative faction within the Muslim Brotherhood.) The series included titles like *Epistle from the Fifth Conference* by Hasan al-Banna; *The System of Life in Islam*, *The Four Topics*, and *Islamic Political Theory* by Maududi; *This Religion* and *The Religion of the Future* by Sayyid Qutb; a compilation of assorted writings by al-Banna, Qutb, and Maududi called *Jihad on the Path of God*; two epistles by Sheikh al-Sha'rawi; a book by Yusuf al-Qaradawi; *Exegesis on the al-fatiha Verse* by Ibn Qayyim and *The Muslim Woman's Hijab* by Salafi Sheikh Nasir al-Din al-Albani; and several publications by Sheikh 'Abd al-Rahman 'Abd al-Khaliq, an Egyptian by birth who inspired the Salafi movement in Kuwait.[175] According to 'Abd al-Mun'im Abu al-Futuh, the committee also regularly republished books by Saudi ulema.[176]

At Minia University, the local jama'a islamiyya whittled down *The Twenty Principles of Hasan al-Banna* to just eighteen; two were considered too "Sufi." The school's jama'a islamiyya was particularly inflexible: Its members were the last to join student union elections because they rejected a structure perceived as too Western and thus contrary to Islam.[177] One of the books published at Alexandria University bore the school's logo and was titled *Gender Mixing According to Islam* (the practice was naturally denounced); another, inscribed "jama'a islamiyya—Faculty of Liberal Arts," was called *The Unique Quranic Generation*.[178] No author was identified, but the title clearly brings Qutb to mind.

In literature on the subject, we find mentions of other texts published or distributed by the jama'at islamiyyat in the 1970s, including a volume called *Islam's Position on Music and Singing* (*Hukm al-islam fi-l-musiqa wa-l-ghina'*); 'Abd al-Rahman 'Abd al-Khaliq's *The Scientific Foundations of the Salafi Call*; a book by Ahmad Al Butami, Qatar's former Wahhabi mufti; as well as the *Epistle on Faith* by Salih Sirriyeh, who had recently been executed for his role in the 1974 attack.[179] Some students, including Muhammad Isma'il al-Muqaddim and Ahmad Farid, the Alexandrians who would cofound the Salafi Call at decade's end, also used the services of the local jama'a islamiyya to publish their first epistles.

The groups frequently held book fairs and clothing sales. There one could find Islamic books, more often from the Salafi tradition than from that of the Brotherhood, sold at substantial discounts negotiated with the publishers.[180] Racks were stocked with all the essentials for conspicuous piety, and at wholesale prices: tunics for the men, long robes (*'abaya*) and veils both partial (hijab) and complete (niqab) for the women, alongside sticks of *siwak* and perfume.[181] The jama'at islamiyya also put on "Islamic weeks" with themes such as "Muslim Minorities of the World," "Palestine," or (after 1979) "Afghan Jihad."[182] Finally, to extend their reach, the jama'at islamiyya took charge of collective prayers for Eid—first on campuses and then in stadiums, which allowed them to break out of the student circle to attract a wider audience.[183]

Starting in the mid-1970s, another major activity of the jama'at islamiyya involved organizing both great and small pilgrimages (*hajj* and *'umra*) to Mecca—a steal at just 25 to 35 pounds per student.[184] Tens of thousands of students took advantage. Many chose to stay a few extra weeks in Saudi Arabia to "seek knowledge" (*talb al-'ilm*) from the kingdom's ulema, who gladly welcomed the jama'at islamiyya as the "Egyptian outgrowth of the movement they embodied."[185] This allowed the young Egyptians to get in touch with Salafism's "homeland," which would have a direct influence on them going forward. Large shipments of Salafi books began arriving, both for students fresh back from pilgrimage and for the jama'at islamiyya, which industriously distributed and sometimes republished them, according to

'Abd al-Mun'im Abu al-Futuh. This means that, despite oft-repeated assertions to the contrary, the Saudi influence reached a generation that was already part-Salafized and thus only reinforced an existing trend—although the effects of this sway were undeniable.[186]

Although many analyses paint a different picture, the jama'at islamiyya politicized their rhetoric only at a later stage, embracing increasingly hostile public postures toward the regime.[187] They appeared relatively indifferent to the January 1977 bread riots, sometimes even sabotaging the organizing efforts of leftist groups on campuses.[188] Even if there were earlier signs of politicization, the turning point for the jama'at islamiyya truly came when Sadat visited Jerusalem in November 1977. Three events in 1979 added to the momentum: the signing of the peace treaty with Israel, Sadat's decision to welcome the exiled Shah of Iran, and finally the passage of controversial legislation (known as Jehan's laws, after Sadat's wife) that expanded women's rights. This was also when the authorities—who had until then treated the jama'at with a degree of goodwill—began to repress the groups, severely restricting their summer camps and then wresting back control of student unions in June 1979.[189] The repression radicalized some of the student activists—especially in Upper Egypt, where the local divisions of jama'at islamiyya soon enlisted with the proponents of armed violence.

THE SPLIT: THE BROTHERHOOD ENTERS THE FRAME WHILE THE SALAFI MOVEMENT CHARTS ITS OWN COURSE

The prior section began with a description of how the 1970s activist generation was socialized in a cultural breeding ground that thoroughly blended Salafism (in its definition of both orthodoxy and orthopraxy) with Brotherhood thought—sometimes al-Banna's version, but more often in its Qutbist variation. Among most young activists, this bricolage happened unconsciously—they built on what they heard and read without necessarily perceiving (at first glance, anyway) the possible contradictions lurking within. As Salafi Call cofounder Ahmad Farid tells it, "We didn't know the word 'Salafism,' just as we didn't know the word '*ikhwani*' [of the Brotherhood], . . . even as we studied and taught Salafi books."[190]

In this context, it was the return of the Muslim Brotherhood—now as an organization, no longer simply a diffuse ideology—that would stir up the hornet's nest. At the dawn of the 1970s, the Brothers had become a myth in every sense: Their battle against Nasser and the suffering they had endured were remembered sympathetically by the new activists, but almost none of them had met a Brother in the flesh. Between 1973 and 1974, Sadat finally decided to free the bulk of the organization's imprisoned members.[191] The "victory of 1973" had placed the president in a comfortable enough position that he could be openly magnanimous toward the regime's former enemies—plus, he felt that the Brothers might be useful reinforcements in combatting the vestiges of Nasserism.

Right out of the gate (literally and figuratively), the Brothers were surprised to discover that a new generation of activists had emerged in their absence and decided to connect with the jama'at islamiyya then flourishing in the universities.[192] Meanwhile, a rupture was brewing in the Brotherhood's still-regrouping leadership: On one side stood partisans of 'Umar Tilmisani, who, after Hasan al-Hudaybi's death, was the last surviving member of the Brotherhood's 1954 Bureau of Guidance, making him al-Hudaybi's default successor as Supreme Guide in 1974. On the other side stood a conservative element more visibly influenced by Sayyid Qutb (even if the faction had abandoned his revolutionary approach). Some of its members were Brothers who had participated in the movement's paramilitary branch (called the "Special Apparatus" or *al-nizam al-khass*) in the 1940s and/or the Organization of 1965 and remained in the Brotherhood after these episodes. They were led by Mustafa Mashhur, who would become Supreme Guide in 1996 and hold the title until his death in 2002.

Differences ran deep between the two strains.[193] Mashhur's followers were what Husam Tammam calls "organizationists" (*tanzimiyyun*): They believed change would come only through preserving and expanding the Brotherhood organization, which they saw as a "vanguard" (*tali'a*)—an expression used by Sayyid Qutb, who influenced them on this point—of the coming Islamic State.[194] As this subset saw things, the movement should not be too open to society, for fear both of compromising its identity and exposing it to dangers that could threaten its mission. Its partisans encouraged secrecy, and its positions on Islam were more conservative overall.

'Umar al-Tilmisani and his followers, on the other hand, prioritized openness to society and followed a more relaxed version of Islam, closer to that of al-Banna and the early Brotherhood. Tellingly, al-Tilmisani made no secret of his enthusiasm for music, sometimes recounting that he had played the oud as a child; he also had some avowed Sufi tendencies.[195] Finally, starting in 1984, he pushed the idea of permanently renouncing violence in favor of massive participation in the realms of politics and labor unions—against the wishes of prominent members within the rival faction.[196]

As it happened, though, in the 1970s al-Tilmisani—then short on allies—found himself in a somewhat weak position within the Brotherhood. For all intents and purposes, partisans of Mashhur were calling the shots; they accepted al-Tilmisani only as the "face of the organization, a political façade."[197] One of them, Kamal al-Sananiri, who had married Sayyid Qutb's sister while in prison, was the first to go about building a bond with members of the jama'at islamiyya (likely in 1975). He reached out to 'Abd al-Mun'im Abu al-Futuh, then president of the student union at Cairo University, who says the two met under top-secret conditions.[198]

Blown away by his interlocutor, Abu al-Futuh broached the subject with a few colleagues, who began to consider joining the Brotherhood:

> The question sparked long discussions between the leaders of the jama'a islamiyya. We oscillated between admiring these people's history—respect for their fight, efforts and sacrifices—and criticizing them because of our radical Salafi background. We reproached them for what to us seemed like their failure to adopt visible prophetic traditions (*sunan*) like the beard, conspicuous piety, and some other elements—however superficial—that overshadowed our judgment when assessing individuals.[199]

His confrere 'Isam al-'Aryan alludes to their "hesitations regarding the Brothers' behavior, like the fact that some didn't have beards or displayed images in their homes."[200] Ibrahim al-Za'farani, who led the jama'a islamiyya of Alexandria, describes bringing four critical talking points to his first meeting with the Brotherhood leaders: the Brotherhood's position on creed (the divine attributes, intercession, etc.); the Brothers' limited adherence to conspicuous traditions (beards, wearing the *jilbab*, etc.); the degree of religious culture among the Brothers; and their understanding of jihad.[201]

Abu al-Futuh, al-'Aryan, and al-Za'farani ultimately chose to join the Brotherhood, followed by some of the principal figures in the jama'at islamiyya. As Abu al-Futuh acknowledges, the "radicalism" of Mashhur's followers (whom they met through al-Sananiri) had reassured them and smoothed their integration into the Brotherhood; they likely would have been more hesitant had their interlocutors belonged to the organization's competing current.[202]

This decision, however, was not immune to second thoughts. Khalid Dawud, one of the leaders of Alexandria's jama'a islamiyya, recounts that "when we joined the Brotherhood, we did so to reform the organization and right its wrongs—that is, to bring it into line with the Salafism that permeated our existence."[203] The Brotherhood's leaders tried to reassure the youth by growing out their beards, hoping to secure a permanent merger.[204] The organization also led a campaign, through its *al-Da'wa* journal, for restructuring the schedules of students and civil servants to allow for on-time arrival to the *zuhr* prayers. Aaron Rock-Singer sees this as another effort at appealing to the piety of the jama'at islamiyya.[205]

The next step involved negotiating the formal unification of the Brotherhood and the jama'at islamiyya. But Abu al-Futuh and his companions were expecting to face strong headwinds from the movement's base and the second rung of leadership, so they postponed announcing an agreement.[206] 'Isam al-'Aryan even recounts how they sometimes "attacked the Brothers in order to head off any accusation that they had joined."[207] In the end a slip of the tongue—by a leader of the Alexandrian jama'a islamiyya (most likely Khalid Dawud) during a conversation with Usama 'Abd al-'Azim, an important leader in the jama'a islamiyya of Cairo—let the cat out of the bag.[208] This accelerated the movement's split, which seems to have happened around 1978.[209] Most members of the jama'at islamiyya, however, trusted their leaders and joined the Brotherhood.

The influx of new blood allowed the Brotherhood to get back on its feet, its ranks having been decimated under Nasser. This alliance would have contradictory consequences both for the organization itself and for its new members. In its early days, the Brotherhood became more visibly Salafi. As Moaaz Mahmoud recounts, "growing a beard, wearing the *niqab* and following *hadi zaher* [conspicuous piety] became normalized and spread within the Brotherhood, which had become more conservative than ever. . . . Judged too moderate and labeled too permissive by the new arrivals, many of the Brotherhood's touchstones, such as works by Sheikhs Muhammad al-Ghazali and Yusuf al-Qaradawi, became increasingly marginalized."[210]

Back then, many Brothers still regularly attended the sermons of the Jam'iyya Shar'iyya and Ansar al-Sunna.[211] But as the years went by, the lion's share of newcomers came to "desalafize" most aspects of their religious observance. Oum Nour, the wife of a high-ranking Brotherhood leader of the era, recounts how Brothers "stopped growing beards and wearing short white djellabas. They made clear to the Muslim Sisters who wore the niqab that it would be preferable not to. For those who didn't want to give it up, the men requested that they wear white, in order to distinguish themselves from the Salafi women who always wore black."[212]

In the words of lawyer and former Brotherhood parliamentarian Subhi Salih, "The general state of mind had been Hanbali-Wahhabi; the Brothers saved us!"[213] The roots of this evolution lay in the mid-1980s, when 'Umar Tilmisani and his followers prevailed in their approach with support from the last remaining influential religious figures in (or close to) the organization: Muhammad al-Ghazali and Yusuf al-Qaradawi.[214] During this period, the two became the face of what their disciples called *wasatiyya*—a middle ground, in Islam—and the term was waved about as an antidote to the prevailing Salafization and to Qutbist temptations.[215] These sheikhs embraced a wide range of ideas: They were Ash'aris, open to a "moderate" Sufism, to a "reasonable" amount of mingling between sexes, to the arts, and to the democratic system—all within the limits laid out by a still-conservative interpretation of the religious texts.[216] Al-Ghazali even led explicit attacks against the widespread Salafization of the religious discourse. In a book in 1989, he referred to Salafism with the rather unkind term "Bedouin fiqh."[217]

The "al-Tilmisani way" led the Brotherhood to disavow violence and renew its openness to society during the 1980s. It also decided to participate in the existing political system so as to advance the organization's cause. And there was another reason for this evolution: Salafis were rapidly becoming adversaries from whom it was imperative to distance the movement so it could stay "respectable"—especially because, much to the chagrin of its dominant current, the public now increasingly equated Salafism with armed action.[218] Despite this pendulum swing, the merger with the jamaʿat islamiyya left some lasting traces of Salafi practice in the Brotherhood, which would later fuel the movement's return to a dynamic of "Salafization." Sufism, for example, was now more unanimously discredited within the organization.[219]

Two factions within the jamaʿat islamiyya vehemently opposed what they saw as a forced fusion, reflecting the power of local specificities. The first faction was dominant at Assiut University and well established in Upper Egypt. Its members were known for emphasizing Sayyid Qutb's revolutionary ideas, which they interpreted in a particularly intransigent way that often led to violence against their critics. In the later 1970s the group practiced what it called "correction of vice by force" (*taghyir al-munkar bi-l-yad*), a radical take on the Islamic concept of "commanding right and forbidding wrong" (*al-amr bi-l-maʿruf wa al-nahi ʿan al-munkar*).[220] Targeted operations "corrected" improperly veiled students, forcibly separated men and women, and raided liquor stores. The Copts (whom the group denounced, following Salafi logic, for their otherness and threat to "Muslim society") became a favorite quarry.[221]

These activists refused to join the Brotherhood because of its perceived inertia: The organization discouraged violent action and had been "co-opted" by the Sadat regime, which they were duty-bound to combat.[222] In a clever verbal joust, the activists derided the group for becoming the "Muzzled" Brotherhood (*Al-ikhwan al-mustaslimun*, literally the "Brotherhood of Capitulators"). They further reproached the organization's insufficiently Salafi religious practice, especially its lack of conspicuous piety.[223] Confrontations between these students and the Brothers sometimes escalated from verbal to violent.[224]

The split sparked a symbolic battle over the name jamaʿa islamiyya, which both parties would continue to claim for a time—the dissenters by enlivening it with the slogan "there is no God but God" (*la ilaha illa Allah*), and the Brothers with "God is the greatest and to him all praises belong" (*Allah akbar wa lillahi al-hamd*).[225] Only in the mid-1980s would the students who had joined the Brotherhood relinquish the name once and for all.[226] Since then, the term Jamaʿa Islamiyya (which I capitalize in this context) has officially referred only to the dissident group. Official or not, though, the homonymy still stirs confusion: When ʿAbd al-Munʿim Abu al-Futuh, a presidential candidate in 2012, wanted to prove he wasn't tied to a movement the Egyptian public associates with terrorism, he struggled to clarify that despite having been a figure in the jama'a islamiyya back when he was a student, he had never belonged to the Jama'a Islamiyya.[227]

Starting in 1979, most of the dissident group's leaders were wanted by the authorities, especially for their involvement in various incidents of sectarian strife in Upper Egypt.[228] The leaders were thus in hiding when they made contact in 1980 with 'Abd al-Salam Faraj, who had managed to unite the various jihadi circles of Cairo and Alexandria, and chose to join his efforts to overthrow Sadat. To lend credibility to their new organization, they selected Azhari Sheikh 'Umar 'Abd al-Rahman, just back from Saudi Arabia, as their spiritual leader; they had also considered handing the role to Hafiz Salama or Rifa'i Surur.[229] Following a fatwa issued by 'Abd al-Rahman, members attacked Christian-run jewelry boutiques in Upper Egypt, hoping to use their plunder to purchase weapons.[230] On October 6, 1981, when Sadat was assassinated by Khalid al-Islambuli, a member of Faraj's organization, they launched an armed revolt in Assiut that the army extinguished in three days' time.[231] All surviving insurgents were sent to prison with harsh sentences, but this would not deter the group from reincarnating later in the decade with a new generation of activists.

Beyond these radical students, a second group refused allegiance to the Brotherhood, citing its proclaimed attachment to "Salafism." Its members, who condemned violence, weren't drawn to the Jama'a Islamiyya, either. The group started out as a circle of ten or so people, based in the Faculty of Medicine and, to a lesser extent, in the Faculty of Engineering at Alexandria University. A handful of early members came from Cairo, too, including Usama 'Abd al-'Azim and Muhammad al-Dubaysi, former directors of the summer camps run by Cairo's jama'a islamiyya.[232] These "Salafis" had, in late 1977, created a "Salafi School" (Madrasa salafiyya) within the jama'at islamiyya to counter the Brotherhood's "harmful" doctrinal influence and reaffirm the fundamentals of their creed.[233] With the jama'at islamiyya's switch into the Brotherhood camp, they had no choice but to split off.

The Alexandrians who advocated this separation would build an organization, the Salafi Call, that openly wished to rid 1970s Egyptian Salafism of its external influences—notably Brotherhood ones—so the movement could be brought back to "orthodoxy." But this didn't stop them from borrowing their adversaries' models and mobilization methods. I will discuss this in detail shortly.

This chapter has offered a new take on the backstory of 1970s Islamic activism by reintroducing its Salafi components, which academic literature has largely ignored. We saw the central role that Salafi religious socialization—pervasive in circles of religious activists at the end of the Nasser era—played in structuring the ideologies of every movement from that era. Without negating the influence of Qutb (who justified his own revolutionary stance through a specific interpretation of books from the Salafi corpus), it is essential to understand that his ideas operated within a framework already shaped by Salafism. Saudi Arabia played an undeniable role during this decade, but this came later and was less decisive than is often advanced. Moreover, Egyptian Salafism itself initially emerged from the period transformed, particularly because over the decade its texts and concepts had been used to support a revolutionary grammar entirely foreign to its earliest proponents.

Only at the end of the 1970s did the boundaries clarify between Brotherism, jihadism, and Salafism within this new activist generation. Each current then seemed to return, broadly speaking, to the ideal-typical grammar of its roots: Islamist grammar for the Muslim Brotherhood, through a relatively inclusive religious approach focused on politics and the conquest of the state; jihadi grammar for the Jama'a Islamiyya and the violent cells, which abandoned strictly theological debate in favor of political combat via armed struggle; and purist grammar for the Salafi Call, which exclusively applied itself to promoting orthodoxy and orthopraxy from below.

Yet, as a result of the battle for influence that played out across this pivotal decade, each current still left its mark on (and was marked by) its competitors. Jihadi rhetoric remained deeply influenced by the Salafi lexicon, even if—following Qutb's logic—the jihadis primarily used the language to lend religious legitimacy to their revolutionary actions. The Brotherhood tried hard to "de-Salafize" and "de-jihadize" its new recruits, to assimilate them into its original discourse and grammar, but it didn't completely succeed—in part because some of the organization's leaders were still influenced by a Salafi and/or Qutbist worldview. And the Salafi

Call, while endeavoring to revive a Salafism free of political Islam's "harmful" influences, borrowed elements of the Brotherhood's mobilizing strategies, as well as its all-encompassing concept of an Islamic discourse that transcends theology. Given the Call's wide-ranging influence on the development of Egyptian Salafism from the 1980s on, we will examine it more closely in the next chapter.

Chapter Three

THE SALAFI CALL

Salafism Meets Activism

A Call blessed by our Lord,
Respected ulema who protected it,
Here is my advice for you:
Remember to give thanks to those who helped it grow.
Have you seen the *qayyim* Abu Idris,
The reason and wisdom he bestowed upon it?
For my pride it is enough that al-Muqaddim
Has honored it with science and with grace,
And the mufti of the Call, our sheikh Saʿid,
Whose chief concern is its protection,
The sheikh of the creed, Yasir Burhami,
A cry that foils the cunning of his foes,
Our sheikh Hutayba, the jurist,
An Umma unto himself for which he fights,
The Call's man of letters, our Sheikh Farid,
Who has devoted to it his life entire.

—EXCERPT FROM A *NASHID* BY YASIR ABU AMMAR

This chapter chronicles the rise of the Salafi Call, an organization that emerged from the splintering of the jamaʿat islamiyya as the deep ideological reordering of the late 1970s swept Egypt. We will see that the group initially had two objectives. First, it wished to reinstate the purist grammar of early Salafism by freeing it of Brotherhood and jihadi influences; the organization would devote much effort to combatting their resurgence throughout the 1980s and 1990s. With Salafism on the verge of supplanting traditional Islam as the incarnation of orthodoxy (at least for those who believed in activist piety), the battle shifted to the heart of Salafism—and the Salafi Call wanted to represent the creed's only legitimate expression.

But the Call also endeavored to equip Salafism with a true social movement built on the techniques the Brothers, and those they inspired, used to organize and mobilize. Its founders simultaneously got to work "ideologizing" Salafism, another process deeply shaped by their early immersion in a Brotherhood-influenced milieu. What a paradox: The group had formed in opposition to the capital-B Brotherhood, yet in many regards it resembled a lowercase-B Salafi one. As we shall see, the Call was not very close with Saudi Arabia—though too quick a glance at the Egyptian religious landscape might give a different impression. In any case, all these ambiguities place the Call outside the purview of Quintan Wiktorowicz's taxonomy.[1] The group matches neither his concept of "purist Salafism," since it embraces organized activism, nor what he calls "political Salafism," since it continues to follow a purist grammar—even if its techniques differ from those of its predecessors.

In the coming pages, we will retrace the Salafi Call's path from its founding to its institutionalization and expansion. We will identify the organizational and discursive strategies it deployed to supplant Ansar al-Sunna (the Salafi standard-bearer until the end of Nasser's reign), in the span of a few dozen years, as the cornerstone of Egyptian Salafism.

THE BEGINNINGS OF THE SALAFI CALL

As I discussed late in the previous chapter, a handful of students who called themselves "Salafis" separated from the jama'at islamiyya in 1978 as the latter were being absorbed into the Muslim Brotherhood. The resulting group's Alexandrian core included around ten students, most of whom lived in the Moharam Bek neighborhood, a former stronghold of the Egyptian aristocracy now inhabited by middle-class families. Nobody could have imagined that the Salafi School these dissenters founded would so quickly become the movement's foremost organization in Egypt: the Salafi Call (Al-da'wa al-salafiyya, the name it adopted when it became a jama'a, or organized group).

The Call's driving force was Muhammad Isma'il al-Muqaddim, born in 1952, who possessed the strongest activist credentials. He came from the jama'at islamiyya, where he was a respected intellectual figure and directed its summer camp program in Alexandria.[2] But before that he had participated in the first Salafi cell formed in the city's Ansar al-Sunna mosques during the late 1960s; most cell members subsequently turned to jihadism. Because of his seniority, the Salafi Call's small founding circle considered him its most erudite member.[3] "Authorized histories" of the movement emphasize five other originators: Saʿid ʿAbd al-ʿAzim and Ahmad Farid, also born in 1952; Muhammad ʿAbd al-Fattah Abu Idris, born in 1954, who had known al-Muqaddim since high school; and Yasir Burhami and Ahmad Hutayba, born in 1958, both also school friends.[4] Along with al-Muqaddim, they constituted the "founding six" that movement members called the "sheikhs of the Salafi Call" (*mashayikh al-daʿwa al-salafiyya*). The founders' praises were sung in *anashid* (Islamic chants) like the one that opens this chapter.

Almost all were graduates or students of the faculty of medicine (or dentistry, in Hutayba's case) at Alexandria University, with the exception of Abu Idris, who studied at the faculty of engineering. The small initial group actually included several other notable figures who are usually left out of the official narrative because they later withdrew from the movement or had significant disagreements with the "founding six." They include ʿImad ʿAbd al-Ghaffur (b. 1960), who would preside over the Nour Party at its inception in 2011, and his brother ʿAdil ʿAbd al-Ghaffur, who studied and taught for many years in Saudi Arabia, where he was a professor of hadith at Riyadh's Imam Mohammad Ibn Saud Islamic University; ʿAdil ʿAdwi, who would play a leading role in the Call's early days but then faded into obscurity; and Muhammad Yaqut, who would part ways with the group in the 1980s, leaving for Yemen to cofound Iman University, a Salafi educational institution, with Yemeni Sheikh ʿAbd al-Majid al-Zindani.[5]

One might ask why these avowed Salafis would create a separate structure from Ansar al-Sunna. The latter, which regained its autonomy in 1972, was enjoying a period of relative prosperity, with Salafi piety in vogue and Saudi Arabia—whose oil wealth could now fund its proselytism—offering generous financial support.[6] So why strike out on their own? Al-Muqaddim and his colleagues say that Ansar al-Sunna had "difficulty attracting youth."[7] And on a practical level, it seems that the Ansar al-Sunna leadership's distant ties with the group of young Alexandrian activists hindered any cooperation.[8]

Some Call members also point to divergences in the two groups' understandings of Salafism at the time. For instance, Ansar al-Sunna members were accused of refusing to base their judicial rulings on single-narrator hadiths (*hadith al-ahad*) and of relying only on the two canonical hadith collections by Bukhari and Muslim (*al-iqtisar ʿala al-sahihayn*)—an approach that the young activists, guided by the teachings of Sheikh Nasir al-Din al-Albani, rejected.[9] Certain Ansar al-Sunna members consequently cast doubt on the prophecy that the *mahdi* (the Islamic equivalent of the messiah) would descend from the heavens at the end of times: The collections of Bukhari and Muslim make no mention of the *mahdi*.[10] Al-Muqaddim responded with an entire epistle defending belief in the *mahdi*. This messianic figure was clearly in the zeitgeist, as it had just been the driver behind a Saudi Salafi millenarian group's two-week violent occupation of Mecca's Great Mosque in 1979.[11]

These issues are minor enough, however, that they were probably not the breaking point between Ansar al-Sunna and the young Salafis. It's also true that joining Ansar al-Sunna, an officially registered organization, would mean implicitly accepting the government's legitimacy and oversight.[12] But it seems that above all, the youth wished to organize independently because they had set their sights much higher than their elders had: Buoyed by successes as part of Alexandria's jama'a islamiyya, they believed in an activist Salafism (*salafiyya harakiyya*), which they saw as the only path to a mass preaching-based movement. They took inspiration from the Islamist movements' organizational approaches and techniques—which they had experienced within the jama'at islamiyya and in interacting with the Brotherhood—to more effectively spread their message.[13] This made the Salafi Call the first real Salafi social movement in Egypt. While it claimed fidelity to Salafism's trademark purist grammar, it offered an "updated" version.

STEPPING INTO THE RELIGIOUS FIELD

From the outset, the Call's founders strove to emphasize the scholarly, rather than simply activist, character of their approach, both by virtue of their grammar and because it set them apart from the Brotherhood. Their goal, they said, was to study and teach Salafi Islam, hence the group's initial name: the "Salafi School" (Al-madrasa al-salafiyya). To avoid being confused with the Islamist groups that had proliferated during the 1970s, they made sure not to call their chosen leader an "emir" (*amir*), instead referring to him as *qayyim*. This ancient Islamic term for a school's principal or superintendent was particularly popular among Salafis, as one of their favorite authors was named Ibn ("son of") Qayyim al-Jawziyya because his father had directed the school founded by Hanbali scholar Ibn al-Jawzi.[14] 'Adil 'Adwi became the Salafi Call's first *qayyim*; Abu Idris, judged more adept at handling red tape, soon replaced him.[15]

These Salafis prioritized teaching above all else. In the early days, classes were held in the Call's only mosque—at the home of 'Imad 'Abd al-Ghaffur—until al-Muqaddim got a small mosque of his own, the small and dingy 'Ubbad al-Rahman, in the working-class Bolkly neighborhood.[16] Some accounts mention two or three other places of worship the group used at the time.[17] Courses covered both creed and fiqh and were initially based on classics like *The Palmyran Message* (*Al-risala al-tadmuriyya*) by Ibn Taymiyya or *Epistle on Legal Imitation* (*Risala fi hukm al-taqlid*) by al-Shawkani, along with contemporary titles like *Warning to the Genuflector Not to Mistake Tombs for Mosques* (*Tahdhir al-sajid min ittikhadh al-qubur masajid*) by Nasir al-Din al-Albani. Points of difference with competing movements were closely studied so that the students could defend theirs as the only sound approach. The initial objective was to train imams who could expand the young movement's control to the mosques of Alexandria.[18]

In addition to the courses they taught, al-Muqaddim and his colleagues strove to carry on their predecessors' publishing work by reprinting the Salafi classics for a student audience, such as the complete fatwas of Ibn Taymiyya and epistles by Sheikh al-Albani. To this end, they created a book series, initially distributed at Alexandria University, called *The Salafis Speak* (*Al-salafiyyun yatahaddathun*), which also gave young Salafis a forum for publishing their own first books (including al-Muqaddim's epistle regarding the *mahdi*, mentioned earlier).[19]

Al-Muqaddim quickly established himself as the group's most prolific author. In 1979, for instance, he published a short treatise called *Evidence for the Prohibition on Shaking the Hand of a Female Stranger* before embarking upon his best-known work, the three-volume *Return of the Hijab* (*'Awdat al-hijab*).[20] In 1980 twenty-two-year-old Yasir Burhami completed his first book, entitled *The Virtues of the Rich and Praiseworthy in Explaining the Book of Tawhid* (*Fadl al-ghani al-hamid fi sharh kitab al-tawhid*), a teachable summary of Muhammad bin 'Abd al-Wahhab's *Book of Tawhid*.[21]

Each member of the "founding six" soon chose a specialty, as there was much ground to cover: Muhammad Isma'il al-Muqaddim would write books on thought (*fikr*), Yasir Burhami on creed, and Ahmad Hutayba on Islamic jurisprudence. Ahmad Farid would take care of the more

THE SALAFI CALL

pathos-centered offerings in the *raqa'iq* (heart-softening) genre. This literature was then integrated into the curriculum, slowly supplanting the nonmovement authors the Call members had at first assigned in their courses.

This exemplifies a defining characteristic of the "founding six": From the beginning, they were driven by a deep religious ambition that went beyond simply reprinting and distributing existing books. By Ahmad Farid's account, this also differentiated them within the jama'at islamiyya. The "administrative officials" (*kawadir idariyya*), he explains, joined the Brotherhood, while the "religious officials" opposed the fusion.[22]

To be sure, the Call's project relied on the fatwas of the era's foremost Salafi ulema, like Sheikhs Ibn Baz and Ibn 'Uthaymin, who were leading figures in the Saudi religious establishment, or the esteemed Sheikh al-Albani. But the Call's leaders also wanted to establish themselves as full-fledged ulema and so dedicated themselves to strengthening their religious credentials—despite the fact that all had medical or engineering degrees and lacked any formal religious training. At best, they could boast of having attended a few courses or lectures by Sheikhs Ibn Baz and Ibn 'Uthaymin during *hajj* pilgrimages to Saudi Arabia. To compensate early on, the leaders memorized the Quran or Ibn Taymiyya's works on their own.[23]

According to its grammar, the group's affiliation with the religious field legitimized its authority. Al-Muqaddim argued that ulema, who were the "successors of the prophets," deserved "courtesy ... protection of their sacredness, knowledge of their value. One must refrain from attacking them, from insulting the greatness of their standing."[24] Burhami explained that when no legitimate Imam—here meaning a political-religious leader—fulfills the conditions that Islamic tradition prescribes for his role (in Burhami's view, most leaders in the modern Arab world do not make the grade), Muslims are duty-bound to "gather around their ulema because they are the ones who hold the authority [*ulu al-amr minhum*] among them, as the only people capable of guiding them in accordance with the book of God and the sunna of His prophet."[25]

SAUDI ARABIA AND THE SALAFI CALL: A COMPLEX RELATIONSHIP

Let's begin with a reminder, in the hopes of laying to rest a common misconception. Most of the Call founders' first Saudi sojourns happened *after*

THE SALAFI CALL

their conversion to Salafism. While Muhammad Isma'il al-Muqaddim made frequent trips starting in the mid-1970s, Sheikh Ahmad Farid, for example, didn't travel there until 1981.[26] Yasir Burhami, who spent four months in the Kingdom in 1979, was quick to emphasize that the Saudis affected the group only a posteriori: "Salafism already existed, and Ibn Taymiyya and Ibn 'Abd al-Wahhab were massive influences even before we visited Saudi Arabia."[27] Another founding member, Sa'id 'Abd al-'Azim, said: "We were Salafis long before going to Saudi Arabia, even for the *hajj* and the *'umra!*"[28]

I should mention that the Call always had a complicated relationship with the kingdom, despite its founders' initial, almost exclusive reliance on the great Saudi sheikhs to defend their arguments.[29] During the debates over integrating the jama'at islamiyya into the Muslim Brotherhood, Muhammad Isma'il al-Muqaddim, Yasir Burhami, and Ibrahim al-Za'farani all sought the counsel of Ibn Baz, then the main figure in the Saudi religious establishment. The ambiguous phrasing of their questions and the sheikh's elliptical replies offered equally useful justifications for the decisions of al-Za'farani, who would join the Brotherhood, and al-Muqaddim and Burhami, who would not.[30] When followers of 'Abd al-Salam Faraj insisted that al-Muqaddim join his group (which would go on to assassinate Sadat), he used the same logic, refusing with a deceptively simple question: "What do Sheikhs Ibn Baz and al-Albani have to say about it?"[31]

Yet, despite their proclaimed deference, the young Egyptian Salafis' ties to the Saudi establishment sheikhs seem tenuous. They initially had few contacts in the kingdom (one, really: Adil 'Abd al-Ghaffur, brother of 'Imad, who went there in the 1980s to study hadith at the Islamic University of Medina).[32] Biographies of the Call's sheikhs mention no special relationship with Ibn Baz or Ibn 'Uthaymin, but all agree that the founders met both.[33] At most, Call leaders seem to have communicated with relatively marginal establishment figures: Sheikh Ibn Qu'ud, introduced during a brief visit to Alexandria in 1989, who was considered a dissident voice and had been removed from the Saudi Council of Senior Ulema in 1986; Sheikh 'Abd al-Razzaq 'Afifi, a fellow Egyptian; and Abu Bakr al-Jaza'iri, an Algerian sheikh based in Saudi Arabia, who visited them during a stay in Alexandria in 1985.[34] Call sheikhs were likewise distant at the time from Ansar al-Sunna's leaders, who either ignored or mistrusted them—which is notable, considering those leaders' closeness with Saudi Arabia.[35] According to various testimonies from the kingdom and from Egypt, the only Call sheikh with a strong network in Saudi Arabia was Muhammad Isma'il al-Muqaddim, who was well-respected in international Salafi circles. His ties, however, were more personal in nature and did little for his organization.

However often its 1980s and 1990s publications quote Saudi sheikhs (and they do so often), the Call's Egyptian nature always shines through. Member Mahmud 'Abd al-Hamid's telling of the group's history thus places Egypt, rather than Saudi Arabia, at the heart of Salafism. It opens with a historical discussion emphasizing Ibn Taymiyya's visits to Egypt—specifically to Alexandria, where he lived and was imprisoned. The author then highlights that many Ansar al-Sunna members (especially 'Abd al-Razzaq 'Afifi, but also Muhammad Khalil Harras) had trained the great Saudi ulema—and not the other way around. "This is how Egypt became the heart of the Salafi message," he concludes. Many of the Call's publications also situate the movement within a local history, drawing attention to the central roles of Muhammad 'Abduh (despite deep differences between his modernizing approach and the Call's take on Salafism) and Rashid Rida, who is frequently depicted as the true father of Egyptian Salafism.[36] When I asked Sa'id 'Abd al-'Azim, one of the Salafi Call's founders, about Saudi Arabia's influence on the Egyptian movement, he replied: "You've got it backwards, we're the ones who influenced them!"[37]

As for the great ulema of the modern age, the Call's sheikhs always start the discussion with Nasir al-Din al-Albani, the "sheikh of contemporary Salafism," who, like them, was not Saudi (and whose relationship with the kingdom was similarly ambivalent).[38] The leaders stress that he initially drew inspiration from Rashid Rida's texts, independent of any ties with Saudi Arabia.[39] Al-Albani's writings do seem to have strongly influenced these Salafis, especially his *Prayer of the Prophet—May Peace and Blessings Be Upon Him—Description From Beginning to End, As Though You Were Seeing It*. (Abu Ishaq al-Huwayni and Muhammad 'Abd al-Maqsud, Salafi sheikhs I discuss later, also cite this book as the epiphany that sparked their conversion.) Two of al-Albani's non-Saudi students—the Egyptian-Kuwaiti 'Abd al-Rahman 'Abd al-Khaliq (mentioned earlier) and the Yemeni Muqbil al-Wadi'i—are likewise seen as important influences on the movement. Also, with few exceptions, the Call's sheikhs avoid wearing

Saudi garb in public.[40] For example, Muhammad Isma'il al-Muqaddim prefers to cover his head with the karakul, made iconic by father of Pakistani independence Muhammad Ali Jinnah.

Saudi and Egyptian interpretations are separated by deeper differences. The most explicit concerns the "excuse of ignorance" (*al-'udhr bi-l-jahl*):[41] Does ignorance forgive acts of associationism (*shirk*) or impiety (*kufr*), thereby shielding their perpetrators from excommunication (*takfir*)? Many contemporary Saudi ulema tend to be dismissive of this exemption or allow it only in drastic circumstances, taking a particularly strict approach to anything creed-related. In their eyes, for example, Sufis are not Muslims, because they violate the precept of *tawhid al-uluhiyya*, the unicity of worship. Some early Egyptian jihadis adopted this interpretation, arguing that governments that don't implement shari'a cannot plead ignorance.[42]

The Call sheikhs saw how much of a risk this stance could represent in Egypt. It would be politically perilous, as denying the "excuse of ignorance" could land them squarely in the jihadis' camp. And this danger extended to Egyptian society, where not only did Salafism still coexist with Sufism, but many Muslims were not conservative, and certain religious practices were still infused with popular Islam. Denying the excuse of ignorance, then, would mean excommunicating a healthy slice of their co-religionaries. So they argued that in Egypt, unlike in an "Islamic country" such as Saudi Arabia, the "proof of Islam" (the Salafi one, of course) had not yet been established (*lam taqum al-hujja*)—and that this proof was a sine qua non condition for excommunicating.[43] Yasir Burhami explains that this difference with Saudi Salafism moved him to write *The Virtues of the Rich and Praiseworthy in Explaining the Book of Tawhid* in 1980: Muhammad bin 'Abd al-Wahhab's *Book of Tawhid*, which Burhami's work purports to summarize, may have been "misunderstood" on this point.[44]

There are other distinctions as well. For example, some of the Egyptians saw the niqab as preferable but not obligatory–unlike the Saudis, but in the tradition of al-Albani.[45] The Call's sheikhs likewise did not consider that a person who, out of laziness, fails to perform all daily prayers should be excluded from the Muslim community.[46] This was again in line with al-Albani but at odds with many Saudi ulema.[47] In short, the Egyptian context opened the Salafis to accepting a wider range of interpretations. As Bassam al-Zarqa, one of the organization's main figures in Alexandria, said, "We had to free fiqh of societal imperatives that had been sanctified on the Arabian Peninsula."[48] In sociological terms, the Salafi Call was forced to "reframe" the Salafi discourse to ensure better reception in the Egyptian milieu.

The relationship with Saudi Arabia grew still more fraught in 1990, when the Salafi Call opposed the Council of Senior Ulama's fatwa authorizing a request for foreign (mainly American) military forces to protect the kingdom from Saddam Hussein after his invasion of Kuwait.[49] Once again, Sheikh al-Albani's opinion aligned with that of the Call. So did that of the Sahwa movement in Saudi Arabia, which used the issue as a rallying cry against the country's regime. The Call's divergent stance, despite its discretion (the Egyptian Salafis did not use the issue to stir up followers in any way), reinforced the Saudi authorities' misgivings.[50] From that moment on, they increasingly distanced themselves from any actor they lumped in—rightly or wrongly—with political Islam.[51] In the words of a former Call member who studied and lived in the kingdom between 2001 and 2010, "The Salafi Call was not welcome in Saudi Arabia, and could only conduct business there in secret."[52] Taken together, these elements demonstrate why it's a bit far-fetched to imagine that the Saudi government would have directly financed the organization, as is often said in Egypt. It's far from impossible, however, that some independent actors—be they sheikhs or businessmen, tied to the Sahwa movement or not—could have given generously to the Salafi Call.[53]

In the late 1990s, with the passing of the three chief figures in worldwide Salafism—the emblematic Saudi sheikhs Ibn Baz and Ibn 'Uthaymin, who died in 1999 and 2001, and Sheikh al-Albani, deceased in 1999—the ulema of the Alexandrian Salafi Call could finally dispense with direct references to Saudi (or simply non-Egyptian) Salafism. From that point on, they sought to impose themselves as independent authorities capable of creating their own religious material.[54]

THE BROTHERHOOD AS CATALYZING ENEMY

Relations between the Salafi School (as it was initially called) and the Muslim Brotherhood were tense from the start. According to al-Muqaddim and his colleagues, the Brothers were manipulators who took the thoroughly Salafi jama'at islamiyya hostage, shamelessly pursuing their ends and even passing themselves off as Salafi despite not actually believing in the doctrine of the *salaf*.[55] The Brothers, for their part, had first tended to see the Salafis as inconsequential and had accordingly shown them nothing but contempt.[56] The situation was likely complicated by the fact that several founders of the eventual Salafi Call, including Abu Idris and Burhami, are said to have fleetingly joined the Brotherhood soon after the scission of the jama'at islamiyya.[57] Perhaps they had hoped to "reform" the older organization (as some individuals alluded to in the previous chapter), or perhaps they were simply unaware that their group had been absorbed; regardless, they quickly parted ways. Details remain murky, but whatever happened at the time left Burhami in particular—despite family ties to the Brotherhood—bitterly resentful of the organization.[58]

Early on, each camp developed a rhetoric for attacking the other's legitimacy. From the moment of the split, the Brotherhood accused the Salafis—both in sermons and in plays it performed at the university—of being "extremists."[59] The organization lampooned the young Salafis' first book series, joking that "the Salafis speak, but the Brothers wage jihad."[60] The Salafis responded by denouncing what they called elements of religious deviance in the Brotherhood's founding principles. Al-Muqaddim, for instance, gave a series of recorded lectures at the time called *Critique of the Twenty Principles of Imam Hasan al-Banna*.[61]

The Brothers and Salafis were further divided by their stances on the Iranian revolution, and then by Sadat's decision to offer asylum to the Shah of Iran. The Brotherhood, true to its ecumenical outlook, saw the Iranian Islamists' coup de force as an authentic Islamic revolution. The organization sent a delegation to Tehran to congratulate Ayatollah Khomeini and make connections with the new Iranian government; these would endure for decades.[62] And the Brothers weren't the only Egyptian Islamists to react this way. Despite its proclaimed adherence to Salafi values, the Jama'a Islamiyya also hailed the Iranian revolution, if for reasons more political than religious, and held demonstrations against the shah's arrival. Like the Brotherhood, it would maintain ties to Iran throughout the 1980s and 1990s.[63] The Alexandrian Salafis, then, were the only ones to proclaim loud and clear—as early as 1979—that Iran's was "a Shia revolution and an insult to Sunnis that will not help them in the least."[64]

The fight was lopsided at first, since the young Salafis began as a tiny group, while the Brotherhood was backed by a strong, organized movement as it waged an all-out war on them. Al-Muqaddim says the Brotherhood even tried to convince the landlord of the Salafis' main mosque to evict them.[65] Yasir Burhami concurs: "We stayed outside of the mosques because we had been driven out. They didn't want us to be able to teach.... 'Get out of the mosque!' they said, but they weren't even from the Ministry of Awqaf—they were part of the Islamic movement, just like us."[66] Things took a violent turn at the universities, too: Deprived of more official platforms, the Salafis began preaching and teaching in the schools' common areas. The Brothers again tried to evict them; a fistfight ensued, in which the Salafis, outnumbered, were thoroughly thrashed.[67] Having exhausted all campus venues, the ragtag crew made the most of their limited options, however bizarre. Ahmad Hutayba, for example, preached to captive audiences on public transit, particularly on the tram during his morning and evening university commutes.[68]

The way Call sympathizers recount this story bears some resemblance to Ansar al-Sunna's founding myth, except in that case it was the Sufis who persecuted al-Fiqi and company, relegating them to preaching in cafés, while here the Brotherhood plays the role of original enemy. As in the story of Ansar al-Sunna, the period of persecution is said to explain the young Salafis' decision to organize more formally.[69] Between late 1979 and 1980, the founders of the Salafi School resolved to transform it into a jama'a (organized group) named the Salafi Call (Al-da'wa al-salafiyya).[70] Reflecting on that decision, Burhami says: "[The Brotherhood's attitude] surprised us. Some brothers [his Salafi companions, not the Brotherhood] said we should back down, and others said we should respond with violence. To anyone watching, we appeared completely caught off-guard. The brothers in the end agreed that we needed to act in an organized fashion, like a union of preachers."[71]

Despite the apparent initial power imbalance between the two sides, the Brotherhood seemed to take its opponents' attacks very seriously, sensing the increasing symbolic weight of Salafism. The Supreme Guide himself, 'Umar al-Tilmisani, thus penned a volume in 1982 called *A Few of the Things the Brotherhood Has Taught Me*, largely a response to criticisms leveled at the group.[72] He argued that his organization's members had as much right to be called Salafis (*salafiyyun*) as their detractors (whom he never names), insisting that the Brothers' "methods, their interpretation, their style are all *salafi salafi salafi*." Al-Tilmisani even began the book with a long homage to Ibn Taymiyya, while managing to take a passing swipe at him: "One must recognize that he and his students were extremely hard on those who held opposing opinions, describing them with the most insulting of epithets. This is just what the martyr imam [al-Banna] aimed to avoid at all costs."[73]

Al-Tilmisani methodically tackled each critique leveled at the Brothers regarding their creed, supposed lack of religious science, and refusal to excommunicate. And yet he yielded no ground on the fundamentals, always redefining "Salafi" terminology to his advantage, in a style that modernist thinker Gamal al-Banna later described as "imbued with spirituality."[74] The book was among the Brotherhood's last major attempts to appropriate the prestigious label, which had in fact slipped through their fingers long before.

The deep differences between Salafis and Brothers would repeatedly surface over the following decades. When the Brotherhood entered institutional politics, winning seats in the Egyptian parliament starting in 1984, the Salafis added a new verse to their chorus of criticism: The Brothers had no qualms about participating in "parliaments of unbelievers" (*majalis kufriyya*) that recognized the people, rather than God, as the source of their power, and passed laws not based in shari'a. In 1984 Sheikh Sayyid al-Ghubashi—a figure in the Call's early history who later disappeared from public life—wrote a short book on the subject, one of the first by a Salafi sheikh, in which he strongly opposed any Salafi involvement in the elections.[75] The Call followed with a proclamation in 1987 that officially adopted al-Ghubashi's position.[76] The group's leaders forbade members from voting—even for the Brotherhood, which pitched itself as the only "Islamic party" in the running.[77] While the Brothers might have hoped that the growing Salafi movement would yield a reliable constituency for their candidates, things panned out differently.

The Salafi Call sheikhs made a habit of laying into the Brotherhood in their writings—though they typically took care to do so indirectly, in deference to the metarule of proclaimed solidarity, which quashed any overly vitriolic public criticism between Islamic factions; harsher critiques were kept within the organization. A more explicit attack did play out in 2009 when the Call's flagship publishing house, Dar al-khulafa' al-rashidin, released a collection of fatwas and pronouncements from ulema denouncing the Muslim Brotherhood. But however severe its substance, its tone remained measured. Moreover, the book was written by a minor figure in the movement and was merely prefaced by Yasir Burhami.[78]

EXPANSION AND STRUCTURING OF THE SALAFI CALL

The decision had been made a few years earlier, but it took until 1984 for the Salafi school to formally become a jama'a (organized group), taking on its new name of Al-da'wa al-salafiyya, the Salafi Call. Creating a jama'a was no small move in the Egyptian Salafi context at the time. While nobody seems to have questioned the lawfulness of founding Ansar al-Sunna as a jama'a in the 1920s, the issue had since become a topic of passionate debate in Salafi milieus, where some held that any "collective action" (al-'amal al-jama'i, or forming a jama'a) would only sow discord and factionalism (tahazzub) in the Muslim community. And some Egyptian Salafis who had initially been close to the Salafi School were of the same mind. In Cairo, for instance, Usama 'Abd al-'Azim—the former leader of the capital city's jama'a islamiyya camps, who had seceded with the Alexandrians when the Brotherhood took over their movement—rejected formal organization of any kind and thus did not join the Call.[79]

Regardless, the young Alexandrian Salafis decided to forge ahead with a proper structure, arguing that "obligations are only fulfilled through cooperation, and ... cooperation requires orders, obedience, and a military mindset—such is human nature."[80] They emphasized, however, that the hierarchy was purely for organizational purposes, and while it was true that this entailed discipline, Call members were not bound to the leader of their jama'a by an oath of political allegiance (bay'a)—a practice common in other Islamist movements and in the Brotherhood—which would make him the practical equivalent of a caliph.[81] The choice to form a jama'a came soon after the Kuwaiti Salafis decided to found a Society for the Revival of Islamic Heritage (Jam'iyyat ihya' al-turath al-islami), which would see the light in 1981.[82] The Kuwaiti group was under the intellectual leadership of Egyptian-Kuwaiti 'Abd al-Rahman 'Abd al-Khaliq, whose book *The Scientific Foundations of the Salafi Call* had greatly influenced the future founders of the Call in the later 1970s (more on this later).[83] It's quite probable that the Egyptians were following the Kuwaitis' lead.[84]

The Salafi School had been fairly successful right from its late 1970s founding, even without much coordination between members. Its following grew, and the group could distribute as many as fifteen thousand copies of some of its leaflets at Alexandria University, where it was overseen by 'Imad 'Abd al-Ghaffur after the founders graduated.[85] The events of 1981 intervened shortly thereafter, putting on hold any further structuring: First, Sadat ordered more than 1,500 activists arrested in September, after particularly bloody clashes between Copts and Muslims in Cairo's al-Zawiya al-Hamra' neighborhood; most of those detained belonged to one faction or another of the Islamic movement.[86] Then, on October 6, Sadat's assassination precipitated hundreds more arrests in religious circles. Even though they had been openly hostile toward the jihadis, the Salafis suffered repression along with all Islamic groups active in Egypt at the time. Muhammad Isma'il al-Muqaddim and Ahmad Hutayba were imprisoned for several months, and their group was forced to end its activities within the university.[87]

Only in 1984, when the political climate began to cool, did the Call truly manage (and this was the point of becoming a jama'a) to establish an administrative structure, if an informal one, though it did not register with the authorities because of "security concerns."[88] The authorities had indeed spotted this activist, organized Salafism taking shape and seemed to be keeping an eye on it. As early as 1980, a handwritten document from the State Security Investigations Service (referred to in this book as "State Security") had identified the core members of the Salafi School.[89] And in 1983 the service "invited" some of the leading Alexandrian Salafis to participate in a filmed debate with a group of sheikhs from al-Azhar; the goal was to torpedo Salafi arguments.[90]

The year 1984 was when the Salafi Call began creating a plethora of divisions to facilitate its operation. A new "executive committee" (*majlis tanfidhi*) consisted of the six founders.[91] In Alexandria, leaders were named according to a mosque-based hierarchy, with the "weight" of each mosque determined by its sheikh's influence rather than its size.[92] Houses of prayer thus became the Call's base unit, which Bassam al-Zarqa likens to a bigger version of the Brotherhood's activist cells (*usar*, or "families"). Together, these formed the "mosque sector" (*qita' al-masajid*), key to the movement, which fell under the purview of a supervising sheikh. (Each of the Call's many areas of activity was a "sector.")[93] A former member told me how the Salafis extended their influence over mosques:

> Either they or one of their sympathizers founds a mosque that they are asked to run. Or sometimes a new mosque is constructed, or one has no

imam, and they petition neighborhood residents to let them run it—which allows them to teach their courses there, to have Quran study sessions there, to establish a library of Salafi literature—or to have one of their imams officiate there on Fridays. To convince the inhabitants, they explain that he's well educated, has a nice voice, et cetera. Competition with the Muslim Brotherhood is fierce because they usually try to do the same![94]

The Salafi Call also lost no time reinvesting in education, creating a "university sector" (*qita' al-jami'a*) led by a sheikh, with leaders appointed for the various faculties. The educational realm was key: The Call's leaders had emerged from universities in the 1970s, and they hoped the group's future ones would follow a similar path. In the mid-1980s the ink had barely dried on the regime's reauthorization of "clubs" (also called *usar*) when the Salafis started using them as cover for all sorts of activities: The clubs hosted book fairs and distribution events, lectures and (especially during the summer) camps.[95] Some published journals that they posted on walls or passed out in university hallways. "Islamic weeks," each themed around issues dear to Salafis, or "university meetings" were also used as pretexts for spreading their message. Groups of preachers would speak at one faculty after another. All was precisely planned: This massive presence in student life was intended to help the group commandeer the university's mosque or obtain a speaking slot during religious festivals (again in competition with the Muslim Brotherhood, which was just as active).[96]

To lay the groundwork for its university ventures, the Salafi Call implemented a "Pioneers" (*tala'i'*) program for elementary, middle, and high school students—another sector, overseen for nearly its entire existence by schoolteacher Mustafa Dyab.[97] There, children were exposed to the Salafi *Weltanschauung* in the hopes that this early experience would bring them to join the movement as adults. The Pioneers published Islamic-themed magazines and offered recreational outings that encouraged group bonding.[98] Through this youth organization, the Salafis often tried to take over a school's mosque or radio station.[99] Young Salafis with ties to the Call also sometimes participated in school elections to boost the group's influence—but to avoid drawing attention to the link, they didn't run on a "Salafi Call" ticket. Muhammad Nur, who eventually became spokesperson for the Nour Party, was once president of the student union at his secondary school.[100]

When individuals joined the Call, they followed a specific curriculum that was taught in private sessions (*halaqat*). According to Muhammad

Tawfiq, a former Call official in Cairo, three books were considered fundamental in the late 1990s: Yasir Burhami's *The Grace of the Merciful* (*Minnat al-rahman*) and *The Virtues of the Rich and Praiseworthy* (*Fadl al-ghani al-hamid*, mentioned earlier), along with *The Ascents to Divine Acceptance* by Saudi Sheikh Hafiz al-Hakami, also referenced earlier.[101] Note that all three focus on creed, reflecting the subject's centrality for the Salafis. Spiral-bound handouts (*malazim*) addressing five central concepts—jihad, questions of belief and unbelief, commanding right and forbidding wrong, divergences among Muslims, and collective action—were distributed as well. Each student took exams to prove his knowledge. Once the corpus had been mastered, he was promoted and could hope for a chance at preaching in one of the movement's mosques.[102] Further education was à la carte: The student would take courses on his chosen area of focus from specific sheikhs at their own mosques.[103]

With the objective of scaling up education for sheikhs on track to become the movement's future officials, the Salafi Call tried to develop a more methodical and in-depth educational program. In 1985 the group opened the al-Furqan Institute, a training center for preachers, just steps from the train station in Alexandria's Bakos neighborhood. Its first director was Faruq al-Rahmani, who was replaced in 1988 by Ahmad Hutayba, one of the Call's founding sheikhs. The course of study there lasted four years and covered all Islamic disciplines. Fundamental books from the Salafi corpus were taught alongside useful skills for preachers, such as sermon (*khutba*) techniques. A graduating student would obtain a certificate (*ijaza*, which was not recognized by the state) that qualified him to preach in the Call's mosques.[104] The experiment was a hit: Soon, the institute had five hundred students, with around fifty graduating each year until it closed in 1994.[105]

While continuing its grassroots work, in the late 1980s the Call started trying to build a public profile that would expand its audience. It launched *The Voice of the Call* (*Sawt al-Daʿwa*) in 1990, a journal that printed a mix of articles written by movement sheikhs and fatwas by well-known Salafi sheikhs, especially Saudi ones (publication ceased in 1994).[106] Taking inspiration from Tabligh methods, the group also put together "preaching caravans" (*qawafil al-daʿwa*) where a crew of Call members would trek to a given neighborhood and preach in the streets. In districts where it was well established, the organization built stages on public squares for its sheikhs to give sermons during religious festivals. Competition with the Brotherhood, who did likewise, was intense as always.[107]

Finally, the organization established a "social committee" (*lajna ijtima'iyya*), extending its reach into a new realm as it helped widows, orphans, and the ill using donations collected in its mosques at the close of Ramadan (*zakat al-fitr*) through a separate "alms committee" (*lajnat al-zakat*).[108] But unlike the Brothers, who created all sorts of NGOs to support their efforts, this activity mostly took place outside of centralized channels: The organization often dispensed aid to individuals via the mosque's imam, on a case-by-case basis. When one of his followers was in need, for example, he might appeal to the generosity of a well-heeled Muslim who lived nearby.[109] In the 2000s, with the help of sympathetic merchants, the Call also organized affordable food markets, as well as caravans that offered free medical services from doctors who belonged to the movement. This blurring between professional activities and activism was standard practice in the Call. For instance, Yasir Burhami may have been a sheikh, but he continued to work—mostly pro bono—as a pediatrician.

Dispute resolution (*fadd al-munaza'at*) offered the Salafis another opportunity to weave themselves into the fabric of society: When conflicts arise, rural Egyptians often prefer not to go to the authorities, instead seeking the arbitration of a council of "wise men." Such bodies are called customary courts, or *mahakim 'urfiyya*, and their members have historically been village notables and local religious figures. But the Muslim Brotherhood was the first religious movement to take advantage of this niche, offering conflict mediators within what it called "peace committees" (*lijan al-sulh*).

In the neighborhoods and villages they controlled or influenced, the Salafis took the same approach. This was the case, for example, in the tribal regions of Marsa Matruh and al-'Amiriyya, where the leader of the local Call division, Sheikh Sharif al-Hawwari (himself a member of the Hawwara tribal confederation), was the go-to mediator. Unlike the Brothers, who most often adhered to a form of vaguely Islamicized traditional law, the Salafis insisted on judging only based on the shari'a. Their one concession was excluding the Quranic punishments (*hudud*), which would have put them in open conflict with the state.[110] Most important, this role gave the Salafis a way to lead by example as they implemented the shari'a at a hyper-local level.

Women were relegated to the background in the Call's early days, since the organization preached a doctrine that limited their presence in public spaces and forbade all gender mixing. Only at the turn of the 1990s was a "women's committee" created. It was tasked with organizing religious and cultural activities for the movement's female members, who were sometimes able to attend sermons and lessons—separated from the men by a screen. Sheikh Sa'id 'Abd al-'Azim became known for teaching classes specifically for women, who gathered in a different room at his mosque and had to submit their questions in writing (the female voice was considered *'awra*, meaning it had to be concealed around men). Lastly, universities sometimes had "female student representatives." Many of the women who held positions in the movement happened to be wives or sisters of its officials.[111] Hanan 'Allam, a psychiatrist and one of the Call's rare female public faces, gave several interviews to the Egyptian media after the revolution.[112] She directed the "women's division" of the Nour Party at the time, which I will touch on later.[113]

The increasing sway of this "Alexandrian school," as it is sometimes called in Egyptian Islamic milieus, paved the way for its geographical expansion in the 1980s. A "committee of governorates" (*lajnat al-muhafazat*) was created to oversee the organization's outgrowths.[114] Often the Call's representatives were former students of Alexandria University, which enrolled youth from across the country. Trained by the movement during their academic years, they became its ambassadors upon returning to their home governorates. Other representatives had studied at the al-Furqan Institute and chosen to spread the organization's message beyond Alexandria.[115]

A selection of Egyptian regions, notably on the Mediterranean coast and in the Delta, thus became home to divisions of the movement that operated quite independently. Each had a leader; some of these were supported by a hierarchical team (ranked by cities, neighborhoods, and mosques). Until the 2000s Upper Egypt, where the Jama'a Islamiyya still held a monopoly on Salafism, remained largely beyond the Call's reach. The movement would also bloom late in Cairo, where other players were already well established in the Salafi community. All this illustrates the ongoing impact of local specificities on the structure of the Egyptian religious field.

In some cases, the Call expanded by collaborating with similarly inclined independent groups. In Giza, for example, 'Abd al-Fattah al-Zayni, who had been a member of the first Salafi groups of the early 1970s (described in the previous chapter), founded a proto-structure for spreading Salafism with Muhammad al-Kurdi in 1982, based out of a mosque in the al-Talibiyya neighborhood.[116] It ran a Quranic school, collected *zakat al-fitr* to help the area's residents, and regularly hosted classes and lectures by the Alexandrian sheikhs, with whom al-Zayni and al-Kurdi had kept in touch since the late 1970s.

The group took on a more formal structure and increased its activities at the end of the 1980s, turning al-Talibiyya's mosque into one of the main hubs for propagating Salafism in the Cairo region. Because the group coordinated its activities somewhat closely with the Salafi Call, the security apparatus saw it as a branch of the larger organization, but it remained largely independent. It had no qualms about bypassing the Alexandrians to draw on Cairo's network of Salafi sheikhs, who (as we'll see) didn't always share the same approach.

Those I interviewed described Giza-like situations elsewhere in Egypt, including Helwan, where a "Helwan school"—close to but not part of the Call—had existed since the 1990s; Minia, where Sheikh Ibrahim Zakariyya, a student of the Alexandrian sheikhs, maintained a similar relationship with the Call; and Mansoura, where Sheikh Ahmad al-Naqib unofficially represented the Call from the 1990s until the early 2000s, when his relationship with the Alexandrians deteriorated and he went his own way.[117]

The development of such an extensive national organization—second in size to the Muslim Brotherhood, even if its administrative structure was much less developed—prompted questions about its financing, especially after the 2011 revolution. These were understandable given that unlike the Brotherhood, which collects dues (*ishtirak*) from its members, the Salafis (by their own admission) required nothing of the sort. To fund their operations, they explained, they relied only on Egyptian benefactors and on *zakat* collection in their mosques.

In Cairo, one often hears that the movement could never have risen without Saudi financing, a claim vociferously denied by the Call's leaders. We saw earlier why official Saudi support seemed unlikely, but this doesn't rule out the possibility that private Saudi citizens—businessmen or religious figures, close to the Sahwa or not—might have managed to slip generous donations to the movement. Like the Muslim Brotherhood, the Call also benefited from wealthy Egyptians living in the Gulf. What's more, the initially tight bonds between the Call and the Society for the Revival of Islamic Heritage suggest that the Call may have benefited from the largesse of its Kuwaiti Salafi "brothers," at least until the organization's mentor 'Abd al-Rahman 'Abd al-Khaliq was expelled in a 1996–1997 internal "coup." This hypothesis seems all the more likely given the Kuwaiti group's major role in the regional financing of Salafism, as Zoltan Pall demonstrates in the case of Lebanon.[118] And some Call figures, like former Nour Party spokesman Yusri Hammad, worked for the Society for the Revival of Islamic Heritage during their stays abroad.[119] Finally, as we will see later, the Call was able to implant itself in the structures of officially approved associations like Ansar al-Sunna and the Jam'iyya Shar'iyya, thereby benefiting indirectly from their resources.

SALAFISM, UPDATED: THE SALAFI CALL'S DISCOURSE AND GRAMMAR

We have seen how the Salafi Call distinguished itself from Ansar al-Sunna with its activism and aspiration to spark a social movement, taking cues from the organizing and mobilizing techniques of political Islam. What further set the Call apart, this time on a conceptual level, was its formulation of an "all-encompassing" discourse (the group described it as *shumuliyya*, borrowing the Brotherhood's term) presenting Salafism as an exhaustive cognitive system that could guide all aspects of a Muslim's life and society.[120] The Call sheikhs' ambition, then, far surpassed that of their elders, whose published invectives were centered on elements of Muslim creed, and almost exclusively focused on shoring up orthodoxy against the heterodox. Granted, Ansar al-Sunna members frequently penned articles decrying communism or atheism—in fact, this ability to engage with modern intellectual ideas was what initially attracted the attention of Saudi King 'Abd al-'Aziz—but rather than taking a sweeping approach, they based their arguments purely on creed. The Call's message, on the other hand, explicitly embraced both orthodoxy and orthopraxy, which were redefined as parts of an ideological "whole": a system built to counter alternative systems like "secularism," "materialism," or "liberalism," which were denounced as corollaries of an "intellectual invasion" (*al-ghazu al-fikri*) by the West.[121]

This ideological whole demanded its activists' total commitment, in the sense used by modern political organizations like the Communist

Party—or, closer to home, by the Muslim Brotherhood. Whereas an Ansar al-Sunna member in the first half of the twentieth century might have seen his involvement as a part-time scholarly activity—one component of a multifaceted identity—the Call left room for nothing else. To adapt French historian Marc Lazar's characterization of communists, the Salafi Call did not just welcome new arrivals; it wished to make Salafis of all those who happened upon Salafism.[122]

The Call thus rounded out Salafism's ideologization, a process Henri Lauzière adeptly describes. He explains that this evolution inspired the coining of *manhaj*—a term that transcends creed (*'aqida*, which of course remains in use)—to describe Salafism.[123] In the introduction, I suggested that *manhaj*, often translated as "methodology," is close to my concept of grammar. But the word also has a less practically oriented, more theoretical meaning, close to the idea of a "system."

Lauzière sees Mustafa Hilmi, introduced in the previous chapter, as the true architect behind this ideologization.[124] He likely pioneered the effort to conceptualize the worldview with his *Rules of the Salafi Method* (1976), which in some respects reads more as a philosophy book than a study in religious science.[125] Hilmi tried to distill Salafism into a sort of science—or perhaps an antiscience, if we take a modern view of "science." This is precisely what is implied by the polysemy of concepts such as "methodology" or "proof" (*dalil*), which can be applied to both religious science and hard science.

Regardless, the process I describe did not simply result from reading Hilmi, whom the Call's founders never mentioned as a primary inspiration—even if they sing his praises today.[126] Rather, it seems more like a consequence of the sheikhs' early socialization. Like Hilmi, who was close at first with the Brotherhood, they started out as student activists and matured within a Brotherhood-influenced social context. They naturally saw Salafism, then, through the lens of political Islam. A comparable evolution took place simultaneously (and in a similar context) in Kuwait, where Sheikh 'Abd al-Rahman 'Abd al-Khaliq took the same approach in *The Scientific Foundations of the Salafi Call*.[127] His book is devoted to demonstrating that true Salafism is more "all-encompassing" than the Brothers' message, which 'Abd al-Khaliq criticizes for losing itself in political "details" (*juz'iyyat*) at the expense of religious concerns. Published in 1975, the text was already using the term *manhaj* to describe Salafism, which means that Hilmi was not the first to use it in that sense.[128] And unlike Hilmi, 'Abd al-Khaliq and his ideas had a widely recognized impact on the Call's founders.

Meanwhile, the Salafi Call's practical "methodology"—what I call "grammar of action"—remained unmistakably purist. One of the movement's "official" historians describes it as "education and reform, along with purging and purification" (*al-islah wa-l-tarbiya, ma' al-tasfiya wa-l-tanqiya*).[129] His phrasing brings to mind "purification and education" (*al-tasfiya wa-l-tarbiya*), the words Sheikh al-Albani, who also influenced the Salafi Call on this subject, used in describing his own project.[130] This meant "purifying" the Islamic corpus back to its intangible essence, then propagating the distilled result. Yasir Burhami quotes al-Albani directly: "Our obligation is to start with what's most important. This means correcting Muslims' beliefs, purifying their spirits, preaching an Islam free of blameworthy innovations and instilling the *tawhid* in the people."[131]

This purification project transcended theological or even strictly religious issues. As part of the all-encompassing discourse described earlier, the Salafi Call laid out a fairly complex framework touching on many social and political questions. The group also waded into some of the great intellectual battles of the time—regarding the veil, for example, which Muhammad Isma'il al-Muqaddim addressed in the three-volume *Return of the Hijab*, mentioned earlier, which is packed with an assortment of historical and religious references.[132] The Call's arguments partly leaned on the era's reigning Islamist tropes, like the supposed worldwide conspiracy to destroy Islam, led by a group of "Jews," "freemasons," and "crusaders" and carried out by their local agents.[133] In the 1980s, with Mubarak's modest liberalization of the Egyptian political landscape and the Brotherhood participating in elections, democracy was increasingly in the air—but the Call sheikhs assailed the idea in no uncertain terms, publishing several books on the topic. Their reasoning combined theological arguments (democracy challenges the principle of "loyalty and disavowal") with more practical ones (it wouldn't lead to reform; participating in such a system would legitimize it).[134]

Instead of simply sidelining the political question, the Salafi Call offered its ideal vision—Islamic governance, based only on obedience to God—while reaffirming that, important as it was, this was only one issue among many rather than *the* fundamental question, as the Islamist movements would have it.[135] The Call employed the terms *hakimiyya* and *jahiliyya* only sparingly but did not entirely reject them.[136] The meanings of these words were still bound up with Sayyid Qutb and Maududi, authors the group valued to a point but who "used general terms that lend themselves to confusion" and "had a negative influence ... in their discussions of faith, unbelief and judgment of people in a manner that diverges from religious science, which imposes limits, defines distinctions, and clarifies questions based on proofs from the Quran and the sunna that follow the understandings of the pious ancestors and the Umma's ulema."[137] Above all, the Call was aware that using the two terms would put the group and its participants at risk. As a former member explains, "The Sheikhs had written a booklet on *hakimiyya*, but it was only for those in the organization, and they were strictly forbidden from mentioning it in public. If State Security came across it, that could cause problems for everyone."[138]

The Call's Salafis likewise avoided attacking the Egyptian regime directly in their discourse or in publicly released books, keeping instead to abstract rhetoric. Members-only teaching sessions were the sole venue for discussing these topics more overtly. The sheikhs also sometimes circulated handwritten or photocopied commentaries (*sharh*) that made explicit the insinuations in their more widely available books. These "cheat sheets" often touched on sensitive subjects, but only bona fide members were allowed to read them; they sometimes had to be hidden out of fear that the police would seize them. Yet, as a general rule, while the Call's sheikhs openly viewed the regime as impious (*kufr*), they stressed—even in private meetings—the distinction between "generic excommunication" (*takfir al-naw'*) and "individual excommunication" (*takfir al-mu'ayyan*). Their denunciation of actions, they explained, should not lead people to understand that the individuals behind them (especially Mubarak) were impious. The generic excommunication of the regime nonetheless led Call higher-ups to discourage members from joining the police, army, or legal system.[139]

This tiptoeing was justified by the metarule of realism explained in the introduction: The benefits and harms (*al-masalih wa-l-mafasid*) of each action and stance had to be weighed by the Call so as not to endanger the message—or the organization itself, as its ambassador. Clearly alluding to the Brotherhood, the sheikhs explained that taking action makes sense only if one has the ability (*qudra*) to attain one's goals. Thus, each move must first be assessed in terms of the power balance.[140] All these considerations served to justify the Call's only true enduring priority: to build, from the ground up, the "community of believers" (*al-ta'ifa al-mu'mina*) that would catalyze the future Islamic State.[141]

But on the question of how to get there—details that occupy a good amount of Brotherhood literature, including Sayyid Qutb's writings—the Call remained noncommittal: "As for the next steps in establishing the Islamic State, we make no specific demands of God that we see as inevitable or even necessary.... The *tamkin* [ability to bring about the Islamic State] is a gift from God, a promise whose goal is to achieve servitude (*'ubudiyya*) to God for the individual and for the Umma. Our obligation is to do what we can to make this possible, but victory will come only from God, and not because we laid the groundwork."[142] The immediate priority, then, was to take hold of society; the state could be dealt with much later, if ever.

The Salafi Call thus remained radically opposed to the Brotherhood's Islamist grammar of action. Its fundamentally purist grammar largely matched that of its Salafi predecessors, but with adjustments meant to empower the organization and increase its appeal, though without putting it at risk.

BATTLES OVER SALAFI GRAMMAR

While the Call was the first organized social movement in Egypt to declare itself Salafi, it didn't hold exclusive claim to the brand—far from it. In the 1970s Salafism swept in as a shared religious reference point in activist circles; other groups that originated during that decade also claimed affiliation with the doctrine. What's more, several currents and networks emerged during the 1980s to compete directly with the Call, in an approximate microcosm of divisions found within the Salafi movement across Gulf countries during the same period.[143]

The goal of this section is to inventory all the self-proclaimed Egyptian Salafi groups that advocated for grammars of action different from that of the Call, thereby challenging its proclaimed monopoly on the Salafi label. The interplay of local interests amplified these rivalries; most groups had roots in specific regions. I will not discuss Ansar al-Sunna, which continued to operate and expand during this period but had lost hold of its strong early identity; the organization became more and more of a hollow shell as various competitors (discussed later) vied for control of it.

Jihadi Groups

I will first touch on the so-called jihadi groups Jama'a Islamiyya and Islamic Jihad, whose roots predate the founding of the Salafi Call.[144] They too claimed to embody the Salafi message, even though their religious writing was markedly less prolific than that of the Call and despite the fact that most members (aside from a handful of charismatic leaders) did not present themselves as experts in religious science.[145] In accordance with the jihadi grammar that governed their actions, these groups prioritized politics, mainly using the Salafi corpus as a powerful lexicon for expressing the radical transformation they envisioned; the debate over orthodoxy and orthopraxy was not in itself a priority. In accordance with their overall strategy, they readily embraced greater pragmatism than the other Salafi groups on such questions.[146] But this didn't stop the jihadis from using Salafi ideals to taunt the Muslim Brotherhood. They denounced its "un-Islamic" practices and views (regarding the legality of music or images, belief in the divine attributes, etc.), although their loathing for the organization stemmed mostly from its rejection of armed violence.[147]

After all groups involved in Sadat's assassination initially unified under an umbrella organization, there was a split in the mid-1980s. It happened in prison. Ex-jihadi 'Abd al-Mun'ib Munib, who was incarcerated with the groups, says that on one side of the debate sat the Cairo and Delta jihadis, who came from the earliest cells that had emerged in the late 1960s, while on the other sat the Jama'a Islamiyya members, natives of Upper Egypt.[148] The former, who were older (most in their thirties at the time) and more experienced, saw themselves as the logical leaders, since most Jama'a Islamiyya members had been university students when they were arrested. The latter protested, invoking the group's only significant religious figure, Sheikh 'Umar 'Abd al-Rahman, a reliable supporter, who had been freed from prison in 1984. But he was blind, which the Cairo jihadis argued disqualified him from holding legitimate authority (*imama*), pointing to medieval treatises on the conditions for becoming the caliph of the Muslim community.[149] After the groups separated mid-decade, a new organization called Egyptian Islamic Jihad was officially announced in 1988.[150] Most members were jihadis from Cairo and the Delta, and their rising star was Ayman al-Zawahiri. The Upper Egypt activists, meanwhile, held on to the Jama'a Islamiyya name.

Beyond these power struggles, the Egyptian jihadi movement was being torn apart by a more theoretical debate over the excuse of ignorance. Jama'a Islamiyya members were inclined to believe that ignorance excused impiety (even, to a degree, on questions of creed), while some Islamic Jihad members loudly proclaimed the opposite. The son of Rifa'i Surur, one of the foremost jihadi ideologues, called this "the pivotal Islamist debate of the 1980s."[151] Above all, it expressed the strategic differences between the two groups.

Burnt by its 1981 routing, the Jama'a Islamiyya felt it had no choice but to put off, for the time being, violent action aimed at "establishing the caliphate along the prophetic path."[152] The group devoted itself instead to preaching and social action in order to solidify its connection with society.[153] This meant shifting temporarily to more of a purist grammar of action, but even this transformation was incomplete—especially because the group didn't completely relinquish violence. It continued to advocate for "the correction of vice by force" in the name of *hisba*—a concrete application of "commanding right and forbidding wrong."[154] Following Salafi logic, "vice" sometimes included symbols of Sufi observance; in 1987, for example, Jama'a Islamiyya members torched a saint's mausoleum in Damietta.[155] But the organization aimed above all to build a vast grassroots movement for its cause so that, when the "inevitable showdown" (*hatmiyyat al-muwajaha*, from the title of one of the movement's books, published in the mid-to-late 1980s) came to pass, its followers would have the upper hand.[156] In sum, as Roel Meijer demonstrates, the Jama'a Islamiyya was positioning itself as a true social movement, which set it apart from the underground organizations that had made up the jihadi movement until then.[157] In such a context, it made sense for the group to "excuse ignorance" rather than burning bridges with a society it wished to win over—especially in Upper Egypt, where Sufism remained influential.[158]

To the more elitist Islamic Jihad, the issue of societal integration felt less pressing, which may explain why, without offering a definitive answer on the excuse of ignorance, the group was comfortable with more rigid rhetoric on the subject.[159] Instead of pushing for a grassroots Islamic revolution, this movement—true to the "letter" of jihadi grammar—advocated taking power through a secret vanguard equipped to undermine the regime from the highest levels. It also reproached the Jama'a Islamiyya for its attachment to "correction of vice by force," which attracted police attention and thus seemed counterproductive.[160] Islamic Jihad, meanwhile, became known for several failed assassination attempts on Egyptian government figures, including Minister of Interior Hasan al-Alfi and Prime Minister Atef Sidqi in 1993 and President Mubarak in 1995. Under Ayman al-Zawahiri, it merged with al-Qaeda in 1998.

Despite its initial desire to avoid conflict with the Egyptian regime, the Jamaʿa Islamiyya would also get caught up in the wave of violence. Skirmishes first broke out between movement activists and Egyptian police in 1986 when some vice correction missions went off the rails.[161] And repression of the Jamaʿa Islamiyya began in earnest when Zaki Badr became minister of interior in 1987, starting a vicious cycle: In retaliation for Badr's repeated arrests of its members, the group attempted but failed to assassinate him. This sparked an intensified response, which in turn triggered violent actions intended to "protect the preaching movement," according to the former chief of the movement's military wing.[162]

The war of attrition between the state and the Jamaʿa Islamiyya killed hundreds (the dead included police as well as extrajudicially assassinated jihadis) and sent up to fifty thousand to prison, which hints at the movement's deep hold on society.[163] Finally brought to their knees, its leaders announced—from prison—an "initiative to end violence" (*mubadarat waqf al-ʿunf*) in 1997 and cowrote four books offering a religious justification for their change of heart.[164] They were freed over the following years, during which time the Jamaʿa Islamiyya, stripped of its revolutionary ideology, morphed into a "classic" Salafi preaching movement, fully embracing a purist grammar whose practice ended up closely resembling that of the Salafi Call.[165]

The 1980s and 1990s also brought smaller jihadi cells; the press gave them nicknames like *shawqiyyun* (disciples of Shawqi) or *al-najun min al-nar* (hell's survivors), to name just two.[166] Given their limited reach and the fact that most were ephemeral, I won't delve into their stances on the key issues discussed in this chapter.

Critical Salafism

A second type of self-proclaimed Salafis belonged to what might be called the "critical" faction of the movement. Its penchant for openly debating sensitive political questions set it apart from the Call, which either avoided such issues or discussed them only internally. The faction also devoted much effort to denouncing "governance that disregards God's revelations" (*al-hukm bi ghayr ma anzala Allah*) and reaffirming the principle of "loyalty and disavowal." It was thus more inclined to proclaim individual excommunication (*takfir al-muʿayyan*) of a leader—Mubarak, in this case—while the Call would hold its tongue. But unlike the jihadis, the critical Salafis did not call for armed struggle.

Critical Salafism's nonviolent politicization placed it in a unique and, in many ways, paradoxical position within the Egyptian Islamic sphere. On one hand, its approach made it a "radical" strain that openly distinguished itself from mainstream Salafism with its stance toward the regime. But because it was political, critical Salafism could also be much more flexible in its choice of allies, sometimes setting aside religious or theological differences out of a strategic need for unity.[167]

I would argue that the critical Salafis largely borrowed from Islamist grammar and its variations, while continuing to identify with a purist grammar. The few Salafis who remained friendly with the Muslim Brotherhood would indeed come from this group, maintaining ties less out of a shared religious vision than because they believed the Islamist movement could only hope to win as a united front. Since the Brotherhood was the dominant Islamist group, victory without it was impossible. Some in the critical movement even agreed with Sheikh Hisham Al ʿUqda, one of their leading figures, who proclaimed that "we should collaborate with all who act and mobilize to aid the oppressed, defend what's true, and stand up to corruption"—even if this "all" included infidels or secularists.[168] Several currents can be grouped under this heading.

THE CAIRO SCHOOL

The "Cairo School," as some call it, was a group of sheikhs based mainly in the Egyptian capital (especially in neighborhoods such as El Matareya and Shubra) who were known from the late 1980s for opposing the regime of Mubarak, whom they excommunicated by name. They also took up transnational Islamic causes such as Palestine or Chechnya, for which they were not shy about seeking donations. Muhammad ʿAbd al-Maqsud (b. 1947) was the face of the group. He originally studied organic chemistry and botany, then obtained a doctorate and landed a job at the Plant Protection Research Institute. As the 1970s drew to a close, he began immersing himself in religion from the Salafi perspective, which was in vogue at that time.[169] Among other trending books, he suggests that he was particularly influenced by al-Albani's *Prayer of the Prophet*.[170] Like many of his friends then, he was essentially a religious autodidact. But he rapidly established himself as an authority, especially on questions of fiqh, and became known in Salafi circles as *faqih al-qahira* (the jurisconsult of Cairo).[171] Along with other sheikhs, some his former students, he built a network that had no formal structure.

The Cairo School generally aligned itself with critics of organized "collective action," a choice influenced both by security concerns and religious beliefs.[172] Each sheikh focused instead on a group of disciples, in the style of traditional relationships between ulema and students. Notable members of this network included Nash'at Ahmad, Fawzi al-Sa'id (who was among those accused of involvement in the events of 1981), and Mamduh Jabir.[173] Their detractors suggested that they had been influenced by Sayyid Qutb's ideas—which wouldn't be at all surprising, given that Qutb left his mark on most Islamist dissidents. But it must be acknowledged that their religious writing was exclusively Salafi-based and that—like the Salafi Call—they mostly refrained from quoting Qutb.

THE SURURIS

Qutb's influence is more obvious in the two other currents of critical Salafism, whose grammars of action are clearly hybrids. The first current is often called Sururi, named after a subset of the Sahwa ("awakening") movement, an ideological fusion that took place in 1970s Saudi Arabia between Brotherhood thought (mostly its Qutbist variation) and Wahhabism. The Sururis, initially tolerated by the Saudi regime, became some of its highest-profile critics during the early 1990s.[174]

Sururism is grounded in a strong ideological identity, as its organic intellectuals in Saudi Arabia—particularly Sayyid Qutb's brother, Muhammad, who taught starting in 1971 at Umm Al-Qura University in Mecca—had produced a large body of work. In his writings, Muhammad Qutb endeavored to demonstrate the compatibility between Qutbist and Salafi thought, arguing that the Brotherhood's battle for shari'a and the Salafis' struggle for creed were in fact two sides of the same coin. In so doing, he helped normalize Salafi usage of Sayyid Qutb's conceptual framework. He specifically wished to show that *hakimiyya*, Qutbism's trademark concept, was foundational to *tawhid*, which in turn lay at the heart of the Salafi message. To this end, he thought it necessary to add a fourth dimension to Muhammad bin 'Abd al-Wahhab's three pillars of *tawhid*: *tawhid al-hakimiyya* (God's sovereignty due to his oneness and transcendence).[175]

In the Saudi context, Sururism existed as a semisecret organization said to have been founded by Muhammad Surur Zayn al-'Abidin (hence its name, though Surur actually had little to do with it), a former member of the Syrian Muslim Brotherhood who was exiled for a time in the kingdom.[176] In the 2000s Saudi Sururism, having been weakened, broke into two main currents. The first, led by Sheikh Salman al-'Awda, advocated reform; the second, more conservative, followed Sheikhs Safar al-Hawali and Nasir al-'Umar, among others.

In Egypt, the movement began expanding starting in the 1980s, both as an intellectual influence and as a network. The three main figures of Egyptian Sururism—Hisham Al 'Uqda, Muhammad Yusri Ibrahim, and Salah al-Sawi—maintained strong ties with Saudi Arabia, where they had either grown up or taught during a period of strong Sururi influence in the country's educational system.

Al 'Uqda's family left the Damanhur region for Saudi Arabia soon after he was born in 1961. He returned to Egypt only in 1979, at the age of eighteen, to enroll in a university medical program, and joined the fledgling Salafi movement during this period. His connections in the kingdom allowed him to return there often for courses with the era's foremost sheikhs, Ibn Baz and Ibn 'Uthaymin, along with the critical sheikhs Nasir al-'Umar and Salman al-'Awda from the Sururi movement, with whom he would remain close. Unlike other Salafi sheikhs, he managed to register at al-Azhar later in life, where he acquired his master's degree with a thesis on "The Rules and Impact of Imprisonment in the Shari'a," which doubled (implicitly) as a scathing criticism of human rights violations in Egyptian prisons.[177] Starting in the 1980s, Al 'Uqda, who steadfastly believed that collective action was permitted under Islamic law, tried to establish and lead a jama'a in his birthplace of Damanhur. He got on well for a time with the Salafi Call, but the overly "political" nature of his teachings occasioned a split; constant harassment by State Security precluded any expansion beyond his home turf.

Muhammad Yusri Ibrahim followed a similar early path. Born in Cairo in 1966, he moved with his parents to Saudi Arabia and didn't return to

THE SALAFI CALL

Egypt until the mid-1980s, when he enrolled at university. He first studied engineering, then went on to al-Azhar, where he obtained his master's degree in shari'a in 2003 and a doctorate in 2011. As with Al 'Uqda, his Saudi years fostered loyalty to Sururism. He remained close with the movement's sheikhs there, particularly Nasir al-'Umar. Ibrahim was also close with an Egyptian sheikh more than ten years his senior, Salah al-Sawi, who was born in 1954. Al-Sawi studied at al-Azhar, then taught at Mecca's Umm Al-Qura University—Muhammad Qutb's home base and a Sahwa stronghold—from 1981 to 1986, which may be when he embraced the Sururi theses.[178] These guided many books he wrote that looked at highly political subjects through a Salafi lens: pluralism, democracy, secularism, and more. In the mid-1990s al-Sawi and Ibrahim both joined one of the Sururi movement's flagship institutions outside of Saudi Arabia: the American Open University (Al-jami'a al-amrikiyya al-maftuha), founded by Ja'far Shaykh Idris of Sudan. Al-Sawi headed its Egyptian satellite, where Ibrahim oversaw the educational programming. One gets the impression from their trajectories that, unlike Al 'Uqda, in addition to being intellectually aligned with Sururism, the two may have been more directly involved in the movement's operation.

Other Sururi-inspired groups sprang up in early 2000s Egypt, including that of Hisham Mustafa in Alexandria. A member of the Salafi Call, Mustafa came under Sahwa influence during several stays in Saudi Arabia during the late 1980s and the 1990s; he severed ties with the Call around 2002. Following this decision, his group—roiled by debates—then chose a reformist approach and authored ample literature on the topic, pivoting to a fully post-Islamist stance in the wake of the revolution, and even pointing to Fethüllah Gülen's movement as an inspiration.[179]

Another group formed in the early 2000s around Sheikh Ashraf 'Abd al-Mun'im in Mansoura, with influences too eclectic for it to simply be called Sururi (its members also took inspiration from the Cairo School and the Qutbist and jihadi movements).[180] This group would go on to found the Salafi Front during the 2011 revolution.

THE *QUTBIYYUN*

One last critical group gained traction in the 1980s. In activist circles, its members were called *qutbiyyun*, which literally means "Qutbists," but I will use the Arabic term here to avoid confusion between this particular circle and Qutbism as a school of thought. 'Abd al-Majid al-Shazli (1938–2013) was the group's main mover and shaker. A young disciple of Sayyid Qutb, his name appeared eighth on the list of accused in 1965; he had been deeply involved in the plot against Nasser. Sentenced to a lifetime of hard labor, he was one of the last Islamists freed by Sadat in 1975.

While in prison, al-Shazli, who held a chemistry degree, became taken with the works of Ibn Taymiyya, Ibn Qayyim, and Muhammad bin 'Abd al-Wahhab.[181] After his release he spent a period in Saudi Arabia, where some sources say he taught, before returning to Egypt.[182] His departure for the kingdom had likely been arranged by Muhammad Qutb, whom al-Shazli knew well and who, after his own release from prison, had become a professor at Umm Al-Qura University in Mecca four years earlier. Al-Shazli used his time in the country to deepen his knowledge of Salafi Islam by studying with 'Abd al-Razzaq 'Afifi, a prominent Ansar al-Sunna figure who had been appointed to Saudi Arabia's Council of Senior Ulema, as well as with Sheikh 'Abd al- 'Aziz bin Baz.[183]

Al-Shazli's intellectual project would thus consist of reformulating Qutbist ideology using Salafi-compatible terms. This had been happening organically in Egypt since the 1970s, but the *qutbiyyun*, along with the Sururis, would be the first to theorize the fusion in detail. Fellow traveler Rifa'i Surur recounts how al-Shazli became "the one who gave a legal and religious foundation to Sayyid Qutb's thinking" (*al-mu'assil al-fiqhi wa-l-shar'i li fikr Sayyid Qutb*), adding to its power by dismantling "the rhetoric of those who assert that Sayyid Qutb's writings are nothing but literature."[184]

Al-Shazli's approach thus resembled that of Muhammad Qutb in every regard; the latter, working from Mecca, was also doing his best to reconcile Qutbism and Salafism.[185] Both aimed to temper the immediate revolutionary potential of Sayyid's thinking, in order to bring back a grammar that more closely resembled the purist ideal. They emphasized instruction (*tarbiya*) of a vanguard (*tali'a*), which would provide the foundation (*al-qa'ida*) on which the Islamic State was to be built—but just how to establish such a state would be addressed at a later point.[186] At the same time, al-Shazli freely applied excommunication (*takfir*) and based his arguments on the idea of modern-day *jahiliyya*. He also stood out for refusing to accept the excuse of ignorance on the religion's most important issues (more on this later).

Unlike Muhammad Qutb—who was far removed from the Egyptian landscape and whose influence would only bleed over indirectly via the Sururi movement—al-Shazli would do his best to establish a true movement in Egypt, from his hometown of Alexandria. Founded in 1975, it was named the Call of the Sunnis (Da'wat ahl al-sunna wa-l-jama'a) and counted thousands of members in the early 2000s.[187] The group was particularly active in the North Sinai, where it promoted and organized "dispute resolution committees through shari'a" intended to resolve conflicts outside of the state legal system, much like those organized by the Brotherhood and the Salafi Call.[188]

Quietist Salafism and Loyalist Salafism

Quietist Salafism is mostly represented in Egypt by those who follow the school of Cairo-based Usama 'Abd al-'Azim and Muhammad al-Dubaysi.[189] Both had been leaders in the 1970s student activism, but they refused to join the Salafi Call because they opposed collective action. 'Abd al-'Azim, the most prominent of the two, was a Salafi heavyweight among the faculty of al-Azhar, where he taught at the Faculty of Islamic Studies until his death in 2022. His rhetoric focused on spiritual questions and avoided all political subject matter. It has sometimes been described as a form of "asceticism" or even, in an oxymoronic turn of phrase, Salafism with a "Sufi" twist.[190] Thousands of students attended his courses regardless, and he enjoyed significant respect within the Egyptian Salafi community. Another sheikh who more or less shares his outlook is Mustafa al-'Adwi, who studied with Muqbil al-Wadi'i in Yemen. All embrace purist grammar and reject the "adjustments" the Call has made to it.

A "loyalist" Salafism has also emerged since the 1990s that, despite presenting itself as apolitical, is best known for categorically disallowing—under threat of excommunication—any rebellion (*khuruj*) against those in power (*wali al-amr*). It also rejects all forms of collective action, which it sees as synonymous with sedition. The loyalist Salafis go to great lengths to badger any movement they associate with political Islam: jihadis, critical Salafis, the Salafi Call, or their favorite target, the Muslim Brotherhood.[191] This current is often referred to as "Madkhali" or "Jami," after its primary inspirations, Saudi sheikhs Rabi' al-Madkhali and Muhammad Aman al-Jami. The two made a name for themselves in 1990s Saudi Arabia with their radical opposition to the Sahwa-led dissidence and their unflagging support for the Saudi authorities.[192]

In Egypt, the current's main figures are (or were) Usama al-Qawsi, Muhammad Sa'id Raslan, and Tala'at Zahran. Often accused of being mere puppets of the authorities, the group could nonetheless claim a significant following in the 2000s and managed to hold important positions in Ansar al-Sunna's decision-making bodies, where the loyalists used their influence to take down the competition.[193] One both archetypical and paradoxical case is that of Mahmud Lutfi 'Amir, who directed the Damanhur branch of Ansar al-Sunna and was prolific in his attacks on his adversaries' views.[194] In 2010 'Amir was so single-mindedly supportive of Hosni Mubarak (whom he called the "Commander of the Faithful") that he released a fatwa declaring Mubarak's leading liberal opponent Mohamed al-Baradei an infidel, saying that it was therefore lawful to spill his blood. The enormous scandal that followed would embarrass both Ansar al-Sunna's leadership and the Egyptian authorities and ultimately cost 'Amir his job.[195]

THE CALL TAKES ON ITS ADVERSARIES

Facing competition from all sides, the Alexandrian sheikhs sought to present themselves as ambassadors of "Salafi orthodoxy," whose purist grammar they wished to protect from rivals' "excesses" and "aberrations." What's more, the violence of the Jama'a Islamiyya and Islamic Jihad had brought Salafism a flood of bad press, which forced the Call to foreground its differences so the security apparatus wouldn't lump it in with the others.

The Alexandrian sheikhs battled other Egyptian Salafi currents regarding four overarching debates, which hinged on two big questions: that of organization, which played out through controversies over the legitimacy of collective action, and the political question—specifically, what stance to take toward the Egyptian regime. This last question tied into quarrels over "commanding right and forbidding wrong," the larger issue of jihad, and excommunication and the excuse of ignorance.

Ideas were wrangled over in writing or in person, in mosques and in prisons. In carceral settings, State Security typically placed each Islamist current in its own section. But the Salafis—who fell outside the existing categories—shared cells with members of other currents, setting the stage for heated debates; only in 2003 did the prison system begin separating them.[196] On the outside, representatives of various groups also jousted in more formal disputations (*munazarat*) that were sometimes recorded and broadcast.[197]

These dialogues led the Call sheikhs to churn out a flurry of texts for internal distribution, some later expanded on and published, which armed members with responses for critics.[198] The writings offered mostly muted, indirect criticisms, in deference to proclaimed solidarity—the metarule of not explicitly attacking adversaries so as to avoid accusations of sowing fitna in the community—but their subtexts were harsh. To tease out these subtleties, I often sought help from veterans of the Salafi movement who could reconstruct the context of a given concept or apparently anodyne allusion that was actually a snipe at a specific adversary (which everyone involved understood quite well).

The first large debate centered on collective action. On one side stood the Alexandrians; on the other, both the Cairo School and the Salafi quietists and loyalists, who considered the Salafi Call guilty of factionalism (*hizbiyya*) and therefore fitna because it had created an independent structure. Yasir Burhami replied that the Call was simply a "collaboration rooted in virtue and piety" (*al-ta'awun 'ala al-barr wa-l-taqwa*)—unlike the Brotherhood, which represented the germ of an alternative society and was led by an all-powerful guide who demanded allegiance.[199] Burhami supplemented his argument with a booklet for members called *Collective Action: Between Excessiveness and Renunciation*.[200]

In addressing the second debate, over "commanding right and forbidding wrong," the Call challenged the Jama'a Islamiyya, which in the 1980s still saw the "correction of vice by force" as a Muslim obligation.[201] This perspective was largely based on an interpretation of the writings of Ibn Taymiyya, who himself had led "corrections of vice by force" that sometimes landed him in prison. Without questioning the religious legitimacy of these actions, the Call reiterated (following the metarule of realism) that the benefits and harms (*al-masalih wa-l-mafasid*) needed to be weighed. Burhami explained, in a booklet taught to Call members, that acting like the Jama'a Islamiyya would jeopardize the Salafis' safety given that they weren't in a position of strength.[202] Such actions thus crossed a red line.

Regarding the third debate, over jihad, the Call again endeavored to distinguish itself from the Jama'a Islamiyya and Islamic Jihad, which saw armed combat against the Egyptian authorities as a religious duty (although because of strategic considerations mentioned earlier, the Jamaʻa Islamiyya initially hoped to forestall the confrontation). While it wasn't hard for the Call to refute Islamic Jihad's argument that the "apostate" regime and its agents had to be combatted—the Call refused to declare them apostates, thereby removing any such necessity—the Jamaʻa Islamiyya's ideologues advanced a religious argument that was harder to dismiss. In a much-read 1980s book, they used Ibn Taymiyya to argue that there is a duty to combat "the group that refrains [*al-ta'ifa al-mumtaniʻa*] from applying one of Islam's manifest and obligatory laws while possessing the authority to do so . . . even if its members recognize the law's necessity and make both professions of Muslim faith."[203] The strength of this argument lay in the choice not to excommunicate: Muslim they might remain, but those who consciously refuse to apply God's laws must be combatted. The Salafi Call rejected this interpretation, positing, for example, that the "group that refrains" can only lawfully be confronted by a powerful community of believers (*ta'ifa mu'mina*) with the capacity to subdue it.[204] Once again, due to the metarule of realism, its most important criterion was an accurate assessment of the power balance.

The fourth and final debate concerned two aspects of *takfir* (excommunication), a true bone of contention within the Salafi movement. As Daniel Lav demonstrated, this debate was fueled during the 1980s and 1990s by renewed controversy in Salafi circles over the definition of faith and how it relates to actions.[205] In other words, when could actions that violated Islamic principles nullify the culprit's faith, rendering him or her an unbeliever?

One part of the debate revolved around the excuse of ignorance. As we saw, the Alexandrian Salafis had distinguished themselves early on from Saudi Salafism (or at least from a fair number of its representatives) regarding this issue. In the 1980s the controversy resurfaced when ʻAbd al-Majid al-Shazli, the leading ideologue of the *qutbiyyun*, published a book called *The Threshold of Islam and the Reality of Faith* (*Hadd al-islam wa haqiqat al-iman*).[206] He argued that Islam required a high level of religiously conforming actions, severely limiting the extent to which the excuse of ignorance could be applied. As al-Shazli saw it, this argument justified excommunicating Arab leaders who don't govern according to Islamic law. That the book was published by the Umm al-Qura University Press in Mecca and edited by Sayyid Qutb's brother Muhammad enhanced its prestige and extended its reach. Sensing a threat, the Call's sheikhs redoubled their refutations. In 1985 Ahmad Farid wrote a volume reaffirming the Call's position on the issue, and Muhammad Isma'il al-Muqaddim issued a lengthy point-by-point refutation of al-Shazli's positions, geared to the movement's members.[207]

A second question relating to excommunication sparked a dustup of unprecedented scale: Does a person who completely abandons one of Islam's obligations (*tarik jins al-'amal*) remain Muslim? The furor began in 1986 when the young Saudi sheikh Safar al-Hawali published a book entitled *The Phenomenon of Irja' in Islamic Thought*, based on his doctoral dissertation.[208] In classical sources, *irja'* is presented as a heterodox current from the early days of Islam that forbade excommunicating a person who claimed to be Muslim, no matter what that person did. Al-Hawali suggested that *irja'* was more than a bygone historical episode, and that it continued to influence many ulema and Muslim intellectuals. He warned his readers against this trend, implying that it led to excessive tolerance for deviant ideas and practices—for example, sheikhs like al-Albani didn't necessarily consider someone an unbeliever if they fail to pray—and unacceptable indulgence toward governments hostile to Islam.[209]

The book triggered an explosive reaction in Saudi Arabia. Al-Hawali was one of the rising stars of the Sahwa movement, which had developed in Saudi universities out of a fusion between theological Salafism and Qutbist political thinking. And Muhammad Qutb, one of the architects of this synthesis, had advised al-Hawali on his dissertation, which Umm al-Qura University then published. Most significantly, the book was viewed in Saudi religious circles as a calculated attack against the traditional Salafi ulema—as much on Sheikh al-Albani, who promoted an essentially purist approach to Salafism, as on the official religious establishment, whose members unreservedly rubber-stamped the Saudi authorities' actions, even when they weren't the least bit Islamic. The publication set the stage for the "Sahwa insurrection," which started in earnest in August 1990, when King Fahd asked American troops to protect his country from the threat of an Iraqi invasion.[210]

The Sahwa's enormous popularity in the kingdom, particularly after the Gulf War, inevitably affected the Egyptian Salafi sphere. Some readily submitted that, while Saudi establishment ulema were overly conciliatory toward the monarchy, the Call sheikhs' indulgence toward Egyptian authorities was not much different. The Egyptian Sururis, who were directly tied to the Sahwa movement, were naturally the first to adopt al-Hawali's theses. But the Call was even more concerned because these ideas had begun spreading within its own flock, which now used them to challenge the sheikhs' authority.[211]

One such case, in 2001–2002, involved Hisham Mustafa's group (mentioned earlier).[212] The al-Hawali controversy had attracted the attention of the Egyptian security apparatus, in an already tense post-September 11 context, making the Call sheikhs nervous. Mustafa's followers were arrested, and the Call found itself on the hot seat.[213] Reflecting on that period, Yasir Burhami writes that al-Hawali's "book started spreading around the world, and many religious students and common people began to clash over its contents; a dangerous fault line appeared in the Salafi camp, causing completely avoidable clashes."[214] The Call's response was twofold: It sidelined (sometimes only temporarily) any Call members who followed al-Hawali's thinking, and it recorded sermons to refute his ideas.[215] Burhami would publish a book based on these sermons in 2004, called *Critical Reading and Refutation of Certain Ideas in the Book* The Phenomenon of Irja'.[216]

Founded by a handful of students with origins in the jama'at islamiyya, the Salafi Call managed to use the Salafi zeitgeist to its advantage, imposing itself in just three decades as the foremost organized Salafi social movement in Egypt. In so doing, the Call helped bookend the 1970s interlude, during which an intuitive new synthesis was built between Salafi discourse and the Islamist and jihadi grammars that temporarily redefined Salafi thought. The group achieved its goals by drawing on the organizational and mobilizing techniques of its adversary, the Muslim Brotherhood, both to better counter the Brothers on their own turf and to gain an edge over competing groups that also claimed to be Salafi. The Call thus updated Salafi grammar while leaving its fundamentals intact. There was pushback, however: Constant controversies embroiled the organization with its adversaries in the Islamic sphere. These offered opportunities for the Call to elucidate its discourse and grammar of action, which it always took care to distinguish from those of its competitors.

Keep in mind that the debates discussed in this chapter unfolded within a specific niche of Egyptian society: believers in Islamic advocacy who pushed for an activist expression of piety. The true shift came in the 1990s, when Salafism started to become normalized across much wider swaths of Egyptian society. While the Call's activities (like those of its competitors, to a certain extent) helped along this evolution, they alone cannot explain it. The next chapter will examine the other complex processes behind the change.

Chapter Four

SALAFISM'S INELUCTABLE ASCENT UNDER MUBARAK

> They would let their beards grow, ungroomed and uncut, to the breadth of a fist, clip their mustaches so that they wouldn't look like Magians, and not pluck their eyebrows so as not to be mistaken for women. From the pocket of one's jallabiya (which we called a "shirt") peeked the tip of a miswak, or chewing stick, with which we cleansed our mouths... and those same mouths were never used to whistle, as we had to distinguish ourselves from the unbelievers of Mecca, who, before Muhammad's mission, used to whistle as they walked around God's Sacred House—a small thing, but one that helped to deepen our sense of continuity over thousands of years.
>
> —KHALED AL-BERRY, *LIFE IS MORE BEAUTIFUL THAN PARADISE: A JIHADIST'S OWN STORY*

> I am among those who believe that the Muslim world has entered the age of Salafism, which will become—if it isn't already—the lodestar of the coming era. In our Muslim world, Salafism has established itself as the most powerful, active, and influential dynamic. As other forces recede, it fills the voids.
>
> —HUSAM TAMMAM, *ISSUES IN THE SALAFI ERA*

Under Mubarak, Salafi influence spread to society as a whole, pushing beyond the pious activist circles to which it had previously been limited. This was the moment when Salafism truly fulfilled its ambition to redefine the Sunni norm.

Several external factors played into the transformation, as we shall see: While the framework the Call offered was key to bringing the Salafi norm to a wider audience, underlying circumstances deserve some (or even most) credit for the norm's success. One element, a popular form of Salafism that took off in the late 1980s, made its discourse accessible to Egypt's Muslim masses. Its pathos-based message centered on individual piety and was disseminated by dozens of sheikhs who projected independence from all organizations—though many had nebulous relationships with the Call and took cues from its teachings.

In addition, the growing Salafi movement joined a powerful economy in the 1980s that was sustained by the Gulf countries; this placed it on stable financial footing and attracted new recruits. And the Mubarak regime's strategy for controlling religious groups largely proved to be a blessing, as in the long run it gave the movement a helpful boost. Finally, by acting as sheikhs and defining their activity exclusively in religious terms, Salafis seized the limelight in an arena mostly neglected by competitors, Brother and Azhari alike. This chapter tells the story of how these various factors played out, tilting the balance to give Salafism the upper hand in the battle of religious ideas.

THE RISE OF POPULAR SALAFISM

As the 1980s wound down, a new generation of independent Salafi preachers came onto the scene, proliferating in proportion to the era's thirst for Salafism—and intensifying it. This surge was possible because the Salafi approach, by nature, "disrupted" the traditional processes for training ulema. Whereas the Azhari method took decades to make a sheikh, autodidacts well-versed in the Salafi tradition's favorite authors could proclaim themselves sheikhs, so long as they had the right connections and had mastered the tricks of the trade. With a good memory for foundational texts (particularly hadiths) and the ability to quote them on command before an awestruck crowd, all a sheikh needed was a dash of charisma and he was set for success.

Many of these new preachers shared the Call's general outlook (a minority aligned more closely with rival groups), but most did not belong to the organization—despite whatever personal ties they might have with its sheikhs. Their religious backgrounds differed, too: Unlike the Call's founders, most had not experienced the activist wave of the 1970s. And a good number were more directly influenced by visits to Saudi Arabia, as hundreds of thousands of Egyptians had flocked to the Gulf for work starting in the late 1970s.[1]

The new preachers answered the Call's all-encompassing approach with one based wholly on individual observance. Moreover, whereas Call sheikhs favored scholarly rhetoric—their goal was to prepare a clerical elite steeped in doctrine—the newcomers spread a popular, theatrical Salafism that played on emotions and was thus more accessible to the common Muslim. They generally avoided political questions, pontificating instead about faith, prayer, purification of the body, the importance of certain practices (men should grow beards, women ought to wear niqabs, etc.), or final judgment and the apocalypse.[2] Even if the established Salafi sheikhs sometimes criticized these preachers for lacking religious knowledge or for "want[ing] to state the right without explicitly denouncing the wrong," they accepted them as crucial allies capable of expanding their base.[3]

Popular Salafis made up the dourest constituency in the "new preacher" movement, whose more liberal expressions—such as televised preacher 'Amr Khalid, an early 2000s sensation who had once been close with the Brotherhood—have been studied elsewhere.[4] While Khalid's influence faded in the second half of the decade, that of the Salafi sheikhs discussed here rose steadily until the 2011 revolution. The latter even took pleasure in taunting the tele-preacher, a favorite target perhaps because he was their direct competitor. The Salafis emphasized their religious legitimacy as (self-declared) ulema, a title Khalid never claimed for himself.[5]

What also distinguished these new preachers from their Salafi antecedents was their massive public presence, which began with the sale and large-scale distribution of cassettes (and later CDs) of their sermons in the 1990s; with their regular appearances on the religious satellite channels that took off after 2006, they gained nationwide recognition.[6] Such media outlets were now lucrative commercial investments, and the already high demand for Salafism made it a natural programming choice.[7] Qanat al-Nas was the first network to become a household name, soon followed by dozens of others; websites and social networks would then spread their content, maximizing its impact. The media attention was certainly crucial, but the sheikhs' popularity extended far beyond the virtual realm. Followers mobbed their sermons and lectures; the governor of a province where a famous sheikh was to appear had to declare a state of emergency as he saw throngs of humanity teetering on the brink of disaster.[8]

The new Salafi preachers took the nation by storm, transcending the audiences that the Salafi Call or established sheikhs were able to reach, in what Muhammad Yusri Ibrahim (himself a Salafi sheikh) called a "media jihad."[9] In this regard, they were to Salafism what star preacher Sheikh 'Abd al-Hamid Kishk had been to the Brotherhood in the 1970s, when, despite his independence from the organization, his rhetoric had carried its ideas to a broader public. The new preachers brought Salafism to all milieus and classes, breaking it out of the relatively educated circles—students and those who had the time to study at mosques—to which it had been limited. More and more individuals openly adopted Salafi practices, transforming Egypt's social fabric.

So many sheikhs appeared that it would be an arduous task to discuss each one. Instead, I will touch on three who were, by a landslide, Egypt's most popular from any Islamic current in the 2000s—and perhaps the country's three best-known public figures. The first, Abu Ishaq al-Huwayni, was the most atypical of the three because he had a solid scholarly reputation that he bolstered by regularly churning out books for specialists. Named Higazi Muhammad Sharif when he was born in 1956, near Kafr al-Shaykh in the Delta region, al-Huwayni recounts his late 1970s conversion to Salafism in a preface and a recorded lecture.[10]

It happened in Cairo, where he had just moved to study Spanish at university. Each Friday he would pray at the mosque of renowned Sheikh 'Abd al-Hamid Kishk. One day, as he exited the mosque, he passed a group of booksellers just outside. A tome caught his eye: *Prayer of the Prophet—May Peace and Blessings Be Upon Him—Description from Beginning to End, As Though You Were Seeing It*, by Sheikh al-Albani. Reading it, he says, helped him realize that the worship he'd been taught was a far cry from true prophetic prayer. Impressed by al-Albani's arguments, he read other works by the sheikh, including *The Collection of Weak and Forged Hadiths*.[11] He continued attending Sheikh Kishk's sermons, but the hadiths on which they were based began to ring hollow for him. Al-Huwayni, searching for answers, began perusing certain Salafi writings then gaining traction. He discovered that one author, Ibn Qayyim al-Jawziyya, had declared apocryphal one of the hadiths Kishk employed. Unable to contain himself, al-Huwayni shared his concerns with Kishk who, dismissive, essentially admonished him to "study up before you criticize."

That was when al-Huwayni knew that he had to become a hadith expert. In addition to attending classes taught by Salafi-inspired Brother Sayyid Sabiq, he studied with one of the few Cairo sheikhs specialized in the subject: Muhammad Najib Muti'i, who was anything but Salafi (and actually closer to being a traditional Azhari). Al-Huwayni nonetheless continued delving into al-Albani's writings; he saw the sheikh as his true mentor despite never having made his acquaintance. In 1986 he traveled to Jordan to spend a month with al-Albani—the first of just two occasions on which they would meet. His education thus remained a bookish, autodidactic process—which his enemies in the religious field would belittle, though many Egyptian Salafi sheikhs followed a similar path at the time.

Al-Huwayni's fame began to grow after he returned from Jordan, due in part to a persistent (but unattributed) rumor that al-Albani had referred to him as one of a chosen few "heirs."[12] Around this time, he wrote several books on hadith, knitted tight bonds with the Alexandrian sheikhs, and set up shop in Kafr El Sheikh.[13] He preached and taught at various mosques there before founding his own in 1998, named after Ibn Taymiyya.[14] It became his "headquarters," where, in the early 2000s, hundreds (sometimes thousands) of followers gathered for each of his lessons. He became known as Abu Ishaq al-Huwayni. The name Abu Ishaq reinforced his claim to authenticity, as it had been the *kunya* (epithet) of Sa'd bin Abi Waqqas, one of the Prophet's companions. He became popular across the country, especially thanks to recorded sermons where he softened his scholarly persona with a vernacular, almost plebeian style peppered with humorous asides, much as televised preacher Sheikh al-Sha'rawi had done before adoring crowds in the 1970s.[15]

While al-Huwayni had few ties to Saudi Arabia (at least early in his religious journey), this was not the case for the two others I describe here; they fit more neatly into the "ideal type" of Salafi sheikhs who made their names during the 1980s and 1990s.

One was Muhammad Husayn Ya'qub, born in 1956. A certified Arabic language professor, he taught the subject in Saudi Arabia for four years starting in 1980. There, he was influenced by Saudi Islam and began attending classes given by the era's Salafi figureheads, particularly Ibn Baz. Ya'qub returned to the country several times and says that on each visit he studied under prestigious figures from the Saudi religious establishment. During one such stay, he heard talk of an Egyptian Salafi sheikh, Usama 'Abd al-'Azim (mentioned in the previous chapter), a leader in Cairo's movement who had refused to join the Salafi Call because he opposed all types of organization. Back in Egypt, Ya'qub became a devotee of 'Abd al-'Azim, whom he would now call "his" sheikh—a move that garnered him the local networks and credentials he had previously lacked. He pursued a preaching career in the 1990s, and his recorded sermons quickly found a following.[16]

The last figure I will touch on here, Muhammad Hassan, was born in 1962 near Mansoura. Like the others, Hassan began without formal religious training, though he says he learned the Quran early on and started preaching to friends and family at a young age. Despite his interest in religion, he majored in media studies (*iʿlam*) at Cairo University.[17] But Hassan seems to have been drawn to Salafi discourse, because he describes traveling to Jordan during his university years to hear Sheikh al-Albani speak. He became involved with Ansar al-Sunna, and its connections may have facilitated his departure in 1981 for Saudi Arabia, where he spent several years taking courses with the era's most important Salafi sheikhs, Ibn Baz and Ibn ʿUthaymin, along with others closer to the Sahwa movement like Ibn Jibrin.[18] On the recommendation of Ibn ʿUthaymin, he was even hired to teach at the Qassim branch of Imam Mohammad Ibn Saud Islamic University.

The Sahwa movement was enjoying enormous popularity at the time of Hassan's stay in the kingdom, which explains his initial politically tinged rhetoric, later traded for a less controversial Salafism. When he returned to Egypt in the late 1980s, he settled in his home region of Mansoura, preaching and teaching mainly at Ansar al-Sunna's al-Tawhid mosque, along with others operated by the organization. He also founded an institute called the "Sunni Center" (Mujammaʾ ahl al-sunna) in his birthplace of Damuh. It's worth noting that in many ways, he remained the most "Saudi" of the Egyptian Salafi sheikhs: He always wore a *shmagh* or *ghutra* (fabric head coverings used in the Gulf states), spoke in literary Arabic, and mostly avoided Egyptian dialect in his conferences and sermons.[19]

The proliferation of these new religious authority figures signaled a remarkable deepening of Egyptian Salafism's influence. Under Ansar al-Sunna, Salafism had been a scholarly network, which the Salafi Call then built into an organized social movement. And the new preachers had transformed Salafism into a widespread expression of popular piety that almost seemed like a "nonmovement," Asef Bayat's term for the collective actions of dispersed, nonorganized actors. "The power of nonmovements," he says, "rests on the *power of big numbers*, that is, the consequential effect on norms and rules in society of many people simultaneously doing similar, though contentious, things."[20] While the phenomenon certainly helped established groups like the Salafi Call with recruitment, Salafism itself—now more than ever a shape-shifting, diffuse phenomenon—was slipping through their grasp. This latter-day metamorphosis could never have succeeded without support from a powerful political economy with roots in the Gulf region.

THE EGYPTIAN SALAFI ECONOMY

The power of ideas here is undeniable: Salafism's growing hold owed much to the overall religious upswell in Egypt, where the Islamic norm was increasingly expressed in Salafi terms. But the movement's growth also depended on more secular (that is, financial) resources. Whether or not the impression was accurate, visible Salafi observance seemed to promise material advantages to its practitioners. This may also account for the soaring number of sermon-givers: The Salafi preaching market was quite bullish.

Community ideals and mutual aid are cornerstones of any religious movement. The Salafis' growing influence over mosques gave them access to all sorts of resources, including *zakat* and individual donations (especially from the wealthy) that imams brought in, as well as potential aid through each mosque's umbrella organization (Ansar al-Sunna or the Jam'iyya Shar'iyya, for example). Salafi solidarity networks thus developed that were less formal than, yet in many ways just as effective as, those of the Brotherhood. They sometimes played an essential role in Egyptians' everyday lives, filling a void left by the state, which, favoring a neoliberal economic model, had gradually been stepping back since the Sadat era. Some say that this is why the Brotherhood was so successful, but the argument works just as well for the Salafis' ascendancy.[21]

Salafism was also part of an opulent transnational economic and religious space centered on the Gulf countries: Saudi Arabia, along with Qatar and Kuwait, and to a more limited extent the United Arab Emirates. Since the 1960s, the Brotherhood, with its already substantial Gulf diaspora, had likewise profited financially from regional connections.[22] Yet by the 1980s and 1990s, Salafis had become the religious actors best positioned to benefit from Gulf wealth. One common (if mistaken) understanding would have it that this economic and religious space was but an appendage of the Gulf states, and entirely bound to their political will. I showed in an earlier book how, while these states did assent to and even subsidize this space, it remained relatively autonomous.[23] It included many types of institutions, such as state (or state-supported) committees for "spreading Islam"; Islamic universities, NGOs, and banks; businesses owned or managed by Salafi sympathizers; and others. These entities felt it was a religious duty to support like-minded faithful abroad. Becoming Salafi in Egypt thus meant potentially joining this powerful network.

The array of possible benefits could be tempting. As a Salafi, for example, one had better chances of finding work in the Gulf at one of the aforementioned establishments. Crucially, governments in the region required each foreign worker to be vouched for by a sponsor (*kafil*). In some cases, an organization like Ansar al-Sunna could use its many ties in Saudi Arabia to help members.

It has often been said that Salafism surged in Egypt because of the country's mass labor exodus to the Gulf.[24] Once abroad, the theory goes, workers were possessed by the prevailing piety and returned home converted. The hypothesis holds in some cases, including that of Muhammad Husayn Ya'qub, whom I mentioned in the previous section. Anthropologist Samuli Schielke nevertheless emphasizes that when such conversions did take place, they often resulted from the disorienting experience of migration and its concomitant quest for a new identity, rather than from active proselytism.[25]

In many other cases, the Salafi conversion happened on Egyptian soil; the Gulf sojourn simply furthered an existing process that had inspired the departure in the first place. One example was Muhammad Hassan who, convinced by Salafi ideas, left for Saudi Arabia (likely through Ansar al-Sunna's connections). And there was Nash'at Ahmad, who was imprisoned during the waves of arrests in 1981, later left to work in Saudi Arabia, and ended up presiding over a Jeddah mosque for around ten years, until 1995.[26] I should note that Saudi Arabia welcomed—at least until the 2000s—followers of all Salafi currents, which had representatives on the ground.

We can't truly measure the impact that workers' emigration to the Gulf region had on Egyptians' religious outlook without conducting quantitative research. Various anthropological studies, like those of Lucile Gruntz, suggest that it's impossible "to draw a clear link between returning migration from the Gulf and the re-Islamization of Egyptian society."[27] They reject "Salafization caused by the return of expatriate workers" as a simplistic theory advanced by former Nasserists or leftist activists who were disconcerted by the profound societal changes rocking post-Nasser Egypt.[28] Renowned Egyptian sociologist Galal Amin agrees: "Some think that this religious tidal wave happened because Gulf customs were adopted during work-related migration. I entirely disagree with this interpretation. Customs and behaviors do not travel that easily; when such a transfer takes place, it is only when the environment in the host country is poised to embrace them and let them spread."[29]

These departures for the Gulf did not launch the Salafization process in Egypt; we clearly saw that it began much earlier. That said, Gulf ties undeniably helped make Egyptian Salafism economically viable. One of several problems Salafis had encountered was that their faith and practices closed off much of the Egyptian job market. Until the 2000s, for example, it was nearly impossible to get hired as a civil servant if one's beard was too thick—which complicated things, as observant Salafis refused to trim them. But whatever their appearance, for the most devoted, working for a non-Islamic government was simply out of the question. Salafis searching in the private sector typically ran into the same problematic rules; exceptions, while theoretically possible, were made only rarely and after intense negotiation. And sheikhs advised against working in the tourism industry, one of the country's biggest employers, because of inevitable exposure to sin.[30]

If Gulf exile wasn't an option, this left only three choices: working as an independent professional (e.g., as a doctor or taxi driver, two of Salafi Egyptians' most popular professions), getting hired within an establishment of what Carrie Wickham calls the "parallel Islamic sector" (such as a nonstate Islamic association, so long as it wasn't too tightly controlled by the Brotherhood, which preferred to install its own loyalists), or buying and selling goods.[31] Gulf oil wealth helped make the second option possible: Carrie Wickham explains that Egypt's parallel Islamic sector grew partly thanks to funds from that region.[32]

A community of Salafi businessmen likewise developed, at least in some measure, due to Gulf involvement. Many Salafis, for example, ventured into the import-export business (perhaps representing a Saudi company in Egypt), while others put their Saudi connections to use as travel agents specializing in pilgrimages. Trade in honey—often imported from Saudi Arabia for use in the "prophetic medicine" (*al-tibb al-nabawi*) so popular among Salafis—was a favorite niche. Still others got involved in the flourishing Islamic publishing market, where Salafism was prominent. Finally, some—like two Azhari brothers, Sayyid and ʿAbd al-Qadir Rizq al-Tawil—threw themselves into the Islamic banking sector, as Malika Zeghal recounts in detail. The pair founded Daʿwat al-Haqq (which had split off from Ansar al-Sunna in the 1970s) and made sure to back their association's activities with an Islamic bank they directed.[33] In all these activities, connections to the Gulf played a key role.

Even if they didn't yield enormous windfalls, these Gulf relationships allowed part of the emerging Salafi community to live comfortably—better, in some cases, than average Egyptians—which kept the "Saudi dream" (pious profits, ripe for the picking) alive and well. The "star" Salafi preachers, a small minority, did enjoy a flashy lifestyle funded by their satellite broadcasts' ad revenues; they also took a cut for acting as trusted middlemen between Egypt and the Gulf. Stars became recurring tabloid targets, making headlines with their astronomical television salaries or allegedly excessive lifestyles.[34] And the scandal sheets had a field day with sex scandals where such preachers were alleged to have misled young religious girls with promises of marriage, then repudiated them based on religious arguments.[35] But for their followers and many pious Egyptians, these sheikhs stood as models of both moral and societal success—which surely explains some of the careers they inspired.

MUBARAK'S SECURITY STRATEGY GIVES SALAFIS A LEG UP

Salafism's growth in Egypt was helped along by Mubarak's strategy for policing the political-religious field, carried out through two principal institutions. The first was the Ministry of Awqaf, which a law in 1960 had theoretically charged with oversight of all mosques. Through its regional and local divisions, it was supposed to name imams, as well as the preachers who gave Friday sermons (*khatib jumʿa*). From the outset, however, there were exceptions: Certain religious associations—including Ansar al-Sunna, the Jamʿiyya Sharʿiyya, and later the Tabligh movement and some smaller organizations like Daʿwat al-Haqq—were authorized to keep operating and supervising their own mosques.

In the 1970s Sadat's initial show of tolerance vis-à-vis the religious field led to a proliferation of so-called private (*ahliyya*) mosques with no ministry oversight, whose imams and Friday preachers were selected by the local community and/or whoever operated the mosque. To close this loophole, several laws were passed—in 1973, 1982, and 1996—to bring private houses of prayer under the auspices of the Ministry of Awqaf.[36] The final piece of legislation threatened stiff penalties or prison time for anyone giving a Friday sermon or religious lesson without ministry approval (*tarkhis*).[37] But the agency didn't have enough imams to cover all of Egypt, despite various attempts to expand its reach—for example, by using "freelance" (*bi-l-mukafa'a*) preachers paid by the sermon.[38]

The number of mosques in the country had skyrocketed, from 17,000 in 1961 to around 30,000 in 1979, then to 50,000 in 1984 and an astounding 108,000 in 2012.[39] Yet in 1980 just 7,000—less than a quarter—were actually overseen by the ministry. By 2012 that number had grown to only 45,000, still fewer than half.[40] This means that for decades, the greater share of mosques fell into a gray zone: The ministry could impose its legal authority on any given mosque, particularly if it had become too large or influential, but the imams and worshippers it drove out would always find a new refuge. And the ministry faced other constraints: My interlocutors described how its preachers were poorly paid and sometimes given assignments far from home, making no-shows a common occurrence. What's more, sermons given by civil servants weren't necessarily imbued with the same conviction as those delivered by a young preacher who believed in the cause. In such situations, community complaints could well lead—through formal or informal channels—to the new imam's replacement, or even the return of the unlicensed one who had been expelled not long before.

Religious movements mastered the art of exploiting the system's weaknesses. The Salafis, like the Brothers and most other Islamic currents, maintained most of their microsocial presence through private mosques. But these were usually quite small, and this limited the movement's reach. One oft-employed, classic technique for taking over larger places of worship thus involved infiltrating authorized nonstate organizations to gain use of their network of mosques.

For example, Ansar al-Sunna has played host to Salafis of all stripes since the 1980s, be they independent or tied to the Salafi Call, critical Salafism, or loyalist Salafism. Each current aimed to gain enough of a foothold at the organization's governorate or district level to be able to install its members in the mosques Ansar al-Sunna supervised. Muhammad Hassan, Abu Ishaq al-Huwayni, and even critical Salafis Fawzi al-Saʻid and Nashʼat Ahmad all used Ansar al-Sunna mosques as their "headquarters."[41] The al-ʻAziz billah Mosque, considered Cairo Salafis' main meeting space in the early 2000s—a place where representatives of every current came to give sermons (some even taught in its preacher training institute)—also belonged to Ansar al-Sunna.[42] And the Salafi Call managed to capture roles within Daʻwat al-Haqq, an independent association after its 1970s split with Ansar al-Sunna. One found an abundance of Call sheikhs in its mosques, especially those of Damietta, a Daʻwat al-Haqq stronghold.[43]

The struggle within the Jamʻiyya Sharʻiyya—between followers of traditional Islam, the Muslim Brotherhood, and the Salafis—was no less intense. During the late 1970s and 1980s, the Brothers seemed to dominate in the organization's decision-making bodies; its *al-Iʻtisam* journal even served at the time as one of the Brotherhood's unofficial media outlets.[44] But in the 1990s the Salafis dramatically amplified their presence in the association; this trend became particularly pronounced after State Security removed members it considered too close to the Brotherhood.[45] Once again, mosques were parceled out according to the power balance in each of the organization's divisions. For example, Giza's large al-Istiqama Mosque, operated by the Jamʻiyya Sharʻiyya, was known as a bastion of Salafism in the Cairo area. And even if the imam of a Jamʻiyya Sharʻiyya mosque was not himself Salafi, it wasn't uncommon (as we see in an anecdote told by Richard Gauvain) to find Salafi sheikhs among those who taught there.[46] It is also worth reiterating that control of a mosque allowed a given group to manage the resources that passed through it. And there was even more at stake, as many Ansar al-Sunna or Jamʻiyya Sharʻiyya mosques also ran clinics or offered a range of social services.

The second institution tasked with policing the religious field was State Security (formally the State Security Investigations Service, or Amn al-dawla), the armed wing of Egypt's domestic security establishment. The agency amassed enormous power under Mubarak, allowing it to impose its will on the Ministry of Awqaf. To achieve its ends, it sometimes ignored the ministry—or even the law itself. And whereas the ministry was often motivated by doctrinal considerations (defending traditional Azhari Islam against its competitors), State Security was concerned only with battling any movement that might threaten the regime. Its General Administration for Combatting Extremist Activities (Al-idara al-ʿamma li mukafahat al-nashat al-mutatarrif, or GACES), with one division for each player in the Islamic arena (Brotherhood, Salafis, etc.), was exclusively dedicated to this fight. And those Islamists in open conflict with the state were perfectly aware of the administration's role: One of the Jamaʿa Islamiyya's best-known feats was its assassination of GACES chief Raʾuf Khayrat in 1993.[47]

Documents seized by protesters when they raided State Security's buildings in March 2011 offered the public a window into its range of activities: close surveillance of each group via a range of methods, including infiltration and observation of mosques; ad hoc operations (for example to prevent a given lecture at a mosque, or to block a certain book release); promoting individuals, movements, or publications perceived as useful to the regime; arresting and interrogating members of the various currents; placing their leaders under constant pressure; and more.[48] Evidence also suggests (and interviews confirm) a degree of communication or even coordination between most Islamic groups and State Security: Movements (at least the nonviolent ones) often had individuals who managed the relationship with the security apparatus, passing messages in both directions.[49] After the revolution, the Brotherhood and the Salafi Call accused each other of past collaboration with the state—and they were both right, even if this clearly happened under duress.

In the captured documents, it's striking to see that while the Muslim Brotherhood and the jihadis were seen as threats from the start, State Security's attitude toward Salafism was more ambivalent.[50] The agency drew a clear distinction between so-called activist (*haraki*) or extremist (*mutatarrif*) Salafism, considered troublesome, and its "moderate" (*muʿtadil*) counterpart, which it tolerated and even tried to harness. Into the first category fell all forms of critical Salafism, and even (to a lesser degree) the Salafi Call, whose structure unsettled the regime. Loyalist and quietist Salafis, along with popular preachers who avoided political issues—like Muhammad Hassan, Muhammad Husayn Yaqʿub, and (usually) Abu Ishaq al-Huwayni—were described as "moderate." Their lectures were tolerated, and if a young Salafi was arrested, that person would be promptly released by claiming role models such as these.[51]

SALAFISM'S INELUCTABLE ASCENT UNDER MUBARAK

We can broadly identify several phases of State Security intervention in the political-religious field. Beginning in 1984, there was a mellowing in the brutal repression that had followed Sadat's assassination. Many Islamists were freed from prison, although front-line activists directly associated with the events of October 1981 remained behind bars. Student activities, specifically religious ones, were once again allowed on university campuses.

Activists regrouped, making the most of this renewed tolerance: The Brotherhood allied with the Wafd Party to participate in the legislative elections of 1984, then took home impressive results in union elections. The Salafi Call extended its reach in Alexandria and beyond; as compared to others, it emerged relatively unscathed from the repression in 1981, never having truly halted its operations. The Jama'a Islamiyya, which had reprioritized (at least temporarily) preaching over confrontation, expanded its influence to many mosques, especially in Upper Egypt.

Then a new spate of skirmishes between the Jama'a Islamiyya and the authorities broke out in the late 1980s, which led to a policy focused on eradicating the group. In this context, the Brotherhood and the Call were seen as useful since both forcefully denounced violent action.[52] Even critical Salafism, which also rejected violence, was left alone: Muhammad 'Abd al-Maqsud continued to preach relatively unhindered at his mosque in Shubra.[53] But the Salafis were instrumental to the regime in another way, too: As Iran's revolutionary Islam struck fear in the hearts of Middle East autocrats, who dreaded its potential alliance with Sunni Islamism, the Salafis were the only ones to directly condemn the Iranian outcome (and in the harshest of terms), which they saw as little more than an outgrowth of abhorrent Shiism. Salafi publications on the subject proliferated in 1980s Egypt.[54]

During this period, the authorities also exhibited uncharacteristic magnanimity toward political critiques by Gad al-Haqq, al-Azhar's Grand Imam, who had until then been a reliable loyalist. One denunciation came in 1989, when he went so far as to equate "the interest paid by savings banks to usury, a position that aligned with most of the Islamist opposition."[55] Then in 1994, he slammed the International Conference on Population and Development held (under the auspices of the Egyptian state) by the United Nations in Cairo. According to Tamir Moustafa, Gad al-Haqq was allowed this leeway in order to lend legitimacy, in the popular mind, to his repeated condemnations of armed violence.[56]

By 1994 the Jama'a Islamiyya appeared substantially diminished, following fierce repression of members including hundreds of extrajudicial executions and thousands of arrests that often included mistreatment and torture.[57] After an abortive first attempt in 1993 at mediation between the group's imprisoned leaders and religious representatives acting on behalf of the state, the former prepared to make public (with the blessing of State Security) a series of ideological revisions (*muraja'at*) that renounced the use of violence; these were officially proclaimed in 1997.[58]

Having secured this capitulation, the security apparatus realigned its priorities, reducing the autonomy and privileges that had been afforded to religious actors who seemed useful for combatting armed Islamists. The Salafi Call, which according to sympathetic journalist 'Ali 'Abd al-'Al already had tens of thousands of followers, was the first to be targeted: In 1994 most of its leaders—starting with Sa'id 'Abd al-'Azim, then the group's foremost figure—were arrested.[59] State Security ordered that the Call, already well established throughout the country, be dissolved, and it was accused of accepting foreign funding.[60] When its leaders were liberated some months later, they were strictly forbidden from leaving Alexandria; meanwhile, the al-Furqan Institute and the *Sawt al-Da'wa* journal were shut down. The Call group at Alexandria University was allowed to continue its activities, but under intense scrutiny.[61]

This desire to prevent the Call from achieving national stature—by "separating the body from the head," in the words of Ashraf Thabit, a leading figure in the movement—came through loud and clear in State Security's attitude toward Giza's Salafis at the time.[62] Ahmed Zaghloul describes how the agency forbade them all contact with the Alexandrian sheikhs, under threat of arrest.[63] The same blueprint would be systematically applied to the Call's competitors; official policy called for "factionalizing" Salafism. For instance, when Hisham Al 'Uqda tried moving to Cairo from Damanhur in 2005, he was immediately arrested.[64] The leaders of the Salafi Call were forced to keep a low profile for a few years, but this did not by any means slow down their activities. The Call informally maintained the same organizational divisions, now under the leadership of Yasir Burhami, who had become the movement's front man and holds that position to this day.

In 1995 it was the Brothers' turn to be targeted, following a large-scale media campaign intended to associate the group with violence.[65] Mass arrests were carried out, and, for the first time under Mubarak, those detained were brought before military courts. The same year, the Brotherhood won zero parliamentary seats in a rigged legislative election. It subsequently lost control of the unions it had captured in the 1980s.[66] And when the harsher security measures reached al-Azhar's gates in 1996, the recently deceased Gad al-Haqq was replaced by Sheikh Muhammad Tantawi, who had demonstrated his obsequiousness toward the country's leadership since he became Egypt's Grand Mufti in 1986.[67] A zealot among zealots, he would even explicitly endorse the regime's candidates in the 2005 legislative election.[68] The year Tantawi was installed, the deferential Mahmud Hamdi Zaqzuq was named minister of awqaf and immediately announced a new nationalization of all Egyptian mosques—which would fail, like its forebears, due to insufficient manpower.[69]

The tail end of the 1990s saw a regional resurgence of jihadism, now embodied in al-Qaeda, which, from its base in Afghanistan, had merged with Ayman al-Zawahiri's Egyptian Islamic Jihad in 1998. After September 11, 2001, Egypt enthusiastically embraced the rhetoric of the "war on terror" while trying, for strategic reasons, to seem receptive to American neoconservatives' calls for "democratizing" the Middle East—which meant allowing a modicum of tolerance for "moderate Islamists." In the legislative elections of 2005, marked by an unprecedented climate of (relatively) free expression and mobilization, the Brotherhood won a historic eighty-eight seats in Parliament despite meddling at the close of the electoral process.

Behind the scrim of political liberalization, those in power continued to exert pressure on actors throughout the political-religious realm. The Brotherhood was regularly subjected to waves of detentions. The Salafi Call was likewise affected by waves of arrests in 1998 and 2002, because the security apparatus was concerned by its expansion throughout Egyptian university campuses and by Yasir Burhami's repeated trips.[70] (Despite being forbidden to travel, he often ventured beyond Alexandria to build and guide the organization.)[71]

Call members were typically released soon after being taken into custody, but in 2002 some of its sheikhs, Burhami included, spent nearly a year in prison. The regime more directly targeted members of the Cairo School, part of Salafism's critical current: Nash'at Ahmad and Fawzi al-Sa'id, along with dozens of their followers, were tried on charges of forming a jihadi organization with ties abroad (notably in Chechnya), and of planning to assassinate figures in Egypt, including President Mubarak. (Those accused denied the charges, saying that they had simply gathered donations for Palestine and Chechnya.)[72] The Salafi followers of Hisham Al 'Uqda—the "Damanhur School"—also suffered persecution.[73]

Al-Azhar University, meanwhile, adopted new admission requirements in the late 1990s, on the pretext of "limited space"; applications were accepted only from those schooled since childhood at one of the country's many educational institutions affiliated with al-Azhar.[74] The goal was clearly to avoid "infiltration" (*tasrib*)—that is, to prevent Islamic activists, Brothers and Salafis, mostly graduates of secular institutions, from obtaining al-Azhar diplomas later in life, which would earn them prestige and could open doors to state-run mosques. Yasir Burhami had been able to get a degree in shari'a at al-Azhar's Damanhur campus in 1999 despite his training as a doctor because his enrollment predated the prohibition.[75] But the new rules put an end to such career changes, while al-Azhar—aware of its majority Salafi- or Brother-inspired student body—blocked many appointments to assistant professorships.[76]

Then, following the Brotherhood's impressive election results in 2005, the regime brought the full force of Salafism to bear on the organization. There was a precedent for this strategy: State Security had never thought twice about using the movement as a counterweight to the Brotherhood's influence. Certain neighborhoods or districts that had become Salafi strongholds were already reportedly off-limits to Brothers.[77] The new approach, however, went further, promoting Salafism as a form of piety that could be a suitable replacement for Brotherhood Islam. In pursuing this, the regime also had two ulterior motives: Salafi rhetoric was used as a specter to frighten the Coptic community, which no longer reliably supported the regime, having become more openly politicized under Pope Shenouda III.[78] What's more, Salafis would spread anti-Shia discourse that could dampen popular support for Hezbollah and Iran, then both regional favorites (thanks to President Mahmoud Ahmadinejad's anti-Israeli sorties and the Lebanese movement's "divine victory" over Israel in the summer of 2006).[79]

The newfound leniency toward Salafis was felt on every level. At universities, for example, activists describe a period of heightened repression for the Brotherhood, while the Salafis—so tightly surveilled just a few years before—now operated with few constraints.[80] The policy soon bore fruit: A Brotherhood activist tells how at Mansoura University, previously a stronghold of his organization, there were four Salafis for every one Brother by the late 2000s.[81] State Security also sometimes engineered the transfer of Brotherhood mosques to Salafi control, with certain groups being favored—the loyalists, for example, who always received preferential treatment.[82] One State Security memorandum in 2007, leaked after the revolution, recommends "leveraging [the group] to counter the extremist religious currents."[83] Another exposes just how close the agency had been with loyalist Mahmud Lutfi 'Amir, who oversaw Ansar al-Sunna in Damanhur.[84] This was the era when the loyalist current gained stature within Ansar al-Sunna, likely with some State Security support. Another prominent loyalist in the association was 'Adil al-Sayyid, who oversaw its preaching and media department for a time.[85]

The biggest shift came in 2006 when broadcast licenses began to be allocated to a whole slew of primarily Salafi "religious channels" on the NileSat satellite network, a privilege that would have been out of the question for any Brotherhood-affiliated broadcaster. Other countries, particularly Saudi Arabia, already had religious satellite channels, but these did not belong to any particular Islamic current (with the notable exception of the highly Salafi Qanat al-Majd, established in 2002). The oldest example, Iqra'—founded in 1998—gave similar amounts of airtime to Saudi sheikhs and to figures like 'Amr Khalid.

Qanat al-Nas was the first of these Egyptian Salafi channels. It started out in January 2006 as a generalist channel that mostly broadcast music videos, but a few months later its programming schedule was completely reworked. From that point on, it exclusively broadcast shows hosted by the era's foremost Salafi preachers.[86] Its slogan, "the people's channel—for everyone," changed to "the screen that brings you to heaven" (*al-shasha allati ta'khudhak ila-l-janna*). With the phenomenal success of Qanat al-Nas, Egypt's most-watched channel in 2007, others followed suit.[87] Besides the top two newcomers—Qanat al-Rahma (founded by Muhammad Hassan in 2007) and Qanat al-Hikma—there were also Qanat al-Khalijiyya, Qanat al-Baraka, Qanat al-Hidaya, Qanat al-Hafiz, and several more.

At first, this flurry of activity was less an ideological project than a "commercial undertaking that invested in an already-Salafizing audience," explains Husam Tammam.[88] The "religious redemption" of Qanat al-Nas, originally an entertainment channel, illustrates this dynamic perfectly. These channels were often funded by businessmen with few ties to Salafism. State Security, meanwhile, felt they were an asset and so let them operate—under its thumb. The agency meddled in programming choices, allowing only Salafis it considered "moderate"—meaning those who moralized without any political undertones. The three "stars" of popular Salafism—Sheikhs Muhammad Hassan (owner of Qanat al-Rahma), Muhammad Husayn Ya'qub, and Abu Ishaq al-Huwayni—became fixtures on these satellite channels. On the other hand, neither critical Salafis nor even the Salafi Call were allowed anywhere near the satellites, except on a handful of hard-won occasions negotiated with State Security. Ahmad Farid, one of the Call's main figures, was once arrested for making an appearance without prior approval.[89] The Salafi Call was nonetheless permitted to launch first one website, then another: "The Voice of the Salaf" in summer 2006 (*Sawt al-salaf*, at http://www.salafvoice.com), and "I am Salafi" in October 2007 (*Ana al-salafi*, at http://www.anasalafy.com).

Despite State Security's firm hand, the channels' newfound influence had consequences that surely displeased the regime. Indeed, they consummated two long-running processes: the transformation of Egyptian religious practice, and Salafism's crowning as the new orthodoxy of the masses. What's more, now that external displays of Salafi practice had been decriminalized, the channels helped build a new, diffuse Salafism made up of individuals who belonged to no organization and yet openly embraced the Salafi method (*manhaj salafi*). And while the satellite networks did divert some young Egyptians from the Brotherhood, this happened only to a limited extent. More often, they fueled that group's "Salafization"; many of the televised sheikhs' dedicated viewers never left the Brotherhood. These channels also benefited groups like the Salafi Call, whose membership swelled.

All this explains why the regime, perceiving Salafism's meteoric rise, pulled a sudden about-face. "Why don't our honourable [moderate] preachers and intellectuals combat Salafi preachers who call for narrow-mindedness?" Mubarak asked in February 2010. "Why don't they combat the chaos of religious channels and new preachers who issue fatwas without having [the] necessary religious knowledge?"[90] When Muhammad Tantawi died in March 2010, the regime seized the opportunity to appoint Ahmad al-Tayyib, who had called Salafis "Hanbali extremists" (*ghulat al-hanabila*), as al-Azhar's Grand Imam.[91] Barely two months into his term, he organized a large international summit through the al-Azhar Alumni Association (Rabitat kharriji al-azhar), themed around Abu al-Hasan al-Ash'ari—the father of Ash'ari theology and bête noire of the Salafis. The hundreds of participants turned the event into a huge anti-Salafi gathering that focused less on al-Ash'ari as a historical figure than on denouncing his modern-day slanderers.[92]

Various Salafi mosques across the country were raided in June 2010, and Cairo's al-'Aziz billah Mosque was placed directly under Ministry of Awqaf control.[93] Under government pressure, NileSat announced in October that twelve channels were coming off the air, including the top Salafi ones. Speculation in the Egyptian press at the time suggested the upcoming parliamentary elections (scheduled for late 2010) as a possible motive, given that the channels could potentially help the Brotherhood campaign.[94] Other commentators tied the closures to their coverage of the Kamilia Shehata scandal. Shehata, the wife of a Coptic priest, was said to have converted to Islam and then been forcibly detained by the church. Concerns about her fate sparked interfaith tensions, fueled by the Salafi preachers' anti-Christian rhetoric. The authorities were particularly concerned because, for the first time, Salafis were protesting in the streets, an episode that foreshadowed the "revolutionary Salafism" discussed in the final chapter. While all these factors likely played into the shutdown of Salafi channels, the decision stemmed above all from the regime's harsher approach to Salafism, initiated several months earlier.

On New Year's Day of 2011, terrorists bombed the Two Saints Church in Alexandria, killing twenty-three Egyptian Copts who had gathered to celebrate. No group claimed responsibility for the attack, and no clear link was ever established; a popular postrevolution theory had the Interior Ministry orchestrating the violence in order to break the resolve of the Coptic Church, which under Pope Shenouda III had consistently maintained independence from Mubarak.[95] Whatever the true story, the police immediately zeroed in on the Salafis, jumping at the chance for a coup de grâce. Despite the Call's official denunciations of the attack, hundreds of Alexandrian Salafis—Call members and independents both—were arrested, and one, Sayyid Bilal, died while being tortured.[96] On January 15 the newspaper Ruz al-Yusuf, a tabloid close with the regime and known for its deep hostility toward political Islam, trained its headline on the Call's leading light: "Yasir Burhami—The Most Dangerous Man in Egypt."[97] Ten days later, the revolution would rescue the Salafis, just in the nick of time, from the unprecedented repression that was about to be unleashed on them.

THE RELIGIOUS FIELD AS A WINNING GAMBLE

Several factors, then, help explain the rise of Salafism: an organized movement comprising groups both scholarly (Ansar al-Sunna) and activist (the Salafi Call), and their outgrowths within what I call popular Salafism; the movement's economic viability; and the relative indulgence of the security apparatus. But this leaves out one more key consideration: Any Islamic actor capable of advancing a competing narrative—be it close to the establishment (primarily al-Azhar) or external to it (primarily the Muslim Brotherhood)—had its religious authority undermined. So from the very start, the Salafis, who were positioned exclusively in the religious field, had hardly a detractor in sight.

This brings me to an initial observation: Following the release of *Muslim Politics* by Dale Eickelmann and James Piscatori, the idea spread that the "fragmentation" of religious authority in the Muslim world had led to a situation where almost anyone could now speak in the name of Islam and be heard.[98] This strikes me as questionable, at best. Discourses have certainly proliferated, but they have never carried equal weight. As religious normativity has taken on renewed importance over the past few decades, sheikhs—or those recognized as such—have continued to be seen as the legitimate authorities. In the Egyptian case, the only difference, perhaps, is that al-Azhar membership is no longer a must. So authority has indeed been deinstitutionalized, but when it comes to defining the religious norm, the only voices that truly matter are those of sheikhs or sheikh-like figures. The Salafis' strength resided in their strong religious footing, whereas their competitors were much less present in this domain.

While al-Azhar remained a powerful symbol, it never fully recovered from Nasser's cooptation. It revived a semblance of credibility under ʿAbd al-Halim Mahmud (Grand Imam, 1973–1978) and then during the latter part of the leadership of Gad al-Haqq (Grand Imam, 1982–1996), but this fizzled out in 1996.[99] And Azhari sheikh (and interviewee) Anas Sultan points out a major problem at the institution: It had become an assembly line that churned out "religious bureaucrats" rather than "messengers."[100] Al-Azhar graduates, poorly trained, often lacked charisma and panache. They couldn't hold a candle to highly motivated activists who had made preaching (*da'wa*) their life's work.

One exception was Muhammad Mitwalli al-Sha'rawi, born in 1911, who served as the Grand Imam's chief of staff in the 1960s and then minister of awqaf from 1976 to 1978. He was known for being Egypt's first successful televised preacher; his program, first broadcast in the 1960s, was one of the most widely watched in the country. Al-Sha'rawi was adored by the masses for his ability to explain the Quran humbly, in simple language, freely flowing between literary and vernacular Arabic. When he died in 1998, no representative of Azhari Islam could adequately carry on his legacy.[101] Sheikh Khalid al-Jundi, a somewhat charismatic (and possibly self-proclaimed) al-Azhar graduate, did try to launch a channel called "Azhari" in 2009 that would serve as the institution's mouthpiece.[102] But the media climate of the late 2000s, when a plethora of mostly Salafi satellite channels came online, was extremely competitive, and his initiative was a total dud. The channel failed to garner the expected viewership, and al-Jundi was swiftly disowned by al-Azhar—perhaps because the venerable institution wanted to distance itself from the embarrassing flop.[103]

The Brotherhood, meanwhile, was anything but weakened. The 1980s saw the organization build on its 1970s renaissance, with a surge in membership and mounting political sway. But the Brotherhood's political pursuits had cost it influence in the religious field. Admittedly, the organization's relationship with ulema had never been simple: Its founders were lay effendis, not clerics, and its message had always contained criticism (even if rarely explicit) of the ulema, who the Brothers felt had failed to contain the parallel trends of Westernization and secularization in Egyptian society. In a rare jab at Islamic clerics, al-Banna once proclaimed that they "saw and observed and heard and did nothing."[104] In many cases, ulema also regarded the Brotherhood with a degree of suspicion, especially as the organization's rise would mean a significant challenge to their authority.

The Brotherhood's relationship with al-Azhar in particular remained fairly paradoxical: The Brothers' Islam was not too far removed, at a strictly theological and religious level, from its Azhari counterpart; the Brothers largely identified with the corpus of traditional Islam championed by the institution. What's more, Brothers and Azharis both consistently maintained that Islam is *din wa dunya* (religion and world).[105] The Brotherhood's popularity within al-Azhar can be seen in generally strong student election results over the past few decades.[106] The problem, though, was that once al-Azhar graduates joined the ranks of the ulema, they tended to resist supporting any one group, feeling that to do so would compromise the universality of their mission.[107]

Consequently, each time the Brothers looked to al-Azhar for allies in a time of crisis, they were disappointed at the paltry response. As one Brotherhood official bitterly confided, "The ulema of al-Azhar always betrayed us!"[108] The year 1954, when Nasser turned against the organization, was one such moment of truth. Some of the most prestigious ulema who had previously supported the movement now pulled back and pledged allegiance to the new regime instead. But this wasn't because of some sudden infatuation with Nasserism. As a general rule, ulema tend to believe they should avoid confronting temporal power—however dubious it may be—so they can continue serving Islam.[109]

Three individuals exemplify this pattern: Hasan al-Baquri, once expected to assume the role of Supreme Guide after al-Banna's 1949 death, along with 'Abd al-'Aziz and Kamil al-Bahi al-Khuli.[110] The first two led Nasser's Ministry of Awqaf, where al-Khuli became a senior official. And they weren't alone: Two other respected ulema, Muhammad al-Ghazali and Sayyid Sabiq, both expelled from the Brotherhood in 1953 due to internal discord, also went to work for Nasser's religious affairs administrations.[111] Though rarely discussed in public, the "treason of the clerics" remained an open wound in the Brotherhood.[112]

To make up for their chronic lack of support in the religious field, the Brothers made do with support from "peripheral" Azhari ulema, to use Malika Zeghal's term. One indirect example (he was not officially a Brother) was Sheikh 'Abd al-Hamid Kishk, a star preacher in the 1970s and 1980s whose tapes reached millions. The organization also showcased a handful of "exceptional" religious figures. These were the lone representatives of the Brotherhood's religious authority—especially the enormously popular Sheikh Yusuf al-Qaradawi, whose reputation peaked in the late

1990s when he hosted the weekly *Shariʿa and Life* show on Al Jazeera. He had officially left the Brotherhood in 1988, embracing the universality of his role as "global mufti," but the public clearly still associated him with the organization.[113]

The Brothers also played on the ambiguity of their relationships with Muhammad al-Ghazali and Sayyid Sabiq, who, while technically unaffiliated, remained close to the organization both philosophically and personally. The organization's final strategic plank involved cultivating a network of local religious figures who solidified its standing on a microsocial level. But these players lacked national stature, and the power grab by Brotherhood "organizationists" marginalized ulema within the movement's leadership, says former Brother ʿAbd al-Sattar al-Milligi, who describes how the clerics "deserted" en masse during the 1990s.[114]

At the close of the twentieth century, several national-scale religious luminaries passed away who had been associated with the Brotherhood in the popular mind: Salah Abu Ismaʿil, a parliament member and Azhari who tirelessly pushed to apply shariʿa, died in 1990, followed by Muhammad al-Ghazali in 1996 and Sayyid Sabiq in 2000.[115] Azharis who publicly represented the Brotherhood were now few and far between—essentially, Sheikh Yusuf al-Qaradawi and a smattering of lower-ranking figures like ʿAbd al-Rahman al-Barr and Sayyid ʿAskar, who could boast of brilliant careers at al-Azhar but lacked charisma and name recognition. The same was true of ʿAbdallah al-Khatib (d. 2015), a former teacher at al-Azhar's Faculty of Arabic Language, who was sometimes referred to as the "mufti of the Brotherhood" despite his limited celebrity and even more limited influence within the organization.[116]

Beyond the Azharis' reluctance to publicly identify as Brothers, the scarcity of religious eminences also stemmed from Mubarak's maneuvering, which carefully circumscribed the organization's access to national media outlets and pulled out all stops to prevent charismatic leaders from emerging within. It was thus no accident that the Egyptian al-Qaradawi acquired his iconic stature in Qatar instead, via the country's Al Jazeera satellite channel. But this paucity of recognizable religious figures also dovetailed with a persistent perspective within the organization, as Moaaz Mahmoud explains: "The Brotherhood's strategy for Islamizing society was not primarily based on this style of 'mass-appeal preaching.' For them, Islamization meant 'ikhwanization' [Brotherization]. The Muslim Brothers planned to Islamize society by bringing more people into the organization."[117]

Then there was the phenomenon sparked in the 2000s by ʿAmr Khalid, a "new preacher" clad in suit and tie whose rhetoric revolved mostly around morals and personal development.[118] He was quite popular among the young, pious bourgeois, to whom he dispensed an "open, proactive Islam with a specific interest in the economy"—what Patrick Haenni calls "market Islam."[119] Khalid long belonged to the Brotherhood but then gradually went his own way, both to symbolize the independence of his views and to avoid any issues with the security apparatus. This meant that while his audience included many Brothers, Khalid, who actually created his own movement in the early 2000s—the "Life Makers" (Sunnaʿ al-hayat), named after his program on the channel Iqraʾ—was not seen as a Brotherhood spokesman.[120] Most important, he wasn't Azhari and presented himself as a popularizer rather than a religious authority, even though his audience looked to him as a role model.[121] His popularity crested in the mid-2000s and had begun to ebb by decade's end.

Brotherhood leaders, concerned about the organization's lack of religious representation, launched a media "infiltration plan" (khittat ikhtiraq) sometime around 2008, at the initiative of Khayrat al-Shatir.[122] One prong involved training an elite circle of Brothers as a new generation of preachers equipped to compete with the Salafi sheikhs. The other involved trying to raise the profile of Brotherhood-friendly preachers on Islamic satellite channels—which, as I have noted, were Salafi-dominated at the time. To this end, the organization worked its existing connections in the media world and ordered members to seek leadership positions at the broadcasters. The plan would help establish figures like Safwat Higazi, a member of the Brotherhood's Salafi wing, who managed to carve out a place for himself on satellite television. The irony, however, was that given their highly Salafi rhetoric, Higazi and his peers hardly seemed like Brothers to anyone watching; more on this in the following section.

Lastly, the Brotherhood's participation in electoral politics starting in 1984 (at first in a mind-boggling alliance with the nationalist Wafd Party, its former rival) sparked an overhaul of the organization's rhetoric, as the Brothers—at least those in the group's "visible element" that did "public-facing work"—now wanted to be seen as politicians. They traded what was left of the preacher's garb and verbiage for those of a trade unionist or a parliamentarian. As legislators, "the Brotherhood now talked mostly of free expression and press freedom, of respect for democratic principles and protections for human rights," writes Egyptian scholar Amr Elshobaki. And in the unions, a Brother was seen not as "an ideological theorist or religious missionary far removed from the daily experience of union members, but rather as an 'embedded politician' who had earned the confidence of a subset of the group through the services he provided." Overall, Elshobaki concludes, the "Brothers stopped playing the role of moral entrepreneurs—to paraphrase Becker in *Outsiders*—and tried to present themselves as typical political candidates."[123]

The Brothers' retreat from the religious field—whether it was by choice or by force—thus helps explain the omnipresence of (and lack of competition for) Salafi discourse. The Brotherhood itself did not escape unscathed from this transformation; effects were felt both within its base and within the organization's new generation of sheikhs. The Salafis' normative hegemony thus revived the "Salafization of the Brotherhood" that had been stopped in its tracks during the 1980s.

THE SALAFIZATION OF THE BROTHERHOOD

The "Salafization of the Brotherhood" (*tasalluf al-ikhwan*, to use Husam Tammam's expression) was nothing new. Since the 1940s there had been reports of Brothers influenced to varying degrees by Salafi discourse, which was increasingly woven into the Islamic norm. One person's religious practice might be guided by Salafi prohibitions, while another's understanding of his faith might be rooted more directly in Salafi theology. Sayyid Qutb fell into the second category, and for him this understanding carried politically revolutionary implications (which most Salafis, however, rejected).

As Egyptian Islam's religious corpus changed profoundly during the twentieth century, that of the Brotherhood underwent a parallel transformation: Ibn Kathir's *tafsir* now overshadowed all others—everywhere, even to some extent at al-Azhar—and had joined the Brotherhood's canon. Ibn Taymiyya, meanwhile, had earned universal respect and admiration but remained less central to the Brothers than he was to the Salafis. Such changes did not always have direct consequences; interpretations of these books vary, and the Brothers' take still differed overall from that of the Salafis. What's more, education for the Brotherhood's grassroots remained mostly intact. Training (*tarbiya*) in activist cells (*usar*, literally "families") was based on textbooks that largely stayed true to the group's original outlook on questions that were strictly religious.

The late-1970s integration of most jama'at islamiyya members into a struggling Brotherhood did pose a significant challenge to the latter's identity.[124] But as 'Abd al-Mun'im Abu al-Futuh explains, most of the leaders who joined soon strayed from their Salafi theological frameworks and practices under the leadership of Supreme Guide 'Umar al-Tilmisani, who wished to uphold al-Banna's vision, and that of Muhammad al-Ghazali and Yusuf al-Qaradawi, the last religious "heavyweights" still tied to the Brotherhood. Within a few years, the new arrivals had forgone their "conspicuous piety" and returned to a less fraught style of dress and general appearance, signaling respectability as the Brothers threw themselves into the political arena.

Backgrounds varied, then, among the rising figures of the Brotherhood's so-called Salafi wing in the 1980s. Some were "survivors" of 1970s Salafism who hadn't completely rejected the era's religious teachings. Others were Brothers back from or still based in Saudi Arabia, where thousands of the group's leaders had flocked—first in the 1950s and 1960s to flee Nasser's repression, and then in the 1970s, hoping to use the movement's established network there to find professional opportunities.[125] All were experiencing, or even furthering, Salafi rhetoric's diffuse influence on the Brotherhood, at a time when such rhetoric was gaining traction in the broader Islamic sphere. These Salafi-oriented Brotherhood figures, then, both indicated a changing religious climate and represented an asset for the Brotherhood, in that they kept the organization's religious discourse (or part of it, anyway) up to date on societal demand.

An early example of these Salafi Brothers was 'Abd al-Sattar Fath Allah, an Azhari born in 1931 who was among those imprisoned in 1965. He then taught for years in Saudi Arabia at both Riyadh's Imam Mohammad Ibn Saud Islamic University and at Mecca's Umm Al-Qura University. At one point Fath Allah joined the Brotherhood's Bureau of Guidance but quit in a huff when the organization chose to run female candidates in the 1987 elections.[126] He denounced "politicians' stranglehold on the Brotherhood and their disregard for Azharis," reflecting the tensions described in the previous section.[127] Twenty years later, he would accuse the reformist Brother 'Abd al-Mun'im Abu al-Futuh of violating the creed by paying a courtesy call to writer Naguib Mahfouz.[128]

Mustafa Hilmi was another interesting case. One of the "theorists" of Egyptian Salafism (prior to his first stay in Saudi Arabia, where he later taught), he nonetheless remained close to the Muslim Brotherhood and released his best-known books during the 1970s and 1980s through a Brotherhood-affiliated publishing house.[129]

Several more recent figures from this current were among the "new preachers" who gained fame largely through the Salafi satellite channels. The most famous was Wagdi Ghunaym, born in 1951, who participated in Alexandria's early Salafi cells, later becoming active in the jama'at islamiyya and then joining the Brotherhood. He made a name for himself in the 1990s with his sermons on tape, known for their virulent tone and references that were atypical for the Brotherhood. Having relocated outside Egypt in the early 2000s, he continued to intervene in the country's debates from abroad via the satellite channels, where he was extremely popular, as well as through social media (where he expressed himself more freely). Ghunaym again made waves in 2017 when he celebrated the death of Tunisian president Beji Caid Essebsi, whom he accused of being an infidel.[130]

On the Salafi satellite channels, many of these Brothers got airtime by squeezing into slots that were of little interest to more traditional Salafi preachers—particularly history programs. On Qanat al-Nas, for example, Safwat Higazi (b. 1963) hosted "The Glory Days" (*Zaman al-'izza*), which served up a staunchly Salafi perspective on Islamic history.[131] Raghib al-Sirjani (b. 1964), a doctor by training, oversaw other historical programming at the channel, offering a Salafi-style take on the past that was deeply hostile to the Shia.[132] He also founded the Civilization Institute for Historical Studies (Markaz al-hadara li-l-dirasat al-tarikhiyya) and a specialty website (http://www.islamstory.com), and authored books including a highly laudatory biography of Muhammad bin 'Abd al-Wahhab.[133]

Gamal 'Abd al-Hadi, born several decades earlier in 1937, also exploited this programming niche, hosting "Pages of History" (*Safahat min al-tarikh*) on Qanat al-Nas. He appeared in a *ghutra* without an *'iqal* (a fabric head covering not affixed with a string), which among Saudi Salafis signifies affiliation with the religious sphere. Indeed, in addition to their similar trajectories within the Brotherhood, Higazi and 'Abd al-Hadi both spent time in Saudi Arabia. Higazi, who holds a degree in cartography, had moved there in 1990 for a government job. Most of his religious education took place in Medina, where he studied at the Prophet's Mosque and at the Dar al-Hadith Institute before returning to Egypt in 1998. 'Abd al-Hadi majored in humanities and philosophy in Cairo, then taught in the kingdom between 1973 and 1987, first at King Abdulaziz University and later at Umm Al-Qura University in Mecca.

Last, Hazim Abu Isma'il, born in 1961, began gaining prominence in the mid-2000s. His father, Salah Abu Isma'il, had been a Brother-aligned Azhari (despite quitting the Brotherhood under Nasser, he never truly broke off ties) and one of the first Islamist members of Parliament elected in the late 1970s. Hazim became well-known as a preacher on Qanat al-Nas, where he hosted several programs wearing a tunic with a *ghutra* or turban. He ran as a Brotherhood candidate in the parliamentary elections of 2005, losing by a slim margin following widely recognized fraud. Hazim would leave the Brotherhood in 2011 and become the figurehead of the revolutionary Salafis; I will discuss this at length in the final chapter.

All these preachers differed from most Brothers because of (in no particular order) their fierce hostility toward Shiism and Sufism, their anti-Christian rhetoric, their long, scraggly beards (except for Higazi), their rejection of music, and their ultraconservative views on the role of women. The current they represented, however, remained a minority in the official Brotherhood hierarchy. After the revolution, some attempts were made to replace the existing curriculum in Brotherhood cells with Salafi-compatible books on creed, but these efforts fell flat due to intense internal resistance.[134]

The new preachers' enormous popularity with the Brotherhood's base in the early 2000s, particularly among junior members, nonetheless demonstrates that, at a time when Salafism was emerging as the new orthodoxy, their stances clicked perfectly with the younger generation. In fact, during the later 2000s the young Brothers—like most pious Egyptians—became devoted viewers of the Salafi channels and often quoted preachers such as Muhammad Hassan.[135] Some, dissatisfied with the "impoverished" religious education they were getting from the Brotherhood, even chose to simultaneously attend courses at Salafi mosques.

There was also a marked return of outwardly visible religious observance among members: men with scruffy beards and no mustache or women choosing to wear a niqab—the "conspicuous piety" that had mostly fallen by the wayside in the 1980s. Brothers interviewed in the late 2000s recounted how during weekly meetings, younger members frequently questioned their superiors on issues of orthopraxy rather than political or intellectual questions. Orthopraxy-centered debates likewise dominated online Brotherhood discussion boards at the time.[136] Salafi practices were often chosen à la carte; their adoption didn't imply an unmitigated embrace of Salafi thought, but it did attest to its diffuse influence. The Salafization of the Brothers' appearance seemed more generalized in neighborhoods where Salafis were well established. This was often because the local Brotherhood leaders recommended such practices to their flocks, both to ward off criticism by competitors and to preserve religious credibility with the pious masses.[137]

The competition pushed the Brothers, almost despite themselves, to wade into Salafi territory. Under attack by the latter, impelled by their young "Salafi-leaning" activists, they now had to come up with religious arguments grounded in the sacred texts (ta'sil shar'i) to justify stances—for example, on the role of women or the legality of participating in democratic institutions—that until then had been taken for granted.[138] It was, explained a young Brother, a "tyranny of the proofs" where "Salafis were always asking us: 'Such and such a practice is a blameworthy innovation (bid'a); where exactly do the Quran and the sunna justify it?' Our leaders then had to formulate proofs with which we could defend ourselves."[139]

Such questions prompted Muhammad Husayn 'Isa of Alexandria to publish a short treatise in 2006 called *The Sparks in the Revelation of Innovations (Al-lama' fi tajliyat al-bida')*. 'Isa himself had no degree from al-Azhar but made sure to have one of its sheikhs provide the preface. Armed with hadiths, Quranic quotes, and the words of Ibn Taymiyya, Ibn Kathir, and various schools of fiqh, the text refuted Salafi critiques of certain Brotherhood practices by redefining the concept of blameworthy innovations so as to "clarify what is missed by those who generalize religious rules indiscriminately and without reflection," as the author of the preface explains. This allows the author to justify the legality of collective *dhikr* prayers, celebrating the Prophet's mawlid, friendly relations with Christians, long garments (versus the Salafis' preferred short tunics), or even beard trimming.[140] Still hot off the presses, the book received a scathing response from the Alexandrian Salafi Sheikh Shahata Saqr.[141]

Along the same lines, in 2010 'Abd al-Rahman al-Barr, the Brotherhood's highest-ranking Azhari (and not a part of its "Salafi wing"), published a long text that used the Quran and the sunna as well as citations by classical Islamic authors to legitimize the Brotherhood's participation in elections.[142] Facing a highly critical response by the Salafis dominant on social media (they denounced the "Brotherhood's tenuous grasp on religion"), he was forced to publish a defense.[143]

This reflected a seismic shift in the Brotherhood's posture. Since the 1940s the organization had participated in elections without ever feeling compelled to justify its choice. Members had simply accepted the decision as legitimate because it came from the Bureau of Guidance, which was presumed to draw on religious knowledge that need not be made explicit. But in what Husam Tammam called the "age of Salafism," this no longer sufficed.[144] 'Isam al-Talima, a young sheikh who studied under al-Qaradawi, expressed his surprise in a book in 2008: "I don't understand why so many Brotherhood authors feel that whenever they address a point of discord between Brothers and Salafis, they absolutely must pacify critics with an Ibn Taymiyya quote. Some of them have enough religious standing that they should not have to quote anyone!"[145]

Finally, elective affinities with aspects of Salafi discourse facilitated its increasing hold on the Brotherhood. They were found in the group's "organizationist" (*tanzimi*) current, whose members viewed the organization as a vanguard that was laying the foundation of the coming Islamic state—and felt that any openness to society threatened both the Brothers' identity and their plan to build a tightly controlled organization (*tanzim*). In addition to Mustafa Mashhur (Supreme Guide from 1996 until his death in 2002), others historically associated with this current included Brothers who had been arrested in 1965, such as Mahmud 'Izzat, Jum'a Amin, and Mahmud Husayn, as well as figures from the following generation like Mahmud Ghuzlan.[146]

After a period of ascendancy in the 1970s, this current was temporarily weakened by al-Tilmisani's strategy—which struggled at first but ultimately seemed to succeed—of "normalizing" the Brotherhood through involvement in the realms of unions and politics. This experiment gave birth to the "reformist" current, advanced by a young group of political and union activists from the Brotherhood who seemed intent on consummating the Brothers' metamorphosis into a "standard" political party, complete with democratic slogans, that would be open to compromises and alliances.[147]

These reformists seemed to be making good headway during the 1990s, but the "organizationists" returned in force over the following decade.[148] "While we were focusing on public-facing work," explains former reformist Brother Khalid Dawud, "they concentrated on the internal structure. They were bound to prevail, because that's where the power lies."[149] The organizationists' resurgence was spearheaded by Khayrat al-Shatir, who became the Brotherhood's new driving force, even if one relegated to the shadows; he would never become the organization's Supreme Guide.[150]

The December 2009 ousting of the last reformists from the Bureau of Guidance, 'Abd al-Mun'im Abu al-Futuh and Muhammad Habib, and the January 2010 election of Muhammad Badi' as Supreme Guide evidenced an internal power grab by the organizationists.[151] Throughout their increasing success in the 2000s, they kept the reformists at bay by maintaining a strategic alliance with representatives of the Brotherhood's "Salafi wing," which shared their mistrust of Brothers who seemed too liberal. This partnership was also founded on shared ideological reference points: The organizationists still felt an affinity with Sayyid Qutb's thinking—stripped of its short-term revolutionary accents, perhaps, but we have seen how it resonated with one aspect of the Salafi mindset. What's more, many of them had spent time in Saudi Arabia during the 1970s and 1980s, where Salafism had influenced their religious culture.

With the organizationists at the wheel, the Brotherhood adopted some untraditional stances.[152] Guidance Bureau member Mahmud Ghuzlan, for example, published a harshly anti-Shia text in 2009 that sparked a virulent debate with the organization veteran Youssef Nada. The latter lambasted the degree of "intolerance and fanaticism" toward the Shia and refused to accept that they be "called *rafida*" ("rejectors," a Salafi pejorative).[153] That same year, the Brothers led the charge against a fatwa issued by Muhammad Tantawi, al-Azhar's Grand Imam, that forbade the niqab from the university—even though Brotherhood women had never been obligated to wear one, and only a minority (a growing one, to be sure) did so.[154] Also in 2009, Ghuzlan wrote an open letter that reproached Yusuf al-Qaradawi—despite his status as the movement's foremost religious authority—for complaining about the "new ideas" coming from Salafism and asserting that "the expulsion of reformists is a betrayal of our mission, of the Brotherhood and of the Umma as a whole."[155]

Two years earlier, the organizationist current had arranged for the leadership to publish a political platform geared to a hypothetical Muslim Brotherhood party that would never end up becoming a reality (at least until the 2011 revolution). The text caused an uproar both within the Brotherhood and without, for two reasons: It refused to accept a president who was female or Christian, and it recommended organizing a committee of ulema to oversee Parliament.[156] No such concerns had been raised in 1952 when the Brothers had issued a draft constitution that granted full political rights to Christians.[157]

During the Mubarak era, Egyptian Salafism pushed beyond activist religious circles and began redefining the Islam of the masses. We saw how this was enabled by several factors, including a new generation of popular preachers–normative entrepreneurs, who offered a simplified version of Salafi religious discourse that could convince a wider audience. This, paired with their style and the platforms offered by new media, made the transformation possible.

All this transpired in a propitious regional and national context. The Gulf countries sustained a powerful Salafi economy, placing the movement on sound financial footing. This bolstered the "Saudi dream" (which, for many, was a "Salafi dream"), making the movement more enticing. Meanwhile the Egyptian regime, with its mostly security-driven approach to managing the political-religious field, took a rather hands-off attitude toward the majority of Salafis, who did not seem like a direct threat.

Finally, the diminished standing of every religious competitor—Azhari or Brother—who could have countered Salafism's redefinition of the Islamic norm only helped entrench the Salafi monopoly. A widely distributed books series published by Salafis in the latter 2000s (by 2010 they could be found at nearly any Islamic bookstore in Cairo) put on the finishing touch by reframing Salafi perspectives as those of al-Azhar. The operation involved selecting Salafi-compatible fatwas by somewhat marginal sheikhs historically associated with the institution and presenting their opinions as pure Azhari orthodoxy. Books in this vein were published on Sufism, Shiism, female circumcision, and the niqab.[158] In a sign of

Salafism's deep influence, it also found its way into the Muslim Brotherhood, where it was promoted by a growing internal faction and gained some traction among the movement's broader base.

In 2010 the regime seemed to realize that its declining control over religious discourse could be a vulnerability. It launched a short-lived counteroffensive that clattered to a halt in January 2011, when the revolution broke out and Mubarak was overthrown. This moment would put Salafism to the test, along with the movements that identified with it. The two final chapters will tell this story.

Chapter Five

SALAFISM FACES REVOLUTION

The Nour Party and Its Rivalry with the Brotherhood

When the revolution happened and the Salafis popped up, people were asking, "Wait, where did you come from?" (*Laughter*) My response was, *you* were the ones living on Saturn, totally oblivious to the folks down below! You always imagined you were superior, thought you were the elite, flattered yourselves while disparaging your inferiors.... They said, "The Brothers? Fine, we're familiar with them. But what do these Salafis want?" People had no idea who they were. And when the Salafis stayed mum, they thought: "OK, we'll provoke them; we'll make them talk."... They said: "The Salafis destroy mausoleums!" They think that the Egyptian people have always been Sufi, that they go to mawlids. That there are four million people who go to al-Badawi's mawlid, three million to al-Dasuqi's, et cetera. They thought they understood the ways of the people—but they didn't realize that the situation had changed! That most of the generation that had done whatever it pleased was now dead! The youth of this generation are no longer lost; the world changed, but they weren't paying attention.

—ABU ISHAQ AL-HUWAYNI, MAY 18, 2011

Preaching involves many duties, and one entity cannot handle them all. That is the role of the Umma as a whole: to protect religion, and to govern the world through religion. We focus on the first aspect and make great strides with God's help. And we will throw our weight behind the second—if the two can work in harmony. But I must warn our brothers that, should politics prove incompatible with—and thus threaten—the fundamentals of our religious approach, we will always prioritize the well-being of our mission and the safekeeping of our ideas.

—MUHAMMAD ISMA'IL AL-MUQADDIM, FEBRUARY 8, 2011

In Egypt, the new millennium's first decade was defined by two parallel but starkly different processes. The first, a political shift, saw the rise of a new generation of activists opposed to Mubarak's rule, who would instigate the revolutionary uprising of January 25, 2011. The second process was religious, as Salafism was becoming the new de facto basis for the Sunni norm in Egyptian Islam. Revolution broke out when the movement was at the height of its influence, which the regime's belated counteroffensive in 2010 had done nothing to diminish. And over the course of 2011, these two processes began to clash.

First off, the Salafis were caught flat-footed. The revolution was a stroke of luck, in that it snatched them from the jaws of the regime's crackdown. But it also posed a major challenge, as it unmoored some fundamentals of their grammar, which—for most Salafis, anyway—had always presupposed long-term change, and this could come only from below. Then Mubarak's fall set off an interim period of great political fluidity.[1] When all the guideposts are shifting, it is especially challenging for actors to strategize, and the Salafis, like everyone else, had no choice but to reinvent themselves.

The revolutionary dynamic and subsequent political transition were affected in equal measure by Salafism's galvanizing power and by the dominance of its normative discourse. Egypt was, after all, particularly pious, and its political actors existed at the mercy of religious influences—and Salafism's influence was reflected both in the Nour Party's early success and in the Muslim Brotherhood's political strategy. The latter, keen on keeping the upper hand, was forced into a game of conservative one-upmanship.

This chapter begins with a look at the Salafi Call. Earlier we observed how the group's status as an organized social movement distinguished it from the rest of the current—and how it managed to become the country's foremost Salafi organization. But now the Call found itself torn between its sheikhs' conservative caution—they wished to remain true to their grammar, no matter what—and a more revolution-oriented faction that wanted the Salafis to jump into the political field. The story of the Nour Party, created against the wishes of the same Call sheikhs who later forcibly annexed it, perfectly illustrates these competing instincts. The chapter concludes with a discussion of how the Brother-Call conflict between 2011 and 2013 hinged on control of the Salafi brand: When the Brotherhood tried to weaponize it against detractors, this fueled the polarization that ultimately brought the organization down.

THE SALAFI CALL GRAPPLES WITH THE REVOLUTIONARY UPRISING

This chapter is not meant to rehash how the Egyptian revolution of January 25, 2011, came to pass; many others have already written on the subject.[2] Suffice it to say that the moment "burst forth" from the work of activists with no direct ties to the Islamic movement, at a time when the latter was lying low due to intense government pressure.[3] The Brothers had just suffered a veritable thrashing in the November 2010 legislative elections—a humiliation orchestrated by the Interior Ministry, of course, in what was then described as the most rigged election in recent Egyptian history. Meanwhile the Salafis, fast becoming the regime's "enemy number one," were stripped of the satellite channels that since 2006 had helped swell their ranks. This context helps explain the silence and/or initial vagueness of Islamic movement organizations over the week preceding January 25 and in the first days of the uprising. Only on January 28 did the Muslim Brotherhood officially join the revolution, directing its activists to come out in force; most figures in the critical Salafi current soon followed suit.

The Salafi Call's reaction to the events of late January was by turns consistent and ambivalent. Unsurprisingly, its sheikhs felt at first that no good could come of the planned street protests against the regime, as the Salafi milieu traditionally frowned on such modes of action.[4] In a communiqué issued January 21, 2011, the sheikhs ordered their flocks not to join, "in accordance with our religion and out of responsibility to our country: to protect its interests, its people and the land during this tense period and foil enemy plans to sow discord."[5]

True to its grammar, the Call felt that transformation could come only through preaching (*da'wa*, its namesake)—from the grassroots—and that it was fanciful to think the regime could be transformed without first changing people's minds. Muhammad Isma'il al-Muqaddim had put this quite explicitly in a speech recorded just months before:

> Substituting one evil for another, replacing what's bad with something worse. . . . We are tired of liberalism, of secularism, of the whole lot. Don't let just anyone ensnare you, usher you blindfolded down a dark tunnel that leads to a dead end! What a waste! You are the only ones who can make a difference. True change is born only in the Salafi mosques. If you want something meaningful, study the Quran or deepen your knowledge of religious science—things that achieve true change, help the Umma, bring it blessings. . . . Forget politics with its lies, hypocrisy and duplicity. Believe in the approach you chose for yourself; true change comes in the mosques![6]

Caught off guard on January 25, the Call initially made no political demands, instead assuming a stance that emphasized preserving order and protecting property, both public and private, from the threat of chaos and looting.[7]

Keep in mind that following the January 1, 2011, attack on Alexandria's Two Saints Church, the Call had been subjected to the worst repression in its history, and Sayyid Bilal, a man in his thirties who had been close with the group, had been tortured to death.[8] The Call was unaccustomed to such brutality, and there was an immense outpouring by its base, some of which called for a commensurate response.[9] Sticking to their grammar, its sheikhs did their best to keep the peace. Muhammad Isma'il al-Muqaddim declared that "we are preachers, not one regime facing another. Some people want to push us into a confrontation with the government, but we have our activities, our preaching work, and our mosques to consider."[10]

The unease the sheikhs felt vis-à-vis their base may, however, explain their decision to place new banners on the Call website that read (with no further explanation), "May God welcome our fallen as martyrs" and "May God take vengeance upon our oppressors."[11] What's more, they felt obliged to append an uncharacteristic public criticism to their January 21 message: "This does not mean we are happy about the injustices, both large and small, that people endure, the most serious of which is the lack of shari'a. We are simply passing on God's orders."[12] The sheikhs grew more ambivalent by the day, likely due to anger among Call members. Some—especially the younger ones—joined the demonstrations despite their leaders' objections. In a statement dated February 1, the first to explicitly broach the political question, the sheikhs demanded an end to the state of emergency, the repression, and corruption—while still calling for a return to order and expressing hope for peace between citizens and police.[13]

On February 5, when Mubarak had already begun to pull back, Burhami, al-Muqaddim, and 'Abd al-'Azim—along with around twenty representatives of critical Salafism (most of whom had openly supported the protests from the early days of demonstrations, unlike the Call)—cowrote an open letter: "The Umma's many constituents have chosen the path of change and reform. Their approach should not be impeded in any way and leaves no choice but to rapidly implement these objectives. The people have chosen justice, development, and reform of the state and its institutions; the hoped-for stability will only come if this choice is respected. These peaceful and responsible demands are not illegitimate, nor do they run counter to the shari'a."[14]

On February 8, flanked by his comrades from the Salafi Call, Muhammad Isma'il al-Muqaddim hailed the "youth" who "have given the Umma the most beautiful of gifts."[15] But Yasir Burhami felt compelled to clarify a few days later. "The Call's position on the protests has not changed," he said.[16] Muhammad Isma'il al-Muqaddim's remarks had been misinterpreted; he had "never suggested that anyone join the demonstrations."[17]

Whatever their public line, it took little time for the Call's sheikhs to see that the revolution offered them a whole host of opportunities. First, it gave them a chance to prove their skill at mobilizing—especially since they could move freely about the country now that the stringent police restrictions they had faced were a thing of the past. From Alexandria to Cairo, from Tanta to Damanhur, huge gatherings were held, each featuring a Call figure—this, even before Mubarak had officially stepped down.[18] The events reunited the sheikhs with their flocks, from which they had sometimes been sequestered for many long years, and let them take stock of how much support they had in the various governorates. To maintain a presence in the streets without joining the protests, the Call also formed neighborhood committees (lijan sha'biyya) to "protect public and private property" in Alexandria and other strongholds.[19] These committees also picked up trash, sold affordable staples, and ensured that merchants weren't price-gouging during the crisis. Videos on the Call's website faithfully documented each action.[20]

In early February the Salafi activists rallied around one central theme: defending the "Islamic identity" of Egypt, which was supposedly threatened by looming changes.[21] On February 13, as Egyptians were still celebrating their president's downfall, the Call launched its official-sounding "Campaign for the Defense of Egypt's Islamic Identity" with a nationwide signature drive.[22] With the political conversation focused on the Constitution—a referendum was planned for March to ratify modifications proposed by an army-appointed commission—the Salafis took up the cause of Article 2, which they felt had to be preserved at all costs.[23]

Introduced under Sadat in 1971 and updated in 1980, the article decreed that "the principles of the shari'a are the primary source of legislation." Conveniently phrased to preclude any practical application in Egyptian law, Article 2 nonetheless stood as a powerful symbol because it recognized the shari'a as the foundational legal principle. No sooner had the referendum been scheduled than the Call's Salafis struck up a loud "YES" campaign, based solely on the fact that the amendments left Article 2 intact, whereas a small handful of liberals had called for it to be jettisoned. The referendum passed with 77 percent of the vote, a victory for which the Salafis took credit even though the "YES" camp also included the Brotherhood and most traditional political forces.[24]

The Salafi Call also seized on the climate of openness to emerge from the semiclandestine status under which it had always operated. On March 14, 2011, the group announced the formation of its "presidential council" (*al-majlis al-ri'asi*)—which included the *qayyim* 'Abd al-Fattah Abu Idris, along with Yasir Burhami and Muhammad Isma'il al-Muqaddim—and of its twelve-member all-Alexandrian "executive council" (*al-majlis al-tanfidhi*).[25] There was also an "advisory board" (*majlis al-shura al-'amm*) consisting of 203 members. On July 1, at the first board meeting, Abu Idris officially became the organization's chief executive, Yasir Burhami its first vice president, and Sa'id 'Abd al-'Azim its second.[26] Together with the three other sheikhs of the "founding six" (Ahmad Hutayba, Ahmad Farid, and Muhammad Isma'il al-Muqaddim), they constituted the Call's "board of trustees" (*majlis al-umana*).

These efforts at administrative formalization served a second (but not at all secondary) purpose: The new structure validated the control of Yasir Burhami, who had held sway over the organization since the mid-1990s and already enjoyed the loyalty of most of its leaders. And in one final institutional innovation—the Call's first ever gesture of openness toward the rest of the Salafi scene—Muhammad Yusri Ibrahim of the Sururi current was named president of the advisory board.[27] This symbolic decision had little impact on the Call's governance, but it reflected the organization's initial strategy for stepping in to lead the larger Salafi movement.

The Call also resumed its activities, now quite officially. In early March 2011, the group announced the reopening of the al-Furqan Institute, which had been shut down since 1994. The school soon founded outposts in several Egyptian cities. In parallel, the sheikhs were giving more speeches across the country and making regular appearances on the Salafi channels (which had lost no time coming back online once Mubarak was out of the picture). The organization also ventured into new territory, launching the "House of Business" (Bayt al-a'mal) in 2012 as the Call's economic arm—a sort of union for Salafi (or Salafi-supportive) businessmen who wished to invest in religiously licit enterprises.[28] The entity was duly registered with the relevant authorities. After so many years underground, the Call also went on the books—as the Preachers' Charity Association (Jam'iyyat al-du'at al-khayriyya).[29]

PUSH-PULL BETWEEN THE NOUR PARTY AND THE CALL

An unparalleled broadening of the party landscape began after March 28, 2011, when the law governing political parties was amended. Of the Islamists, the Brothers were the first to take the plunge, creating the Freedom and Justice Party. But the Salafis weren't far behind—with the notable exceptions of loyalist and quietist Salafis, who maintained their initial opposition to any form of political participation and kept up uncompromising counterrevolutionary rhetoric.[30]

Of the Salafis, those in the critical camp were the first to jump into the fray. Given the strong political undertones of their hybrid grammar, some in this camp had long discussed the idea of political participation; the time had now come to put theory into practice.[31] Acolytes of Cairo's Muhammad 'Abd al-Maqsud joined forces with Mansoura-based affiliates of the Salafi Front to form the al-Fadila (Virtue) Party. Led by 'Abd al-Maqsud's brother 'Adil, it pledged to "spread the values of justice and equality, and return Egypt to its centrality in every sphere, in compliance with the shari'a."[32] 'Abd al-Maqsud's followers, mostly from Cairo, would then quit al-Fadila in July to found the al-Asala (Authenticity) Party, once again headed by his brother.[33] In Damanhur, followers of Sheikh Hisham Al 'Uqda founded the al-Islah (Reform) Party under 'Atiyya 'Atlan, who had earned his doctorate at the American Open University, a Sururi institution par excellence.[34] Last, in Alexandria, the small group of Hisham Mustafa, the former Salafi Call member who had left the group in 2002, created the al-Islah wa-l-Nahda (Reform and Revival) Party.

More surprisingly, the former jihadis of the Jama'a Islamiyya—some had been released from prison after the ideological revisions (*muraja'at*) issued in the late 1990s, while others had been freed only after the revolution—announced their movement's own offering: the al-Bina' wa-l-Tanmiya (Construction and Development) Party, whose mostly aging base resided primarily in Upper Egypt, former stomping ground of the Jama'a Islamiyya. Other ex-jihadis also announced forthcoming political organizations, including Kamal Habib's al-Salama wa-l-Tanmiya (Security and Development) Party, but few of these plans made it off the drawing board.[35] Each party's following stayed fairly local, and the resulting political scene mirrored the existing factionalism among the critical and jihadi currents.

The real shock came with the May 24, 2011, announcement of a new party with ties to the Salafi Call, which the party commission validated in mid-June. This, despite the Call sheikhs' repeated confirmations—in line with their historical rejection of the democratic system—that they hadn't the slightest intention of founding one. The party would be named al-Nour (*Hizb al-nur*, the Party of Light, often called the Nour Party in English).[36]

It's true that a March 22 statement had signaled the Call's decision to "participate positively in the political process."[37] But 'Abd al-Mun'im al-Shahhat, the recently appointed Call spokesperson, had clarified this position on April 18: "We will not create any parties, nor will we present candidates. We will simply support certain candidates and advise people to choose the most suitable option from the Islamic current—someone competent and trustworthy."[38] Meanwhile, as leaks circulated in the press about an imminent Nour Party, Yasir Burhami reaffirmed that this would not be the Salafi Call's political arm.[39] On June 3 the Call held a seminar at the al-Fath Mosque in Cairo entitled "The Salafi Call and Political Participation," at which its sheikhs offered the group's first-ever explicit arguments for participating in party politics.[40] One speaker, Sheikh Mahmud 'Abd al-Hamid, announced that "having examined the Nour Party's platform, we have decided to endorse it in the upcoming elections, and if God so wishes, we will throw our weight behind it, because its methodology (*manhaj*) agrees with that of the Salafi Call."

Keep in mind that the Call's sheikhs never revised in the slightest the theoretical basis for their earlier antagonism toward the democratic system. In 2012 one could, for example, still find Sheikh Sa'id 'Abd al-'Azim's harsh indictment of democracy at any decent Salafi bookstore in Egypt.[41] The sheikhs limited themselves—in what was more rhetorical sleight-of-hand than ideological realignment—to citing an opinion from Egypt's Supreme Constitutional Court in 1996 that interpreted Article 2 as forbidding any law that violated shari'a. Presented as such, this made Egypt a de facto Islamic State, which would justify the Call's participation therein.[42] No explanation was given, however, for the fact that this opinion had never found a real-world application, nor for the sudden evaporation of the Call's hostility to political participation—which had not changed in 1996.

Let's return for a moment to Mahmud 'Abd al-Hamid's remarks at the June 3 seminar. After expressing his support for the Nour Party, he added that "the Call will never become a party, nor will our preachers ever join one." By supporting Nour, 'Abd al-Hamid said, the Call hoped (1) to push through shari'a-based laws instead of leaving an opening for the secularists who, unopposed, "would pass—and impose on us—whichever laws they pleased, and we would be helpless to do anything about it," and (2) to obtain "a framework through which to protect the Call by having members in Parliament."[43] We will see later that these objectives proved incompatible, and that the second, which more closely matched the Call's purist grammar, would win out in the end.

To understand both the Call's change of heart and its initially ambiguous attitude toward Nour, we must first retrace the party's story. The drive to create it came not from deep within the Call, but from its fringes. Fault lines, then largely invisible to the casual observer, had formed during the revolution: The sheikhs and their most dedicated disciples were attached to the organization's public wait-and-see attitude, while some more peripheral figures had no issue expressing support for the revolutionaries—and they made this clear, both from their pulpits and in the streets.

One such individual was Muhammad Yusri Salama, a brilliant young sheikh who had studied with Muhammad Isma'il al-Muqaddim and was known in Salafi circles for his encyclopedic knowledge of all things Ibn Taymiyya.[44] But the most important voice belonged to 'Imad 'Abd al-Ghaffur, who had helped found the Call before going his own way in the 1980s. While his departure likely had something to do with his conflict at the time with Yasir Burhami, the official line was that 'Abd al-Ghaffur had left for Afghanistan because his surgical skills were needed there by Islamic aid groups.[45] After a sojourn in the Gulf region, where he may have been influenced by the Sahwa movement's critical brand of Salafism, he settled in Turkey, married there, and worked in pharmaceutical distribution; he did not permanently return to Egypt until 2011.[46] The diverse life experiences of 'Abd al-Ghaffur and of Salama—who traveled widely and spent a period in the United States—may help explain their unique outlook.

Feeling vindicated by Mubarak's fall, the two began reasserting themselves within the organization, as its sheikhs fumbled with the challenges that recent events posed to their grammar. 'Abd al-Ghaffur, who had witnessed the Justice and Development Party (also known as the AK Party) gain a foothold in Turkey, wished to see a Salafi equivalent emerge in Egypt. Through an intense lobbying campaign with the Call sheikhs—enabled by his seniority in the movement and the respect he still enjoyed—he advocated creating a political party.[47]

His efforts bore fruit: The sheikhs, some more enthusiastic than others, gave him a green light—while refusing to take responsibility for a project whose failure could be detrimental to the Call. And so the Nour Party was born, led by its new chairman 'Abd al-Ghaffur and a small group of committed followers who, by and large, had the same profile: They had been involved in the Call without holding official roles; skewed young and somewhat worldly thanks to their studies or travels; and most had supported the revolution and could legitimately call themselves revolutionaries.[48] Muhammad Yusri Salama was named cospokesman with Yusri Hammad, a graduate of the al-Furqan preaching institute, who had himself spent nine years abroad in India, Bangladesh, Sri Lanka, and Pakistan.[49] Meanwhile Bassam al-Zarqa, another figure with an atypical story (he had become involved with critical Salafism in the 1990s) became the party's leader in Alexandria.[50]

After Salama's dramatic resignation in August 2011, he was replaced by Muhammad Nur, who had a background in the Call but had lost touch with the group in 1995. Nur had lived a long spell in Bosnia, where he married. In an interview, he talked at length about his participation in the revolution and sang the praises of Muhammad 'Abd al-Maqsud (even though he is not one of Nur's sheikhs), telling me that "after the revolution, I wanted to join a Salafi party. If the Nour Party hadn't already existed, I would have started one myself."[51] As mentioned earlier, no Call officials participated in the project at first due to an explicit prohibition by its leaders.[52]

Both this small founding group and those who joined later received training from specialists—some Salafi, others wholly unrelated to the movement. 'Abd al-Fattah Madi, for example, an Alexandria University political science professor with conservative (but not at all Salafi) leanings, oversaw political courses. For economic education, the Nour Party brought in al-Mursi Higazi, another university professor whose profile closely resembled Madi's.[53] These experts played a key role in writing the political platform, which didn't look much different from that of a typical conservative party, although Nour—like most of the newly formed parties—remained quite vague, offering just a handful of concrete proposals.

The document began by reaffirming the importance of Egypt's "Arab-Islamic identity" and the need to solidify its standing, but the scope of this plank went no further than the Constitution's Article 2, which established the "principles of shari'a" as Egypt's "primary source of legislation." None of the platform's societal recommendations reflected a Salafi worldview. What's more, it specified that "the party calls for a modern state (*'asriyya*) to be built on modern foundations (*al-usus al-haditha*), respecting each citizen's right to peaceful coexistence and rejecting both the theocratic model, in which the political leadership claims its power comes from God and asserts a monopoly on truth, and the secular one, which wants to deprive the nation of its roots and its cultural identity." It went on: "The party calls for a state comprising several branches, with separation between its legislative, executive and judicial powers, which should play equal and complementary roles. This state should protect the rights of all citizens and guarantee them justice, with equal opportunity for all."[54]

Upon closer examination, however, a specialist would note certain concessions to Salafi rhetoric: "Sons of the nation" (*abna' al-watan*) replaced the more common "citizens" (*muwatinun*), a term that never sat right with the Salafi sheikhs because it seemed to gloss over religious differences. By the same token, the document spoke of a "modern state" (*'asriyya*) rather than the "civil state" (*madaniyya*) referred to by all other parties, including the Brotherhood. Bassam al-Zarqa explains that this was because "in political contexts the word *madaniyya* means 'secular' [*'ilmaniyya*], which is unacceptable to us."[55]

Still, the platform did represent a major break with traditional Salafi discourse. It also indicated that going forward, the party would comply with the rules of a democratic system, even if 'Abd al-Ghaffur later clarified that while the Nour Party accepted the "procedures of democracy," it rejected the "philosophy."[56] The law obliged Nour, like its peers, to have a small percentage of Christian members, an obligation it mostly fulfilled with people from the small Egyptian evangelical community who already had business ties with the Salafis.[57]

The party got off to a rocky start. As Mahmud 'Abbas, one of the earliest participants, recounts, "We had no money, since the Call didn't want to fund us. We had to appeal to our founding members for donations."[58] The law on political parties mandated a minimum founding membership, and 'Imad 'Abd al-Ghaffur tirelessly traveled Egypt to gather the necessary number. Despite its ambivalent relationship with the Call's sheikhs at the time, Nour likely owed its ultimate success to the organization's support—which was at first grudgingly parceled out. As other Salafi parties were still struggling to scrape together the requisite five thousand members from ten governorates, the Nour Party managed to reach its goal. Within a few months it counted tens of thousands across the country and opened hundreds of offices, including thirty-five in Alexandria alone.[59] A national-scale structure gradually took shape, even as it harbored contradictions that would eventually tear the party apart. Nour leadership and spokesperson roles were still held by figures peripheral to the Call, and many of the party's local recruits had no ties to the religious organization (even if most had preexisting connections to Salafism).

But the Call was not simply watching from the sidelines: It was getting more involved by the day, having picked up on Nour's popularity and sensed its potential. What's more, the need to establish the party nationwide made its organization chart indistinguishable in some regions from that of the Call, as it had no choice but to rely on the local leaders already in place. Further muddying the waters, certain Call figures were nominated to key roles like that of "membership director" (*mas'ul shu'un al-'adawiyya*), which Ashraf Thabit secured thanks to pressure from his mentor, Burhami. An array of the latter's confidants was likewise parachuted into the party's campaign leadership a few weeks before the legislative elections, replacing founders who had labored there for months.[60] In August Burhami had also torpedoed a planned merger with a small party led by Nidal Hammad, a politically minded Salafi intellectual well-known in the movement, fearing that this fusion might diminish the Call's pull within Nour.[61]

In September 2011 the selection process began for legislative candidates. Ground rules were set: Candidates had to be virtuous (but not necessarily capital-S Salafi), have specific skills, and possess a local base. Most important, they had to be able to finance at least part of their campaign, with the party covering the rest.[62] Mahmud 'Abbas explains that three committees were responsible for selecting the candidates: a local one that assembled the preliminary list of names, a governorate-level group that examined these proposals, and a ten-member high commission (*lajna 'ulya*) that made the final decisions. At each successive rung sat a greater percentage of Call proxies who could veto one candidate or shoehorn in another. This was how Call spokesman 'Abd al-Mun'im al-Shahhat landed the candidacy for Alexandria's Montaza district, says 'Abbas. Burhami had purportedly planned for al-Shahhat to be named leader of the Nour Party's parliamentary caucus, but he was eliminated in the second round of the election.[63]

The Nour Party's list of contenders was quite diverse in the end, featuring Call notables from the various governates and many independent Salafis who had joined out of ideological affinity, alongside other independents whose religious practice was not truly Salafi.[64] A good example was Muhammad al-Mislawi, an ill-fated candidate from Cairo, who openly described his values as "liberal" while emphasizing his admiration for Salafis. "I would love to be like them," he told me, "but to be human is to be weak." Illustrating this point, al-Mislawi shared a photo of himself cleanshaven, taken six months before.[65] Nour's increasing visibility starting in the summer of 2011 likely inspired some opportunism: Unlike the Brotherhood and other fixtures of the political landscape, Nour had no natural candidates; this tempted strivers who wanted a fast track to political renown.

For all these reasons, Nour candidates were younger overall than those in the other parties—and especially in that of the Brotherhood, where age was extremely important: It reflected a person's seniority in the movement and thus his likelihood of holding a post. An analysis of the Nour MPs' biographies (sadly, such information is unavailable for its complete candidate list) shows that on average they were 43.5 years old, as compared to 49.5 in Parliament as a whole. Seventeen Nour MPs were younger than 35, whereas it was nearly impossible to find a Brotherhood MP under 40.[66]

The Nour Party entered the fall 2011 parliamentary elections as part of a coalition formed in extremis with two smaller partners from the Salafi current: the al-Asala Party (an offshoot of critical Salafism) and the al-Bina' wa-l-Tanmiya Party (the political arm of the reformed Jama'a

Islamiyya), which joined forces with Nour only after failing to build alliances with the Brotherhood.[67] Nour won 112 seats to al-Asala's 3 and al-Bina' wa-l-Tanmiya's 13, bringing the coalition total to 128, or 25.2 percent of parliamentary seats. Barely six months old, Nour was now Egypt's second largest party, coming in behind the colossal 43.7 percent of seats amassed by the Brotherhood's Freedom and Justice Party. This remarkable success whetted appetites and ignited intraparty disputes; these came across loud and clear in my interviews in 2011 with Nour leaders, who did not mince words in their critiques of Call sheikhs.

Conflict at first centered on who deserved credit for the Nour Party's electoral success. Yasir Burhami and the Call felt that the organization's networks and resources—without which the undertaking would have been inconceivable—were entirely to thank.[68] The campaign was costly, especially since Nour's strategy involved occupying as much public space as possible with its posters, slogans, and electoral *nashid*, "*Ya masr sabah al-nur*" (Good morning Egypt), which seemed to ring throughout the streets of Egypt's major cities in the fall of 2011.[69] Such publicity had been possible only with support from the Call's financial backers. The Salafi satellite channels, where the Call leaders had strong connections, also did their share by offering more or less explicit support for the party. As far as the sheikhs were concerned, these factors made Nour's success a victory for the Call.

'Abd al-Ghaffur and his followers saw things a little differently. They underscored their early and ongoing dedication to the project—despite the sheikhs' skepticism—and the appeal of the party's political discourse, which had swayed a sizable segment of the electorate.[70] And it's true that Nour ran a very effective campaign, based largely on the party's novelty, that presented its political inexperience as a plus: Our hands are clean, its candidates repeated, since we are pious and have never been involved in any way with the prior regimes—thinly veiled disparagement of the Brothers, who had served in Parliament since 1984.

Interviews and observations during the campaign in the working-class Cairo suburb of Shubra al-Khayma, where Brotherhood MP Muhammad al-Baltagi was seeking reelection, showed that this argument had hit the nail on the head. Asked about their votes, many residents seemed to prefer the Nour Party because "al-Baltagi has been an MP for so long, and he hasn't done anything for us." The MP's devotees countered that this was because Mubarak had always blocked Brotherhood initiatives—but the harm had been done.[71]

Another theme permeated the Nour candidates' discourse. Muhammad al-'Adli, director of a party outpost in Tanta, put it this way: "We are of the people, we experience their problems... unlike the politicians in Cairo who see only their own problems."[72] Once again, this critique targeted the liberals and the left as much as it did the Brothers, whom the Salafis often accused of elitism, of having lost touch with the common people. Some Salafi candidates infused their assertions with leftist undertones, once again to distinguish themselves from a Brotherhood that they insinuated had become "gentrified." Such arguments allowed the Nour Party to capture an audience well beyond its strictly Salafi base. With Salafism on the verge of becoming the country's normative reference point, everyday Egyptians could also more easily identify with the party's religious discourse even if they did not practice conspicuous piety.

As the stakes grew higher, the party's internal disputes—mostly involving how the Nour leaders expressed their political approach—spilled into the public arena. Interviewed in the press or during his then-frequent talk show appearances, 'Imad 'Abd al-Ghaffur did adopt some bold stances. In mid-December 2011 he declared that shari'a would not be used to restrict civil liberties and said that all citizens, Christians included, shared equal rights and obligations.[73] Asked shortly thereafter about the lack of Christians on the party's electoral lists, he lamented this fact and said he hoped that some would run in the next election. Yasir Burhami quickly set him straight via a fatwa on the Call website that reaffirmed the prohibition on Christians in Parliament; such a role would give them authority over Muslims, who are the only people eligible to hold authority (*wilaya*).[74]

More flare-ups followed. On another occasion, 'Abd al-Ghaffur declared the party open to alliance-building with any other political group, including the Free Egyptians Party—which was led by Naguib Sawiris, a Copt. In short order, Burhami published his response in the Call's recently created *al-Fath* journal (which, as an aside, remained separate from the Nour Party's journal, *Jaridat Hizb al-Nur*): "Any alliance with groups that reject God's Law is expressly forbidden."[75] A subsequent scandal broke out when party spokesman Muhammad Nur attended a reception hosted by the Iranian Embassy; after pressure from Burhami, he was suspended as punishment.[76] And it was déjà vu a few months later when 'Abd al-Ghaffur accepted an invitation from the Turkish Embassy to a gala for the country's national holiday. Burhami accused 'Abd al-Ghaffur of participating in what amounted to a "celebration of the fall of the Caliphate."[77]

By all accounts, Nour's leaders were trying to build an Islamist "political party like any other," to quote Muhammad Nur.[78] They openly called themselves "politicians" (*siyasiyyun*) and explained to all who would listen how different this role was from that of "sheikh," essentially presenting politics and religion as separate realms of activity governed by different sets of rules. As Mahmud 'Abbas explained, "We consult the Call sheikhs, whom we deeply respect, when we need a fatwa on a specific question. But we do not want them meddling in the party's everyday business because this is politics, and politics is not their area of expertise."[79] In making this assertion, the Nour leaders cast doubt both on the authority of the Call's ulema and on the purist grammar that guided their every action. Burhami, then, wasn't wrong to see this as a threat to the Call, at least in the form it had taken. Burhami's string of fatwas charged 'Abd al-Ghaffur with what amounted to repeated "grammatical mistakes."

REAFFIRMING PURIST GRAMMAR

The dominant narrative of the Nour Party's internal discord, both among the Salafi base and in the Egyptian press, gives star billing to individual and psychological explanations: This was nothing but a power struggle between two men, Yasir Burhami and 'Imad 'Abd al-Ghaffur, who we are reminded never got on well in the first place.[80] While the duo's mutual animosity almost certainly played a role, the true stakes were much higher.[81]

The Nour Party's arrival shifted the Salafi center of gravity away from the ulema and toward a new category of actors: Salafi politicians who felt that—within the confines of this separate political field—they should no longer be strictly bound by the religious principles that had brought the movement to life. And they were clear about this: As we have seen, while they had no problem recognizing the sheikhs as their religious guideposts, they were unwilling to accept their interference in party political decisions. Nour leaders visibly contrasted themselves with the sheikhs by donning suits; according to a founder, 'Abd al-Ghaffur encouraged this practice in one of Nour's prelaunch meetings.[82] One can imagine how this power transfer must have discomfited the Call's founders, whose movement centered entirely on religious figures. When Burhami attacked 'Abd al-Ghaffur over his deviations (real or imagined) from the letter of the Salafi corpus, it was chiefly to reassert the sheikhs' primacy.

Above all, the Nour Party's desire to become a "political party like any other" challenged the grammar that had reigned within the Call. It meant believing that top-down change was possible—and thus trying to make it to the top (which 'Abd al-Ghaffur often repeated was the Nour Party's goal). It also meant standing up when necessary to the existing authorities, who in the postrevolutionary context were the army and its allies. With such an approach, the Nour Party would essentially be following an Islamist grammar while maintaining a Salafi veneer. In taking on 'Abd al-Ghaffur, Burhami was acting as guardian of the purist grammar on which Salafism was built.

Yasir Burhami's actions reveal a radically different take on Nour's role. He felt it should be more than just the Call's political arm; the party should function as part and parcel of the religious organization, entirely at its bidding. Granted, the sheikhs had acquiesced to the argument that, in a postrevolutionary context where power balances were being renegotiated within the field of party politics, the Call now needed representation there. But the Nour Party should be limited to the role of "advocacy group" for Call interests, for example, by forming a parliamentary bloc that advanced the interest of the religious group or obstructed decisions harmful to the organization. "The good of the Call"—*maslahat al-da'wa*, which could also be understood as "the good of the call" (lowercase c), meaning the overall need to bring Muslims to Salafi Islam—became the catchphrase the sheikhs used in justifying their stances to their followers.[83]

Given the country's existing power balance, Burhami and his followers felt that Nour should also appease the army, a still-powerful force, and make stability its utmost priority—which would render the party a politically conservative force.[84] This explains why Abu Idris lauded the military council in May 2012 for its "restraint in the face of agitation, its desire to protect Egyptians' lives, and its success in organizing the elections."[85] Sure, the party should encourage the Islamization of the Constitution or of Egyptian law, given the right circumstances. But this shouldn't be

Nour's raison d'être; bottom-up Islamization remained far preferable to its top-down alternative. Running a presidential candidate would therefore be useless, at best, and at worst could even damage the Nour Party by inviting tension with the army. Just after the party joined Parliament, this outlook was detailed by Ashraf Thabit, an eminent Call official close to Burhami who, as mentioned earlier, rode the latter's influence into a job as Nour's membership director:

> As far as we are concerned Parliament is not—and will never be—the solution. We believe in grassroots change, and changing laws is not enough to make that happen. Parliament is simply a way to practice what we see as the starting point for everything else: preaching (*da'wa*). That is our methodology (*manhaj*) for bringing about change. We must purify the beliefs of the Umma. When people talk about us, they say: "They're going to make changes, they're going to impose laws"—but that is not at all our methodology. That has never been, nor will it be, our way, and this would not have changed even if we had won the majority.[86]

This perspective led to a unique relationship with the political field, which represented a means rather than an end: This field was not important *in itself*. Taken to the extreme, such reasoning would authorize the Nour Party to embrace an entirely pragmatic approach, offering its support to whomever would best serve "the good of the Call" in a given circumstance. Such behavior might bring to mind—in a substantially different context— the conduct of Israel's ultraorthodox parties, which, like the Call, emerged from an education-centered religious movement and have formed coalitions with those both on the left and (more frequently today) the right who were willing to give favorable treatment to their schools.[87]

At face value, this pragmatism might seem to contradict Burhami's fatwa on the "unnatural" alliances that 'Abd al-Ghaffur had said he was open to making with a range of political actors. But 'Abd al-Ghaffur saw these alliances as tools for political change rather than for helping the Call. Again, Burhami's reprimands were less about the limitations imposed by the Salafi corpus than about reasserting the sheikhs' (and the Call's) authority over the party. His stance thus fit perfectly into the purist grammar he had always defended: Politics couldn't bring about political change, because reform could only be effected by educating society according to

Salafi principles. Protecting (and reinforcing) the entity responsible for this mission—the Call—was therefore the only worthwhile objective.

This outlook gained traction within the Nour Party starting in the spring of 2012, when Burhami managed to maneuver his disciples into nearly all key party roles, making 'Imad 'Abd al-Ghaffur and the group of founders a minority. Over the following months, Burhami tried several times to replace 'Abd al-Ghaffur with one of his own loyalists as party leader.[88] The Nour president had announced that he would seek a new term in the intraparty elections planned for after the national ones, although the two sides could not see eye to eye on election protocol. 'Abd al-Ghaffur knew the Call, whose sheikhs now had tentacles throughout the party hierarchy, was a formidable opponent. But he was banking on his popularity among Nour's base, much of which had no ties with the Call.

The election was initially scheduled for September 2012, but at the last minute Burhami's allies managed to certify a motion mandating that party members pass a political literacy exam before they could vote. According to 'Abd al-Ghaffur's camp, the test was planned via an extremely secretive process, at the initiative of Call-affiliated leaders who conveniently invited only their own disciples—and shared the answers with them.[89] In retribution for vehement opposition by 'Abd al-Ghaffur and company to holding the vote under such conditions, the party's high commission—now mainly Call officials—announced that 'Abd al-Ghaffur was being removed and would be replaced by Sayyid Mustafa, a Burhami loyalist. 'Abd al-Ghaffur challenged the decision and continued to call himself the party's legitimate president.[90] But in December 2012, after months of controversy, 'Abd al-Ghaffur and his followers threw in the towel, spitefully quitting Nour to found a new party according to their model. Its name, al-Watan ("The Homeland," an unusual allusion for Salafis) said much about the road they had traveled. The party immediately announced a "separation of preaching and politics" (*fasl al-da'wa 'an al-siyasa*) and a "preference for skill over loyalty to the sheikhs."[91] Entire chapters of the Nour Party split off to join the new group; overall, however, only a minority defected.[92]

With the Call's commandeering of the Nour Party and the return of a purist grammar stripped of hybrid influence, the Muslim Brotherhood—which 'Abd al-Ghaffur had regarded as the competition rather than a sworn enemy—was reinstated as nemesis. In the handful of studies on the Nour Party, this interorganizational feud is often explained in terms of personal relationships or overall history: The late 1970s split had inaugurated a three-decade-long rivalry between the two movements, leaving the groups plenty of reasons to hate each other.[93]

Without denying the significance of this backstory, it's important to shed light on the rivalry's deeper roots. From the Call's perspective, the Brothers posed an existential threat because they wanted more than political power: They also wished to seize the nation's mosques for what Salafis saw as a perverted form of Islam. If the Brotherhood managed to become the ruling force, it could install its own disciples in houses of prayer, poaching the Call's "market share" and placing the group—and its mission—in mortal danger. In short, a "Brotherization" of the Ministry of Awqaf would be the Salafis' worst nightmare. On April 30, 2012, 'Abd al-Mun'im al-Shahhat described the "deep fear disquieting large segments of society, especially the Salafis, at the thought that a single organization could take control, which would pave the way for a new authoritarian regime."[94] Direr still was the picture that Burhami painted his followers: "The Brotherhood will destroy the Salafi Call if they get the chance!" he said during a lesson at his mosque on February 6, 2013.[95]

This explains why the Call tried so fervently, starting in spring 2012, to prevent its rival from coming to power. With a presidential election scheduled for May and June, the Brotherhood's early April announcement that it would present a candidate (first Khayrat al-Shatir, whose candidacy was invalidated, and then Mohamed Morsi in his place) set off alarm bells, especially since another Islamist candidate was already enjoying a striking amount of popularity: Hazim Abu Isma'il, to whom part of the next chapter is devoted. The candidate referred to himself as Salafi (while departing from the movement's grammar), but he was a rebel with too little regard for the Call's authority to be considered as an alternative.

Defying expectations, Burhami and his allies in the Nour Party threw their support behind the most liberal of the Islamist candidates: 'Abd al-Mun'im Abu al-Futuh, an Islamo-centrist who had unceremoniously exited the Brotherhood the prior year and was trying to build his own cross-ideological alliance; his candidacy was actually backed by several big names from the revolutionary left.[96] The Salafis had four fairly simple reasons for endorsing Abu al-Futuh: He came from the Islamic movement—a minimum, as it would otherwise have been difficult to justify support for a liberal or leftist candidate to Call members; he had a dreadful relationship with the Brotherhood; he would be a weak president, dependent on the alliances that brought him to power; and he seemed to have a decent chance at winning. After a show of institutional procedures, where all Islamist candidates were interviewed and voted on by committees from the Nour Party and the Call, official support was given to Abu al-Futuh.[97]

Many followers of 'Abd al-Ghaffur, whose views still carried weight despite their increasing marginalization, said they would have preferred to endorse Morsi, whom they saw as the only Islamist candidate with a chance of winning—a difference of opinion that speaks to the two factions' grammatical distinctions. But Abu al-Futuh seemed a sound enough choice, so 'Abd al-Ghaffur's camp relented and agreed to support him. For months they had been pushing for political normalization, and endorsing Abu al-Futuh represented the culmination of this effort—radically different reasoning from that of the sheikhs. The only initial opposition to Abu al-Futuh came from sheikhs less directly involved in leading the Call. Some preferred Morsi, some Abu Isma'il,[98] but all ultimately united behind the organization's decision.[99]

Abu al-Futuh's performance was respectable but fell short. He was eliminated in the first round of the presidential election, having placed fourth with 17.47 percent of votes. Nour and the Call bore some responsibility for this failure, as Abu al-Futuh himself lamented when I interviewed him. For one thing, the Salafi support had scared away some of the liberals and leftists who had planned to vote for him. And for another, the Nour Party had struggled to sufficiently mobilize its base for its chosen candidate.

This fact was hard to ignore at an Abu al-Futuh rally, held by the Call's Alexandrian branch, that I observed on May 18, 2012. The candidate mounted the podium alongside several figures from the organization, including Yasir Burhami and Nadir Bakkar. As Abu al-Futuh, with his short white beard, talked of revolution, consensus, and democracy, the Salafi crowd seemed skeptical. Once he had spoken for perhaps fifteen minutes, the sheikhs took the floor and hammered home, ad nauseam, one single message: "Supporting Abu al-Futuh means standing up for the good of the Call" (that same catchphrase: *maslahat al-da'wa*). The Call was visibly struggling to convince its own base, which only compounded the challenge already posed by the many "noncardholding" (and thus less disciplined) Salafis in Nour's ranks. For a good number of them, it would have been inconceivable to vote for this man who seemed too liberal, and whose positions the Call had often criticized in the past—which the Brotherhood made sure nobody forgot during the campaign.[100] Many Salafis thus voted for Morsi or—to avoid directly contradicting their sheikhs' preferences—abstained.

Abu al-Futuh's elimination thus presented the Call with a serious conundrum, as the second round would pit Brotherhood candidate Mohamed Morsi (who had taken first place in the first round), against Ahmad Shafiq, Mubarak's final prime minister and an embodiment of the former regime. To avoid a mutiny by its base, the Nour Party publicly announced support for Morsi, the only candidate in the running who came from the Islamic current. Neither Nour nor the Call, however, did any real campaigning for Morsi. And as Egypt awaited results from the second round, Yasir Burhami visited Shafiq—perhaps believing, as did many of his compatriots, that the army wanted the Brothers to lose and would announce Shafiq as victor, no matter the actual vote count. We are not privy to the details of their meeting, but one might imagine that Burhami's goal was to negotiate favorable conditions for the Call in such an outcome.[101]

THE CALL'S RISKY BET AGAINST THE BROTHERHOOD

When the votes were tallied, Mohamed Morsi had just over 51 percent, and the Call-Nour tandem found itself in a tight spot. The groups immediately tried to exact promises—including of roles in the incoming administration—from Morsi as recompense for their belated support. After much negotiation, 'Imad 'Abd al-Ghaffur (who had not yet quit Nour) was named the presidential advisor on societal relations, and two Nour officials, Bassam al-Zarqa and Khalid 'Alam al-Din, were appointed to a twenty-person presidential advisory team.[102] These nominations were purely symbolic, as the roles in question were anything but central to the government. And the Brotherhood, which closely followed its opponent's internal disputes, was doubtless trying to stir the pot by choosing 'Abd al-Ghaffur and al-Zarqa, two Nour founders who had testy relationships with the Call.

A tenuous peace between Brothers and Call would hold until the end of 2012, thanks partly to their overlapping perspectives on one issue: In

November 2012, Morsi had adopted a series of presidential decrees to force through a new constitution—an attempt to override the authority of the constitutional court, which, finding fault with the process, repeatedly stood in the way. The controversy centered on the fact that the constituent assembly, named by Parliament, largely reproduced the latter's power balance. The Islamist movement—Brotherhood, Nour, and independents—controlled a majority of seats, which meant chances were good that the resulting constitution would be heavily Islamicized. And although the Salafis, in accordance with their grammar, didn't see this as the immediate goal of their political involvement, the chance to reinforce the centrality of shariʿa to the constitution was too good to squander. "Moderate" Brotherhood members at first considered allying with the liberals (and against the Salafis) to pass a more consensus-based text, but the potential partners' deteriorating ties made this less and less likely.[103] The Brotherhood's more conservative faction, meanwhile, was on the rebound as this once-in-a-lifetime opportunity came within reach: Now was the moment to turn its dream of an authentically Islamic constitution into a reality. In the end, the text was written by Brothers and Salafis—who together held a majority on the committee—and without most of the liberals, the leftists, and the Copts, who boycotted the debates in protest.[104] Morsi then decided to legitimize this strong-arming via a popular referendum, on which the Salafis and the Brotherhood vocally campaigned for the populace to vote "YES."

The measure passed easily, winning 63.8 percent of votes, but with turnout at a meager 33 percent. Article 2, which states that "the principles of the shariʿa are the primary source of legislation," was preserved as is. But the freshly minted Article 219 spelled out these "principles" so as to ensure that vague phrasing didn't stymie the Islamization of Egyptian law, as it had under the previous regime: "The principles of Islamic shariʿa include general evidence, foundational rules, rules of jurisprudence, and credible sources accepted in Sunni doctrines and by the larger community."[105] It was now impossible to pretend that Article 2 referred to general principles rather than Islam's textual sources.

In addition, Article 4, which reaffirmed al-Azhar's independence and granted it an advisory role on anything shariʿa-related, codified the permanent tenure of its Grand Imam. In a leaked internal conversation that sparked a scandal, Yasir Burhami described this as an initial concession to the liberals and to the Christians who were reassured by the presence of then–Grand Imam Ahmad al-Tayyib (who, one will recall, had deemed Salafis "Hanbali extremists" and was no fan of the Brotherhood either).[106] The tradeoff was necessary to get the text passed without other significant changes, but he added that the Salafis were taking the long view: They planned to legislate a maximum age for the role so they could eliminate their nemesis and seize power at al-Azhar.

No sooner had the Constitution been ratified than Brotherhood and Call found themselves back at each other's throats. In January 2013, the Nour Party (which since the December defections had a new executive team chaired by one of Burhami's most loyal allies, Yunis Makhyun) joined with Morsi's liberal critics in denouncing the Brotherhood's domineering tendencies, which they called a "Brotherization of the state" (*akhwanat al-dawla*).[107] Nour's leaders went so far as to announce that they had assembled a dossier with every instance of Brotherization and threatened to publish it.[108] When Iranian president Mahmoud Ahmadinejad visited in February 2013, the Nour Party made a fuss about "Shia proselytism."[109] The accord that soon followed, which allowed Iranian tourists to visit Egypt and Egyptians to visit Iran without a visa, reignited the controversy; Burhami accused the Brothers of "selling out their religion to make room for the expansion of Shiism."[110] For the Salafis, this was an ideal cause: By blasting the presumed ties between Morsi and Iran, Nour was able to both reassert its doctrinal orthodoxy and attack the Brotherhood. Nour also criticized Morsi for having obtained a loan from the International Monetary Fund (IMF), as interest payments were a form of usury (*riba*) prohibited in Islam.

The controversy illustrates Nour's shifting alliances: In August 2012, during the cold peace between Brothers and Salafis, Yasir Burhami had issued a fatwa greenlighting the IMF's proposal, since the charges it included were "administrative fees" rather than true "interest."[111] Now, the Call's leaders justified their change of heart by claiming they had misinterpreted the issue (due, they said, to "erroneous" information sent by the Brotherhood).[112]

Nour took its anti-Brotherhood campaign to the international stage. A delegation including Nadir Bakkar and Tal'at Marzuq toured various Western countries in the spring of 2013, telling anyone who would listen that Nour embodied moderation and the Brotherhood its opposite.[113]

Everywhere it went, the Nour Party offered a discourse tailored to its audience, portraying itself as a protector—sometimes of "pluralism" and "political consensus," sometimes of "state stability," and sometimes of the "Islamic project."[114]

A united front of Morsi detractors was taking shape, with Nour playing a fairly active role—all while projecting the image of "mediator" between the two camps and proposing a crisis resolution initiative that would "avoid a bloodbath."[115] But the Salafis' greatest fear was already coming to pass: Unable to place their loyalists in the tightly controlled army, Interior Ministry, or judicial system, the Brotherhood had settled for apparently less significant administrations like the Ministry of Awqaf, whose upper echelons were now largely in Brotherhood hands.[116] Fears spread that their organization would get a stranglehold on mosques. Morsi, meanwhile, was calling for a new Azhari-only "preachers' union" (*niqabat al-duʿat*); only its members would be authorized to preach. The Salafis saw this as an attempt to exclude them.[117]

The Call-waged war of attrition dragged on, and the Brotherhood responded with escalation: In February 2013 the office of the president accused one of the two remaining Nour members in the executive branch, Khalid ʿAlam al-Din, of misappropriating funds, and he was swiftly removed from his role on the advisory team.[118] The other Nour member within the team, Bassam al-Zarqa, then resigned in solidarity with his colleague, who denounced the accusations as a baseless political maneuver.[119] Nour was now bereft of any formal representation within the executive branch, as ʿImad ʿAbd al-Ghaffur, still the presidential advisor on societal relations, had quit the party in December and now led al-Watan instead. Things took an even more serious turn in May when Yasir Burhami was briefly detained at Alexandria's airport after a flight from Saudi Arabia, a move Nour took as a declaration of all-out war.[120] Sheikh Ibrahim Zakariyya, a leading figure of the Call's Minia division, wrote on his Facebook page at the time that "the Brothers are trying to throw the Salafis—especially Nour Party members—in prison, and replace them with a so-called Salafi current that's really just an extension of the Brotherhood." In behind-the-scenes conversations at the Call, many voiced similar suspicions.[121]

Starting in May 2013, the anti-Morsi Tamarod campaign—in which we now know the Egyptian security apparatus played a role—began gathering momentum, bringing together the president's liberal and leftist detractors with notables from the former regime.[122] A large protest was planned for June 30 to demand early elections. As the fateful date approached, Nour clarified its position, offering some passive support for the anti-Morsi movement: Burhami stated that the party would not call for people to protest (little surprise, as such advocacy fell outside its grammar) but added that "if millions of protesters take to the streets, we will call for Morsi's resignation."[123] Burhami had laid the religious groundwork for this several months before by explaining that Morsi was no caliph, and the presidency was nothing more than a contract (*'aqd*) with the people. One understood (even if Burhami didn't quite spell it out) that such a contract could be broken if its terms were not respected.[124]

When General Abdel Fattah el-Sisi, then chief of the Supreme Council of the Armed Forces, announced on July 3 that Morsi was no longer president and a new political era was beginning, a coterie of political and religious leaders stood behind him: the Tamarod campaign's young founder, the liberal Mohamed al-Baradei, al-Azhar's Grand Imam, the Coptic Pope ... and none other than Galal Murra, a Nour Party executive, whose presence visibly demonstrated the party's support for the coup d'état. In an internal document, Burhami said that this had been the only way "to protect the Islamic identity in the Constitution and to guarantee that there would be a party capable of preserving all of the Islamic movement's accomplishments."[125]

Once again, Nour's stance makes perfect sense through the lens of the party's own grammar and context. Morsi represented an existential threat to the Salafi Call, whose leaders thus felt there was no choice but to neutralize him. And the army struck them as a far better partner, because (the Salafi leaders believed at the time) it had no designs on the religious field and might even look to the Call for help in regaining control of the mosques that remained loyal to the Brothers. The sheikhs lent Islamic legitimacy to the new regime, so they assumed they were indispensable. They hoped for a power-sharing arrangement like in 1980s Pakistan under military dictator Muhammad Zia-ul-Haq, or in Sudan after a coup d'état in 1989 brought military officer Omar al-Bashir and Islamist ideologue Hassan al-Tourabi to power. In such a scenario, the army would govern while a religious movement maintained social control. The Call's confidence in the army also stemmed from a personal relationship Burhami appears to have developed with General el-Sisi. The two had interacted several times since 2011, as part of dialogues el-Sisi had been tasked with organizing between the army and political forces.[126]

But things didn't quite go according to plan for the Call. The organization's support for the coup d'état immediately precipitated a mass defection from the Nour Party, despite repeated attempts to justify the stance with religious arguments.[127] An internal document, for example, explained to members that "ulema throughout history have seen individuals take power by killing and imprisoning their predecessors, and they accepted the need to work with the victors [*al-mutaghallib*]."[128]

It seems that the first to jump ship were independents who had joined after the revolution, hoping that Nour would be in a position to build an Islamic State on Salafi principles. Often guided by a hybrid grammar that was a far cry from the Call's purism, these individuals could more easily identify with the Brothers—and many headed their way after the coup d'état, followed by another wave after the notorious massacre at Rabaa al-Adawiya Square on August 14, 2013, where nearly a thousand Morsi supporters were killed in a single day. Other Salafis saw Nour's position as an inexcusable trespass of proclaimed solidarity among Muslims, always a metarule. As the new regime's anti-Brotherhood violence intensified and Nour feared for its base, the party tried to reimplement some semblance of this solidarity by distancing itself from the repression.[129]

But once the Call realized that it could easily become the regime's next target, the metarule of realism soon won out. El-Sisi's increasing intolerance for dissent of any kind forced the Call-Nour duo into ever more committed allegiance. The sheikhs gave unqualified support to his candidacy in the 2014 and 2018 presidential elections, posting their efforts (and photos of their followers marching in lockstep to vote for the military strongman) on social media. During the legislative elections of 2015, the Nour Party also had to accept all the conditions it had denounced just a few years before, like Christians among its candidates, as mandated by the new election law.[130] Facing criticism, Nour president Yunis Makhyun declared that the party had made this concession only under "duress," sparking a controversy in the Coptic community that was lapped up by the press.[131] To be fair, as those close to the Call told us in interviews, the group's sheikhs had concluded that with the regime's ever-lengthening list of enemies, the Call would suffer the same fate as the Brotherhood if its efforts fell short.[132] The organization's underlying grammar still centered on protecting the Call and its ability to retain at least some influence in society—even if such a pursuit sent it down a hellish spiral with the authorities and incited yet more defections.

Only "card-carrying" Call members now remained, as much out of loyalty to the organization and its sheikhs as because their background gave them better insight than others might have into its guiding grammar. And yet fissures appeared even among the holdouts. The most overt rebellion deep within the Call came from Sa'id 'Abd al-'Azim, an eminent member of its "founding six," who condemned its support for the coup d'état and quit the organization he had helped found thirty-five years before. He lived in exile until his death in 2024.

To understand his decision, one must consider the personal ties he had developed postrevolution with certain Brotherhood figures, particularly Khayrat al-Shatir, and his historically tense relationship with Yasir Burhami. ('Abd al-'Azim had been the face of the organization until Burhami unseated him in 1994.) Two other founding sheikhs, Muhammad Isma'il and Ahmad Hutayba, took a more discreet approach, returning to full-time preaching after summer 2013 without any public pronouncement about the ongoing events.[133] Some branches of the organization took a similar tack: Its Marsa Matruh chapter announced that it would remain affiliated but was ending its political activities in order to concentrate exclusively on religious ones.[134] For all these Salafis, Nour had become an albatross; if they wished to restore the movement's original operating principles, they absolutely had to break free of the party.

All this naturally limited the movement's ability to mobilize. In the parliamentary elections in 2015, Nour—the only religious party to run—won just 12 of 550 seats. While this was likely due to security apparatus meddling during the campaign and the election, it also reflected a real loss of interest in the party, at least as compared to its 2011 returns. The Call thus saw Nour's utility as an advocacy group for its religious priorities reduced to almost nil. And it soon became apparent that, despite the Salafis' displays of loyalty, the new regime had no intention of according them the role they had longed for. Their pull on the new constituent committee, convened in the summer of 2013 by the incoming regime, was negligible—one seat out of fifty—and they had little say over the final text. The Islamicized constitution passed under Morsi was thus replaced by one that more closely resembled the Mubarak-era one on religious issues.[135]

Rather than relying on the Call, the new regime now looked to a reinvigorated al-Azhar in its quest to retake the religious realm.[136] New regulations imposed by the mosque-university and the Ministry of Awqaf dictated that only Azharis were now authorized to preach, briefly threatening the Call's control of its own mosques until the Interior Ministry intervened on behalf of the organization.[137] The Salafi sheikhs no longer dreamed of expansion; now, they could only hope to salvage the core of their religious infrastructure—a feat they managed to pull off, at least partially. But they remained under considerable pressure, as did the Jam'iyya Shar'iyya and Ansar al-Sunna, who had no choice but to comply with the edicts of the Ministry of Awqaf.[138]

The Call can certainly boast of being the only prominent Islamic movement to have survived in Egypt and maintained seats in Parliament, and of having held onto its main mosques. But this came at a significant cost to its credibility and hold on society. The group also faced particularly biting attacks from the world's eminent Salafi authorities—especially from one of its early inspirations, the Kuwaiti-Egyptian sheikh 'Abd al-Rahman 'Abd al-Khaliq. In a December 2013 open letter to Burhami, he wrote: "You used to be a soldier of Satan. But you perfected your depravity, and now you are his master."[139] And in January 2014 dozens of Saudi sheikhs from the Sahwa movement attacked the Nour Party's actions.[140] How far the party had fallen: A role model in 2011, inspiring similar initiatives from Gaza to Morocco, Nour was now seen by many as a stain on the movement to which it belonged.[141]

BROTHERHOOD AND CALL BATTLE FOR CONTROL OF SALAFISM

In the postrevolutionary period, the subject of Salafism was by no means limited to the Call and the Nour Party. With the Salafi norm becoming hegemonic in the religious sphere, control of it became one of the chief objectives in the competition between Brothers and Salafis. Earlier, we saw how the Brotherhood itself became partially Salafized when a religious Salafi wing established itself within the group. And the organizationist current, which had completed its takeover of the Brotherhood in 2009, shared elective affinities with the Salafi discourse without fully embracing it. The group would come to view these Salafi connections as valuable tools for widening its base and countering its competitors, Nour and the Call.

One of the most emblematic battlegrounds of this rivalry was an association created in the midst of the revolution: the Religious Council for Rights and Reform (*al-hay'a al-shar'iyya li-l-huquq wa-l-islah*), which—while presenting itself as the new voice of Egyptian Islam—positioned itself as a forum for Salafi or Salafi-compatible ulema who wished to "share a free religious voice with the Umma that condemns all vice, especially political ... and offers Islamic solutions to contemporary problems and concerns."[142] Muhammad Yusri Ibrahim, a leading figure in critical Salafism's Sururi current, became the council's secretary general.

The critical Salafis—unlike the Call and many of the Salafi sheikhs who had established their authority through satellite television—committed to the revolutionary movement early on, in late January 2011. Ibrahim saw the Religious Council as a way to push his less-politicized colleagues into overtly endorsing the revolution; it would also provide the Salafi ulema with a tool for exerting political pressure. Indeed, when the Alexandrian sheikhs signed the council's inaugural statement on February 5, 2011, this was their first expression of support for the revolution. The Religious Council also took on the job of crafting a religious basis for the Salafis' new political involvement. It published a series of books by Ibrahim and some close collaborators (printed by his own publishing house, Dar al-Yusr, and emblazoned with the council logo) that addressed, among other topics, "political participation" and "political pluralism and alliances with secular parties."[143]

Ibrahim's hybrid grammar borrowed as much from Islamism as it did from Salafism, making him an ideal go-between for the two branches of the Islamic movement. He always appeared in Azhari attire, and his formal affiliation with the institution (as a graduate, not a professor) enhanced his credibility. The Call had grasped this early on; the group had placed him in charge of its "advisory board" in spring 2011, hoping to expand the group's influence to the broader Islamic sphere. As I noted earlier, this appointment was symbolic—the board had no power—but the gesture illustrates Ibrahim's centrality during this period. And he was once again acting as a bridge when he founded the Religious Council.[144] To bring together individuals from divergent currents, he played equally on the metarule of proclaimed solidarity—which obligated at least a show of cooperation between the factions of the Islamic movement—and on the aspirations of all who wished to use the council as a means to their ends.

Its six executives and thirteen board members reflected the spectrum of Egyptian Salafism.[145] There were Salafi-inclined Azharis like Tal'at 'Afifi; critical Salafis like Muhammad 'Abd al-Maqsud, Nash'at Ahmad, and Hisham Al 'Uqda; Salafi-friendly Brothers like Safwat Higazi, 'Abd al-Sattar Fath Allah, and the organizationist Khayrat al-Shatir (a central Brotherhood figure who, like other organizationists, was said to have Salafi leanings); Call members like Sa'id 'Abd al-'Azim and Muhammad Isma'il al-Muqaddim; Salafi "new preachers" like Muhammad Hassan; Tariq al-Zumur of the Jama'a Islamiyya; Ansar al-Sunna's president, 'Abdallah Shakir; and the Tabligh movement's Muhammad Hisham Raghib.

In the beginning, the Religious Council strategically placed itself under the symbolic auspices of al-Azhar by naming the Salafi-compatible Azhari Nasr Farid Wasil as its president. Born in 1937, he had taught some fifteen years in Saudi Arabia and was the former Grand Mufti of Egypt (1996–2002).[146] He was known at al-Azhar both for his wide-ranging connections (as a member of its Academy of Islamic Research) and for his sometimes dissenting stances toward the former regime, which reportedly cost him his post as Grand Mufti in 2002.[147] Yet, when Muhammad Yusri Ibrahim accused al-Azhar in the press of "continuing to support corruption through its allegiance to the state" and "trying to divide and fragment the Islamic movement," this elicited a strong reaction within the institution, which was unaccustomed to public condemnations. And when he faced pressure from his peers, Wasil prioritized Azhari solidarity, abruptly resigning from the council in July 2011 and accusing it of "straying from the legitimate objectives for which it was created."[148] The council carried on, but without the credibility he had lent it.

As conflicts grew between Brotherhood and Call, control of the Religious Council—and the potential legitimacy it offered—became a priority for all involved. Khayrat al-Shatir leaned on his close relationship with Muhammad Yusri Ibrahim, working tirelessly to transform the council into an extension of the Brotherhood. But the balance truly tipped when the critical Salafis chose sides. Unlike the Call sheikhs, these hybrid-grammared Salafis had been friendly with the Brothers since the Mubarak era, and the bond deepened as a Salafi wing established itself within the Brotherhood. It's true that the largest critical Salafi party, al-Asala, had picked up a few seats by allying with Nour for the legislative elections in late 2011. Starting in spring 2012, however, and especially after Hazim Abu Isma'il had been eliminated from the presidential race—which I will discuss at length in the next chapter—most critical Salafis openly endorsed the Brotherhood instead, judging it the only Islamist organization strong enough to win the election. This was crucial for the Brothers, whose religious authority had been undermined by the Salafis, and thus the critical Salafis' support for Mohamed Morsi would play a central role in the presidential campaign. A two-thirds majority of the Religious Council voted to endorse Morsi—much to the chagrin of the Salafi Call which, for reasons discussed earlier, supported Abu al-Futuh.[149] At each of Morsi's campaign events, several Salafis—critical figures as well as members of the Brotherhood's Salafi wing—would address the crowd before the candidate spoke. For example, at Morsi's last major Cairo rally before the first round of elections, Salafi-leaning Brother Safwat Higazi took the stage alongside Muhammad 'Abd al-Maqsud.[150]

It is striking to note that the Brotherhood almost exclusively advanced Salafi religious rhetoric in the months leading up to the election. Sheikh Yusuf al-Qaradawi, however, who many considered the organization's foremost religious authority on the international stage, played no role in the campaign—despite having been the first sheikh to deliver a Friday sermon on Tahrir Square after Mubarak's fall, in front of an enormous crowd on February 17, 2011.[151] Of course, as early as 2008 he had denounced the "new ideas coming into the Brotherhood, some of which are from the Salafi movement," making it highly unlikely that he would choose to participate in a campaign with Salafi overtones.[152] Al-Qaradawi had indeed expressed his personal preference for presidential candidate Abu al-Futuh.[153]

Once elected, Morsi pursued the same strategy, which helped deepen the divide between the Brothers and their critics. His first nominee for the Ministry of Awqaf was Muhammad Yusri Ibrahim, who, since the critical Salafis had joined forces with the Brotherhood, had acted as the latter's loyal ally. But this nomination sparked an uproar at al-Azhar; Grand

Imam Ahmad al-Tayyib and Grand Mufti 'Ali Jum'a supposedly paid a personal visit to Morsi to register their protest.[154] The president walked back his decision in the end, appointing Tal'at 'Afifi instead—whose profile wasn't so different. Like Ibrahim, 'Afifi was a Salafi and a member of the Religious Council, but his status as an eminent professor at al-Azhar (where he had led the Faculty of Islamic Preaching, or *da'wa*), made him a tougher target.[155] In January 2013 the Saudi Salafi sheikh Muhammad al-'Arifi was welcomed with great ceremony at Cairo's 'Amr bin al-'As Mosque. His Friday sermon there celebrated Egypt and called for investment in the country; given the tense circumstances, this was interpreted as a political endorsement of President Morsi.[156]

The Brothers' strategy seemed to be justified by the open war waged by their detractors, which now included the Call and the Nour Party (whose members permanently quit the Religious Council in February 2013, charging that it was controlled by the Brotherhood).[157] This strategy culminated on June 15, 2013, when, against a backdrop of large, planned anti-Morsi protests, a gathering was held at Cairo International Stadium in support of the Syrian revolution, co-organized by the council and the office of the president—represented by Morsi himself. A who's-who of Salafis—from both the regional level (Muhammad al-'Arifi of Saudi Arabia) and the national one (Sheikhs Muhammad Hassan and Muhammad 'Abd al-Maqsud)—held forth, defending the jihad in Syria and vilifying Shia and Alawites. Notably absent were the Call sheikhs, who boycotted the event to indicate their rejection of the Brotherhood.[158] The participants sang Morsi's praises, and some—including Sheikh 'Abd al-Maqsud—used their speeches to disparage those gearing up to protest the president.[159]

We now know that the coup d'état that ousted Morsi had been in the works since the spring. Yet, in its wake, the June 15 episode would offer the Brotherhood's detractors an a posteriori justification that they kept playing up as proof of Morsi's mortal threat to Egypt.[160] Above all, this event illustrates the shortcomings of the Brotherhood strategy: Whether inspired by true ideological affinity or by more tactical calculations, the Brothers—short on meaningful religious figures and facing fierce competition from the Call—were forced to entrust their fate to Salafi sheikhs who gradually replaced the Brotherhood's ideological agenda with their own.

At a time of growing polarization and with the government looking weaker than ever, the Brotherhood's discursive excesses offered ample fodder to its opponents, who could not have asked for better luck. Far from the consensus-based strategy followed by the Tunisian Islamists (which some Brotherhood dissidents, like 'Abd al-Mun'im Abu al-Futuh, looked to as a model for Egypt), the Egyptian Brothers' choice to escalate ended up doing some of the legwork for those in the army, state agencies, and the non-Islamist camp who had vowed to take down Morsi.

Salafi religious rhetoric, and those who advanced it, loomed large during the period of institutional transition that stretched from Mubarak's ouster until the authoritarian takeover by General Abdel Fattah el-Sisi. This is just further evidence of the normative dominance that Salafism and its promoters had acquired by 2011.

And yet beneath this near hegemony lurked divisions that predated 2011 and were aggravated by the postrevolutionary context. Confronted with the possibility of top-down change, which it had never envisaged, the Salafi Call's grammar was at first knocked off balance. Its historic—and at first reluctant—decision to authorize the creation of Nour, a political party tied to the group, stirred a debate over the role of such a party and caused a rift within the organization.

The question, in short, was whether Nour should be an "Islamist party" like any other, which would mean breaking with the purist grammar that had always oriented the organization. Alternatively, Nour could limit itself to being an advocacy group for the religious organization's interests, which would only require a more minor grammatical update. This is what the party became in the end, making it a political entity radically different from the traditional Islamist parties; even the label "Islamist party" did not quite fit. Under cover of political intrigue, the Salafis continued to do what they had always done—preaching their creed in order to transform the social fabric—although intensified state repression after the events of 2013 forced them to scale back their ambitions.

We also saw how the Salafi brand was increasingly appropriated by the Brotherhood, which was already being influenced internally by Salafism. The organization tried to beat the Call at its own game by allying with figures from the critical Salafi movement; the ensuing one-upmanship fed the polarization that characterized this transitional period in Egypt, and which was one factor in Morsi's downfall.[161]

To round out the picture of Salafism's many post-2011 manifestations, the final chapter is dedicated to a current that chose to occupy streets rather than institutions: revolutionary Salafism.

Chapter Six

THE POPULIST ROUTE
Revolutionary Salafism

Have you heard about the man who rose alone, with neither partners nor followers, and in a few months' time found himself carried to within a hair's breadth of the presidential palace by those who believed in him and his message?

Do you know the story of the man who shattered the glass ceiling, who lifted the call for "implementing the shariʻa" to such heights that neither friend nor enemy could believe their eyes as all of society—even those from the most humble backgrounds—united behind him? . . .

What do you know of this sheikh, but a minor figure on the religious channels, who then so quickly revived and incarnated the image of those true sheikhs and ulema who guide the masses, who liberate them from oppression and from the worship of anyone but God?

The story of Sheikh Hazim Abu Ismaʻil is so incredible . . . and that of the Islamic movement all the more so!

. . . As Imam Hazim Abu Ismaʻil looked to the future, battling to earn his place, all the Islamic movements were still living in the past: The Salafis, fresh from their theological skirmishes with the Maturidis, the Muʻtazilis and the Kallabis, found themselves thrown into a world that made no sense to them. . . . And as for the old Brotherhood, whose historical pendulum swung from victim to victor, then from victor to victim, everyone was dumbfounded to see that it had not lost its incredible gift for repeating history and all its hardships.

—AL-MIQDAD GAMAL AL-DIN, *YAQAZAT AL-IMAM: MAQALAT FI-L-FIKR AL-ISLAMI AL-THAWRI*

As we have seen, the revolution presented both an opportunity and a challenge for the established Salafi currents. But it was also a time when new actors took up the Salafi brand, imbuing it with new meaning and grammar a world apart from those of the "official" sheikhs. This was further proof of the normative power Salafism had amassed: It now served as the default operational framework for a significant subset of Islamic actors. This invited all sorts of reinventions. One example (and a favorite topic in the media, especially the Western press) were the Salafis of Costa (Salafiyyu Costa), a group of self-proclaimed Salafis who tried to demonstrate the "ordinariness" and open-mindedness of their religious practice. Their strategy? Associate it with Costa Coffee, a coffee chain where they—and many in the Egyptian middle class—were loyal customers. The Salafis of Costa raised their public profile by holding soccer matches with Copts and posting humorous videos denouncing clichés about Salafis.[1]

But in 2011 an entirely different (and more significant) entity appeared on the horizon: what I call revolutionary Salafism, which in a matter of months stirred up a massive popular movement intent on seizing power in order to champion shari'a and revolution, the two most popular themes in the aftermath of Mubarak's fall. Under the banner of its charismatic leader, presidential candidate Hazim Abu Isma'il, the movement adopted a populist grammar as much in phase with the revolutionary moment—where the street and the people had become effective political forces—as it was the polar opposite of Salafism's traditional modus operandi.

This chapter will journey to the earliest days of revolutionary Salafism. We will examine its emergence, then study its manifestations between 2011 and 2012. Like any populist movement, it would be confronted with the challenges of institutionalization, especially after Abu Isma'il was unexpectedly knocked out of the presidential race. Its desire to chart a different course from that of existing Islamist groups would be complicated by the political tensions under Morsi, which relegated the revolutionary Salafis to serving as unwieldy reinforcements for a regime they resented. The July 3, 2013, coup d'état did nothing to alleviate the dilemma, as the revolutionary Salafis risked fading into obscurity among the crowd of el-Sisi opponents.[2]

THE GENEALOGIES OF REVOLUTIONARY SALAFISM IN THE BUILDUP TO 2011

We saw in the preceding chapters how, during the Mubarak era, Salafism was confronted with an atmosphere of cross-pollination. This gave rise to groups whose hybrid grammars of action stirred in equal doses of original Salafi purism and Brotherhood Islamism, making them more inclined toward political opposition and thus more likely to be repressed by the regime. Their modes of action fell into two categories: Critical Salafis delivered public condemnations in mosques, and jihadis used violence. These groups had never before looked to street politics—rallies or protests—as a tactic for expanding their audience, both because this fell outside the scope of their activist culture and because such visibility would expose them to further regime repression. This type of activism had gained currency in the 1970s, particularly at universities, but no parallel had appeared under Mubarak—at least until 2010.

Granted, a rare instance of "Salafi protest" was reported in 2005 in Alexandria, when rumors spread that a play said to disparage the Muslim religion had been performed in a Coptic church. Called *I Was Blind but Now I See*, it told the story of a young Christian who converts to Islam but later returns to Christianity. Thousands of demonstrators, some with ties to Salafism, surrounded the church, and three people died when police dispersed the crowd.[3] This incident, however, was more an instance of what the Egyptian press calls "sectarian strife" (*fitna ta'ifiyya*): supposedly spontaneous outbursts of rage stemming from local tensions between Christians and Muslims. No single group was identified as the instigator of the protests, which the Salafi Call publicly condemned as it appealed for calm.[4]

Things were a good deal different in 2010, even if the mobilization was once again triggered by sectarian strife. To grasp the situation, one must first understand the Salafis' perception of their Christian compatriots, whom they insist on calling *nasara* (a Quranic term, literally "Nazarenes") rather than *masihiyyun*, as the Christians call themselves—the choice of one term or the other having become a strong indicator of the speaker's ideology. With the 1970s rise of a broad-based Salafi movement, the sheikhs seized on the Coptic question, making it a central motif in their writing and sermons—a visible contrast with earlier, Brotherhood-dominated periods when it had figured much less prominently.

For Egyptian Salafis, the "religious hatred" of Christians—an extension of "loyalty and disavowal"—was an article of faith. But in the predominant grammar of action among Salafis, this did not translate into physical attacks or any other provocation that risked societal unrest.[5] (I should clarify that this was not the case for the Jama'a Islamiyya, which took up anti-Copt violence starting in the late 1970s.) This religious antagonism was reinforced by a narrative that Christians were an "obstacle to carrying out the Islamic project" and enjoyed foreign protection and special standing with the authorities, who supposedly treated them better than Muslim citizens.[6] Naguib Sawiris, a Coptic businessman who is among the richest Egyptians, had connections both within the regime and abroad and seemed to prove this theory. Many Salafis also believed that Copts were stockpiling arms in their churches for a war on Muslims that would make Egypt a Christian state.[7] Christian activism, both linked to the Coptic Church and independent, was on the rise at the time, further amplifying the perceived threat.[8]

Interfaith tensions were inflamed on several occasions by stories of Christian women purportedly detained by the church because they had converted to Islam. The 2000s were periodically punctuated by such affairs; the most recent involved Kamilia Shehata, the wife of a Coptic priest, who the Egyptian authorities were said to have forcibly returned to the church after she became a Muslim.[9] The protests inspired by her story lasted from August to October 2010. Both their number and their scale were unprecedented, and tensions were exacerbated in September when Bishop Anba Bishoy, secretary of the Copts' Holy Synod, made statements that seemed to question the authenticity of certain Quranic verses.[10] The Salafi movement's investment in the affair can partly be explained by its connection to both her Muslim conversion and her escape attempt, which Salafis had allegedly organized.[11]

Two factors made this new context unique. For one, the political climate had shifted: The government was tolerating a greater degree of opposition, as evidenced in the recurring protests held by the Kefaya (Enough) movement and the April 6 Youth Movement against the planned transfer of power from Hosni Mubarak to his son Gamal, among other things. For several years, Salafis had specifically benefited from increased state indulgence (until this policy's mid-2010 reversal). The other novelty—our primary focus here—was the appearance of new actors and collectives that called themselves Salafi but, in marked contrast to their forbears, sought to politicize the public space. Many among them were connected with critical Salafism, and with Sheikhs Muhammad 'Abd al-Maqsud and Fawzi al-Sa'id in particular; others had been influenced by the writings of the *qutbiyyun*, especially 'Abd al-Majid al-Shazli.[12] But the most active were students of Rifa'i Surur, an independent but widely respected figure.

In the 1970s Surur, who made several appearances in chapter 2, had helped reframe Egyptian Salafism from a thoroughly jihadi perspective. Surur's students inherited more than his hybrid grammar, which interwove Salafi and Qutbist influences: They also took on his deep mistrust of the narrow-minded factionalism among established Islamist organizations (*tanzimat*). Unlike some other sheikhs, he did not see the organizations' existence as contrary to Islam but rather criticized their approach in terms of political strategy.[13] His students likewise embraced his idea that a large popular movement was needed, with many entities united around a common "political vision" (*tasawwur siyasi*), to overthrow the existing order. Preaching and violence were equally legitimate means to this end; the choice hinged solely on an accurate assessment of the context.[14]

Rifaʻi Surur consequently criticized the Brotherhood and the Salafi Call (without naming names, so as not to break the metarule of proclaimed solidarity) in equal measure. He argued that "defining the Islamic movement's political vision will avoid dangerous pitfalls in the methodology that is adopted. The two gravest risks are: straying from the commandments of the shariʻa when practicing the call, [on the pretext that this was] 'for the good of the call' ... and giving up on confrontation by force because political action is supposedly a suitable replacement."[15] Ahmad Mawlana, a figure from the current, says this was, in a way, a return to 1970s Salafism—what he calls the "true" Salafism—which was unconcerned with organizations and embraced political action, participating in the public sphere while keeping violence on the table.[16]

For these disciples of Surur, Muslim-Christian tensions became a focal point, both for religious reasons and because they grasped the topic's political potential: it also drew attention to the Egyptian state's murky role in the matter.[17] Surur's protégés included Khalid Harbi, who would found the Islamic Observer of Resistance Against Christianization (Al-marsad al-islami li-muqawamat al-tansir) in late 2008; Husam Abu al-Bukhari, who would zero in on Christian texts in the pages of his *Critical Journal* (*Al-jarida al-naqdiyya*) and create the Coalition of Support for New Muslims in March 2011; and Khalid Saʻid, Hisham Kamal and Ahmad Mawlana, all three based in Mansoura, who would establish the Salafi Front (Al-jabha al-salafiyya) in January 2011. In September 2010 Hisham Kamal dedicated a website to Shehata called *Kamilia's Story* (*Hikayat Kamilia*) that called for boycotting Christians in Egypt.[18] In parallel, a Salafi Call dissident named Rida Samadi reactivated the Salafi Movement for Reform (Al-haraka al-salafiyya li-l-islah, or HAFS), an organization he had founded in 2005, which also took up the cause of Kamilia Shehata.

While most Salafi sheikhs were opposed to protest as a pressure tactic for reasons both religious and security related, these new actors and groups considered it a perfectly legitimate technique. Starting in August 2010, there was an upswell of activity around the Shehata affair, with activists covering it almost daily on websites and Facebook pages that passed along calls to protest. The movement received assistance from the League of Muslim Lawyers and from the always provocative Sheikh Hafiz Salama, who even headed up some of the demonstrations.[19] Thanks to this activism, the cause elicited such an outpouring among Salafi youth that the Call sheikhs themselves felt obliged to jump on the bandwagon, authorizing participation in the rallies—with a fair number of ground rules: Women could not participate; the events could target only the church, never police or bystanders; and they should be held only where they wouldn't cause trouble (for example, the Call leadership forbade a gathering outside of Alexandria's Qa'id Ibrahim Mosque).[20] Sheikhs from the satellite channels, eager to please their audience, also largely supported the movement.

This first surge of Salafism as a force in street protests was cut short, in part due to its unexpected success: For three months, thousands of people had demonstrated every Friday in both Cairo and Alexandria.[21] This helped convince the regime to abruptly trade its Salafi-friendly strategy for a more repressive one and to shutter the satellite channels. But the experience had been formative for a new generation of Salafis with backgrounds outside of the established groups, whose repertoire of action now included street protest. Unsurprisingly, in January 2011, they would be among the first Salafis to join those at Tahrir Square—some as early as day one of the revolution.

SHARI'A AND REVOLUTION: HAZIM ABU ISMA'IL AND THE BIRTH OF A MOVEMENT

For the pioneering activists just described, the "eighteen days of Tahrir" represented another seminal moment. At the square, they rubbed shoulders with Brothers and critical Salafis, who had joined the movement starting January 28, 2011, as well as with various figures from the jihadi movement who regularly visited the protest site.[22] They also spent long hours talking with the liberal and left-wing activists who had initiated the mobilization. And in this swirling melting pot of movements and ideas, one person caught their attention with his charisma and with the intransigence of his Islamist rhetoric: Hazim Abu Isma'il, who had some renown from his time preaching on the Salafi channels and had been a regular visitor to Tahrir Square from the very dawn of the uprising. These hybrid-grammared activists would be the first to coalesce around him.[23]

Born in a comfortable Cairo suburb in 1961, Hazim Abu Isma'il came from a noble bloodline in the Islamist milieu. His father was Salah Abu Isma'il (1927–1990), an Azhari sheikh and one of the handful of significant religious figures in the Muslim Brotherhood's entourage. The elder Abu Isma'il had been among the first Islamists elected to the People's Assembly in the late 1970s, where he fought tooth and nail for the shari'a to be implemented, earning him nationwide celebrity status. Hazim studied law and became a lawyer while continuing his activism within the Muslim Brotherhood, where he inherited his father's role. He ran unsuccessfully as a Brotherhood candidate in the 1995 and 2005 legislative contests but was elected to the Lawyers Syndicate in 2005.[24] In parallel with his professional and political activities, the younger Abu Isma'il took on the trappings of a sheikh, officiating at mosques and in customary courts (in religious arbitration councils).[25]

His Salafi-accented rhetoric also made him a rising star in the Brotherhood's Salafi wing. After the satellite landscape opened up to Salafis in 2006, Abu Isma'il took to the airwaves, preaching in a tunic paired with a *ghutra* or turban. While he rarely ventured into political waters (given the constraints imposed on television personalities, he wasn't expected to), he did occasionally take the liberty of criticizing the Mubarak regime—particularly during Israel's bombing campaign in the Gaza strip in winter 2008. This earned him points with Islamists but apparently no trouble from the authorities, which suggests that State Security viewed him as a lesser figure in the Islamic movement.[26]

In 2011 he was still relatively unknown, even within the religious sphere. And unlike many of Cairo's more established critical Salafi sheikhs, he did not have a formal network supporting him—especially after he distanced himself from the Brotherhood, which he quit soon after the revolution broke out. It was this independence and "outsider status" (*zahira kharij al-anmat*, as Khalid Harbi described it in an interview) that attracted the aforementioned activists, who saw him as an off-ramp from the organizational (*tanzimi*) mindset: someone who could help restructure the Islamist movement from the grassroots. Through him, they also hoped to "bring the conversation back around to shari'a."[27]

Over the following months, two interwoven processes took shape: A sui generis Salafi rhetoric developed that I call revolutionary Salafism, and Hazim Abu Ism'ail came to incarnate this discourse. A turning point arrived on May 24, 2011, when Abu Ism'ail, who by then had officially quit the Brotherhood, announced he would run for president (although no election date had yet been chosen). Many in the Islamist movement assumed his candidacy was merely a tool for pressuring the established Islamist groups into entering the race—particularly the Brotherhood, which had reassured its liberal adversaries with statements that it was not contemplating a presidential bid.[28]

And yet, whatever its initial justification, Abu Ism'ail's campaign slowly picked up steam as endorsements rolled in from independents in the Salafi movement. The earliest came from the collectives and individuals mentioned in the previous section: Khalid Harbi and his Observer; Husam Abu al-Bukhari, who had just launched his Coalition of Support for New Muslims in March with the support of Hafiz Salama and others (he would also create a second group, *Al-tayyar al-islami al-'amm*, or the General Islamic Current); and the Salafi Front, which had announced its formation early in the revolution in a communiqué calling for people to rise up.[29] These would become more or less the "organic intellectuals" of the movement personified by Abu Isma'il, whom they promoted at every opportunity. They began by introducing Abu Isma'il to Rifa'i Surur, their sheikh, who then officially announced his endorsement. Surur enjoyed immense respect among jihadis; some of them decided—given the current state of affairs—that taking to the streets made more sense than taking up arms and threw in their lot with the candidate.[30] The new allies included Egyptian figures long tied to the al-Qaeda movement, as well as individuals from small jihadi groups of just a few dozen followers, many of them founded after 2003, that had endured ruthless governmental oppression.[31] Many of their members had been freed only after the 2011 revolution.

At the same time, a good number of jihadis continued to oppose Abu Isma'il because of "his desire to affect change through secular constitutions, which deprive God of his authority and his right to legislate," as it was put by Ayman al-Zawahiri, who took over al-Qaeda's leadership after Osama bin Laden's death in May 2011.[32] But most of these opponents nonetheless accorded the candidate a degree of respect. Al-Zawahiri in fact appealed directly to Abu Isma'il in winter 2012—along with "his supporters and all goodhearted people of Egypt"—encouraging him to "start a preaching and outreach campaign for the people in order to complete the revolution, which was cut short . . . and force the corrupt elements in Egypt to acquiesce to the people's demands."[33] Ayman's brother Muhammad al-Zawahiri, who was freed after the revolution and held some symbolic authority over the Egyptian jihadi movement, "did not endorse Hazim, but he didn't oppose him either," recounts the son of Rifa'i Surur.[34]

The *qutbiyyun* who followed 'Abd al-Majid al-Shazli and his association, the Call of the Sunnis, did also choose to endorse Abu Isma'il. And of course there was the veteran Hafiz Salama, who was only too happy to appear with the candidate. Simply put, Abu Isma'il became a uniter of radical forces.

Perhaps most important, he was backed by an abundance of "ordinary," mainly younger people. Some came from the various Salafis currents, while others were drawn from outside of the movement, attracted by what the candidate symbolized.[35] To them, he looked like what Khalil el-Anani calls the "sheikh president": a perfect synthesis of sheikh—given who his father was, as well as his history preaching at his mosque and on the Salafi channels, where he really looked the part—and politician, with his Brotherhood background, profession, and apparent ease discussing politics and economics (even if he kept the conversation general).[36] Abu Isma'il's strength lay in his ability to gather the two dominant themes of 2011 Egypt under one umbrella discourse, without compromising either: Islam and revolution, or, more precisely, shari'a and *karama*—the call for dignity carried by the revolution.

The candidate's signature theme was a demand for full implementation of shari'a.[37] Incanted like a mantra, it was not rooted in a detailed political vision.[38] At most, the rhetoric of Abu Isma'il and his backers made it clear that they felt the purpose of both Islam and the revolution was to defend those of little means. "I don't know how we can accept," he said, "the ravaging and humiliation of our country's poor, not just by the police but by every arm of the state."[39] In October 2012 some revolutionary Salafi intellectuals, most of whom belonged to the Salafi Front, would take such thinking to its logical end, announcing what turned out to be an ephemeral "People's Party" (Hizb al-sha'b) geared "to the workers and farmers"; some observers labeled its rhetoric "leftist Salafism."[40]

Dignity, the second motif in Abu Isma'il's discourse, tied in directly with the first. Starting in late 2011, posters featuring the words "we will live in dignity" (*sanahya kiraman*, his campaign slogan) were plastered throughout Cairo and cities across Egypt. The theme was primarily expressed through an oft-repeated commitment to the January 25 revolution, which was seen as the germ of a revolutionary process rather than its culmination. For revolutionary Salafis, this idea was nearly an article of faith. They believed that "religion is fundamentally about defying oppression," says Ahmad Mawlana, a member (and spokesman) of the Salafi Front's political bureau and an Abu Isma'il supporter.[41] As 'Ali al-Raggal notes, this stance also stems from the intense repression suffered until 2011 by the milieus from which many of revolutionary Salafism's founding activists came.[42] Like the self-proclaimed Youth of the Revolution (Shabab al-thawra), and unlike most established political parties, Abu Isma'il and his followers thus regarded Mubarak's February 11 departure as just one step in—rather than the end of—a revolution that had to march on until all traces of the former regime had been eliminated.[43] This made the Supreme Council of the Armed Forces (SCAF), which ruled during the transitional phase, their new enemy; they continually derided it as a vestige (*feloul*, in Egyptian dialect) of the Mubarak era, a threat to the revolution.

Abu Isma'il's fight for dignity also entailed an unyielding nationalism that played on a mix of Islamic and Egyptian symbols and perpetually denounced the "foreign powers"—with the United States and Israel at the top of the list.[44] Indeed, Abu Isma'il was the only Islamist candidate who promised to annul the peace treaty that had bound Egypt to the Jewish state since 1979.[45] And when Osama bin Laden was killed in May 2011, Abu Isma'il celebrated him in a heartfelt tribute as one of the "*mujahideen*," in the tradition of "'Abdallah 'Azzam and Ahmed Yassin."[46]

In the eyes of his supporters, what distinguished Abu Isma'il from every other candidate was his lack of ambiguity. As blogger and supporter Muhammad Ilhami put it in January 2012:

> Sheikh Abu Isma'il is the perfect example of a man who speaks to the soul of those Muslims who love clarity and sincerity, who have no compunctions about expressing their goals and vision.... He doesn't try to please—not the foreign powers, nor the Egyptian power centers, nor the

revolutionary currents, nor the Islamists who gravitate to him. Because of this coherence, there are no contradictions in his declarations, there is no backtracking on his positions; these seem clearer and purer with each passing day![47]

REVOLUTIONARY SALAFISM BECOMES A TRUE POPULIST MOVEMENT

The earliest rumblings of revolutionary Salafism as a freestanding force (or very nearly so) in the public arena can be traced back to Friday, July 29, 2011, the first demonstration since the revolution to be organized only by religious forces.[48] Referred to as "Friday of the People's Will" (Jum'at al-irada al-sha'biyya), the event—held by the leading Islamic groups, including the Muslim Brotherhood and the Salafi Call—aimed to reaffirm the centrality of shari'a and demonstrate the power of the "religious camp."

Soon enough, though, its Brotherhood- and Call-affiliated organizers were drowned out by the throngs of independent Salafis: jihadis waving black flags and chanting "We are all Osama," loyalist Salafis with Saudi flags and signs that read "O Field Marshal, you are our leader" (meaning Field Marshal Mohamed Tantawi, then head of the SCAF), and a revolutionary Salafi contingent shouting anti-army slogans—much to the chagrin of Brotherhood and Call, who were tiptoeing around the SCAF at the time.[49] Over one stage hung a large banner with the likeness of Abu Isma'il.

From the way Midhat al-Haddad, leader of Alexandria's Brotherhood branch, tells it, one senses that the experience left the organization traumatized: "The Muslim Brotherhood had agreed to participate as long as it was allowed to share the stage and every voice was represented. But the Salafis monopolized the whole thing. They took over and tried to sideline the Brothers," who left early in protest.[50] The gathering, which liberal media outlets quickly dubbed "Kandahar Friday" (Jum'at Qandahar), would help set off parallel processes: polarization between liberals, shaken by the spectacle they had witnessed, and Islamists; and polarization between the Brotherhood and the Salafi Call, with the former accusing the latter of trying to outdo it and of letting its troops get out of hand—even though these "troops" did not exactly look to the Call for their marching orders.

Revolutionary Salafism's second public appearance (more orderly this time) took place during the so-called Mohamed Mahmoud Street events in late November 2011. On the eighteenth of that month a large demonstration was held in Cairo, with wide-ranging demands: power transfer to a civil authority, an end to military tribunals for civilians, and the retraction of supraconstitutional articles that some thought the army would try to impose without any democratic process. Nearly every faction of the political opposition participated, Islamist or otherwise.

As night fell, the Brotherhood left Tahrir Square along with the Call's Salafis; both still desperately wished to avoid escalation with the SCAF. But revolutionary activists, prepared for a showdown with the military, held their ground. Observers were surprised to note that even though the large Islamist parties had all abandoned ship, a surprising number of the remaining "die-hards" were indeed Islamists. These were mostly revolutionary Salafi followers of Abu Isma'il, who visited the square several times over the following days as clashes with the authorities intensified, leaving dozens dead. Each time he stopped by, usually addressing the crowd from a hastily mounted rostrum, a hush would fall over large sections of the plaza as people listened to, then cheered for, this increasingly unassailable revolutionary figure.[51] Despite their profound differences of opinion with Abu Isma'il, even the activists of the April 6 Youth Movement were enthralled by his bravery and determination in the face of the SCAF.[52] Muhammad Yusri Salama, who had resigned from his role as Nour Party spokesman a few months before these new Tahrir Square protests, later wrote that this was the moment when Abu Isma'il became "a strong bridge between the Islamist youth and the revolutionary youth."[53]

With the protests as backdrop, Abu Isma'il's presidential campaign truly took flight. As the Brotherhood and the Nour Party tried to appease the SCAF, hoping to tip the political balance by winning seats in the upcoming parliamentary election, they became the perfect foil for Abu Isma'il, the Steadfast Revolutionary. Moreover, the Brotherhood and Nour, eyes on the legislative prize, were daily watering down their Islamist rhetoric with soothing words for their detractors. The Nour Party assented to democratic procedures; explained that shari'a would be implemented only gradually; reaffirmed that—if it came to power—neither alcohol nor women's swimsuits would be banned (at least not universally); and included women on its parliamentary electoral lists, although it placed roses where their faces would have appeared on political brochures. Each compromise directly contradicted the vision advanced by Salafism in the prerevolutionary era. On an international level, Nour additionally mirrored the Brotherhood in announcing that it would not upend any existing treaties—a tacit acceptance of the peace agreement with Israel. In short, like the Brothers, the Nour Salafis seemed to have abandoned (or indefinitely postponed) plans for establishing the Islamic State.[54]

After the late 2011 swearing-in of a significant Islamic parliamentary majority comprising the Brotherhood and the Nour Party—and especially given the postrevolutionary context, when the population's hopes still ran high—both parties were paying dearly for their failure to address Egyptians' everyday problems. In reality, however, politicians' hands were pretty well tied as long as the executive branch remained under military control. Meanwhile, morality scandals took down two Nour legislators. First, Anwar al-Balkimi was forced to resign in early March 2012 because he got a nose job, which Salafism expressly forbids (the body is God's work), then lied that his face was bandaged due to an attack.[55] And in early June, 'Ali Wannis, another Salafi parliamentarian, was arrested after being caught roadside in a compromising position with a young woman.[56]

Next to the Brotherhood and the Nour Salafis, then, the "incorruptible" Abu Isma'il seemed like the last hope for the Islamist utopia that the others had given up on.[57] His movement bore every trait of populism, making him unique (and partly explaining his success) among Egyptian political candidates. Cas Mudde and Cristóbal Rovira Kaltwasser define populism as "a thin-centered ideology that considers society to be ultimately separated into two homogeneous and antagonistic camps, 'the pure people' versus 'the corrupt elite,' and which argues that politics should be an expression of the *volonté générale* (general will) of the people."[58]

Here, the "pure people" were the revolutionaries motivated by Islam and the call for shari'a, which expressed the *volonté générale*. ("The people," *al-sha'b*, was a concept that Abu Isma'il evoked surprisingly often for an Islamist.) The former regime and SCAF represented the primary "corrupt elite," but the category was gradually expanded to encompass all established political forces, including both the Brotherhood and the Call.[59] And Abu Isma'il's "ideology" did have a bit of a "thin center": It called itself Salafi—in 2011 Egypt this was the normative symbol in vogue—but it also borrowed from nationalism and from the left's demands for social justice, two other ideals that hadn't lost their cachet. Last, the charismatic leader, played here by Abu Isma'il, is a hallmark of populist movements.

Early on, Brothers and Salafis alike sensed the danger of such a phenomenon. It was out of fear that Abu Isma'il (or, to a lesser extent, Abu al-Futuh) might carry the election that the Brotherhood—which had sworn up and down that it wouldn't submit its own presidential candidate—in the end decided to run Khayrat al-Shatir, then Mohamed Morsi. For the Call sheikhs, the peril was greater still because Abu Isma'il, like them, identified with Salafism, but he bent its meaning to allow for a populist grammar of action, thereby jeopardizing their organization's symbolic authority. This made him an unacceptable alternative to Mohamed Morsi, whom the Call also saw as an existential threat. This ultimately led it to endorse Abu al-Futuh, a candidate with no apparent ambition to seize the religious field. To those Call members entranced by Abu Isma'il's charisma, Yasir Burhami would insist time and again that the man was no Salafi: He was a "Brother in disguise" and should be treated as such.[60]

Despite—or perhaps thanks to—opposition by the Brotherhood and the Call, Abu Isma'il's adoring crowds swelled as the presidential election neared, and his many evening talk show appearances bolstered his popularity. The candidate always came off as resolute but respectful of the host, offsetting his intransigence with a gentleness that seemed to soften his ideas. The smile he flashed at each interview and his signature preface—"I'm so glad you asked me that question" (*ana sa'id giddan annak sa'alt al-su'al da*)—furnished his critics, especially liberal comedian Bassem Youssef, with ample material for their caricatures.[61] Salafi television, meanwhile, was constantly abuzz with talk of Abu Isma'il; he was officially backed by the popular al-Hikma channel at the initiative of its president, Wisam 'Abd al-Warith.[62]

Abu Isma'il enjoyed so much support that tens of thousands of his admirers took to Salah Salim, the street that led to the Presidential Election Commission (PEC), as he submitted his candidacy on March 30, 2012, transforming a bureaucratic formality into a bona fide demonstration.[63] His application carried more than 150,000 signatures gathered by supporters; the other candidates' numbers seemed paltry in comparison. As early as March, several surveys predicted that he would win 20 percent of votes in the first round, and a few even had him leading the tally.[64]

The groundswell of support for Abu Isma'il sent waves that reached as far as the established Islamist political forces, some of whose members (or, more unnervingly, officials) defected or expressed support for him. Several Nour MPs, for example, veered from the party line and signed his electoral petition, while some of the most influential Salafi sheikhs also expressed their admiration for the candidate.[65] They included the Egyptian-Kuwaiti 'Abd al-Rahman 'Abd al-Khaliq, popular Salafi preacher Abu Ishaq al-Huwayni, Salafi-leaning Azhari Sheikh Mazin al-Sirsawi, critical Salafis Fawzi al-Sa'id and Hasan Abu al-Ashbal, and even Muhammad Isma'il al-Muqaddim and Ahmad Farid of the Salafi Call. Most telling was a March 28, 2012, announcement by the Consultative Council of Ulema (Majlis shura al-'ulama'), created just after the revolution, that after an internal vote it had decided to endorse Abu Isma'il.[66] (The council was made up of ten Salafi ulema from outside the critical movement, including three stars from the satellite channels—al-Huwayni, Muhammad Hassan, and Muhammad Hussein Ya'qub—along with ulema from Ansar al-Sunna and Call figure Sa'id 'Abd al-'Azim.)

Herein lies the paradox of Abu Isma'il's candidacy: His uncompromising, shari'a-centered rhetoric left Salafi sheikhs no choice but to support him, at least in appearance—and the Salafi youth were always there to apply pressure, lest the sheikhs forget their obligation. At the same time, Abu Isma'il represented a direct, significant challenge to their authority, hence their reluctance to offer him more than ephemeral gestures of support. The two Call sheikhs who had at first expressed approval of Abu Isma'il (whether guided by personal inclinations or by pressure from some of their base) would later retract it, falling in line with the Call's choice of Abu al-Futuh. But the tensions Abu Isma'il's candidacy had stoked within the Salafi movement remained extremely high.

Then came a spectacular turn of events, though typical for 2011–2013 Egypt. On April 14, 2012, with Abu Isma'il at his peak, seemingly on the verge of shattering the whole Islamist field and perhaps even winning, the PEC invalidated his candidacy. His mother had allegedly acquired American citizenship during her time in United States—a violation of the electoral regulations, which barred any candidate with a foreign-born or dual-citizen parent. Abu Isma'il cried foul, but there was no changing the commission's verdict; he was eliminated from the race.[67] A huge sigh of relief swept through all who had feared he would win: the Nour Party, the Brotherhood, and the vast majority of Egyptian political players.

The incident did nothing to quell the revolutionary furor of Abu Isma'il's followers, most of whom believed his removal was a conspiracy. A new wave of mobilization started gathering momentum: First, thousands of revolutionary Salafis besieged the PEC and the State Council in protest of the decision.[68] Abu Isma'il's angry supporters then moved on to Abbassia Square, not far from their ally Hafiz Salama's al-Nour Mosque and across from SCAF headquarters. In so doing, they crossed a line from which the Tahrir Square protestors had so far kept their distance.

The Abbassia protesters called for a new revolutionary uprising against these "military men who snatched back the revolution," but only a smattering of non-Islamist activists joined them—mostly from the "ultras" (soccer fans who became politicized during and after the events of 2011) and the April 6 movement. It's worth noting that the polarization had become quite severe between Islamists and non-Islamists by April 2012, and activists willing to stand shoulder-to-shoulder with those from the opposing camp were few and far between. Several revolutionary Salafis died and dozens were injured in violent confrontations with the army, which cleared the occupied square in a matter of days.[69] This was deeply traumatic to the participants, who felt betrayed by the other political forces and now saw themselves as the only "true" revolutionaries.

To round out its revolutionary credentials, the movement attempted to appropriate, and Islamicize, symbols of the uprising.[70] One closely associated online figure created a web page in 2012 called "We Are All Khalid Sa'id—Islamic Edition" to compete with the more liberal page "We Are All Khalid Sa'id" (*Kulluna Khalid Sa'id*), which had posted the first calls to demonstrate on January 25, 2011, in memory of the young Alexandrian whose death at the hands of police in June 2010 had so deeply moved activists.[71] Readership of the new page skyrocketed to the tens of thousands, making it among the most widely read by movement members.[72]

The revolutionary Salafis also extended their list of declared enemies to include all "secular" forces. Journalists, collectively accused of hostility toward the Islamic movement, bore the brunt of the criticism, which was indiscriminately trained on both broadcasters like Tawfiq 'Ukasha, who owned (and hosted on) the al-Fara'in channel, where he waxed nostalgic for the former regime, and Bilal Fadl, a liberal journalist and revolutionary since day one.[73] In December 2012 the activists held a sit-in at Media Production City (Madinat al-intaj al-i'lami), where all nonreligious media outlets were targeted regardless of political leaning.[74] Sheep named for the reviled "secularists" were sacrificed at the event, in what the press deemed a dangerous symbolic escalation.[75]

QUESTIONS OF HOW AND WHY: THE CHALLENGE OF ORGANIZING REVOLUTIONARY SALAFISM

As compared with established Islamic movements like the Brotherhood, the Salafi Call, or even the Jama'a Islamiyya, revolutionary Salafism stood out for its organizational fluidity and intricate networks. We saw how the movement was initially made up of individuals and small collectives who, on principle, rejected the idea of a centralized and structured group. They chose a leader who seemed confident that a large grassroots social movement would spring up around him, almost of its own accord. Mudde and Kaltwasser explain that this is another classic trait of populism, at least in its fledgling phase.[76] As Abu Isma'il's followers grew in number, new, mostly youth-based collectives formed that became the movement's most visible element, all loosely organized and with a rotating cast of leaders and spokespeople.

Al-Miqdad Gamal al-Din, a founder of the foremost collective, Hazimun (literally "The Determined Ones," although the term also evoked Abu Isma'il's first name), says it was created in September 2011 as a "mobile lobby for the message of Hazim Abu Isma'il."[77] His narrative is worth quoting at length, as it evokes the hope that these youth placed in Abu Isma'il.

> After listening to just an hour and a half of [Abu Isma'il's] lecture "Message to the Great People of Egypt," my friend and I were confident that this man was destined for greatness, that God had saved him especially for this historical moment in Egypt. When I left the gathering, I was a changed man. This was the first time someone had ever made me cry by speaking of slums and the plight of women. The first time I had encountered someone with both a vision and a true mission, someone both sincere and pious, and blessed with a captivating charisma. As I stepped out, I felt I was in a wonderful dream—and that's when the painful reality hit me. My friend said to

me, "You know that the Muslim Brotherhood will never endorse him. There's very little chance he'll be elected." I replied, "We will support and endorse him, whatever the cost, and God will forgive us if he loses."

Gamal al-Din then turned to the future:

Hazim Abu Isma'il will grow more popular; his message will draw great crowds because he speaks the truth. Every position Abu Isma'il takes will differ from the classic Islamist leaders: on street protests, on major crises, and on key issues like the constitution, the presidency, and even shari'a. And that is why this man will become a movement in his own right. His followers will evolve from simple voters into messengers and missionaries. But before long, there will be a drastic betrayal by all of the Islamist currents, stirring up a tidal wave within political Islam and leading to the fragmentation of every old-guard institution, from the Brotherhood to the Salafi Call. Those who defect will seek out other groups that exemplify this new message, which contrasts with all we have today.... This is why we decided to found the "Hazimun" movement. We chose the name, which is perhaps not the most fitting, to emphasize "Hazim," and to show that he now has disciples who take orders from him alone. The idea has spread, and the name has been increasingly used to refer to Hazim's followers, who with time have begun to feel that they are more than just voters or campaign workers. That way, whenever Hazim dies, history will carry on his message—because the Hazimun will live on.[78]

Other, similarly intentioned collectives appeared around the same time. Like the Hazimun, most of their names included a direct reference to Abu Isma'il, such as "Lazim Hazim" (We Need Hazim), a group founded by neighborhood sheikh Gamal Sabir. Along the same lines, Facebook pages appeared with names like "Awlad Abu Isma'il" (Children of Abu Isma'il) and "Hazim li kull al-masriyyin" (Hazim for All Egyptians).[79]

With all this focus on Abu Isma'il himself, however, questions had begun surfacing even within the movement—especially because, as one of his backers stated, "the heart of the matter isn't support for or opposition to Abu Isma'il; it is shari'a, nothing more and nothing less."[80] In addition, most of his followers readily admitted that the presidential election was but a pretext. They believed neither in the democratic system nor in its rules. The campaign offered an opportunity to take to the streets, to spread the message of revolutionary Salafism far and wide. Abu Isma'il personified this message, but it transcended both him and the election—which, in a nutshell, was the whole paradox of revolutionary Salafism: While the movement was out in the streets fighting the power, its leader was auditioning to *be* the power. After Abu Isma'il was removed from the race in April 2012, the question of which methods to employ became more pronounced.

Gradually, a consensus formed that revolutionary Salafism needed a structure independent of its charismatic figurehead—a stumbling block that most populist movements run into sooner or later.[81] Some activists felt that creating a political party would resolve the issue. This possibility had first been discussed a few days before the candidate's removal, when Sheikh 'Abd al-Rahman 'Abd al-Khaliq argued that "for the president to be strong, he must be supported by a strong, organized party."[82] Two days after Abu Isma'il's ejection, it was announced that a forthcoming party would "represent those who identified with his mission."[83] The Party of the Egyptian Nation (Hizb al-umma al-masriyya) would be led by the independent Islamist intellectual Muhammad 'Abbas, who since the 1980s had earned a reputation for both his political radicality and his religious intransigence.[84] More declarations were made over the following weeks, each suggesting that the party was about to become a reality—but it never did.[85]

In late 2012 it was announced that another party representing Abu Isma'il's political stances would soon be created. Called al-Raya (The Flag), its name referred to the variety of nationalistic symbolism that characterized the movement; the flag stood as much for Egypt as it did for the caliphate. Unlike the earlier initiative, this party would be overseen by Abu Isma'il himself. Lo and behold, in March 2013 came simultaneous announcements of the party's creation and of a new electoral alliance called "Coalition of the Nation." (Tahaluf al-umma can also be translated "Coalition of the Umma"; Abu Isma'il was again playing on homonymous references.) The coalition united al-Raya with six other small Salafi parties that were in conflict with Nour, most of which came from the critical Salafi movement (al-Fadila, al-Islah, al-'Amal, al-Hizb al-Islami, Hizb al-Sha'b, and Hizb al-Taghyir).[86] There had been talks with the al-Watan Party as well, but they were not successful.

Keep in mind that, while both the party and the coalition that had crystallized around it certainly planned to compete in the forthcoming legislative elections (initially scheduled for April 2013), this entry into party politics did not replace their street-based strategy. At the party announcement, Abu Isma'il even declared to loud cheers: "We will no longer keep off the streets, as we have done over the past months.... Starting today, we're taking them back. We will begin with Tahrir Square, and we won't stop until every single square is occupied."[87]

Al-Raya opened party offices in cities across Egypt and held initial meetings, but it never fully took shape; in fact, it never even got the party commission's stamp of approval. Indeed, barely had it been announced when the pace of political events began to accelerate: First the legislative elections were postponed, and then the anti-Morsi movement took center stage. Within a few months, the president had been removed and the political process recaptured by the army.[88] There were deeper reasons, however, for revolutionary Salafism's difficulty transitioning to the logic of party politics.

One problem was that while the movement had plenty of seasoned activists, it lacked leaders with the political experience—and the institutional and administrative know-how—necessary for such a conversion.[89] That, according to interviews with movement intellectuals, is what doomed the forever-postponed Party of the Egyptian Nation.[90] And then there was a more structural problem: Since revolutionary Salafism's raison d'être (again, like that of any populist movement) was of course to forgo institutional politics in favor of radical change—carried out by a "savior" said to embody the general will of the people—any acceptance of standard party politics could mean political suicide for the movement. As Yahya Rifa'i Surur, son of Sheikh Rifa'i Surur and an early Abu Isma'il backer, put it: "We are against the party structure. Parties kill ideas."[91] His comrade Khalid Harbi added that "the party structure imposes its rules on you; you've got no choice but to become a new iteration of the Muslim Brotherhood."[92]

In the spring of 2012, Al-Miqdad Gamal al-Din, mentioned earlier, had already said in no uncertain terms that "because we are revolutionaries, we refuse to allow the sheikh to create a party. It would be fated to repeat the Nour Party disaster. And if he chooses to do so—well, we won't go along with it. Because we want to become a revolutionary movement capable of exporting the revolution, and for that we first need the January revolution to succeed."[93] This explains why so many of Abu Isma'il's supporters (and the candidate himself) were at first so reluctant to enter into party politics, the pitfalls of which their rhetoric incessantly denounced. And when he ultimately decided to take the leap in March 2013, he took pains to clarify: "We are not announcing a new party as though this were an end in itself. What we're setting in motion is bigger than a party: It is a movement. The party is just one element of this movement, and depends on it.... Whatever our chosen name, whatever our stated cause, what matters is our common objective."[94]

It was also difficult to separate the almost messianic figure of Abu Isma'il from the revolutionary Salafism he represented. The earlier quote from al-Miqdad Gamal al-Din hints at the lingering ambiguity on this point: The revolutionary Salafi message may well have be fated to transcend Abu Isma'il, who was merely its vector, but it remained stubbornly intertwined with his person. Matters were further complicated by the fact that Abu Isma'il was no textbook politician. Rather than sticking to activism, pure and simple, he communicated with his followers through a mix of preaching and political commentary, whether from the pulpit of his Asad bin al-Furat Mosque (in Dokki, across the Nile from downtown Cairo) or on Salafi television shows.[95]

The debate over creating a party led some Abu Isma'il supporters to choose other forms of organization.[96] Some young activists from the Hazimun movement, for instance, recognized that revolutionary Salafism needed a structure and identity independent of its figurehead but prioritized keeping it popular and far removed from institutions—otherwise, it would become meaningless. Several movements (*harakat*) that formed starting in 2012 adopted this strategy. Unlike the decentralized Hazimun movement, these new groups took on leaders, skeletal structures, symbols (logos, slogans, etc.), and easily identified imagery. Among the new movements was Tullab al-Shari'a (which translates to either "Those Who Demand Shari'a" or "Students of Shari'a"), coordinated by Walid al-Haggag, which became increasingly visible starting in mid-2012. The larger Ahrar movement (Harakat ahrar, the "Freemen Movement"), which carried revolutionary Salafism toward new horizons, had similar roots and inspirations.

Ahrar was founded in the fall of 2012 by Hazimun youth, but the group immediately set its sights on a much broader unification; its stated goal was to reach across ideological frontiers.[97] It defined itself as "a youth movement uniting all young people who love freedom, in the truest and fullest sense of the word: Their own freedom, that of their country and homeland—the liberty that they find in following the path of authentic Islam, which should fill every Muslim with pride."[98] Political, economic, and cultural liberation (*taharrur*) were thus central to Ahrar's rhetoric, and the movement—borrowing directly or indirectly from a body of far-left Western literature (including authors like Noam Chomsky and Susan George), as well as from the writings of Salafi sheikhs like Safar al-Hawali of Saudi Arabia—thought of itself not just in terms of Egyptian concerns, but as part of a no-holds-barred fight against the hegemony (*haymana*) of the "new world order."[99] Ahrar, one of whose slogans was "Borders Are Just Dust" (*Al-hudud turab*), indeed advocated leaving behind the system of nation-states and embracing true, Umma-scale internationalism. This idea figured prominently in imagery the movement developed and in the words of its leaders—for example, the book *The Battle of the Freemen* by Ahmad Samir, which served as the organization's de facto handbook.[100] Ahrar also played on symbols from Islamic history, for example, with calls for long-lost Andalusia to be returned to the Umma and a sit-in at the Citadel of Saladin in Cairo.[101]

While Ahrar repeated that its goal was to "see Islam implemented in all its beauty and in its entirety," the group asserted—in accordance with revolutionary Salafi thinking—that it was "independent of all organizations, parties, and religious or political groups" and would "support the oppressed, whatever their religious, political or intellectual identity."[102] This open-ended rhetoric broke through to new audiences, for example, yielding some success with the ultras, the soccer supporters mentioned earlier who led street battles with the army and police during and after the revolution. Sayyid 'Ali Fahim, known as Sayyid Mushaghib (Sayyid the Troublemaker)— the "capo" of the Ultras White Knights, which supported the Zamalek Sporting Club—was among the movement's most emblematic recruits.[103] The Ultras culture actually played an important role in Ahrar: As a way of broadcasting its message, the movement composed a cappella anthems (which made them acceptable for the Salafis, who consider music illicit) that echoed the rhythms of football chants. In addition, Ahrar's Facebook page and its followers' graffiti adopted the symbols of the global "Anonymous" movement—especially the mask from the film *V for Vendetta*.[104]

These ties with "youth culture" allowed Ahrar to establish a noticeable presence among students, particularly at Cairo University and Mansoura University.[105]

REVOLUTIONARY SALAFISM, BROTHERHOOD RULE, AND THE COUP D'ÉTAT

Mohamed Morsi's presidential victory put the revolutionary Salafis in a position as uncomfortable as it was paradoxical. They continued to think of themselves as the opposition and maintained their harsh critiques of the president, yet they ended up siding with the Brotherhood whenever it clashed with liberals or members of the former regime.[106] This dynamic was particularly clear during the constitutional referendum in December 2012: While dissatisfied with the proposed text of the constitution, which they felt favored the military and considered insufficiently Islamic (even as the Brothers' liberal detractors complained it was too much so), the revolutionary Salafis refrained from criticizing it publicly for fear that their words could benefit their rivals.[107] At the time, Yahya Rifa'i Surur summed up the dilemma as follows: "We have profound disagreements with Morsi, but there is a conspiracy against him, and if he falls we will all go back to prison."[108]

Abu Isma'il's discourse reflected the same ambivalence. He had positioned himself as a fierce opponent of Brotherhood rule at the beginning of Morsi's term, denouncing the group's willingness to compromise with the former regime and its propensity toward ideological concessions.[109] But as a broad anti-Morsi contingent coalesced over the fall of 2012, bringing together liberals and those nostalgic for the old regime, Abu Isma'il softened his critiques, now casting them as simple recommendations. Soon before the June 30, 2013, demonstration—which would take down the Brotherhood president—Abu Isma'il joined the Islamist counteroffensive, slamming the "criminal" and "counterrevolutionary" mobilization. Meanwhile, the anti-Morsi crowd was busy appropriating symbols of the revolution. They were somewhat successful in this, which left the revolutionary Salafis—who were stuck acting as auxiliaries to the current regime and defending its institutions—feeling a little less, well, revolutionary.[110]

There was one exception within revolutionary Salafism: the Ahrar movement, which signaled its independence by refusing to compromise with the Brotherhood.[111] Ahrar unambiguously opposed the December 2012 constitution and, as the fateful date of June 30 drew near, refused to take sides, instead offering tongue-lashings to both the "merchants of blood" (*tujjar al-dam*) in the opposition and the "merchants of religion" (*tujjar al-din*) in the pro-Morsi camp.[112] "The revolution lives on," chanted Ahrar in an anthem called "They Betrayed" (*khanu*), written in June 2013, with "they" referring to Brothers, liberals, and the army.[113] The Brotherhood-Ahrar relationship had been particularly acrimonious since April of that year, when the movement blamed the Brothers for the arrests of several of its activists after violent protests at Mansoura University.[114]

The July 3 coup d'état caught the revolutionary Salafis off-guard; they now found themselves in the sights of the new regime, right along with the Brotherhood. Abu Isma'il was the first figure to be arrested, on charges that he had falsified the documents attesting to his mother's citizenship.[115] The new regime clearly understood that he was the only true charismatic leader in the Islamist camp—and thus the only person who could effectively galvanize the masses against the coup d'état.

The army's return to power offered the revolutionary Salafis, bereft of their mentor, a new chance to unfurl the flag of revolution that they had been forced to stow away. Ironically, though, nearly every one of their actions aligned with Brotherhood positions. Stripped of its elected president, the Brotherhood was now calling for an uprising against the military leadership, its stance approaching the radicality of Abu Isma'il's followers. Many revolutionary Salafis participated in the July 2013 sit-ins against the coup d'état, and some of their leaders addressed the crowds gathered in support of Morsi.

Soon, though, signs of a partial divide began to reappear: There was a much larger revolutionary Salafi presence at the first sit-in, on al-Nahda Square, than at the second one, on Rabaa al-Adawiya Square, where the Brotherhood was out in force. After August 14, when the authorities massacred participants at both locations, the revolutionary Salafis carried on protesting for months alongside the Morsi supporters, even though their objective (unlike that of the Brotherhood) wasn't so much to restore Morsi to power as to turn the tide and finally make their utopian dream a reality. And their agenda would sometimes steal the limelight, as in November 2014 when revolutionary Salafi activists, particularly from the Salafi Front, called for a "Muslim youth insurrection" (*intifadat al-shabab al-muslim*), a step toward an "Islamic revolution" against the regime.[116] The Brotherhood distanced itself from this appeal, continuing instead to insist on Morsi's electoral "legitimacy" (*shar'iyya*)—which the revolutionary Salafis couldn't have cared less about.[117] In any case, the "insurrection" failed, along with all the Brotherhood's attempts to restore "its" president.

In the wake of the coup d'état, Ahrar was, once again, the only movement born out of revolutionary Salafism to remain independent.[118] Rather than joining the bulk of Islamists at the al-Nahda and Rabaa al-Adawiya sit-ins, its activists launched their own protest on Sphinx Square, where they tried to organize a "third current" (*al-tayyar al-thalith*) hostile to both the Brotherhood and the army. Ahrar made connections with the followers of Islamo-centrist 'Abd al-Mun'im Abu al-Futuh, who had likewise dismissed both Morsi and his adversaries and was trying to present himself as an alternative to the two factions. But reconciling the one group's democratic slogans with the other's Islamist radicalism proved too tough a task, and the attempted collaboration fizzled out. In the fall of 2013 Ahrar played a major role in the demonstrations that blazed across Egyptian campuses, as confirmed by dozens of videos posted on social media at the time.[119] Despite the repression bearing down on it, the movement managed to continue mobilizing its followers until the end of 2014, at which point it fell off the radar.[120]

After years of persecution, the revolutionary Salafi movement (at least in its 2011–2013 form) now lies dormant. The context that catalyzed it—a public arena in which it could campaign for radical Islamic change—has vanished from present-day Egypt. Some of the movement's activists withdrew, discouraged, while others are imprisoned or living in exile, often in Istanbul, where they mingle with the Brothers. And then there are those who turned to armed violence.

One popular theory in el-Sisi's Egypt holds that revolutionary Salafism was nothing but a Trojan horse for jihadism, and so it was only natural that Abu Isma'il's followers should be among the first to join armed groups after the summer of 2013.[121] There is likely some truth to this suggestion.[122] Revolutionary Salafis represented the most radical force among the groups active in the Egyptian public sphere between 2011 and 2013, and most of the movement's organic intellectuals did not object to the idea of violence as a tool; whether it should be used depended on context. The Brotherhood's strong identity and solid hierarchy—whose word was law—ensured that relatively few Brothers took up arms.[123] But the revolutionary Salafi movement was more a collection of independent spirits that had no authority figure after Abu Isma'il's arrest.

What's more, while many within the jihadi current maintained their distance from Abu Isma'il, I described earlier how others had joined him. For these individuals, that meant renouncing violent tactics in favor of a "democratic" strategy. Some, like the jihadi Sheikh Ahmad 'Ashush, a fierce opponent of Abu Isma'il, attacked this abrupt shift to "democracy."[124] Therefore, rather than simply regarding revolutionary Salafism as one radicalized element of the Islamic field, I would also suggest that it helped deradicalize another element by bringing it around to nonviolent political action (even if in a populist style) rather than armed action. In postdemocratic Egypt, however, such considerations were no longer relevant.

What became of revolutionary Salafi activists after 2013? Few sources exist to help us piece together their story. Those that do are problematic: mostly articles published by a press that had lost all independence, some based on reports from state security agencies—and all this at a moment when the "Islamist question" was being highly politicized by a government laser-focused on taking down the Muslim Brotherhood and its supporters. But they do offer a window into a few telling trajectories, including that of Islam Yakin, a sports coach who apparently had been a devoted follower of Abu Isma'il starting in 2012 but left for Syria after the Rabaa al-Adawiya massacre, joining the Islamic State (IS) organization and making a name for himself with the brutal content of his social media posts.[125] Then there was Muhammad Nasr, a university professor described—again, by the Egyptian media—as one of Abu Isma'il's campaign managers, who is said to have founded a jihadi organization in the Sinai, which then joined Ansar Bait al-Maqdis, which in turn pledged its allegiance to IS.[126] The proregime Egyptian media published many other articles that described Abu Isma'il followers joining IS or al-Qaeda.[127]

Absent other sources, it is hard to judge the extent of this phenomenon. But I will say this: When revolutionary Salafis did shift to a violent approach, they didn't always join groups that identify with global jihad. It seems a subset of those who chose this path joined local organizations instead that advocated a more targeted form of "revolutionary violence" against Egyptian state agencies. These groups, which also attracted young

Brotherhood members at odds with their leadership's strategy of avoiding armed conflict with the new regime, included the Popular Resistance Movement (Harakat al-muqawama al-shaʿbiyya), Revolutionary Punishment (Iʿqab thawri), and Soldiers of Egypt (Ajnad masr).[128] An activist interviewed after many years in prison described how the Salafi Front members and their close collaborators—including some of Abu Ismaʿil's main backers—in fact acted as a major counterweight against the spread of IS ideology among the incarcerated.[129]

Today, revolutionary Salafi ideas are no longer embodied in an active structure. A handful of its exiled intellectuals, some of whom regrouped around online journals, nonetheless carry on the legacy of a moment when an Islamic revolution in the Sunni world—framed in terms of Salafism, the religious language of the moment—had seemed within reach.[130] The memory will no doubt live on among future generations of Islamists, in Egypt and beyond.

Rather than becoming a firmly established current, revolutionary Salafism symbolized a moment in Egypt's recent history as powerful as it was ephemeral, made possible by a perfect storm: open democratic transition in a climate where Salafism defined the norm among the religious field's dominant forces. It represented an attempt to merge Salafi discourse with populist grammar; the contradictions inherent to such a fusion surfaced as the movement wrestled with its longer-term approach. Strategic postponements paralyzed the movement, and history galloped onward without the revolutionary Salafis. When Abu Ismaʿil was finally forced to make a half-hearted venture into party politics, the democratic process was already on its way to the scrap heap. As Hazimun founder al-Miqdad Gamal al-Din—whose words opened the chapter and will help bring it to a close—bitterly writes, "Hazim could have been the Khomeini of the Egyptian revolution, or even of the Sunni world. Sadly, he decided to settle for being the sheikh of a party tied to an ideology that he had outgrown by far."[131]

More than anything, this moment epitomizes the Pyrrhic nature of Salafism's ascent to quasi-hegemonic norm. As their religious rhetoric became predominant, the sheikhs watched the grammar of action for the very movement they claimed to personify slip through their grasp, despite great effort to protect it. Meanwhile, competing interpretations of this grammar contradicted their own and subverted its meaning. Put simply, politics regained the upper hand. Olivier Roy writes that "when everything is religious, nothing is religious anymore."[132] In this case, one might say that "when everything is Salafi, nothing is Salafi anymore."

CONCLUSION

The Fortunes and Misfortunes of Egyptian Salafism

In less than a century, a normative revolution swept across Egypt, handing Salafism near-total symbolic dominance over the religious field. The preceding chapters have tried to pinpoint the primary motivations and processes that drove this transformation.

We saw how the rise of Salafism began with the work of normative entrepreneurs, who with dazzling success were able to harness the resources, both material and symbolic, that their undertaking required. The heart of the Salafi message remained untouched, but the activism that advanced it changed shape several times as it adjusted to each era's specificities: Whereas Ansar al-Sunna resembled a society of ulema (at least at first), the Salafi Call's mission was always to build Salafism into an organized social movement. These evolutions in form also expanded the message from the Salafism of Ansar al-Sunna—primarily a theological stance—to that of the Salafi Call, which became an all-encompassing ideology, a framework for all aspects of a believer's life that demanded total commitment.

But whatever its form, Salafi activism benefited throughout this period from largely favorable winds. The various currents received funding at critical moments in their histories from public or private actors in the Gulf region (though not always the Saudi state, especially for the Salafi Call). While there is no question that such financial support existed, and while its impact should not be underestimated, neither should it be viewed as the sole driver of Egyptian Salafism, which was mostly the product of a homegrown dynamic. Nonetheless, being able to plug into such an opulent transnational economy undeniably helped make the movement viable.

Throughout the decades, political circumstances also tended to smile on the Salafis. Regime after regime considered them the "lesser evil" as compared to their apparently more threatening competitors. The periods when the Muslim Brotherhood faced repression were actually a boon for Salafis, who deftly made the most of them. This makes sense when seen through the "purist" grammar of action that reigned within Salafism—a grammar based entirely on religious purification and which, unlike the Islamist grammar, always saw "top-down" Islamization as a pointless or even perilous endeavor whose methods only risked ruffling the authorities' feathers.

Last, the Salafis were able to take advantage of the vacuum left in the religious field by the simultaneous decline of official Islam's representatives, discredited by their close ties with successive regimes, and of the Brotherhood, whose attention and efforts were quite literally consumed by politics starting in the 1980s. With the others nowhere to be found, Salafis simply filled the void; they alone took up the mantle of the ulema, in a post-1967 society where religion was more and more in demand.

I identified three key periods in the development of Egyptian Salafism. During the first, from the 1920s through the 1960s, the Salafis waged a tireless campaign within the nascent religious publishing industry to promote authors who corresponded to their theological notions, starting with the triumvirate of Ibn Taymiyya, Ibn Qayyim, and Ibn Kathir. Despite the initially hostile reactions by Azhari ulema, who realized that this initiative could weaken their authority, the Salafis' efforts paid off with time. More agile and enterprising than their competitors, they largely won this "battle of the corpora"—a victory enhanced by the revolution of 1952, in whose aftermath they were the only religious actors still able to operate independently of the state; all others had either been co-opted or crushed.

The second period began in the late 1960s, when an "Islamic awakening" rose from crumbling Nasserism. Because the Salafis already had the upper hand in the battle of the corpora, and their mosques were the only ones not under direct state control, this awakening emerged from within their own movement. The Islamic advocacy that defined the 1970s was

CONCLUSION

mostly expressed in Salafi terms, which at that point had almost a complete normative hold on activist Islam.

The third period, which spanned Mubarak's reign (1981–2011), saw Salafism extend its reach beyond the milieus of religious activism to the larger community of believers—thanks to the Salafi Call's efforts to make Salafism a true social movement by breaking it free of narrower scholarly circles. The proliferation of Salafi "new preachers"—media "stars" who transformed Salafism into a universally accessible popular religious idiom via emerging technology (cassettes, then compact discs, and finally satellite channels, the internet, and social media)—also helped accelerate the movement's expansion.

In the late 2000s Egyptian Salafism was at the height of its influence. It represented the grassroots of a new orthodoxy and now defined the norm, which had several consequences. In the religious field, a new order of ulema was on the verge of replacing its forebears. The earliest members of this class were most often autodidacts, but its power began to be institutionalized, with newer Salafi elite now educated in preacher training institutes and/or at Gulf universities. This transition was taking place without the blessing of official bodies, but Salafism still gained influence—diffuse, but no less real—at al-Azhar and beyond. The Salafis managed to impose their authors and language, even on critics like the Muslim Brotherhood, which gave in to pressure from its "Salafi wing."

The beliefs and behaviors of the Egyptian Muslims were thus transformed as well—but to a lesser degree than one might imagine. A significant gap remained between what each individual saw as the norm and how he applied it to himself. And yet millions of Egyptians found a way to visibly unite theory and practice: These were the people one frequently saw in the late 2000s wearing short tunics with scruffy beards and no mustache, who flocked to the movement sheikhs' Friday sermons. Even when diffuse, this Salafi influence had a tangible impact on society: Relationships with Christians were dialed back to a strict minimum (the Salafi norm held that such mingling was harmful), and participation dropped in the large *mawlid*s, which often lost their festive atmosphere. A society guided by the Salafi religious norm must above all be austere.

On a political level, it wasn't clear at first how Salafism's increasing power would play out. The authorities had long seen the movement as an ally of convenience, as it seemed to offer an apolitical option to those searching for an observant Islamic practice. And it somehow remained apolitical—so long as purist grammar held sway. The problem was that, as Salafism became the norm, it matured into a common language to which anyone, from loyalist to critical Salafi, could help themselves. Starting with Sayyid Qutb, politicized and even revolutionary interpretations began to appear and, with them, a grammar of action far from the purism of the established sheikhs, who—especially at the Salafi Call—dedicated whole volumes to dismantling such interpretations and pushing purism over any sort of hybrid grammar.

In 2010 it dawned on the Egyptian regime that Salafi religious hegemony was not, in fact, benign. There were the crowds its preachers drew and their television audience; the expansion of an organization like the Salafi Call that, however purist its action, nonetheless represented an opposing social power; and, more than anything, the first demonstrations organized by the more politicized Salafi fringe. All this disquieted the aging Mubarak, aware that his power was simultaneously being challenged by a rising tide of antiregime sentiment within Egyptian society. His counteroffensive would be short-lived, interrupted within a matter of months by the Egyptian revolution of January 2011.

The two parallel but distinct processes that defined the 2000s would be set on a collision course by the transition following Mubarak's February 11 departure. The first process, political, involved a swath of Egyptian society increasingly hungry for freedom and rule of law within a representative system freed once and for all of nepotism and corruption. The second, religious, consecrated Salafism as the dominant religious idiom. As the processes intersected, democracy and Salafism would each push the other to its limit.

Given that politics in Egypt are rarely disentangled from religion (except as regards a minority of political actors), Salafism was poised to have a major impact on the transitional period. Whether through Nour—the Call-affiliated political party and the Muslim Brotherhood's chief competitor in parliament—or through the revolutionary Salafi movement epitomized by Hazim Abu Isma'il, Salafism's pervasiveness fed cutthroat political and religious competition that made it impossible for the Brotherhood to act as a centrist force, as the Ennahda Party had managed to do in Tunisia. Thus, rather than trying to bridge the perilous divide between Islamists and non-Islamists, the Brotherhood actively widened it, for fear of appearing insufficiently Islamic. This polarization ultimately played into the hands of the military and security officials behind the July 3, 2013, coup d'état.

Salafism itself emerged profoundly changed from those two interminable years. The abortive political transition confirmed the hypothesis that as Salafism became the norm, controlling its grammar of action would prove increasingly difficult—hence the tensions within the Nour Party and, in a more dramatic turn of events, the phenomenally successful poaching of Salafi discourse by a populist leader like Abu Isma'il. During the transition, nearly every possible political stance—pro- and anti-army, pro- and anti-Brotherhood, pro- and antirevolution—was adopted by one Salafi sheikh or another. In hindsight, those of the Call appear to have maintained a relatively consistent position amid the chaos by tailoring their actions to the purist grammar that had always guided them. But consistent or not, they did not fare much better than their competitors: Their chronic violations of the metarule of proclaimed solidarity—most flagrantly on July 3, when they supported the coup d'état, throwing the Brothers under the bus "for the good of the Call"—alienated a large share of their base. After the coup, Call leadership was forced to endorse a succession of religious opinions they had always opposed, and they fell from the pedestal on which many had placed them. The military regime of Field Marshal el-Sisi offered no recompense for the sheikhs' support, dashing their hopes as he slashed their influence while backing a reinvigorated al-Azhar.

Suffice it to say that the Salafis lost big by getting mixed up in politics. Indeed, how could the movement claim to be the interpreter of immutable religious rules when circumstances forced it to offer completely contradictory interpretations? And how to survive under an omnipresent state less tolerant than previous regimes of a nonstate organization like the Call and its potential social influence? But Salafism is not necessarily losing ground as the religious norm. Much time has elapsed since the movement first refashioned even its rivals' understanding of Islam. We should not, then, expect to see a sudden resurgence of mawlids; nor is an author like Ibn Taymiyya about to fade into the annals of history.

If the Salafi discourse faces any existential challenge today, it comes from the Gulf. For about fifteen years now, the United Arab Emirates (UAE) has been trying to support and export what some have called "neo-traditional Islam."[1] This updated incarnation of "traditional Islam" is Ash'ari, Sufi, attached to the canonical legal schools, and (most important to its Emirati advocates) fundamentally opposed to every twentieth-century Islamic movement, Brotherhood and Salafi alike, instead embracing political loyalism with the trappings of respectable "moderation." The UAE has introduced a plethora of institutions for this purpose; the highest-profile one in the Arab world is the Muslim Council of Elders (Majlis al-hukama' al-muslimin), presided over by al-Azhar's Grand Imam, Ahmad al-Tayyib, himself. This well-funded Emirati offensive supports—officially or officiously—a range of religious actors from most Arab countries, particularly Egypt.

With the rise of Crown Prince Mohammed bin Salman (MBS), Riyadh's new strongman, Saudi Arabia—the homeland of Salafism—is now being overtaken by the rhetoric of religious reform. Make no mistake: The prince wants to centralize authority in his own hands by shattering all extant opposing forces. This is a central purpose of his "Vision 2030," presented as a plan for radically transforming the kingdom, an initiative that has cost Saudi Salafism dearly. Ulema have largely been deprived of the autonomy they had enjoyed since the kingdom's founding. They have also lost a huge share of the financial backing for their proselytism, as MBS has little incentive to spread the "good word" abroad when this offers no immediate strategic gain. Government repression has eradicated the country's critical Salafi currents, which had long coexisted with the more official loyalist brand. Those loyalists who remain thus have no choice but to rubber-stamp the prince's decisions, even when these violate their own principles. With varying degrees of enthusiasm, they have become the spokesmen for an "open" Salafism—a far cry from the intransigence of yesteryear. Like the Egyptian Salafis before them, they have lost much of their religious credibility as they're forced to directly contradict their past positions.

The Emirati and Saudi offensives will certainly affect Salafism's normative status, although it is hard to predict by how much. And these attacks paralleled another development that had major consequences for Salafism: An Islamic State, founded by an eponymous organization (IS) according to Salafism's most unyielding ideals of "purity," took the fusion between jihadi and purist grammars to a new level. The demise of the group and its "state" in 2017 no doubt tempered the project's appeal. But IS leaves a powerful legacy within Salafism, whose zeitgeist it managed to capture at least for a time—despite repeated condemnations by all the movement's sheikhs.

We have entered the post-Salafi era, write researchers Ahmad Salim and 'Amr Basyuni, themselves close to the current.[2] I would not go that far, but I can say with certainty that one chapter is coming to a close. Salafism won the battle for the religious norm, even if this victory is now threatened in some quarters. The Salafi utopia, however, in both its purist and jihadi versions, has collapsed. In neither case did this happen under the weight of its contradictions alone. Rather, it was pummeled by its adversaries: one version by the Arab world's authoritarian regimes, and the other by Western armies. This is why Salafism—not as the embodiment of the religious norm, but as the activist expression of deep dissatisfaction with the world as it stands—will carry on, likely in new and unexpected forms.

NOTES

INTRODUCTION

Epigraph: Cyril Lemieux, *Le devoir et la grâce* (Paris: Economica, 2009), 24.
1. Max Weber, *The Vocation Lectures* (Indianapolis: Hackett, 2004).
2. For Bourdieu's discussion of fields, see, for example, Pierre Bourdieu, *Sociology in Question*, trans. Richard Nice (London: SAGE, 1993), 72f.
3. For more on this subject and on the discrepancy between normative statements and actual practices, see Samuli Schielke, *The Perils of Joy: Contesting Mulid Festivals in Contemporary Egypt* (Syracuse, NY: Syracuse University Press, 2012).
4. Field observations by the author, fall 2011.
5. Jonathan A. C. Brown, *Hadith: Muhammad's Legacy in the Medieval and Modern World* (Oxford: Oneworld Publications, 2009), 57.
6. Saba Mahmood, *Politics of Piety: The Islamic Revival and the Feminist Subject* (Princeton, NJ: Princeton University Press, 2005); Schielke, *The Perils of Joy*.
7. Carrie Rosefsky Wickham, *Mobilizing Islam: Religion, Activism and Political Change in Egypt* (New York: Columbia University Press, 2002), 157f.
8. François Burgat, *Understanding Political Islam* (Manchester, UK: Manchester University Press, 2020), 2.
9. Michel Foucault, "The Political Function of the Intellectual," *Radical Philosophy* 017 (Summer 1977), https://www.radicalphilosophy.com/article/the-political-function-of-the-intellectual.
10. For example, this is the definition 'Abd al-Mun'im al-Shahhat gives in his lecture "Salafism and the Methodologies of Transformation" (*al-salafiyya wa manahij al-taghyir*), 1st audiocassette. See also *Ma hiya al-salafiyya?*, https://ar.islamway.net/fatwa/77460/ال-السلف-فهم-عن-الخروج-يجوز-وهل-تنسب-من-إلى-و-السلفية-معنى-ما. صالح-في-تفسير-النصوص-الشرعية

INTRODUCTION

11. Henri Lauzière, *The Making of Salafism: Islamic Reform in the Twentieth Century* (New York: Columbia University Press, 2015), 21.
12. Lauzière, 37-40.
13. An eminent Azhari sheikh such as Muhammad Abu Zuhra (1898–1974) could thus, as early as 1971, employ the word "Salafism" unambiguously in his *History of the Islamic Schools*: "We use the term *salafiyyun* to designate those who have made the word their own. They appeared in the fourth century of the Hijra. They were Hanbali, and they said that all of their opinions could be traced back to Ahmad bin Hanbal. *Salafiyyun* reemerged in the seventh century of the Hijra, inspired by 'Sheikh of Islam' Ibn Taymiyya, and the very same views reappeared on the Arabian Peninsula in the twelfth century of the Hijra at the impetus of Muhammad 'Abd al-Wahhab." Muhammad Abu Zuhra, *Tarikh al-madhahib al-islamiyya fi-l-siyasa wa-l-'aqa'id wa tarikh al-madhahib al-fiqhiyya* (Cairo: Dar al-fikr al-'arabi, 1971), 177.
14. For more on this, see, for example, Bernard Haykel, "On the Nature of Salafi Thought and Action," in *Global Salafism: Islam's New Religious Movement*, ed. Roel Meijer (London: Hurst, 2009), 45-46.
15. Hamit Bozarslan, *Révolution et état de violence—Moyen-Orient 2011–2015* (Paris: CNRS Éditions, 2015), 91.
16. For more on Hanbalism as a theological school, see George Makdisi, *L'Islam hanbalisant* (Paris: Geuthner, 1983).
17. The four schools are the Maliki, Shafi'i, Hanafi, and Hanbali. Hanbalism is both a legal and a theological school.
18. The goal here is not to caricaturize "traditional Islam," which brilliant studies have demonstrated was anything but monolithic and rigid—see, for example, Khaled El-Rouayheb, *Islamic Intellectual History in the Seventeenth Century* (Cambridge: Cambridge University Press, 2015). But it can be said that, like Salafism, it held fast to a certain number of fundamentals.
19. Michael Cook, "The Origins of Wahhabism," *Journal of the Royal Asiatic Society* 2, 3rd series, no. 2 (July 1992): 191-202.
20. Khaled El-Rouayheb, "From Ibn Hajar al-Haytami (d. 1566) to Khayr al-Din al-Alusi (d. 1899): Changing Views of Ibn Taymiyya Among Non-Hanbali Sunni Scholars," in *Ibn Taymiyya and His Times*, ed. Yossef Rapoport and Shahab Ahmed (Oxford: Oxford University Press, 2010), 269-318.
21. Ahmed El Shamsy, *Rediscovering the Islamic Classics: How Editors and Print Culture Transformed an Intellectual Tradition* (Princeton, NJ: Princeton University Press, 2020), 166.
22. Lauzière, *The Making of Salafism*, 210.
23. Louis Gardet, "Les noms et les statuts. Le problème de la foi et des œuvres en Islam," *Studia Islamica*, no. 5 (1956): 78; Daniel Lav, *Radical Islam and the Revival of Medieval Theology* (Cambridge: Cambridge University Press, 2012), 28.
24. Haykel, "On the Nature of Salafi Thought," 40.
25. Henri Laoust, *Essai sur les doctrines sociales et politiques de Taqi ed Din Ahmad b. Taimiya* (Cairo: IFAO, 1939), 529-30.
26. Michael Crawford, *Ibn 'Abd al-Wahhab* (London: Oneworld Publications, 2014), Kindle ed., 1785/2779.

INTRODUCTION

27. Cole M. Bunzel, "Manifest Enmity: The Origins, Development and Persistence of Classical Wahhābism (1153–1351/1741–1932)" (PhD diss., Princeton University, 2018), 202.
28. Alexei Vassiliev, *The History of Saudi Arabia* (London: Saqi Books, 2000), 70-71.
29. Bunzel, "Manifest Enmity," 276.
30. In this text I am omitting the "al-" that would typically be required for Ibn al-Qayyim, thus simplifying the name as Ibn Qayyim to ensure consistency.
31. Crawford, *Ibn 'Abd al-Wahhab*, 1785/2779.
32. El-Rouayheb, "From Ibn Hajar al-Haytami," 306-7.
33. Quoted in Muhammad Qasim Zaman, *The Ulama in Contemporary Islam: Custodians of Change* (Princeton, NJ: Princeton University Press, 2002), 4.
34. Jon Hoover, "Ibn Taymiyya Between Moderation and Radicalism," in *Reclaiming Islamic Tradition: Modern Interpretations of the Classical Heritage*, ed. Elisabeth Kendall and Ahmad Khan (Edinburgh: Edinburgh University Press, 2016), 177-203.
35. El Shamsy, *Rediscovering the Islamic Classics*, 188, 197.
36. This was especially true starting in the nineteenth century. See Michael Cook, *Forbidding Wrong in Islam* (Cambridge: Cambridge University Press, 2003), 125-26.
37. Haykel, "On the Nature of Salafi Thought," 42-44.
38. Henri Laoust, "Le réformisme d'Ibn Taymiyya," *Islamic Studies* 1, no. 3 (September 1962): 27-47.
39. For example, the Saudi ulema cited this principle when they barred women from driving—not because such an act would go against Islam, but because it would lead to gender mixing on the roads, a slippery slope toward all sorts of "debauchery."
40. Glenn E. Robinson, quoted in Quintan Wiktorowicz, "Introduction," in *Islamic Activism: A Social Movement Theory Approach*, ed. Quintan Wiktorowicz (Bloomington: Indiana University Press, 2004), 3-4.
41. John D. McCarthy and Mayer N. Zald, "Resource Mobilization and Social Movements: A Partial Theory," *American Journal of Sociology* 82, no. 6 (May 1982): 1215.
42. Howard S. Becker, *Outsiders: Studies in the Sociology of Deviance* (New York: Free Press/London: Collier-Macmillan, 1966), 147-48.
43. Donatella della Porta and Mario Diani, *Social Movements: An Introduction*, 2nd ed. (Oxford: Blackwell, 2006), 74f.
44. Della Porta and Diani, 193f.; David S. Meyer and Debra C. Minkoff, "Conceptualizing Political Opportunity," *Social Forces* 82, no. 4 (April 2004): 1457-92.
45. Cyril Lemieux, *La sociologie pragmatique* (Paris: La Découverte, 2018), 58.
46. Lemieux, *Le devoir et la grâce*, 5.
47. Lemieux, *La sociologie pragmatique*, 58.
48. Charles Tilly, "Contentious Repertoires in Great Britain, 1758–1834," *Social Science History* 17, no. 2 (Summer 1993): 253.
49. Lemieux, *Le devoir et la grâce*, 48.
50. Richard P. Mitchell, *The Society of the Muslim Brothers*, 2nd ed. (Oxford: Oxford University Press, 1993), 234-35.
51. A recurring debate appears in the historiography of the Brotherhood about whether there were revolutionary stirrings in the late 1940s. Given the hindsight of nearly a century, potential discussion of a revolt—as yet unproven—would not,

for our purposes, cast doubt on the Brotherhood's predominant grammar. For more on this, see Mitchell, 73-79.
52. For a critical argument about the use of this term to describe Salafism, see Jacob Olidort, "The Politics of 'Quietist' Salafism," *Brookings Analysis Paper* (Washington, DC: Brookings Institution, 2015), https://www.brookings.edu/wp-content/uploads/2016/06/Olidort-Final-Web-Version.pdf.
53. For Gramsci's perspective on these ideas, see Antonio Gramsci, *Guerre de mouvement et guerre de position* (Paris: La Fabrique, 2012). This is a collection of essays taken from Gramsci's prison notebooks, which are available as a complete critical edition in English as *Prison Notebooks, Volumes I-III*, ed. and trans. Joseph A. Buttigieg with Antonio Callari (New York: Columbia University Press, 2011).
54. Quintan Wiktorowicz, "Anatomy of the Salafi Movement," *Studies in Conflict and Terrorism* 29, no. 3 (2006): 207-39.
55. For the debate on limitations, see Joas Wagemakers, "Revisiting Wiktorowicz: Categorising and Defining the Branches of Salafism," in *Salafism After the Arab Uprising: Contending with People's Power*, ed. Francesco Cavatorta and Fabio Merone (London: Oxford University Press, 2017), 7-24.
56. Mu'taz Zahir offers a good overview in his *Min al-masjid ila al-barlaman: dirasa hawla al-da'wa al-salafiyya wa hizb al-nur* (London: Takween, 2015), 132.
57. For example, this is the subject of the controversial book *Preachers at the Gates of Hell*. Islam Anwar al-Mahdi, *Du'a 'ala abwab jahannim* (N.p.: n.d.), https://dawa.center/file/2050.
58. Lemieux, *Le devoir et la grâce*, 81f.
59. Michel Dobry, *Sociologie des crises politiques* (Paris: Presses de la FNSP, 1986), 101, 150f.
60. Bourdieu, *Sociology in Question*, 72.
61. Raymond Boudon, *The Unintended Consequences of Social Action* (London: Palgrave Macmillan, 1977).
62. Jürgen Habermas, "The Public Sphere: An Encyclopedia Article (1964)," *New German Critique*, no. 3 (Fall 1974): 49-55; Armando Salvatore, *The Public Sphere: Liberal Modernity, Catholicism, Islam* (London: Palgrave Macmillan, 2007).
63. Howard S. Becker, "The Life History and the Scientific Mosaic," in *Sociological Work: Method and Substance—Essays by Howard S. Becker* (New York: Routledge, 2017), 69. On biographical illusion, see Pierre Bourdieu, "The Biographical Illusion," trans. Yves Winkin and Wendy Leeds-Hurwitz, in *Biography in Theory*, ed. Wilhelm Hemecker and Edward Saunders (Berlin: De Gruyter, 2017), 210-16.
64. See, for instance, Naïma Bouras, "Émergence d'un discours salafiste féminin en Égypte," *Afrique(s) en mouvement* 1, no. 2 (2020): 25-31.

1. BATTLE OF THE CORPORA

Epigraph: Abu al-Wafa' Darwish, *Sihat al-haqq*, 6th ed. (Beirut: Al-maktab al-islami, n.d.), 15.
1. Editorial from the first issue of *al-Hadi al-Nabawi*, published in 1936. Quoted in Mahmud al-Sayyid Muhammad, *Da'wat Ansar al-Sunna al-muhammadiyya wa sanawat min al-'ata'* (Cairo: Publications of Ansar al-Sunna's Public Center, n.d.), 29.

1. BATTLE OF THE CORPORA

2. Alexei Vassiliev, *The History of Saudi Arabia* (London: Saqi Books, 2000), 70–71. For another example, see the writings of Abu al-Wafa' Darwish, quoted in Ahmad al-'Afifi, "Abu al-Wafa' Muhammad Darwish wa juhuduhu li-dirasat al-'aqida al-islamiyya" (MA thesis, Cairo University, Faculty of Dar al-'ulum, 2009), 42–44.
3. Samuli Schielke, "Hegemonic Encounters: Criticism of Saints-Day Festivals and the Formation of Modern Islam in Late 19th and Early 20th-Century Egypt," *Die Welt des Islams* 47, no. 3-4 (2007): 327.
4. Michael Gilsenan, "Some Factors in the Decline of the Sufi Orders in Modern Egypt," *Muslim World*, no. 67 (1967): 11–8; Michael Gilsenan, *Saint and Sufi in Modern Egypt: An Essay in the Sociology of Religion* (Oxford: Clarendon Press, 1973), 47.
5. Catherine Mayeur-Jaouen, *Histoire d'un pèlerinage légendaire en islam. Le mouled de Tantâ du XIIIe siècle à nos jours* (Paris: Aubier, 2004), 156. See also Samuli Schielke, *The Perils of Joy: Contesting Mulid Festivals in Contemporary Egypt* (Syracuse, NY: Syracuse University Press, 2012), 113–14.
6. The expression was used by Jalal al-Din al-Suyuti, among others (Schielke, *The Perils of Joy*, 113). See also Rachida Chih, "La célébration de la naissance du prophète (al-Mawlid al-nabawi): aperçus d'une fête musulmane non canonique," *Archives de sciences sociales des religions* 2, no. 178 (2017): 177–94.
7. See, for example, the critique in *al-Manar*, 32nd year (Jumada al-ula 1351); also 'Abdallah al-Qasimi, *Shuyukh al-Azhar wa-l-ziyada fi-l-islam*, 2nd ed. (Beirut: Al-intishar al-'arabi, 2007), 12.
8. Itzchak Weismann, "Modernity from Within: Islamic Fundamentalism and Sufism," in *Sufis and Salafis in the Contemporary Age*, ed. Lloyd Ridgeon (London: Bloomsbury, 2015), 15.
9. David Commins, *The Wahhabi Mission and Saudi Arabia* (London: Tauris, 2006), 158.
10. Muhammad Rashid Rida, *Al-wahhabiyyun wa-l-hijaz* (Cairo: Manar Masr, 1344/1926), 13–14.
11. 'Abd al-Razzaq al-Bitar, quoted in 'Abdallah al-Bassam, *'Ulama' Najd khilal thamaniyat qurun*, 6 vols. (Riyadh: Dar al-'Asima, 1419), 3:115.
12. Al-Bassam, 3:114, 116. Al-Bassam evidently made a mistake here, as al-Subki described himself as Maliki.
13. Henri Lauzière, *The Making of Salafism: Islamic Reform in the Twentieth Century* (New York: Columbia University Press, 2015), 40.
14. 'Abduh in fact indicated his strong disagreement with Wahhabism, describing it as "the group that purported to brush off the dust of imitation to unveil the Quranic verses and the contents of the *hadiths*, in order to sift out God's judgments, but which proved to be more narrowminded and intolerant than the imitators themselves." Muhammad 'Abduh, *Al-islam bayna al-'ilm wa-l-madaniyya* (Giza: Wikalat al-sahafa al-'arabiyya, 2019), 156.
15. Malcolm H. Kerr, *Islamic Reform: The Political and Legal Theories of Muhammad 'Abduh and Rashid Rida* (Berkeley: University of California Press, 1966), 111; Catherine Mayeur-Jaouen, "'À la poursuite de la réforme': Renouveaux et débats historiographiques de l'histoire religieuse et intellectuelle de l'islam, XVe–XXIe siècle," *Annales. Histoire, sciences sociales* 73, no. 2 (June 2018): 329.
16. Schielke, *The Perils of Joy*, 114.

1. BATTLE OF THE CORPORA

17. Skovgaard-Petersen, for example, notes that Rida frequently quotes Ibn Qayyim al-Jawziyya in his fatwas, particularly to justify working outside of the schools of fiqh. See Jakob Skovgaard-Petersen, *Defining Islam for the State: Muftis and Fatwas of Dar al-Ifta* (Leiden: Brill, 1997), 75.
18. Barbara Metcalf, *Islamic Revival in British India: Deoband, 1860–1900* (Princeton, NJ: Princeton University Press, 1982), 352; Guido Steinberg, *Religion und Staat in Saudi-Arabien* (Würzburg: Ergon, 2002), 117.
19. David Commins, *Islamic Reform: Politics and Social Change in Late Ottoman Syria* (New York: Oxford University Press, 1990), 25.
20. Khaled El-Rouayheb, "From Ibn Hajar al-Haytami (d. 1566) to Khayr al-Din al-Alusi (d. 1899): Changing Views of Ibn Taymiyya Among Non-Hanbali Sunni Scholars," in *Ibn Taymiyya and His Times*, ed. Yossef Rapoport and Shahab Ahmed (Oxford: Oxford University Press, 2010), 311. While less well-versed in Ibn Taymiyya's writings than Rida would eventually be, Muhammad ʿAbduh, who admired the juridical independence of the Damascene scholar but shared neither his creed nor his intransigence, would all the same call him "the wisest of men regarding the sunna, and the most committed to the religion." See Muhammad ʿImara, *Rawaʾiʿ Ibn Taymiyya* (Cairo: Nur li-l-nashr wa-l-tawziʿ, 2017), 122.
21. Rida, *Al-wahhabiyyun wa-l-hijaz*, 6–8. The collection mostly included articles that had previously appeared in *al-Manar* and *al-Ahram*.
22. Lauzière, *The Making of Salafism*, 65–67.
23. Rainer Brunner, *Islamic Ecumenism in the Twentieth Century: The Azhar and Shiism Between Rapprochement and Restraint* (Leiden: Brill, 2004), 89–92. This transformation is apparent in Rida's collected writings on Shia: Muhammad Rashid Rida, *Al-sunna wa-l-shiʿa aw al-wahhabiyya wa-l-rafida* (Cairo: Dar al-nashr li-l-jamiʿat, 2010).
24. The curriculum of this institution appears in Jamal al-Banna, *Al-sayyid Rashid Rida: Munshiʾ al-Manar wa raʾid al-salafiyya al-haditha* (Cairo: Dar al-fikr al-islami, 2006), 139–54. One section of the curriculum focuses on "the struggle against superstitions and blameworthy innovations."
25. Mentioned in the biography of Muhammad ʿAbd al-Razzaq Hamza, http://www.saaid.net/Doat/gamdi/11.htm. For more on this, see, for example, Yaʿqub bin Yusuf al-Ibrahim, "Li-madha yunkir Jamal al-Banna dur raʾid khaliji min ruwwad al-Islah," *Al-Sharq al-Awsat* (May 29, 2009), https://elaph.com/Web/NewsPapers/2009/5/445459.html.
26. Faysal bin ʿAbd al-ʿAziz al-Samhan, *Al-Imam al-sayyid Rashid Rida fi mayadin al-muwajaha* (Kuwait: Maktabat ahl al-athar, 2011), 154–55.
27. Ibrahim al-Samannudi, *Saʿadat al-darayn fi al-radd ʿala al-firqatayn al-wahhabiyya wa muqallidat al-zahiriyya* (Cairo: Dar al-khulud li-l-turath, 2008), 11–36.
28. Taqi al-Din al-Hilali, *Kitab al-daʿwa ila-llah fi aqtar mukhtalifa* (N.p.: n.d.), 7, http://www.alhilali.net/المكتبة/10719-كتاب-الدعوة-إلى-الله-في-أقطار-مختلفة/.
29. Usama Shahada, "Silsilat rumuz al-islah 19—al-ʿallama Muhammad Hamid al-Fiqi," *Al-Rasid*, no. 127 (Muharram 1435), http://alrased.net/main/articles.aspx?selected_article_no=6412.
30. Nadia Elissa-Mondeguer, "Al-Manâr de 1925 à 1935: la dernière décennie d'un engagement intellectuel," *Revue des mondes musulmans et de la Méditerranée*, no. 95-98

1. BATTLE OF THE CORPORA

(April 2002); Muhammad ʿAbd al-ʿAziz al-Khuli, *Miftah al-sunna aw tarikh funun al-hadith* (Cairo: Dar al-kutub al-ʿilmiyya, 1991).
31. Husayn Ahmad Muhammad al-Sayyid, "Al-ʿilaqa bayna al-Azhar al-Sharif wa quwa wa jamaʿat al-tayyar al-islami fi masr min 1919 ila 1936" (MA thesis, Cairo, al-Azhar University, 2008), 134.
32. "Nubdha ʿan al-Shuqayri sahib al-sunan wa-l-mubtadiʿat" (November 30, 2008), https://www.islamweb.net/ar/fatwa/115548/نبذة-عن-الشقيري-صاحب-السنن-والمبتدعات.
33. Muhammad al-Shuqayri al-Hawamdi, *Al-sunan wa-l-mubtadiʿat al-mutaʿalliqa bi-l-adhkar wa-l-salawat* (Cairo: Maktabat Ibn Taymiyya, n.d.). The book specifically targets the Jamʿiyya Sharʿiyya and its founder, Mahmud Khattab al-Subki. For more on this, see Lauzière, *The Making of Salafism*, 125.
34. "Hiwar maʿ fadilat al-shaykh Safwat Nur al-Din," *Majallat al-Bayan*, no. 162 (Safar 1422): 65, http://islamport.com/w/amm/Web/135/3893.htm.
35. Al-Hilali, *Kitab al-daʿwa ila-llah fi aqtar mukhtalifa*, 16–29.
36. For more on this movement, see Ahmed El Shamsy, *Rediscovering the Islamic Classics: How Editors and Print Culture Transformed an Intellectual Tradition* (Princeton, NJ: Princeton University Press, 2020). See also Ahmad Khan, "Islamic Tradition in an Age of Print: Editing, Printing and Publishing the Classical Heritage," in *Reclaiming Islamic Tradition: Modern Interpretations of the Classical Heritage*, ed. Elisabeth Kendall and Ahmad Khan (Edinburgh: Edinburgh University Press, 2016).
37. For more on this, see, for example, Khan, "Islamic Tradition," 59. Ahmed El Shamsy gives the example of Ibn al-Jawzi, whose book *The Devil's Deception* (*Talbis iblis*, 1922) gave him a reputation for extreme hostility toward Sufism, while other, more moderate texts he wrote on the subject were neglected (and would only be published much later). See El Shamsy, *Rediscovering the Islamic Classics*, 240.
38. Khan, "Islamic Tradition," 60.
39. Khan, 81.
40. Henri Laoust, *Le traité de droit public d'Ibn Taymiyya* (Beirut: Institut Français de Damas, 1948).
41. ʿAʾida Ibrahim Nusayr, *Al-kutub al-ʿarabiyya allati nushirat fi masr fi-l-qarn al-tasiʿ ʿashar* (Cairo: American University in Cairo Press, 1990). See entries on Ibn Taymiyya, Ibn Qayyim, and Ibn Kathir.
42. Some books by Ibn ʿAbd al-Wahhab, such as *Thalathat al-usul fi-l-tawhid* (Cairo: Matbaʿat Mustafa al-Babi al-Halabi, 1900), seem to have been published at the turn of the twentieth century, but with limited distribution. See ʿAʾida Ibrahim Nusayr, *Al-kutub al-ʿarabiyya allati nushirat fi masr bayna ʿamay 1900–1925* (Cairo: American University in Cairo Press, 1983).
43. Nusayr, *Al-kutub al-ʿarabiyya allati nushirat fi masr bayna ʿamay 1900–1925*; ʿAʾida Ibrahim Nusayr, *Al-kutub al-ʿarabiyya allati nushirat fi masr bayna ʿamay 1926–1940* (Cairo: American University in Cairo Press, 1980).
44. Ami Ayalon, *The Arabic Print Revolution: Cultural Production and Mass Readership* (Cambridge: Cambridge University Press, 2016), 154–55.
45. ʿAbd al-ʿAziz Al Saʿud only formally adopted the title of king in 1932, but I use it throughout the book for consistency.
46. Less formal relationships continued, however. King ʿAbd al-ʿAziz even visited Cairo in 1931.

1. BATTLE OF THE CORPORA

47. Daniel Crecelius, "Saʿudi-Egyptian Relations," *International Studies* 4, no. 4 (October–December 1975): 571.
48. Stéphane Lacroix, *Awakening Islam: The Politics of Religious Dissent in Contemporary Saudi Arabia*, trans. George Holoch (Cambridge, MA: Harvard University Press, 2011), 14.
49. Al-Samhan, *Al-Imam al-sayyid Rashid Rida*, 141–48; for more on the relationship between Rida and ʿAbd al-ʿAziz, see Lauzière, *The Making of Salafism*, 1509/12282f.
50. See, for example, Sulayman bin Sahman, *Irshad al-talib ila ahamm al-matalib* (Cairo: Matbaʿat al-Manar, 1921); Sulayman bin Sahman, *Al-hadiyya al-saniyya wa-l-tuhfa al-wahhabiyya al-nadjiyya* (Cairo: Matbaʿat al-Manar, 1923); and the foundational *Majmuʿat al-rasaʾil wa-l-masaʾil al-najdiyya* (Cairo: Matbaʿat al-Manar, 1927).
51. Walid Saleh, "Preliminary Remarks on the Historiography of *Tafsir* in Arabic: A History of the Book Approach," *Journal of Qurʾanic Studies* 12 (2010): 15.
52. *Al-Manar* 6, no. 28 (1926): 472, quoted in Al-Samhan, *Al-Imam al-sayyid Rashid Rida*, 143.
53. Ahmad Zaghlul Shalata, *Al-hala al-salafiyya al-muʿasira fi masr* (Cairo: Madbuli, 2011), 192.
54. Henri Lauzière, "The Construction of *Salafiyya*: Reconsidering Salafism from the Perspective of Conceptual History," *International Journal of Middle East Studies* 42, no. 3 (August 2010): 383.
55. Usama Shahada, "Silsilat rumuz al-islah 18—al-ʿallama al-muhaqqiq Muhibb al-Din al-Khatib," *Al-Rasid*, no. 126 (Dhu al-Hijja 1434), http://alrased.net/main/articles.aspx?selected_article_no=6381.
56. See his biography on the Dar al-Iftaʾ website, "Fadilat al-shaykh Muhammad Bakhit al-Mutiʿi," http://www.dar-alifta.gov.eg/ar/ViewScientist.aspx?sec=new&ID=12&LangID=1.
57. Mahmud ʿAbd al-Hamid, *Tarikh al-daʿwa al-salafiyya*, lecture, www.anasalafy.com; https://www.youtube.com/watch?v=bEW4xxoj66Q (part 1); https://www.youtube.com/watch?v=Nv5X25yAcyM (part 2).
58. ʿAbd al-Hamid, *Tarikh al-daʿwa al-salafiyya*.
59. Catherine Mayeur-Jaouen, "Les débuts d'une revue néo-salafiste: Muhibb al-Dîn al-Khatîb et Al-Fath de 1926 à 1928," *Revue des mondes musulmans et de la Méditerranée*, no. 95-98 (April 2002), https://remmm.revues.org/234#ftn9.
60. Lauzière, "The Construction of *Salafiyya*," 377; Joseph H. Escovitz, "'He Was the Muhammad ʿAbduh of Syria'—a Study of Tahir al-Jazaʾiri and His Influence," *International Journal of Middle East Studies* 18, no. 3 (August 1986).
61. Mayeur-Jaouen, "Les débuts d'une revue néo-salafiste." For more on Yusuf al-Dijwi, see Muhammad Rajab al-Bayyumi, *Al-nahda al-islamiyya fi siyar aʿlamiha al-muʿasirin*, 2 vols. (Beirut: Al-dar al-shamiyya, 1995), 2:143–60.
62. Muhibb al-Din al-Khatib, *Al-khutut al-ʿarida li-l-usus allati qam ʿalayha din al-shiʿa al-imamiyya al-ithna ʿashariyya* (Cairo: Al-maktaba al-salafiyya, 1959), https://waqfeya.com/book.php?bid=5085.
63. El Shamsy, *Rediscovering the Islamic Classics*, 172.
64. Muhammad Munir ʿAbduh Agha al-Dimashqi, *Namudhaj min al-aʿmal al-khayriyya fi idarat al-tibaʿa al-muniryya* (Riyadh: Maktabat al-imam al-Shafiʿi, 1349/1930).

1. BATTLE OF THE CORPORA

65. Nusayr, *Al-kutub al-ʿarabiyya allati nushirat fi masr bayna ʿamay 1900–1925*; Nusayr, *Al-kutub al-ʿarabiyya allati nushirat fi masr bayna ʿamay 1925–1940*.
66. El Shamsy, *Rediscovering the Islamic Classics*, 168, 173f, 186–88. For example, the *maktaba zahiriyya* of Damascus holds many manuscripts written by Ibn Taymiyya and Ibn Qayyim (El Shamsy, 184).
67. ʿAbd al-Munʿim Munib, *Dalil al-harakat al-islamiyya* (Cairo: Maktabat Madbuli, 2010), 53.
68. Al-Bassam, *ʿUlamaʾ Najd khilal thamaniyat qurun*, 3:114.
69. James Heyworth-Dunne, *Religious and Political Trends in Modern Egypt* (Washington, DC: Self-published, 1950), 29.
70. Mahmud Khattab al-Subki, *Al-din al-khalis aw irshad al-khalq ila-l-din al-haqq*, 4th ed. (Cairo: Al-maktaba al-mahmudiyya al-subkiyya, 1977); "Al-jamʿiyya al-sharʿiyya ... miʾat ʿam min al-ʿataʾ," http://islamstory.com/الجمعية_الشرعية_مائة_عام_من_الدعوة_والتنمية-.
71. Mahmud Khattab al-Subki, *Fatawa al-ʿulamaʾ al-muslimin bi-qatʿ lisan al-mubtadiʿin* (Cairo: Al-matbaʿa al-husayniyya bi kafr al-tamaʿin, n.d.). Al-Subki did not categorically reject the mawlid; he was mostly critical of its wild celebrations and dedicated a book to the subject. See Mahmud Khattab al-Subki, *Al-maqamat al-ʿaliyya fi-l-nashʾa al-fakhima al-muhammadiyya* (Cairo: Matbaʿat al-saʿada, n.d.). For al-Subki's definition of "proper Sufism" (*al-tasawwuf al-sahih*), see Mahmud Khattab al-Subki, *Al-ʿahd al-wathiq li-man arada suluk ahsan tariq* (Cairo: Matbaʿat Hassan, 1980).
72. Frederick De Jong, "Opposition to Sufism in Twentieth-Century Egypt (1900–1970): A Preliminary Survey," in *Islamic Mysticism Contested: Thirteen Centuries of Controversies and Polemics*, ed. Frederick De Jong and Bernd Radtke (Leiden: Brill, 1999), 316; Sarah Ben Néfissa, "Citoyenneté morale en Égypte: une association entre État et Frères musulmans," in *ONG et gouvernance dans le monde arabe*, ed. Sarah Ben Néfissa et al. (Paris/Cairo: Karthala-CEDEJ, 2004), 213–71.
73. Al-Subki, *Al-din al-khalis*, 1:16.
74. Regarding conflicts with Ansar al-Sunna, see Ahmad Muhammad al-Tahir, *Jamaʿat Ansar al-Sunna al-muhammadiyya: Nashʾatuha, ahdafuha, manhajuha, juhuduha* (Riyadh: Dar al-fadila/Dar al-hadi al-nabawi, 2004), 149.
75. Mahmud Khattab al-Subki, *Ithaf al-kaʾinat bi-bayan madhhab al-salaf wa-l-khalaf fi-l-mutashabihat*, 2nd ed. (Cairo: N.p., 1974). For more on this book, see also Lauzière, *The Making of Salafism*, 123f.
76. Interview with Usama al-Azhari.
77. Aaron Rock-Singer, "The Salafi Mystique: The Rise of Gender Segregation in 1970s Egypt," *Islamic Law and Society*, no. 23 (2016): 286–88. Regarding how the prohibition on gender mixing became such a central feature of Salafism, in both Saudi Arabia and Egypt, see Aaron Rock-Singer, *In the Shade of the Sunna: Salafi Piety in the Twentieth Century Middle East* (Oakland: University of California Press, 2022), 137–69.
78. Ben Néfissa, "Citoyenneté morale en Égypte"; "Raʾis al-jamʿiyya al-sharʿiyya bi-masr: nushrif ʿala 6000 masajid" (April 6, 2005), http://almoslim.net/node/86714.
79. Heyworth-Dunne, *Religious and Political Trends in Modern Egypt*, 90.
80. "Raʾis al-jamʿiyya al-sharʿiyya bi-masr."
81. *Al-Hadi al-Nabawi*, no. 17–18, 6th year (Ramadan 1361): 29.

1. BATTLE OF THE CORPORA

82. Muhammad Yusri Salama, "Al-salafiyyun wa-l-aqbat fi masr—ru'ya fi-l-judhur wa-l-ishkaliyyat wa-l-tahaddiyat," in Al-Misbar, *Al-aqbat fi Masr ba'd al-thawra* (Dubai: Markaz al-Misbar, 2012), 207.
83. Rock-Singer, in *In the Shade of the Sunna*, eloquently describes how Ansar al-Sunna placed increasing importance on these issues, in line with transformations occurring in Saudi religious discourse throughout the second half of the twentieth century.
84. Al-Tahir, *Jama'at Ansar al-Sunna al-muhammadiyya*, 87; Shahada, "Silsilat rumuz al-islah 19."
85. For example, see the article in *al-Hadi al-Nabawi*, no. 1 (Rabi' al-Thani 1356), republished at http://www.alukah.net/culture/0/55069/.
86. Al-Tahir, *Jama'at Ansar al-Sunna al-muhammadiyya*, 87.
87. "Tarjamat al-shaykh Muhammad Hamid al-Fiqi," http://www.ansaralsonna.com/web/play-1622.html.
88. Al-Hilali, *Kitab al-da'wa ila-llah fi aqtar mukhtalifa*, 10.
89. Al-Tahir, *Jama'at Ansar al-Sunna al-muhammadiyya*, 88.
90. Shahada, "Silsilat rumuz al-islah 19."
91. 'Abdallah bin 'Ali al-Najdi al-Qasimi, *Al-buruq al-najdiyya fi iktisah al-zalamat al-dijwiyya* (Cairo: Matba'at al-Manar, 1931); 'Abdallah al-Ghumari, *Qat' al-'uruq al-wardiyya min sahib al-buruq al-najdiyya* (Leiden: Dar al-Mustafa, 2007), 45.
92. Sulayman bin Salih al-Kharashi, *'Abdallah al-Qasimi... wijhat nazar ukhra!* (Beirut: Rawafid li-l-tiba'a wa-l-nashr wa-l-tawzi', 2008), 35; Jürgen Wasella, *Vom Fundamentalisten zum Atheisten: Die Dissidentenkarriere des Abdallah al-Qasimi, 1907–1996* (Gotha: J. Perthes, 1997), 50.
93. Wasella, *Vom Fundamentalisten zum Atheisten*, 49.
94. 'Abdallah al-Qasimi, *Shuyukh al-azhar wa-l-ziyada fi-l-islam* (Cairo: Matba'at al-Manar, 1932); *Al-fasl al-hasim bayna al-wahhabiyyin wa mukhalifihim* (Cairo: Matba'at al-Tadamun al-Akhawi, 1934); *Al-thawra al-wahhabiyya* (Cairo: Matba'at Masr, 1936); *Al-sira' bayna al-islam wa-l-wathaniyya* (Cairo: Al-Matba'a al-Salafiyya, 1937); *Kayf dall al-muslimun* (Cairo: Matba'at Ansar al-Sunna al-Muhammadiyya, 1940).
95. Al-Kharashi, *'Abdallah al-Qasimi*, 246.
96. Wasella, *Vom Fundamentalisten zum Atheisten*, 53.
97. See the many refutations of his writings gathered by Sulayman al-Kharashi: Al-Kharashi, *'Abdallah al-Qasimi*.
98. Biography of Muhammad 'Abd al-Razzaq Hamza, http://makkahscholars.com/scholar/mo-hamza/.
99. 'Adil al-Sayyid, *Al-hakimiyya wa-l-siyasa al-shar'iyya 'inda shuyukh jama'at Ansar al-Sunna al-muhammadiyya* (Cairo: Dar al-Ibana, 2009), 63-64.
100. Shahada, "Silsilat rumuz al-islah 19."
101. Quote from an interview with Jamal al-Murakibi in *Majallat al-Bayan*, no. 256 (December 2008).
102. Al-Tahir, *Jama'at Ansar al-Sunna al-muhammadiyya*, 98.
103. *Al-Hadi al-Nabawi*, no. 1 (Rabi' al-thani 1356): 23, quoted in Al-Tahir, *Jama'at Ansar al-Sunna al-muhammadiyya*, 91.
104. Undated interview of Safwat Nur al-Din in the Yemeni journal *al-Furqan*, http://www.altawhed.net/article.php?i=397.

1. BATTLE OF THE CORPORA

105. Munib, *Dalil al-harakat al-islamiyya*, 55.
106. Al-Fiqi himself published works such as *Fath al-Majid*, by Wahhabi Sheikh 'Abd al-Rahman bin Hasan, as well as *Ijtima' al-juyush al-islamiyya*, by Ibn Qayyim. See al-Sayyid, *Al-hakimiyya wa-l-siyasa al-shar'iyya*, 25-26.
107. 'Abd al-Rahman al-'Aql, *Jamharat maqalat al-'allama al-shaykh Ahmad Muhammad Shakir* (Riyadh: Dar al-Riyadh, 2005), 66-108.
108. Muhammad Hamid al-Fiqi's critical edition of the book by 'Abd al-Rahman bin Hasan Al al-Shaykh, *Fath al-majid sharh kitab al-tawhid*, 7th ed. (Cairo: Matba'at al-sunna al-nabawiyya, 1957), 282.
109. Al-Sayyid, *Al-hakimiyya wa-l-siyasa al-shar'iyya*, 65, 67, 119, 102.
110. Al-Sayyid, 106.
111. Zaghlul Shalata, *Al-hala al-salafiyya al-mu'asira fi masr*, 210.
112. Malika Zeghal, *Gardiens de l'islam: les oulémas d'al-Azhar dans l'Égypte contemporaine* (Paris: Presses de Sciences Po, 1996), 81.
113. *Al-Hadi al-Nabawi*, no. 1-2, 6th year (Muharram 1361): 21-25, 26-30, 32-34, 35.
114. Al-Sayyid, *Al-hakimiyya wa-l-siyasa al-shar'iyya*, 127, 141.
115. Muhammad, *Da'wat Ansar al-Sunna al-muhammadiyya*, 38; 'Abd al-Rahman al-Wakil, *Hadhihi hiya al-sufiyya*, 4th ed. (Beirut: Dar al-kutub al-'ilmiyya, 1984), 12. One of the sources he cites is Goldziher, the Islamicist. See Al-Wakil, 101.
116. Al-Wakil, *Hadhihi hiya al-sufiyya*, 124, 16, 93, 180. See also Richard Gauvain, "Egyptian Sufism Under the Hammer: A Preliminary Investigation into the Anti-Sufi Polemics of Abd al-Rahman al-Wakil (1913-1970)," in *Sufis and Salafis in the Contemporary Age*, ed. Lloyd Ridgeon (London: Bloomsbury, 2015), 33-57.
117. Gauvain, "Egyptian Sufism Under the Hammer," 48-51, for example.
118. Gauvain, 48-49.
119. Muhammad, *Da'wat Ansar al-Sunna al-muhammadiyya*, 38.
120. Sulayman al-Kharashi, "Al-nasiha al-dhahabiyya li-l-asha'ira al-mu'asirun . . . li-l-shaykh 'Abd al-Rahman al-Wakil Rahamahu Allah," http://www.saaid.net/Warathah/Alkharashy/mm/52.htm.
121. 'Abd al-Rahman al-Wakil, *Al-baha'iyya: Tarikhuha wa 'aqidatuha wa silatuha bi-l-batiniyya wa-l-sahyuniyya* (Cairo: Dar al-madani, 1962).
122. "Ansar al-Sunna tutalib bi-ilgha' mawlid al-Sayyid Zaynab wa tasif al-ihtifal bihi bi-l-takharif," *Al-Masri al-Yawm* (July 15, 2009). See also Zaghlul Shalata, *Al-hala al-salafiyya al-mu'asira fi masr*, 229.
123. Al-Sayyid, *Al-hakimiyya wa-l-siyasa al-shar'iyya*, 189.
124. "Antum sufara'una al-diniyyun fi kulli makan." See Al-Sayyid, 153-54.
125. Al-Sayyid, *Al-'ilaqa bayna al-Azhar al-Sharif wa quwa wa jama'at al-tayyar al-islami*, 111.
126. Al-Sayyid, *Al-hakimiyya wa-l-siyasa al-shar'iyya*, 100; Al-Tahir, *Jama'at Ansar al-Sunna al-muhammadiyya*, 92.
127. Al-Sayyid, *Al-hakimiyya wa-l-siyasa al-shar'iyya*, 148.
128. Muhammad Hamid al-Fiqi, *Athr al-da'wa al-wahhabiyya fi-l-islah al-dini wa-l-'umrani fi jazirat al-'arab wa ghayriha* (Cairo: Matba'at al-nahda, 1935); Muhammad Khalil Harras, *Al-haraka al-wahhabiyya: radd 'ala maqal Muhammad al-Bahi fi naqd al-wahhabiyya* (Beirut: Dar al-kitab al-'arabi, 1985).
129. Muhammad Hamid al-Fiqi, *Azhar min Riyadh: sirat al-imam al-'adil 'Abd al-'Aziz bin 'Abd al-Rahman al-Faysal Al Sa'ud* (Cairo: Dar 'ilm al-salaf, 2008).

1. BATTLE OF THE CORPORA

130. Ahmad Salim, "Al-wahhabiyya fi Masr," in *Al-wahhabiyya wa-l-salafiyya: awraq bahthiyya* (Beirut: Al-shabaka al-'arabiyya li-l-abhath wa-l-nashr, 2016), 289.
131. Shahada, "Silsilat rumuz al-islah 19."
132. Shahada.
133. One of Muhammad 'Abd al-Razzaq Hamza's biographers suggests that it was Rida who recommended him and Abu al-Samh to King 'Abd al-'Aziz. See 'Abd al-'Aziz bin 'Abd al-Latif bin 'Abdallah Al al-Shaykh, *Mashahir 'ulama' Najd wa ghayruhum* (Riyadh: Dar al-yamama li-l-bahth wa-l-tarjama wa-l-nashr, 1974), 514.
134. Al-Tahir, *Jama'at Ansar al-Sunna al-muhammadiyya*, 91.
135. Al-Shaykh, *Mashahir 'ulama' Najd wa ghayruhum*, 501; Al-Tahir, *Jama'at Ansar al-Sunna al-muhammadiyya*, 92–93.
136. "Hiwar ma' al-shaykh Fathi 'Uthman," *Majallat al-Bayan*, no. 277 (November 7, 2010), http://www.albayan.co.uk/mobile/MGZarticle2.aspx?ID=368; Al-Tahir, *Jama'at Ansar al-Sunna al-muhammadiyya*, 93.
137. According to Safwat Nur al-Din's biography of him in *al-Tawhid*, no. 3, 28th year (Rabi' al-awwal 1414); Nabil Mouline, *Les Clercs de l'islam: autorité religieuse et pouvoir politique en Arabie Saoudite XVIIIe–XXIe siècle* (Paris: PUF, 2011), 178.
138. Lacroix, *Awakening Islam*, 47.
139. Al-Tahir, *Jama'at Ansar al-Sunna al-muhammadiyya*, 91.
140. Al-Sayyid, *Al-hakimiyya wa-l-siyasa al-shar'iyya*, 153.
141. Al-Tahir, *Jama'at Ansar al-Sunna al-muhammadiyya*, 93–94.
142. As Jamal al-Murakibi explained in an interview. See *Majallat al-Bayan*, no. 256.
143. Muhammad, *Da'wat Ansar al-Sunna al-muhammadiyya*, 96. The author does, however, mention donations from "certain upstanding people" (*ba'd ahl al-khayr*), whose nationality is not specified.
144. *Al-nas al-kamil li-taqrir lajnat taqassi al-haqa'iq hawla al-tamwil al-ajnabi li-l-jam'iyyat al-ahliyya bi-masr*, https://aljaras.wordpress.com/2012/01/04/الكامل-لتقرير-لجنة-تقصى-الحقائق-ح/.
145. See, for example, Ahmad al-Tahir's discussion in *Jama'at Ansar al-Sunna al-muhammadiyya*, 139f.
146. See, for example, Al-Sayyid, *Al-'ilaqa bayna al-Azhar al-Sharif wa quwa wa jama'at al-tayyar al-islami*, 154.
147. Al-Fiqi, for example, signs most of his books as follows: "Muhammad Hamid al-Fiqi, member of the venerable al-Azhar (*min jama'at al-azhar al-sharif*) ... and president of the Ansar al-Sunna al-Muhammadiyya Association."
148. *Al-Hadi al-Nabawi*, no. 2, 1st year (Jumada al-ula 1353): 6–7. Quoted in Al-Sayyid, *Al-'ilaqa bayna al-Azhar al-Sharif wa quwa wa jama'at al-tayyar al-islami*, 108.
149. Al-Sayyid, *Al-'ilaqa bayna al-Azhar al-Sharif wa quwa wa jama'at al-tayyar al-islami*, 118. The fatwa in question is included in the book's annex (no. 5). Followers of theological Hanbalism use the term *mu'attila* pejoratively to attack those they accuse of "invalidating" the divine attributes (especially by interpreting them as metaphor).
150. Al-Sayyid, 126, 128–29.
151. Al-Sayyid, 129. Some of these articles were assembled and republished as *Maqalat wa fatawa al-shaykh al-Dijwi* (Cairo: Dar al-kitab al-sufi, 2011).
152. Al-Sayyid, 130.

1. BATTLE OF THE CORPORA

153. The complete title is *Radd al-Imam al-Darimi 'Uthman bin Sa'id 'ala Bishr al-Marisi al-'anid*, ed. Muhammad Hamid al-Fiqi (Beirut: Dar al-kutub al-'ilmiyya, n.d.).
154. Al-Sayyid, *Al-'ilaqa bayna al-Azhar al-Sharif wa quwa wa jama'at al-tayyar al-islami*, 147.
155. Shahada, "Silsilat rumuz al-islah 19."
156. Al-Sayyid, *Al-'ilaqa bayna al-Azhar al-Sharif wa quwa wa jama'at al-tayyar al-islami*, 134-35, 138. The book in question is 'Abdallah al-Ghumari, *Qat' al-'uruq al-wardiyya min sahib al-buruq al-najdiyya* (Leiden: Dar al-Mustafa, 2007).
157. Al-Sayyid, *Al-'ilaqa bayna al-Azhar al-Sharif wa quwa wa jama'at al-tayyar al-islami*, 142, 146, 148, 131.
158. Al-Tahir, *Jama'at Ansar al-Sunna al-muhammadiyya*, 142-44.
159. Al-Wakil would even tell Shaltut that "the members of the association consider him their religious guide." See Al-Tahir, 144.
160. Brunner, *Islamic Ecumenism in the Twentieth Century*, 320.
161. Al-Sayyid, *Al-'ilaqa bayna al-Azhar al-Sharif wa quwa wa jama'at al-tayyar al-islami*, 147-48.
162. Shahada, "Silsilat rumuz al-islah 19."
163. Ansar al-Sunna dedicated an entire journal issue to sharing its side of the story. See *al-Hadi al-Nabawi*, no. 21-22, 6th year (Dhu al-qa'da 1361).
164. In his book *The Moulids of Egypt*, McPherson laments the Wafd government's efforts to control, and sometimes suppress, the mawlids. See J. W. McPherson, *The Moulids of Egypt* (Cairo: Ptd. N. M. Press, 1941), 11-12.
165. François Burgat, *L'Islamisme en face* (Paris: La Découverte, 2007), 69f.
166. Hasan al-Banna writes: "Islam is a total system that encompasses every aspect of life. It is state and motherland, government and nation." See Ibrahim al-Bayyumi Ghanim, *Al-fikr al-siyasi li-l-imam Hasan al-Banna* (Cairo: Markaz madarat li-l-abhath wa-l-nashr, 2012), 243.
167. "Al-ikhwan al-muslimun wa-l-sufiyya," https://www.ikhwanwiki.com/index.php?title=الإخوان_المسلمون_والصوفية.
168. Husam Tammam, *Tasalluf al-ikhwan: takul al-utruha al-ikhwaniyya wa su'ud al-salafiyya fi jama'at al-ikhwan al-muslimin* (Alexandria: Maktabat al-iskan dariyya/wahdat al-dirasat al-mustaqbaliyya, 2010), 8.
169. Richard P. Mitchell, *The Society of the Muslim Brothers*, 2nd ed. (Oxford: Oxford University Press, 1993), 214-15.
170. Tammam, *Tasalluf al-ikhwan*, 8.
171. Tammam, 7; Brunner, *Islamic Ecumenism in the Twentieth Century*, 180.
172. Youssef Nada (with Douglas Thompson), *Inside the Muslim Brotherhood: The Truth About the World's Most Powerful Political Movement* (London: Metro Publishing, 2012), 51-68.
173. Even if this sentence does not appear in al-Banna's writings, the Muslim Brotherhood often attributes it to him. See Mitchell, *The Society of the Muslim Brothers*, 217.
174. Quoted in Mitchell, 14. See also Hasan al-Banna, "Al-ikhwan fikra islahiyya shamila," in *Rasa'il al-imam al-shahid Hassan al-Banna*, https://www.ikhwanwiki.com/index.php?title=رسائل_الإمام_الشهيد_حسن_البنا.
175. Tammam, *Tasalluf al-ikhwan*, 16.

1. BATTLE OF THE CORPORA

176. Tammam, 9. In 1920s Egypt the effendis were the educated middle class who emerged from the modernization that began in the nineteenth century. See, for example, Lucie Ryzova, *L'Effendiyya ou la modernité contestée* (Éditions du CEDEJ, e-book, 2013), https://books.openedition.org/cedej/923.
177. Tammam, *Tasalluf al-ikhwan*, 9. See Beth Baron, *The Orphan Scandal: Christian Missionaries and the Rise of the Muslim Brotherhood* (Stanford, CA: Stanford University Press, 2014).
178. Zakariyya Sulayman Bayyumi, *Al-Ikhwan al-muslimun wa-l-jama'at al-islamiyya fi-l-haya al-siyasiyya al-masriyya 1928–1948*, 2nd ed. (Cairo: Maktabat Wahba, 1991), 272.
179. "Al-ikhwan al-muslimun wa-l-jam'iyya al-shar'iyya wa ansar al-sunna," http://ikhwanwiki.org/index.php?title=الإخوان_المسلمون_والجمعية_الشرعية_وأنصار_السنة.
180. "Al-ikhwan al-muslimun aw al-ikhwan al-masriyyun bayna al-ams wa-l-yawm," *Al-Hadi al-Nabawi*, no. 6 (Jumada al-Ula 1365).
181. Muhammad bin 'Awad bin 'Abd al-Ghani, *Lamahat 'an da'wat al-ikhwan al-muslimin* (Cairo: Dar sabil al-mu'minin, 2010), 10.
182. "Uqim wajhak li-l-din hanifan ya fadilat al-ustadh!!," in 'Abd al-Ghani, *Lamahat 'an da'wat al-ikhwan al-muslimin*, 25–26.
183. "Al-Iman qayd al-fatak," in 'Abd al-Ghani, *Lamahat 'an da'wat al-ikhwan al-muslimin*, 20.
184. Muhammad Nasir al-Din Al-Albani, *Silsilat al-huda wa-l-nur*, no. 37, cassette no. 1; see also http://kulalsalafiyeen.com/vb/showthread.php?p=285903.
185. This is what Samuli Schielke demonstrates regarding mawlids, against which modernists and Salafis united, sometimes even borrowing the others' arguments. See Schielke, *The Perils of Joy*, 123–26.
186. Khan, "Islamic Tradition," 61–62, 71; El Shamsy, *Rediscovering the Islamic Classics*, 212.
187. Saleh, "Preliminary Remarks on the Historiography," 29–30; Ignaz Goldziher, *Die Richtungen der Islamischen Koranauslegung* (Leiden: Brill, 1920). See J.J.G. Jansen, *The Interpretation of the Koran in Modern Egypt*, 2nd ed. (Leiden: Brill, 1980), 6.
188. El Shamsy, *Rediscovering the Islamic Classics*, 182.
189. For more on the relationship between language and power, see Pierre Bourdieu, *Language and Symbolic Power*, trans. Gino Raymond and Matthew Adamson (Cambridge: Polity Press, 1991).

2. EGYPT AFTER NASSER

Epigraph: Lecture by Sheikh Abu Ishaq al-Huwayni, *Al-kiyasa fi-l-siyasa*, part 2, https://www.youtube.com/watch?v=H3maLmagEY4.
1. One example is Gilles Kepel, *Muslim Extremism in Egypt: The Prophet and Pharaoh* (Berkeley: University of California Press, 1985).
2. Emmanuel Sivan, *Radical Islam: Medieval Theology and Modern Politics*, enl. ed. (New Haven, CT: Yale University Press, 1990).
3. Richard P. Mitchell, *The Society of the Muslim Brothers*, 2nd ed. (Oxford: Oxford University Press, 1993), 105–62.

2. EGYPT AFTER NASSER

4. Kepel, *Muslim Extremism in Egypt*. In Arabic, see Ahmad Ra'if, *Al-bawwaba al-suda'* (Cairo: Al-zahra' li-l-i'lam al-'arabi, 1985).
5. Law 247 of 1953. This was followed by a second law in 1957 that allowed this money to be spent for purposes that were not exclusively religious. See 'Amr 'Izzat, *Li-man al-manabir al-yawm? Tahlil siyasat al-dawla fi idarat al-masajid* (Cairo: Al-mubadara al-masriyya li-l-huquq al-fardiyya, 2014), 17.
6. Law 157 of 1960. 'Izzat, *Li-man al-manabir al-yawm?*, 18.
7. Malika Zeghal, *Gardiens de l'islam: les oulémas d'al-Azhar dans l'Égypte contemporaine* (Paris: Presses de Sciences Po, 1996), 102f.
8. Tamir Moustafa, "Conflict and Cooperation Between the State and Religious Institutions in Contemporary Egypt," *International Journal of Middle East Studies* 32, no. 1 (February 2000): 5-6.
9. Zeghal, *Gardiens de l'islam*, 103-4.
10. 'Ammar 'Ali Hasan, *Al-tanshi'a al-siyasiyya li-l-turuq al-sufiyya fi masr: thaqafa dimuqratiyya wa masar al-tahdith lada tayyar dini taqlidi* (Cairo: Dar al-'ayn li-l-nashr, 2011), 155-56.
11. Zakariyya Bayyumi, *Al-sufiyya wa lu'bat al-siyasa fi masr al-haditha wa-l-mu'asira: dirasa tarikhiyya watha'iqiyya* (Desouk: Al-'ilm wa-l-iman li-l-nashr wa-l-tawzi', 2009), 68.
12. Interview with Zakariyya Bayyumi.
13. Muhammad 'Izz al-'Arab, "Al-tawajjuhat al-siyasiyya li-l-turuq al-sufiyya fi masr," *Aswat Masriyya*, no. 33 (Summer 2006).
14. Husam Tammam, *Tasalluf al-ikhwan: takul al-utruha al-ikhwaniyya wa su'ud al-salafiyya fi jama'at al-ikhwan al-muslimin* (Alexandria: Maktabat al-iskandariyya /wahdat al-dirasat al-mustaqbaliyya, 2010), 12.
15. 'Adil al-Sayyid, *Al-hakimiyya wa-l-siyasa al-shar'iyya 'inda shuyukh jama'at Ansar al-Sunna al-muhammadiyya* (Cairo: Dar al-Ibana, 2009), 217-19, 174.
16. The Brotherhood had nearly 500,000 members at the time. See Salih al-Wardani, *Al-haraka al-islamiyya fi masr: al-waqi' wa-l-tahaddiyat* (Cairo: Maktabat dar al-kalima, 2000), 360.
17. Michael Gilsenan, *Recognizing Islam* (London: Tauris, 1993), 242.
18. Ahmad Muhammad al-Tahir, *Jama'at Ansar al-Sunna al-muhammadiyya: Nash'atuha, ahdafuha, manhajuha, juhuduha* (Riyadh: Dar al-fadila/Dar al-hadi al-nabawi, 2004), 149.
19. Ministerial decree (*qarar wizari*) no. 71 of 1967, May 22, 1967.
20. 'Abd al-Ghaffar Shukr, ed., *Al-jam'iyyat al-ahliyya al-islamiyya fi masr* (Cairo: Dar al-amin li-nashr wa-l-tawzi', 2001), 33; interview with Jamal al-Murakibi, *Majallat al-Bayan*, no. 256 (December 2008).
21. Sarah Ben Néfissa, "Citoyenneté morale en Égypte: une association entre État et Frères musulmans," in *ONG et gouvernance dans le monde arabe*, ed. Sarah Ben Néfissa et al. (Paris/Cairo: Karthala-CEDEJ, 2004): 213-71; Muhammad al-Sarwi, *Tanzim 65—al-zalzal . . . wa-l-sahwa* (1955-1975), part 1, http://www.ikhwanwiki.com/index .php?title=(1965)_الجزء_الأول_:_الواقع_المصري_بين_عامي_1954_-_1965)_ونشأة_تنظيم .&direction=next&oldid=29364, 73.
22. Shukr, *Al-jam'iyyat al-ahliyya al-islamiyya fi masr*, 33.
23. Ministerial decree no. 1 of 1973, January 3, 1973.
24. Al-Tahir, *Jama'at Ansar al-Sunna al-muhammadiyya*, 148.

2. EGYPT AFTER NASSER

25. Al-Tahir, *Jama'at Ansar al-Sunna al-muhammadiyya*, 149. Interviews with Usama al-Azhari and with Anas Sultan touched on the point as well.
26. Based on informal examination of *al-Tawhid* issues published between 1973 and 2013.
27. Al-Tahir, *Jama'at Ansar al-Sunna al-muhammadiyya*, 148.
28. Muhammad Jamil Ghazi mainly published critical editions of Ibn Qayyim al-Jawziyya and Ibn Taymiyya. See Muhammad al-Majdhub, *'Ulama' wa mufakkirun 'araftuhum*, 3 vols. (Riyadh: Dar al-shawwaf li-l-nashr wa-l-tawzi', 1992), 3:181, 182, 183f; Muhammad Jamil Ghazi, *Al-sufiyya—al-wajh al-akhar* (Alexandria: Dar al-iman, 2007).
29. My observations, September 2010.
30. In 1961—during the period when Egypt and Syria were united as the United Arab Republic—a large Ibn Taymiyya festival (*mahrajan al-imam Ibn Taymiyya*) was held in Damascus with support from the highest levels. Participants included a large number of Egyptian and Syrian intellectuals and ulema. See Muhammad Yusri Salama, *Mu'jam ma tubi'a min musannafat shaykh al-islam Ibn Taymiyya* (Alexandria: Dar al-tawhid li-l-turath, 2010), 44.
31. See, for example, Muhammad Rashad Salim, *Muqarana bayna al-Ghazali wa Ibn Taymiyya* (Kuwait: Dar al-qalam, 1992).
32. Tala'at Radwan, *Al-thaqafa al-masriyya wa-l-usuliyya al-masriyya qabl wa ba'd thawrat yulyu 1952* (Cairo: Al-dar li-l-nashr wa-l-tawzi', 2010), 101.
33. *Al-shaykh al-duktur Muhammad Rashad Salim*, https://al-maktaba.org/book/31616/79611.
34. Salama, *Mu'jam ma tubi'a*, 45–46. For a biography of Salim, see http://www.alukah.net/culture/0/3189/.
35. Husam Tammam, "Mustafa Hilmi: Ba'th wa tajdid al-salafiyya falsafiyyan" (August 2, 2003), http://www.onislam.net/arabic/islamyoon/salafists/95743-2003-08-02%2000-00-00.html; Ahmad Farid, *Hadith al-dhikrayat* (Alexandria: Dar al-Majd, 2008), 31.
36. Husam Tammam, "Muhammad Rashad Ghanim: madrasa salafiyya fi mahall antikat" (June 27, 2007), http://www.onislam.net/arabic/islamyoon/salafists/119470-2007-06-27%2017-02-54.html.
37. Al-Sarwi, *Tanzim 65*, 82.
38. 'Abdallah al-'Aqil, "Al-da'iya al-rabbani... al-shaykh Ibrahim 'Izzat," http://alaqeelabumostafa.com/charDetails.asp?CharID=12583.
39. 'Urabi Faruq, "Ibrahim 'Izzat... mu'assis al-tabligh fi masr," in Al-Misbar, *Suwwah min ajl al-da'wa: jama'at al-tabligh* (Dubai: Markaz al-Misbar, 2012), 320; Al-Sarwi, *Tanzim 65*, 83.
40. Muhammad Faraj, "Al-tabligh wa-l-da'wa fi masr: ishkaliyyat wa qadaya," in Al-Misbar, *Suwwah min ajl al-da'wa*, 148. As a reminder, the niqab is a full face veil.
41. Marc Gaborieau, "Tablīghī djamā 'at," in *Encyclopaedia of Islam*, ed. P. Bearman et al., 2nd ed. (Leiden: Brill, 1998).
42. 'Abd al-Mun'im Munib, *Dalil al-harakat al-islamiyya* (Cairo: Maktabat Madbuli, 2010), 56–57.
43. Ra'if, *Al-bawwaba al-suda'*, 321–33.
44. Salah al-Din Hasan, *Al-salafiyyun fi masr* (Giza: Dar awraq, 2012), 125–34.

2. EGYPT AFTER NASSER

45. Munib estimated that there were around 250,000 Egyptian Tabligh members when his book was published in 2010. Munib, *Dalil al-harakat al-islamiyya*, 57; "Jama'at al-Tabligh... i'tizalat al-siyasa fa-i'tazalatha Amn al-Dawla," *Al-Wafd* (September 22, 2011), https://alwafd.news/اعتزلت-التبليغ-جماعة-98965/وملفات-حوارات. السياسة-فاعتزلها-أمن-الدولة.
46. Al-Sarwi, *Tanzim* 65, 76.
47. Al-Sayyid, *Al-hakimiyya wa-l-siyasa al-shar'iyya*, 220.
48. "Salafization" is Husam Tammam's expression. See Tammam, *Tasalluf al-ikhwan*.
49. 'Abbas al-Sisi, *Fi qafilat al-ikhwan al-muslimin*, 2, https://www.ikhwanwiki.com /index.php?title=في_قافلة_الإخوان_المسلمين_الجزء_الثاني
50. Mahmud Jami', *Wa 'araft al-ikhwan* (Cairo: Dar al-tawzi' wa-l-nashr al-islamiyya, 2003), 141.
51. Jami', 142.
52. Al-Sarwi, *Tanzim* 65, 159.
53. Al-Sarwi, 199. Muhammad al-San'ani (1688–1759) was a Yemeni scholar and contemporary of Muhammad bin 'Abd al-Wahhab. Some of his writings are popular among Salafis.
54. Tammam, *Tasalluf al-ikhwan*, 12.
55. Rainer Brunner, *Islamic Ecumenism in the Twentieth Century: The Azhar and Shiism Between Rapprochement and Restraint* (Leiden: Brill, 2004), 184; Aaron Rock-Singer, "The Salafi Mystique: The Rise of Gender Segregation in 1970s Egypt," *Islamic Law and Society*, no. 23 (2016): 289.
56. *Sawanih al-dhikrayat ma' al-duktur Yasir Burhami* (biographical interview with Sheikh Yasir Burhami on the al-Dalil channel), part 1 (September 2011), https:// www.youtube.com/watch?v=8g1ENaBUBAI.
57. Olivier Carré, *Mystique et politique: Lecture révolutionnaire du Coran par Sayyid Qutb, Frère musulman radical* (Paris: Presses de Sciences Po, 1984).
58. For more on *hakimiyya*, see Stéphane Lacroix, "Ḥākimiyya," in *Encyclopaedia of Islam*, ed. Kate Fleet et al., 3rd ed. (Leiden: Brill, 2017).
59. For a fairly thorough discussion of Qutb's ideas, see Kepel, *Muslim Extremism in Egypt*, 36-59. See also Carré, *Mystique et politique*; John Calvert, *Sayyid Qutb and the Origins of Radical Islamism* (London: Hurst, 2010).
60. Kepel, *Muslim Extremism in Egypt*, 43.
61. Sayyid Qutb, "Siha fi wajh wizarat al-ma'arif ... sahhahu akazib al-tarikh," *Majallat al-Risala*, no. 1001, Cairo (August 9, 1952). Quoted in 'Ali Fahd al-Zumay', *Fi-l-nazariyya al-siyasiyya al-islamiyya* (Kuwait: Waqf Nuhud, 2018), 220.
62. Ahmad 'Abd al-Majid, *Al-ikhwan wa 'Abd al-Nasir: al-qissa al-kamila li tanzim 1965* (Cairo: Al-Zahra' li-l-i'lam al-'arabi, 1991), 75-77.
63. 'Abd al-Majid, *Al-ikhwan wa 'Abd al-Nasir*, 79.
64. Daniel Lav, *Radical Islam and the Revival of Medieval Theology* (Cambridge: Cambridge University Press, 2012), 54-55, 57.
65. Sivan, *Radical Islam*, 102.
66. Itzchak Weismann, "Modernity from Within: Islamic Fundamentalism and Sufism," in *Sufis and Salafis in the Contemporary Age*, ed. Lloyd Ridgeon (London: Bloomsbury, 2015), 17.
67. Carré, *Mystique et politique*.

2. EGYPT AFTER NASSER

68. See, for example, Salafi author Ihsan al-'Utaybi's *Waqafat ma' kitab "Fi zilal al-qur'an,"* https://www.saaid.net/Doat/ehsan/74.htm, where he lists Qutb's theological errors.
69. The fact that Qutb wasn't truly a Salafi—again, at least not as the term is defined in this book—also explains why his works managed to travel so far beyond Salafi-like circles. In Morocco, for example, the Sufi and Ash'ari sheikh 'Abd al-Salam Yassin looked to Qutb's example when he founded the Islamist al-'Adl wa-l-Ihsan movement.
70. For more on this episode, see Barbara H. E. Zollner, *The Muslim Brotherhood: Hasan al-Hudaybi and Ideology* (London: Routledge, 2009).
71. Kepel, *Muslim Extremism in Egypt*, 61.
72. Lav, *Radical Islam*, 72.
73. Sivan, *Radical Islam*, 104, 107.
74. Karl Mannheim, "The Problem of Generations," in *Essays on the Sociology of Knowledge*, ed. P. Kecskemeti (London: Routledge and Kegan Paul, 1952), 276–320.
75. This is according to Muhammad Habib, a former Brotherhood figure who was a young adult (and close to Ansar al-Sunna) during that era. See Muhammad Habib, *Dhikrayat al-duktur Muhammad Habib 'an al-hayat wa-l-da'wa wa-l-siyasa wa-l-fikr* (Cairo: Dar al-shuruq, 2012), 106.
76. "A primary source" became "*the* primary source" when the constitution was amended in 1980.
77. Interview with Zakariyya Bayyumi.
78. Muntasir al-Zayyat, *Al-jama'at al-islamiyya: ru'ya min al-dakhil* (Cairo: Dar Masr al-mahrusa, 2005), 77–78. There were 21,000 of these by 1980, for a total of 28,000 mosques in all; see Shukr, *Al-jam'iyyat al-ahliyya al-islamiyya fi masr*, 58.
79. Al-Subki's son in fact added four pages on the prohibition against gender mixing to his father's magnum opus. See Rock-Singer, "The Salafi Mystique," 286–88.
80. See, for example, Ahmad bin Taymiyya, *Iqtida' al-sirat al-mustaqim li mukhalafat ashab al-jahim* (Riyadh: Maktabat al-rushd, n.d.), 1:81.
81. Al-Zayyat, *Al-jama'at al-islamiyya*, 79.
82. Interview with al-Samawi in *al-Masri al-Yawm* (November 21, 2007).
83. Interview with Khalid al-Za'farani.
84. See the report on Sukri Mustafa's testimony to the judges in Rifa'at Sayyid Ahmad, *Al-nabi al-musallah (1)—al-rafidun* (London: Riad El-Rayyes Books, 1991), 55.
85. Ahmad, 57, 56.
86. Gilles Kepel explains that some of Mustafa's followers had initially been drawn to him by "the way he practiced the *sunan.*" See Kepel, *Muslim Extremism in Egypt*, 76.
87. Mukhtar Nuh, *Man qatala al-shaykh al-Dhahabi? qira'a fi-l-watha'iq al-sirriyya li-tanzim al-takfir wa-l-hijra* (Cairo: Al-mahrusa, 2008), 16.
88. Ahmad, *Al-nabi al-musallah (1)*, 60–61, 70–71.
89. Interview with Khalid al-Za'farani.
90. Rifa'at Sayyid Ahmad, *Al-nabi al-musallah (2)—al-tha'irun* (London: Riad El-Rayyes Books, 1991), 115–60.
91. Ahmad, *Al-nabi al-musallah (1)*, 67, 95.
92. Interview with Khalid al-Za'farani.

2. EGYPT AFTER NASSER

93. Interview with Hasan al-Halawi in Nuh, *Man qatala al-shaykh al-Dhahabi?*, 109.
94. Kepel, *Muslim Extremism in Egypt*, 91f.
95. He refused to be called Taha because he believed the name was reserved for the Prophet. See Al-Zayyat, *Al-jama'at al-islamiyya*, 45; interview with al-Samawi in *al-Masri al-Yawm* (November 21, 2007).
96. For more on al-Samawi's outlook, see his interview with the newspaper *Al-Ahali*, the French translation of which appears in *Revue de la presse égyptienne* 2, no. 23, CEDEJ (1986): 13-22.
97. Ahmad, *Al-nabi al-musallah (1)*, 194.
98. Al-Zayyat, *Al-jama'at al-islamiyya*, 45, 47.
99. Al-Samawi's text appears in Rifa'at Sayyid Ahmad's collection. See Ahmad, *Al-nabi al-musallah (1)*, 193-97.
100. Al-Zayyat, *Al-jama'at al-islamiyya*, 56-57; Munib, *Dalil al-harakat al-islamiyya*, 115.
101. This is recounted in the interview he gave to *al-Masri al-Yawm* (November 21, 2007).
102. Al-Zayyat, *Al-jama'at al-islamiyya*, 50, 52-53, 57.
103. 'Ali 'Abd al-'Al, "Al-Shaykh alladhi lam yantami li-jama'a" (January 24, 2009), http://www.odabasham.net/تراجم/72970-الشيخ-الذي-لم-ينتم-لجماعة.
104. 'Adil Hamuda, *Qanabil wa masahif*, 3rd ed. (Cairo: Sina li-l-nashr, 1989), 126.
105. 'Ali 'Abd al-'Al, "Al-Shaykh alladhi lam yantami li-jama'a." For more on this affair, see *Revue de la presse égyptienne* 2, no. 23, CEDEJ (1986): 102-5.
106. Regarding Kishk and al-Mahallawi, see Zeghal, *Gardiens de l'islam*, 214-21. Gilles Kepel also describes Sheikh Kishk at length in Kepel, *Muslim Extremism in Egypt*, 172f.
107. Kepel, *Muslim Extremism in Egypt*, 276-80.
108. Mitchell, *The Society of the Muslim Brothers*, 18.
109. Al-Majdhub, *'Ulama' wa muthaqqafin 'araftuhum*, 2:115-17.
110. Mamduh Isma'il, "Al-shaykh Hafiz Salama wa-l-shuyukh," http://ar.islamway.net/article/7748/الشيخ-حافظ-سلامه-والشيوخ; "Masjid al-Nur . . . nuqtat intilaq al-masirat wa malja' li-l-mutazahirin wa shahid 'ala ahdath al-'abbasiyya," *Al-Ahram* (May 5, 2012).
111. Zeghal, *Gardiens de l'islam*, 337-58.
112. Al-Zayyat, *Al-jama'at al-islamiyya*, 221.
113. 'Abd al-Mun'im Munib, "'Umar 'Abd al-Rahman azhari zalamahu Nasir wa-l-Sadat wa Mubarak wa sajanatahu al-wilayat al-muttahida muddat al-hayat" (June 2, 2015), https://ar.islamway.net/article/48223/و.س. عبد-الرحمن-أزهري-ظلمه-ناصر-والسادات-ومبارك- جنته-الولايات-المتحدة-مدى-الحياة عمر-.
114. 'Umar 'Abd al-Rahman, *Kalimat haqq: murafa'at al-shaykh 'Umar 'Abd al-Rahman fi qadiyyat al-jihad*, 9, http://www.tawhed.ws. See also Zeghal, *Gardiens de l'islam*, 347.
115. "Masjid al-'aziz billah . . . min huna kharajat jama'at al-tatarruf fi masr," *Al-Mujaz* (December 16, 2013), http://www.elmogaz.com/node/118237.
116. Talal al-Ansari, *Safahat majhula min tarikh al-haraka al-islamiyya al-mu'asira: min al-naksa ila-l-mashnaqa* (Cairo: Markaz al-mahrusa li-nashr wa-l-khadamat al-sahafiyya wa-l-ma'lumat, 2006), 17.

2. EGYPT AFTER NASSER

117. Ahmad Zaghlul Shalata, *Al-daʿwa al-salafiyya al-sakandariyya: masarat al-tanzim wa malat al-siyasa* (Beirut: Markaz dirasat al-wahda al-ʿarabiyya, 2016), 29, mentions Basyuni's expulsion.
118. ʿAli ʿAbd al-ʿAl, *Rifaʿi Surur . . . min al-jihad ila al-tanzir*, http://www.arabtimes.com/portal/article_display.cfm?ArticleID=13254.
119. Al-Ansari, *Safahat majhula*, 18.
120. Al-Ansari, 19.
121. Al-Ansari, 20-21; interview with Khalid Dawud.
122. Interview with Khalid Dawud.
123. Mukhtar Nuh, *Qadiyyat al-fanniyya al-ʿaskariyya: awwal muhawalat inqilab islami ʿaskari fi-l-qarn al-ʿishrin* (Cairo: Al-mahrusa, 2006), 15.
124. Al-Ansari, *Safahat majhula*, 24.
125. Al-Ansari, 40-41.
126. Nuh, *Qadiyyat al-fanniyya al-ʿaskariyya*, 15; Nuh, *Man qatala al-shaykh al-dhahabi?*, 105; Saad Eddin Ibrahim, "Anatomy of Egypt's Militant Islamic Groups: Methodological Note and Preliminary Findings," *International Journal of Middle East Studies* 12, no. 4 (December 1980): 435; Muhammad Muru, *Tanzim al-jihad: afkaruhu, judhuruhu, siyasatuhu* (Cairo: Al-sharika al-ʿarabiyya al-duwaliyya li-l-nashr wa-l-iʿlam, 1990), 24-25.
127. Kepel, *Muslim Extremism in Egypt*, 93. See also Husam Abu Hamid, "Tawjih al-din didd al-dawla: bayna Sayyid Qutb . . . wa Salih Sirriya," *Al-ʿArabi al-Jadid* (April 23, 2015), https://www.alaraby.co.uk/amp//opinion/2015/4/22/والم-الدولة-ضد-الدين-توجيه. جتمع-بين-سيد-قطب-وصالح-سرية
128. For the story of Sirriyeh's life, see Al-Ansari, *Safahat majhula*, 54-55.
129. Ahmad, *Al-nabi al-musallah (1)*, 31f.
130. Ahmad, 36-37.
131. Al-Ansari, *Safahat majhula*, 61.
132. Nuh, *Qadiyyat al-fanniyya al-ʿaskariyya*, 14.
133. Munib, *Dalil al-harakat al-islamiyya*, 81; Muru, *Tanzim al-jihad*, 32.
134. Sources differ on the date: Muhammad Muru mentions 1960, ʿAbd al-Munʿim Munib says 1964, and Ayman al-Zawahiri writes 1966.
135. Muru, *Tanzim al-jihad*, 16, 17.
136. Kamal Al-Saʿid Habib, "Jamaʿat al-jihad: al-masar wa-l-afkar wa-l-shakhsiyyat," in Al-Misbar, *Al-fitna al-ghaʾiba: jamaʿat al-jihad fi masr* (Dubai: Markaz al-Misbar, 2012), 11.
137. "Al-islami al-masri Hani al-Sibaʿi yarwi qissat taʾsis tanzim al-jihad," *Al-Hayat* (September 1-4, 2002), http://ilmway.com/site/hansib/ar/news.php?readmore=34.
138. Biography of Muhammad Khalil Harras, http://shamela.ws/index.php/author/159; Munib, *Dalil al-harakat al-islamiyya*, 75.
139. "Al-islami al-masri Hani al-Sibaʿi yarwi qissat taʾsis tanzim al-jihad."
140. Munib, *Dalil al-harakat al-islamiyya*, 77.
141. Ayman al-Zawahiri, *Al-tabriʾa: tabriʾat ummat al-qalam wa-l-sayf min manqasat tuhmat al-khawr wa-l-daʿf* (N.p.: n.d.), 27.
142. Habib, "Jamaʿat al-jihad," 13.
143. Nuh, *Man qatala al-shaykh al-Dhahabi?*, 103-4.
144. Habib, "Jamaʿat al-jihad," 15.
145. Al-Ansari, *Safahat majhula*, 18.

146. Munib, *Dalil al-harakat al-islamiyya*, 83.
147. Al-Zayyat, *Al-jama'at al-islamiyya*, 95-96.
148. Muru, *Tanzim al-jihad*, 29-30.
149. Munib, *Dalil al-harakat al-islamiyya*, 84.
150. Al-Zayyat, *Al-jama'at al-islamiyya*, 108.
151. Al-Zayyat, 94.
152. Al-Zayyat, 127. For more on Juhayman al-'Utaybi, see Thomas Hegghammer and Stéphane Lacroix, "Rejectionist Islamism in Saudi Arabia: The Story of Juhayman al-'Utaybi Revisited," *International Journal of Middle East Studies* 39, no. 1 (February 2007): 103-22.
153. Ahmed Abdalla, *The Student Movement and National Politics in Egypt 1923–1973* (London: Al Saqi Books, 1985), 149f.
154. Kepel, *Muslim Extremism in Egypt*, 129f.
155. Interview with Khalid Dawud; Husam Tammam, *'Abd al-Mun'im Abu al-Futuh: shahid 'ala tarikh al-haraka al-islamiyya fi masr 1970–1984* (Cairo: Dar al-Shuruq, 2010), 33.
156. Tammam, *'Abd al-Mun'im Abu al-Futuh*, 34; Salah Hashim, "Shihada 'an nash'at al-jama'a al-islamiyya fi masr," http://www.murajaat.com/trajuaat_akra_data/14.DOC; 'Abduh Mustafa Dasuqi and al-Sa'id Ramadan al-'Ubadi, *Tarikh al-haraka al-tullabiyya bi jama'at al-ikhwan al-muslimin (1933–2011)*, http://www.ikhwanwiki.com, 197.
157. Hashim, "Shihada 'an nash'at al-jama'a al-islamiyya fi masr."
158. Tammam, *'Abd al-Mun'im Abu al-Futuh*, 47.
159. Badr Muhammad Badr, *Al-jama'a al-islamiyya fi jami'at masr: haqa'iq wa watha'iq* (N.p.: 1989), 23.
160. Sivan, *Radical Islam*, 134.
161. Tammam, *'Abd al-Mun'im Abu al-Futuh*, 45.
162. Tammam, 65, 69.
163. Tammam, 64.
164. 'Abd al-Salam Faraj, for example, was invited to speak at a camp run by the *jama'a islamiyya* of Assiut University as early as 1979—even before it joined his group in the summer of 1980. See Al-Zayyat, *Al-jama'at al-islamiyya*, 92.
165. Salwa Muhammad al-'Awwa, *Al-jama'a al-islamiyya al-musallaha fi masr 1974–2004* (Cairo: Maktabat al-shuruq al-duwaliyya, 2006), 71.
166. Kepel, *Muslim Extremism in Egypt*, 134. See also Abdullah al-Arian, *Answering the Call: Popular Islamic Activism in Sadat's Egypt* (Oxford: Oxford University Press, 2014), 127-28.
167. Kepel, *Muslim Extremism in Egypt*, 138f.
168. Tammam, *'Abd al-Mun'im Abu al-Futuh*, 54, 71.
169. Kepel, *Muslim Extremism in Egypt*, 139.
170. Al-Arian, *Answering the Call*, 141.
171. Farid, *Hadith al-dhikrayat*, 26; Tammam, *Tasalluf al-ikhwan*, 15; Al-Zayyat, *Al-jama'at al-islamiyya*, 130; Al-sayyid 'Abd al-Sattar Al-Milligi, *Tarikh al-haraka al-islamiyya fi sahat al-ta'lim 1933–1993* (Cairo: Maktabat Wahba, 1994), 41; Al-Arian, *Answering the Call*, 141. Yasir Burhami says that the camps he visited in 1977, 1978, and 1979 followed the Salafi *manhaj*. See 'Ali 'Abd al-'Al, "Yasir Burhami fi shihadatihi 'an nash'at al-da'wa al-salafiyya fi-l-iskandariyya," part 2,

2. EGYPT AFTER NASSER

http://www.arabtimes.com/portal/article_display.cfm?Action=&Preview=No&ArticleID=13519. Al-Jaza'iri was invited to the camp in Alexandria in 1977, but it was canceled at the last minute by the authorities. See "Tullab al-ikhwan wa khawd al-intikhabat al-tullabiyya," https://www.ikhwanwiki.com/index.php?title= طلاب_الاخوان_وخوض_الانتخابات_الطلابية.

172. Farid, *Hadith al-dhikrayat*, 26.
173. "Tarjamat al-shaykh al-'allama Usama 'Abd al-'Azim," http://www.forsanhaq.com/showthread.php?t=111707.
174. Kepel, *Muslim Extremism in Egypt*, 141.
175. Tammam, *'Abd al-Mun'im Abu al-Futuh*, 45–46; Abul A'la Maududi, *Nizam al-hayat fi-l-islam* (Cairo: Cairo University, Faculty of Medicine, 1978, Sawt al-Haqq series); Tammam, *Tasalluf al-ikhwan*, 16. *Jihad on the Path of God* was published in 1977 by the jama'a islamiyya of the Faculty of Medicine (copy in my possession).
176. Tammam, *'Abd al-Mun'im Abu al-Futuh*, 67.
177. Al-Arian, *Answering the Call*, 132, 124.
178. Copies of both are in my possession (undated, no author identified).
179. Badr, *Al-jama'a al-islamiyya fi jami'at masr*, 29; Farid, *Hadith al-dhikrayat*, 26; 'Ali 'Abd-'Al, "Yasir Burhami fi shihadatihi 'an nash'at al-da'wa al-salafiyya fi-l-iskandariyya," part 2; Ahmad Al-Butami, *Tathir al-jinan wa-l-arkan 'an darn al-shirk wa-l-kufran*, quoted in Yasir Burhami, *Sawanih al-dhikrayat ma' al-duktur Yasir Burhami*, part 2; Al-Zayyat, *Al-jama'at al-islamiyya*, 93; Muru, *Tanzim al-jihad*, 29.
180. Interview with Subhi Salih; "Tullab al-ikhwan wa khawd al-intikhabat al-tullabiyya."
181. Hashim, "Shihada 'an nash'at al-jama'a al-islamiyya fi masr"; Badr, *Al-jama'a al-islamiyya fi jami'at masr*, 27; Kepel, *Muslim Extremism in Egypt*, 146. *Siwak* is a natural toothbrush sourced from the *Salvadora persica* (toothbrush) tree, used during Prophet Muhammad's time and thus popular among Salafis.
182. Badr, *Al-jama'a al-islamiyya fi jami'at masr*, 29.
183. Kepel, *Muslim Extremism in Egypt*, 145.
184. Al-Arian, *Answering the Call*, 133; Tammam, *'Abd al-Mun'im Abu al-Futuh*, 68.
185. Tammam, 68; interview with Yasir Burhami by the (defunct) website Islamonline, http://www.arabtimes.com/portal/article_display.cfm?ArticleID=6971; Tammam, *Tasalluf al-ikhwan*, 15.
186. Al-Arian, *Answering the Call*, 133; Tammam, *'Abd al-Mun'im Abu al-Futuh*, 67, 68.
187. Al-'Awwa, *Al-jama'a al-islamiyya*, 75, 79–80. See also Al-Sayyid 'Abd al-Sattar, *Tajrubati ma' al-Ikhwan: min al-da'wa ila al-tanzim al-sirri* (Cairo: Al-zahra' li-l-i'lam al-'arabi, 2009), 133f.
188. Hashim, "Shihada 'an nash'at al-jama'a al-islamiyya fi masr."
189. Kepel, *Muslim Extremism in Egypt*, 147f.
190. Farid, *Hadith al-dhikrayat*, 22.
191. Until this point only a handful of members had been freed, including Supreme Guide Hasan al-Hudaybi, who was released in 1971 for health reasons.
192. Al-Arian, *Answering the Call*, 93.

2. EGYPT AFTER NASSER

193. The conflict was so pronounced that when Alexandria University students invited 'Umar al-Tilmisani to speak, a leader of Alexandria's Brotherhood reproached them: "He doesn't represent the Brothers!" See Farid, *Hadith al-dhikrayat*, 27.
194. Tammam, *Tasalluf al-ikhwan*, 17; in English, see Khalil al-Anani, *Inside the Muslim Brotherhood: Religion, Identity and Politics* (Oxford: Oxford University Press, 2016), 146.
195. Tammam, *'Abd al-Mun'im Abu al-Futuh*, 83, 87; see also 'Isam al-Ghazi, *'Umar al-Tilmisani—min al-tanju fi 'Imad al-Din ila za'amat al-ikhwan al-muslimin* (Giza: Hala, 2008).
196. Tammam, *'Abd al-Mun'im Abu al-Futuh*, 129.
197. 'Abdallah al-Nafisi, Hamid al-Quwaysi, *Al-naqd al-dhati li-l-haraka al-islamiyya: ru'a mustaqbaliyya* (Cairo: Maktabat al-shuruq al-duwaliyya, 2009), 114.
198. Tammam, *'Abd al-Mun'im Abu al-Futuh*, 74-75.
199. Tammam, 79.
200. Dasuqi and al-'Ubadi, *Tarikh al-haraka al-tullabiyya*, 197.
201. "Hikayat al-Za'farani" (interview with Ibrahim al-Za'farani on the website of Wagdi Ghunaym), episode 3 (April 8, 2007). The entire series is available at https://www.ikhwanwiki.com/index.php?title=حكايات_الزعفراني.
202. Tammam, *'Abd al-Mun'im Abu al-Futuh*, 95.
203. Interview with Khalid Dawud.
204. Tammam, *'Abd al-Mun'im Abu al-Futuh*, 79.
205. Aaron Rock-Singer, *Practicing Islam in Egypt: Print Media and Islamic Revival* (Cambridge: Cambridge University Press, 2019), 113.
206. Interview with Khalid Dawud.
207. Dasuqi and al-'Ubadi, *Tarikh al-haraka al-tullabiyya*, 198.
208. Tammam, *'Abd al-Mun'im Abu al-Futuh*, 89-90.
209. Abu al-Futuh says this happened in 1979 or 1980, as does Abu al-'Ala' Madi, another figure in the jama'at islamiyya at the time; see Dasuqi and al-'Ubadi, *Tarikh al-haraka al-tullabiyya*, 175-76. Yasir Burhami refers to 1979; see 'Ala' Bakr, *Al-sahwa al-islamiyya fi masr fi al-sab'iniyyat* (Alexandria: Dar al-khulafa' al-rashidin, 2013), 67. But this seems fairly late compared with other accounts: Khalid Dawud says 1976 or 1977 (interview with Khalid Dawud), and Husam Tammam even mentions the date as 1975 or 1976 and suggests this followed the publication of the *al-Da'wa* journal; see Tammam, *Tasalluf al-ikhwan*, 3. Given the conflicting narratives, I selected a date in the middle—which also happens to be the one chosen in Munib, *Dalil al-harakat al-islamiyya*, 144.
210. Moaaz Mahmoud, "Les Frères musulmans en Égypte face à la montée du salafisme" (MA thesis, Sciences Po, Paris, 2009), 35.
211. Mahmoud, 36.
212. Oum Nour, quoted in Mahmoud, 40.
213. Interview with Subhi Salih.
214. Abu al-'Ala' Madi, "Dawr al-Qaradawi fi tarshid al-sahwa al-islamiyya fi awsat jil al-sab'inat fi masr," unpublished manuscript shared with me.
215. Raymond William Baker, *Islam Without Fear: Egypt and the New Islamists* (Cambridge, MA: Harvard University Press, 2003).

2. EGYPT AFTER NASSER

216. Jeffry R. Halverson, *Theology and Creed in Sunni Islam: The Muslim Brotherhood, Ash'arism, and Political Sunnism* (New York: Palgrave Macmillan, 2010), 74. Regarding al-Qaradawi and Sufism, see, for example Weismann, "Modernity from Within," 26-27.
217. He wrote: "This is how Bedouin *fiqh* spread, with its childish understanding of the beliefs and rules." See Muhammad al-Ghazali, *Al-sunna al-nabawiyya bayna ahl al-fiqh . . . wa ahl al-hadith*, 6th ed. (Cairo: Dar al-shuruq, 2007), 15. Other al-Ghazali books target Salafism, including Muhammad al-Ghazali, *Humum da'iya*, 6th ed. (Cairo: Nahdat masr, 2006). In 1999 al-Qaradawi also set pen to paper in response to the Salafi attacks on the Brotherhood; see Yusuf al-Qaradawi, *Al-ikhwan al-muslimun: 80 'aman fi-l-da'wa wa-l-tarbiya wa-l-jihad* (Cairo: Maktabat wahba, 1999), 314f.
218. Mahmoud, *Les Frères musulmans en Égypte*, 41.
219. Tammam, *Tasalluf al-ikhwan*, 19.
220. Al-'Awwa, *Al-jama'a al-islamiyya*, 84-86.
221. Al-Zayyat, *Al-jama'at al-islamiyya*, 89; Kepel, *Muslim Extremism in Egypt*, 156f.
222. Tammam, *'Abd al-Mun'im Abu al-Futuh*, 90; Al-Zayyat, *Al-jama'at al-islamiyya*, 84, 90.
223. Interview with Nagih Ibrahim.
224. Al-'Awwa, *Al-jama'a al-islamiyya*, 82.
225. Dasuqi and al-'Ubadi, *Tarikh al-haraka al-tullabiyya*, 200.
226. Al-'Awwa, *Al-jama'a al-islamiyya*, 83, n. 86.
227. *Musa yas'al Abu al-Futuh: dawruka fi jara'im al-jama'a al-islamiyya*, https://www.dailymotion.com/video/xu3x6e.
228. Al-'Awwa, *Al-jama'a al-islamiyya*, 85.
229. Munib, "'Umar 'Abd al-Rahman azhari zalamahu Nasir wa al-Sadat wa Mubarak."
230. Mukhtar Nuh, *Mawsu'at al-'unf fi-l-harakat al-islamiyya al-musallaha* (Cairo: Sama li-l-nashr wa-l-tawzi', 2014), 493, 500.
231. Al-'Awwa, *Al-jama'a al-islamiyya*, 100-103.
232. Usama Muhammad 'Abd al-'Azim Hamza, http://www.ahlalhdeeth.com/vb/showthread.php?t=112250.
233. Zaghlul Shalata, *Al-da'wa al-salafiyya al-sakandariyya*, 49.

3. THE SALAFI CALL

Epigraph: A *nashid* is an a cappella chant, considered the only religiously acceptable singing by the Salafis. This *nashid* is chanted in honor of the sheikhs of the Salafi Call. *Nashid Yasir Abu 'Ammar—al-da'wa al-salafiyya*, https://www.youtube.com/watch?v=d9PcBJ_vy1Y.

1. Quintan Wiktorowicz, "Anatomy of the Salafi Movement," *Studies in Conflict and Terrorism* 29, no. 3 (2006): 207-39. See the introduction for a discussion of these categories.
2. Lecture by Haytham Tawfiq, *Tarikh nash'at al-da'wa al-salafiyya*, https://www.youtube.com/watch?v=YohcU25JICg

3. THE SALAFI CALL

3. Tawfiq, *Tarikh nash'at al-da'wa al-salafiyya*.
4. These "authorized histories" were the work of three middle-ranking Call sheikhs: Mahmud 'Abd al-Hamid, Haytham Tawfiq, and Ahmad Hamdi. After 2011, as the Call became a prominent participant in Egyptian public debate, its leaders decided it was necessary for the group to write its own history rather than allowing sometimes unsympathetic journalists to do so in their stead. Tasked with this mission, the three young sheikhs booked lectures across the country to introduce the public to the Call. Along the same lines, 'Ala' Bakr, a Burhami confidant known as the "historian of the Call," wrote a book titled *The Islamic Awakening in Egypt in the 1970s* in which the Call offered its vision of this pivotal decade. 'Ala' Bakr, *Al-sahwa al-islamiyya fi masr fi al-sab'iniyyat* (Alexandria: Dar al-khulafa' al-rashidin, 2013). In an interview in *al-Watan* (May 28, 2012), Abu Idris mentioned his high school connection with al-Muqaddim.
5. Mahmud 'Abd al-Hamid, *Tarikh al-da'wa al-salafiyya*, lecture, www.anasalafy.com, https://www.youtube.com/watch?v=bEW4xx0j66Q (part 1); https://www.youtube.com/watch?v=Nv5X25yAcyM (part 2); Ahmad Farid, *Hadith al-Dhikrayat* (Alexandria: Dar al-Majd, 2008), 163.
6. Bakr, *Al-sahwa al-islamiyya*, 69.
7. Interview with Sa'id 'Abd al-'Azim. See also 'Abd al-Hamid, *Tarikh al-da'wa al-salafiyya*.
8. 'Ali 'Abd al-'Al, "Yasir Burhami fi shihadatihi 'an nash'at al-da'wa al-salafiyya fi-l-iskandariyya," part 3, http://www.arabtimes.com/portal/article_display.cfm?Action=&Preview=no&ArticleID=13520.
9. Ahmad Zaghlul Shalata, *Al-da'wa al-salafiyya al-sakandariyya: masarat al-tanzim wa malat al-siyasa* (Beirut: Markaz dirasat al-wahda al-'arabiyya, 2016), 55. See Stéphane Lacroix, "L'apport de Muhammad Nasir al-Din al-Albani au salafisme contemporain," in *Qu'est-ce que le salafisme?*, ed. Bernard Rougier (Paris: PUF, 2008).
10. Tawfiq, *Tarikh nash'at al-da'wa al-salafiyya*.
11. Muhammad Isma'il al-Muqaddim, *Al-mahdi haqiqa la khurafa*, 11th ed. (Alexandria: Al-dar al-'alamiyya li-l-nashr wa-l-tawzi', 2008).
12. Salah al-Din Hasan, *Al-salafiyyun fi masr* (Giza: Dar awraq, 2012), 27.
13. Tawfiq, *Tarikh nash'at al-da'wa al-salafiyya*. Burhami himself acknowledged this in a July 2006 interview on the website Sawt al-Salaf, http://www.salafvoice.com/article.aspx?a=217.
14. Tawfiq, *Tarikh nash'at al-da'wa al-salafiyya*.
15. 'Abd al-Hamid, *Tarikh al-da'wa al-salafiyya*.
16. 'Abd al-Hamid; Tawfiq, *Tarikh nash'at al-da'wa al-salafiyya*.
17. 'Abd al-'Al, "Yasir Burhami fi shihadatihi," part 2.
18. 'Abd al-Hamid, *Tarikh al-da'wa al-salafiyya*.
19. 'Abd al-Hamid.
20. "Stranger" here refers to a woman without a religiously legitimate connection to the man presumed to be reading the book. Muhammad Isma'il al-Muqaddim, *Adillat tahrim musafahat al-mar'a al-ajnabiyya*, 14th ed. (Cairo: Dar al-khulafa' al-rashidin, 1993).
21. 'Abd al-'Al, "Yasir Burhami fi shihadatihi," part 3.
22. Farid, *Hadith al-dhikrayat*, 75.

23. Tawfiq, *Tarikh nash'at al-da'wa al-salafiyya*. For more on these youth's self-guided learning, see Zaghlul Shalata, *Al-da'wa al-salafiyya al-sakandariyya*, 80–81.
24. Muhammad Isma'il al-Muqaddim, *Hurmat ahl al-'ilm* (Cairo: Dar Ibn al-Jawzi, 2005), 8.
25. Yasir Burhami, *Fiqh al-khilaf bayn al-muslimin* (Alexandria: Dar al-'aqida, 2000, 2nd edition), 56.
26. Tawfiq, *Tarikh nash'at al-da'wa al-salafiyya*; Farid, *Hadith al-dhikrayat*, 77.
27. Interview with Yasir Burhami on the Jama'a Islamiyya website, part 1, http://www.salafvoice.com/article.aspx?a=2489; Zaghlul Shalata, *Al-da'wa al-salafiyya al-sakandariyya*, 145.
28. Interview with Sa'id 'Abd al-'Azim.
29. A section in each *Sawt al-Da'wa* issue reprinted selected fatwas of Ibn Baz, Ibn 'Uthaymin, or Salih al-Fawzan.
30. Yasir Burhami describes the moment when "each person asked a question of Ibn Baz according to his desired response" by "phrasing the question in a certain way." Al-Za'farani asked: "Sheikh, there is a group that is making several errors. May we continue participating so we can reform it or should we leave?" "If it is possible to reform it," the sheikh more or less replied, "then you can remain part of it." Al-Muqaddim then added: "And if they have pledged allegiance to the Shia?" "In that case, no!" replied Ibn Baz. "You must leave them!" See *Sawanih al-dhikrayat ma' al-duktur Yasir Burhami* (interview with Sheikh Yasir Burhami about his life story, on the *al-Dalil* channel), part 2 (September 2011), https://www.youtube.com/watch?v=R-14EN2n8qg.
31. 'Abd al-Mun'im Munib, *Dalil al-harakat al-islamiyya* (Cairo: Maktabat Madbuli, 2010), 93.
32. For some background on 'Adil 'Abd al-Ghaffur, see http://majles.alukah.net/t112881/.
33. Farid, *Hadith al-dhikrayat*, 145–52; *Sawanih al-dhikrayat ma' al-duktur Yasir Burhami*, part 2, https://www.youtube.com/watch?v=R-14EN2n8qg.
34. Farid, *Hadith al-dhikrayat*, 159; Stéphane Lacroix, *Awakening Islam: The Politics of Religious Dissent in Contemporary Saudi Arabia*, trans. George Holoch (Cambridge: Harvard University Press, 2011), 171; Zaghlul Shalata, *Al-da'wa al-salafiyya al-sakandariyya*, 147. It is worth noting that Farid misspells Ibn Qu'ud's name as Ibn Qa'ud, which seems to suggest that their relationship was never very close. Burhami does likewise in his interview with the website Sawt al-Salaf.
35. Ahmad Farid says that only in 1989 did they meet Muhammad 'Ali 'Abd al-Rahim, a prominent figure in Alexandrian Salafism and the sitting president of Ansar al-Sunna, on the occasion of a visit from Saudi sheikh Ibn Qu'ud. Farid suggests that 'Abd al-Rahim did not think much of the Salafi Call at the time. See Farid, *Hadith al-dhikrayat*, 153.
36. See, for example, the book authored by the "historian of the Call," 'Ala' Bakr, *Thatlathu qurun hijriyya 'ala da'wat al-shaykh Muhammad bin 'Abd al-Wahhab al-salafiyya* (Alexandria: Dar al-khulafa' al-rashidin, 2007), 159–69.
37. Interview with Sa'id 'Abd al-'Azim.
38. Lacroix, *Awakening Islam*, 84–85. See, for example, Farid, *Hadith al-dhikrayat*, 141.

3. THE SALAFI CALL

39. Muhammad Isma'il al-Muqaddim, *Khawatir hawla al-wahhabiyya* (Alexandria: Dar al-tawhid li-l-turath, 2008), 109.
40. One exception is Ahmad Farid, who frequently appeared "Saudi-style" with a *ghutra* on his head.
41. Farid, *Hadith al-dhikrayat*, 80.
42. See, for example, Tariq 'Abd al-Halim, *Al-Jawab al-mufid fi hukm jahil al-tawhid*, http://www.almeshkat.net/book/1357. The book was first published in 1978.
43. *Sawanih al-dhikrayat ma' al-duktur Yasir Burhami*, part 2.
44. Interview with Yasir Burhami on the Jama'a Islamiyya website, part 2, https://www.anasalafy.com/play.php?catsmktba=82634.
45. Interview with Muhammad Yusri Salama.
46. See, for example, Ahmad Farid's fatwa "hukm tarik al-salat," https://www.anasalafy.com/play.php?catsmktba=48163. Burhami wrote a book on this, siding with Ibn Taymiyya over the stance of the Saudi ulema. See Yasir Burhami, *Tahqiq madhhab shaykh al-islam Ibn Taymiyya fi tarik al-salat*, 2nd ed. (Alexandria: Dar al-khulafa' al-rashidin, 2011).
47. Muhammad Nasir al-Din al-Albani, *Hukm tarik al-salat* (Riyadh: Dar al-jalalayn, 1992); Mu'taz Zahir, *Min al-masjid ila al-barlaman: dirasa hawla al-da'wa al-salafiyya wa hizb al-nur* (London: Takween, 2015), 52. See, for example, the fatwa issued by Ibn Baz: "hukm tarik al-salat," https://binbaz.org.sa/fatwas/20429/حكم-تارك-الصلاة.
48. Interview with Bassam al-Zarqa.
49. *Sawanih al-dhikrayat ma' al-duktur Yasir Burhami*, part 2; Zaghlul Shalata, *Al-da'wa al-salafiyya al-sakandariyya*, 147.
50. Interview with Muhammad Yusri Salama.
51. Stéphane Lacroix, "Saudi Arabia's Muslim Brotherhood Predicament," *The Monkey Cage* (March 20, 2014), https://www.washingtonpost.com/news/monkey-cage/wp/2014/03/20/saudi-arabias-muslim-brotherhood-predicament/.
52. Interview with Ahmad Harqan.
53. As a longtime Call figure explained in an interview: "Yasir Burhami always brought back large amounts of cash from his pilgrimages. Everybody knew; it was an open secret."
54. Interview with Muhammad Yusri Salama.
55. 'Abd al-'Al, "Yasir Burhami fi shihadatihi," part 2; see also Tawfiq, *Tarikh nash'at al-da'wa al-salafiyya*. "The *jama'at islamiyya* were entirely Salafi," says Yasir Burhami. See 'Abd al-'Al, "Yasir Burhami fi shihadatihi," part 2. "The Salafi Call is an outgrowth of the *jama'a islamiyya* because the latter followed the Salafi creed," insists Ahmad Farid. See Farid, *Hadith al-dhikrayat*, 7.
56. In 1989 Brother sympathizer Badr Muhammad Badr described the current of Alexandrian Salafis that emerged from the jama'at islamiyya as "a small, uninfluential group." See Badr Muhammad Badr, *Al-jama'a al-islamiyya fi jami'at masr: haqa'iq wa watha'iq* (N.p.: 1989), 104-5.
57. Interviews with Khalid Dawud and Midhat al-Haddad.
58. 'Abd al-'Al, "Yasir Burhami fi shihadatihi," part 1, http://www.arabtimes.com/portal/article_display.cfm?Action=&Preview=no&ArticleID=13518.
59. Tawfiq, *Tarikh nash'at al-da'wa al-salafiyya*.

3. THE SALAFI CALL

60. Munib, "al-tayyarat al-salafiyya fi masr wa mawaqifuha al-siyasiyya" (December 29, 2009), http://moneep.alummah.today/node/160.
61. Tawfiq, *Tarikh nash'at al-da'wa al-salafiyya*.
62. Youssef Nada (with Douglas Thomson), *Inside the Muslim Brotherhood* (London: Metro Publishing, 2012), 54; Nada, *Inside the Muslim Brotherhood*, 58–63, 71, 81.
63. Usama Shahada, *Min tarikh al-harakat al-islamiyya ma' al-shi'a wa Iran*, Kitab al-rasid 7, 137–47, http://www.alrased.net.
64. Tawfiq, *Tarikh nash'at al-da'wa al-salafiyya*.
65. Muhammad Isma'il al-Muqaddim, "Silsila hawla dukhul al-barlaman," lecture, transcription at https://audio.islamweb.net/audio/index.php?page=FullContent&audioid=163387#163391.
66. Tawfiq, *Tarikh nash'at al-da'wa al-salafiyya*.
67. 'Abd al-'Al, "Yasir Burhami fi shihadatihi," part 3. See also Tawfiq, *Tarikh nash'at al-da'wa al-salafiyya*.
68. Tawfiq.
69. Tawfiq; 'Abd al-'Al, "Yasir Burhami fi shihadatihi," part 3.
70. Tawfiq, *Tarikh nash'at al-da'wa al-salafiyya*.
71. Yasir Burhami quoted in Zahir, *Min al-masjid ila-l-barlaman*, 34.
72. The book was republished under its title, *Ba'd ma 'allamani al-ikhwan al-muslimun*, in Jamal [pronounced Gamal] al-Banna, *Min watha'iq al-ikhwan al-muslimin (al-juz' al-khamis)* (Cairo: Dar al-fikr al-islami, 2009), 42–109.
73. Al-Banna, 45, 45.
74. Al-Banna, 43.
75. Sayyid al-Ghubashi, *Iblagh al-haqq ila-l-khalq—risala fi hukm al-musharaka fi majlis al-sha'b al-masri*, http://www.tawhed.ws. For more on Sayyid al-Ghubashi, see Ahmad Salim, *Ikhtilaf al-islamiyyin: al-khilaf al-islami—al-islami (halat masr namudhajan)* (Beirut: Markaz Nama' li-l-buhuth wa-l-dirasat, 2013), 294–95.
76. The contents of the proclamation, entitled "Weighing the Question of Parliamentary Elections" (*Al-intikhabat al-barlamaniyya fi-l-mizan*), are described in Ahmad Salim and 'Amr Basyuni, *Ma ba'd al-salafiyya* (Beirut: Markaz Nama' li-l-buhuth wa-l-dirasat, 2015), 448–49.
77. At the time of the parliamentary elections in 2010, a small white book could be found in the Salafi bookstores of Alexandria and Cairo. Written by a "group of religious scholars" (*jama'a min ahl al-'ilm*), it was called *Islam's Position on Participation in Elections—Why We Did Not Endorse the Muslim Brotherhood*. See *Hukm al-musharaka fi-l-intikhabat wa li-madha lam nusanid al-ikhwan al-muslimin?* (N.p.: n.d.).
78. Ibrahim Fawzi (preface by Yasir Burhami), *Fatawa wa aqwal al-'ulama' fi jama'at al-ikhwan al-muslimin* (Alexandria: Dar al-khulafa' al-rashidin, 2009).
79. Zaghlul Shalata, *Al-da'wa al-salafiyya al-sakandariyya*, 62. For some biographical details, see Usama Muhammad 'Abd al-'Azim Hamza, http://www.ahlalhdeeth.com/vb/showthread.php?t=112250.
80. Zaghlul Shalata, *Al-da'wa al-salafiyya al-sakandariyya*, 76.
81. Yasir Burhami's 2006 interview with the website Sawt al-Salaf (part 2), http://www.salafvoice.com/article.aspx?a=217.

3. THE SALAFI CALL

82. For more on this association's activities in Kuwait, see Carine Abou Lahoud, *Islam et politique au Koweït* (Paris: PUF, 2011); Zoltan Pall, *Kuwaiti Salafism and its Growing Influence in the Levant* (Washington, DC: Carnegie Endowment for International Peace, 2014), 4–11.
83. 'Abd al-Rahman 'Abd al-Khaliq, *Al-usul al-'ilmiyya li-l-da'wa al-salafiyya*, 2nd ed. (Kuwait: Al-dar al-salafiyya, 1977).
84. Interview with Muhammad Yusri Salama.
85. Zaghlul Shalata, *Al-da'wa al-salafiyya al-sakandariyya*, 63.
86. There were 1,536 arrested. Regarding these clashes, see Gilles Kepel, *Muslim Extremism in Egypt: The Prophet and Pharaoh* (Berkeley: University of California Press, 1985), 119f.
87. Zaghlul Shalata, *Al-da'wa al-salafiyya al-sakandariyya*, 64.
88. Zaghlul Shalata, 64.
89. This document, a copy of which is in my possession, is among those taken by protesters during the attack on State Security buildings in spring 2011.
90. *Munazara bayna mashayikh al-da'wa al-salafiyya wa shuyukh al-Azhar*, https://www.youtube.com/watch?v=S6UqcFzXE80.
91. Zaghlul Shalata, *Al-da'wa al-salafiyya al-sakandariyya*, 64.
92. Interview with Ahmad Nagi.
93. Interview with Bassam al-Zarqa.
94. Interview with Ahmad Nagi.
95. Interview with Mahmud 'Abbas, who at the time led one of these university "clubs" named after the Muslim conqueror Khalid Ibn al-Walid; Zaghlul Shalata, *Al-da'wa al-salafiyya al-sakandariyya*, 92.
96. For specifics, see Zaghlul Shalata, *Al-da'wa al-salafiyya al-sakandariyya*, 92, 97–107.
97. Zaghlul Shalata, 87, 90–91.
98. Interview with Hasan Bughdadi, who held various leadership roles in this sector around the turn of the millennium.
99. Zaghlul Shalata, *Al-da'wa al-salafiyya al-sakandariyya*, 87.
100. Interview with Muhammad Nur.
101. *The Grace of the Merciful* was so central for Call members that they often repeated, "Anyone who hasn't read the *minna* can't be one of us (*min-na*)"—a play on words in Arabic.
102. Interviews with Muhammad Tawfiq and Ahmad Nagi.
103. Interview with Ahmad Nagi.
104. Zaghlul Shalata, *Al-da'wa al-salafiyya al-sakandariyya*, 81–2. For a detailed description of the program, see 82–85.
105. Zaghlul Shalata, 82.
106. The first issue was dated Dhu al-Qa'da 1410, or May 1990.
107. Interview with Hasan Bughdadi.
108. Zaghlul Shalata, *Al-da'wa al-salafiyya al-sakandariyya*, 64.
109. Interview with Muhammad al-'Adli.
110. Interview with Khalid Hamza; interview with Sharif al-Hawwari conducted in fall 2013 by 'Abd al-Rahman Yusuf, who shared it with me.
111. Zaghlul Shalata, *Al-da'wa al-salafiyya al-sakandariyya*, 138–39.

3. THE SALAFI CALL

112. See, for example, "Hanan 'Allam aminat al-mar'a al-salafiyya: la yajuz ijbar al-zawj 'ala al-khal'," *Ruz al-Yusuf* (May 17, 2012).
113. Interview with Nadir Bakkar.
114. Zahir, *Min al-masjid ila-l-barlaman*, 35.
115. 'Ali 'Abd al-'Al, "Al-da'wa al-salafiyya al-sakandariyya: al-nash'a tarikhiyya" (January 20, 2016), http://islamion.com/news/الدعوة-السلفية-بالإسكندرية-النشأة-التاريخية/.
116. For more on this group, see Zaghlul Shalata, *Al-da'wa al-salafiyya al-sakandariyya*, 112–15.
117. Interviews with Muhammad Tawfiq, Ayman 'Abd al-Rahim, and Ahmad Mawlana.
118. Pall, *Kuwaiti Salafism*, 12–17.
119. Interview with Yusri Hammad, who, among other roles, worked for the Society in Afghanistan and in Bangladesh.
120. Tawfiq, *Tarikh nash'at al-da'wa al-salafiyya*.
121. 'Ala' Bakr and Yasir Burhami, *Madhahib fikriyya fi-l-mizan: muhadarat fi-l-ghazu al-fikri* (Mansoura: Maktabat fayyad, 2011).
122. Marc Lazar, "Le parti et le don de soi," *Vingtième Siècle. Revue d'histoire* no. 60 (1998): 35.
123. Henri Lauzière, *The Making of Salafism: Islamic Reform in the Twentieth Century* (New York: Columbia University Press, 2015), 201.
124. Lauzière, 216f.
125. Mustafa Hilmi, *Qawa'id al-manhaj al-salafi fi-l-fikr al-islami* (Beirut: Dar al-kutub al-'ilmiyya, 2005); Husam Tammam, "Mustafa Hilmi... ba'th wa tajdid al-salafiyya... falsafiyyan," http://tammam.org/0838-21-11-04-2010-388-/مقالات.html.
126. See the updated edition of Hilmi's *Rules of the Salafi Method*, issued in 2010 by Call publishing house Dar al-khulafa' al-rashidin and prefaced by al-Muqaddim, Burhami, 'Abd al-'Azim, and Farid.
127. Al-Khaliq, *Al-usul al-'ilmiyya li-l-da'wa al-salafiyya*.
128. Aaron Rock-Singer points to the use of the term *manhaj* by Salafi-leaning scholars from the late 1960s in Egypt, although it was apparently used then in a less specific sense. See Rock-Singer, *In the Shade of the Sunna: Salafi Piety in the Twentieth Century Middle East* (Oakland: University of California Press, 2022), 85.
129. Bakr, *Al-sahwa al-islamiyya*, 68.
130. Muhammad Nasir al-Din al-Albani, *Al-tasfiya wa-l-tarbiya wa hajat al-muslimin ilayha* (Riyadh: Maktabat al-ma'arif li-l-nashr wa-l-tawzi', 2007).
131. Yasir Burhami, "Al-salafiyya wa manahij al-taghyir," *Sawt al-Da'wa* 3 (1412, which corresponds to 1991–1992).
132. Muhammad Isma'il al-Muqaddim, *'Awdat al-hijab*, 20th ed. (Alexandria: Dar al-khulafa' al-rashidun, 2011).
133. Al-Muqaddim, 3–9.
134. Sa'id 'Abd al-'Azim, *Al-dimuqratiyya wa nazariyyat al-islah fi-l-mizan* (Alexandria: Dar al-fath al-islami, 2009).
135. 'Abd al-Mun'im al-Shahhat, *Al-hakimiyya* (2nd audiocassette), http://www.anasalafy.com/play.php?catsmktba=53590.
136. Al-Shahhat, *Al-hakimiyya*; Yasir Burhami, *Sharh masa'il al-jahiliyya* (Alexandria: Dar al-khulafa' al-rashidin, 2013); Muhammad Isma'il al-Muqaddim, *Silsilat al-islam wa-l-kufr* (21st audiocassette).

3. THE SALAFI CALL

137. Yasir Burhami, *Qira'a naqdiyya li ba'd ma warada fi kitab "zahirat al-irja'" wa-l-radd 'alayha* (Alexandria: Al-dar al-salafiyya li-l-nashr wa-l-tawzi', 2004), 7.
138. Interview with Hasan Bughdadi.
139. Zahir, *Min al-masjid ila al-barlaman*, 176.
140. Yasir Burhami, *Sharh fiqh al-amr bi-l-ma'ruf wa-l-nahi 'an al-munkar*, photocopied booklet distributed to members of the Call (in my possession); Zaghlul Shalata, *Al-da'wa al-salafiyya al-sakandariyya*, 117-18.
141. Burhami, "Al-salafiyya wa manahij al-taghyir."
142. Burhami.
143. For more on these divisions, see Lacroix, *Awakening Islam*.
144. A convincing and exhaustive account of the formation, institutionalization, and internal debates of these two groups can be found in Jérôme Drevon, *Institutionalizing Violence: Strategies of Jihad in Egypt* (Oxford: Oxford University Press, 2022)
145. Muhammad Abu 'Atiyya al-Sanadbisi, *Al-inqilab al-fikri li-l-jama'a al-islamiyya* (Giza: Dar awraq, 2012), 117.
146. Mahir Farghali, *Al-khuruj min bawwabat al-jahim* (Beirut: Al-intishar al-'arabi, 2012), 116-17.
147. Muhammad Habib, *Dhikrayat al-duktur Muhammad Habib 'an al-hayat wa-l-da'wa wa-l-siyasa wa-l-fikr* (Cairo: Dar al-shuruq, 2012), 135.
148. Munib, *Dalil al-harakat al-islamiyya*, 100f.
149. Regarding this debate, see Malika Zeghal, *Gardiens de l'islam: les oulémas d'al-Azhar dans l'Égypte contemporaine* (Paris: Presses de Sciences Po, 1996), 341.
150. Munib, *Dalil al-harakat al-islamiyya*, 103.
151. Interview with Yahya Rifa'i Surur.
152. Quote from *Charter of Islamic Action (Mithaq al-'amal al-islami)* in Rifa'at Sayyid Ahmad, *Al-nabi al-musallah (1)—al-rafidun* (London: Riad El-Rayyes Books, 1991), 168.
153. Salwa Muhammad al-'Awwa, *Al-jama'a al-islamiyya al-musallaha fi masr 1974–2004* (Cairo: Maktabat al-shuruq al-duwaliyya, 2006), 112f.
154. The Jama'a Islamiyya's *Charter of Islamic Action* defines its activities as follows: "preaching as a tool for changing conceptions, *hisba* as a tool for changing society, and *jihad* as a tool for change when preaching and *hisba* are not enough."
155. Walid Yusuf al-Birsh, *Alihat al-'unf: min manassat al-Sadat ila manassat Rabi'a* (Cairo: Kunuz li-l-nashr wa-l-tawzi', 2015), 99.
156. Rifa'at Sayyid Ahmad, *Al-nabi al-musallah (2)—al-tha'irun* (London: Riad El-Rayyes Books, 1991), 224.
157. Roel Meijer, "Commanding Right and Forbidding Wrong as a Principle of Social Action," in *Global Salafism: Islam's New Religious Movement*, ed. Roel Meijer (Oxford: Oxford University Press, 2009), 189.
158. Al-Birsh, *Alihat al-'unf*, 57.
159. Zeghal, *Gardiens de l'islam*, 341.
160. Meijer, "Commanding Right and Forbidding Wrong," 198.
161. Munib, *Dalil al-harakat al-islamiyya*, 146.
162. Al-'Awwa, *Al-jama'a al-islamiyya al-musallaha*, 124-27, 133.
163. Interview with Nagih Ibrahim.

3. THE SALAFI CALL

164. For a thorough analysis of the process that led to that decision, see Omar Ashour, "Lions Tamed: An Inquiry Into the Causes of De-Radicalization of Armed Islamist Movements: The Case of the Egyptian Islamic Group," *Middle East Journal* 61, no. 4 (Fall 2007): 596–925.
165. Yasir Burhami himself makes this observation in the first part of his interview with the website of the Jama'a Islamiyya, republished at http://www.salafvoice.com/article.aspx?a=2489.
166. Regarding these groups, see for example Munib, *Dalil al-harakat al-islamiyya*, 161f.
167. Salim, *Ikhtilaf al-islamiyyin*, 84–85.
168. Hisham Al 'Uqda, *Al-Ijabat* (Cairo: Dar al-safwa, 2008), 60.
169. A number of interesting biographical details on Sheikh Muhammad 'Abd al-Maqsud can be found at http://www.ahlalhdeeth.com/vb/showthread.php?t=69711.
170. *Man huwa al-shaykh Muhammad 'Abd al-Maqsud*, https://www.youtube.com/watch?v=goSCoA_L4mo.
171. Interview with Ayman 'Abd al-Rahim.
172. 'Abd al-Maqsud argues that collective action is rarely immune to factionalism, in the preface to 'Abd al-Hamid al-Hindawi, *Dirasat hawla al-jama'a wa-l-jama'at . . . kayf al-amr idha lam takun jama'a*, 2nd ed. (Cairo: Maktabat al-tabi'in, 1995).
173. Fawzi al-Sa'id's 1981 involvement is mentioned in Zaghlul Shalata, *Al-da'wa al-salafiyya al-sakandariyya*, 55.
174. Lacroix, *Awakening Islam*, 228.
175. Lacroix, 54.
176. Lacroix, 69.
177. For some biographical details, see http://www.forsanhaq.com/showthread.php?t=91570; also at his now-defunct website, http://www.oqdah.com.
178. For a biography of Salah al-Sawi, see his page on the Islamway website: https://ar.islamway.net/scholar/61/profile.
179. Interview with Hisham Mustafa. For his books that illustrate this shift, see, for example, Hisham Mustafa 'Abd al-'Aziz, *Min huna nabda'—mashru' islahi ijtima'i* (Alexandria: Dar al-huda, 2011); *Nahdat umma* (Alexandria: Dar al-huda, 2008); and *Al-islamiyyun wa-l-dimuqratiyya* (Alexandria: Dar al-huda, 2009).
180. Interview with Hisham Kamal.
181. As told by al-Shazli. See 'Abd al-Majid al-Shazli, *Thawabit al-da'wa wa asbab al-ikhtilaf fi-l-musharaka al-siyasiyya* (part 4), https://www.youtube.com/watch?v=7b2JRHj_lvw. Al-Shazli's degree is mentioned in Ahmad 'Abd al-Majid, "Al-ta'rif bi-fadilat al-shaykh bi-qalam al-ustadh Ahmad 'Abd al-Majid," http://alshazly.info/node/198.
182. Interview with Khalid al-Za'farani.
183. Al-Shazli, *Thawabit al-da'wa*.
184. Rifa'i Surur, "Al-ta'rif bi-fadilat al-shaykh bi-qalam al-shaykh Rifa'i Surur," https://alshazly.info/node/199.
185. Lacroix, *Awakening Islam*, 54–55.
186. Many of these ideas are found in Muhammad Qutb, *Waqi'una al-mu'asir* (Cairo: Dar al-shuruq, 1997).

3. THE SALAFI CALL

187. Today it is named the "Call of the Sunnis for the Rebirth of the Umma" (*Da'wat ahl al-sunna wa-l-jama'a fi tariq ihya' al-umma*). Munib, *Dalil al-harakat al-Islamiyya*, 70.
188. 'Abd al-Rahman Mustafa, "Ahl al-Sunna wa-l-Jama'a: laysa kullu sahib lihya takfiriyyan," *Al-Shuruq* (August 16, 2012), http://abderrahmann.blogspot.com/2012/08/blog-post_16.html; Ismail Alexandrani, "Sinaï: From Revolution to Terrorism," in *Egypt's Revolutions: Politics, Religion, and Social Movements*, ed. Bernard Rougier and Stéphane Lacroix (London: Palgrave Macmillan, 2016), 187.
189. For biographies of these two figures, see Muhammad Hamid 'Abd al-Wahhab, *Al-salafiyyun fi masr* (Riyadh: Maktabat al-ansar, 2012), 334-45.
190. Salim, *Ikhtilaf al-islamiyyin*, 57.
191. See, for example, Abu 'Abdallah Hamdan, *Kashf al-haqa'iq al-khafiyya 'an salafiyyat al-iskandariyya* (Al-mahalla al-kubra: Dar ibn Zayid, 2009).
192. Lacroix, *Awakening Islam*, 211-21.
193. Hasan, *Al-salafiyyun fi masr*, 41.
194. For an anti-Brotherhood book, see Mahmud Lutfi 'Amir, *Tanbih al-ghafilin bi haqiqat fikr al-ikhwan al-muslimin*, 4th ed. (Damanhur: Dar al-mahja al-bayda', 2006).
195. "Sahib fatwa ihdar dam al-Barada'i yastaqil," *Akhbar al-Yawm* (January 1, 2011). For more on this, see also Hasan, *Al-salafiyyun fi masr*, 93. See the statement regarding this incident on page 72 of *al-Tawhid*, no. 470, 40th year (Safar 1432-January 2011). For a summary of the reactions to the ensuing scandal, see pages 2-8 of the same issue.
196. Mahmud Tarshubi, "Tarikh al-salafiyya al-jihadiyya fi masr," in *Al-salafiyyun fi masr ma ba'd al-thawra*, ed. Mustafa Zahran, 'Umar Ghazi et al. (Riyadh: Markaz al-din wa-l-siyasa/Beirut: Al-intishar al-'arabi, 2012), 209-12.
197. Interview with Hasan Bughdadi.
198. Interview with Muhammad Tawfiq.
199. "Hiwar ma' fadilat al-shaykh Yasir Burhami (al-juz' al-thani)" (July 28, 2006), http://www.salafvoice.com/article.aspx?a=217.
200. Yasir Burhami, *Al-'amal al-jama'i bayna al-ifrat wa-l-tafrit*, photocopied booklet distributed to members of the Call (in my possession).
201. In this case, a collective obligation (*fard kifaya*).
202. Yasir Burhami, *Sharh fiqh al-amr bi-l-ma'ruf wa-l-nahi 'an al-munkar*.
203. 'Isam Darbala, 'Asim 'Abd al-Majid, *Al-qawl al-qati' fi man imtana' 'an al-shara'i'* (N.p., 1991), 1. Parts of this book are quoted in Mukhtar Nuh, *Mawsu'at al-'unf fi-l-harakat al-islamiyya al-musallaha* (Cairo: Sama li-l-nashr wa-l-tawzi', 2014), 437-61.
204. 'Abd al-Mun'im al-Shahhat, *Al-salafiyya wa manahij al-taghyir*, 13th audiocassette, transcription at http://www.forsanhaq.com/archive/index.php/t-189768.html.
205. Daniel Lav, *Radical Islam and the Revival of Medieval Theology* (Cambridge: Cambridge University Press, 2012), 87.
206. 'Abd al-Majid al-Shazli, *Hadd al-islam wa haqiqat al-iman* (Mecca: Umm al-Qura University Press, n.d.).
207. Ahmad Farid, *Al-'udhr bi-l-jahl wa-l-radd 'ala bid'at al-takfir* (Giza: Maktabat al-taw'iya al-islamiyya, 2002, 4th edition); photocopied booklet distributed to members of the Call (in my possession).

3. THE SALAFI CALL

208. Safar bin 'Abd al-Rahman al-Hawali, *Zahirat al-irja' fi-l-fikr al-islami* (Rosmalen: Dar al-kalima, 1999). Haytham Tawfiq, a student and confidant of Burhami, describes this "affair" in detail. See Haytham Tawfiq, *Al-irja' taht al-majhar* (Alexandria: Dar al-khulafa' al-rashidin, 2011), 133f.
209. Lacroix, *Awakening Islam*, 148.
210. Lacroix, 151f.
211. Interview with Muhammad Yusri Salama.
212. Interview with Hasan Bughdadi.
213. This seems to be the story that Haytham Tawfiq recounts in his book, written under a pen name, without explicitly mentioning Hisham Mustafa. See Ahad talabat al-'ilm, *Hiwar hadi hawla kitab qira'a naqdiyya wa ma hawlahu min i'taradat* (N.p., 2008), 6–7.
214. Burhami, *Qira'a naqdiyya li ba'd ma warada fi kitab "zahirat al-irja'" wa-l-radd 'alayha*, 313.
215. Interviews with Muhammad Yusri Salama, Bassam al-Zarqa, and 'Imad 'Abd al-Ghaffur.
216. Burhami, *Qira'a naqdiyya li ba'd ma warada fi kitab "zahirat al-irja'" wa-l-radd 'alayha*.

4. SALAFISM'S INELUCTABLE ASCENT UNDER MUBARAK

Epigraphs: Khaled al-Berry, *Life Is More Beautiful than Paradise: A Jihadist's Own Story* (Cairo: American University in Cairo Press, 2009), 53. Husam Tammam, "As'ilat al-zaman al-salafi" (2010), https://tammam.org/0106-14-09-02-2010-283-/مقالات.html.

1. Lea Müller-Funk, "Managing Distance: Examining Egyptian Emigration and Diaspora Policies," *Égypte/Monde arabe*, no. 15 (2017), http://journals.openedition.org/ema/3656.
2. See Jean-Pierre Filiu, *L'Apocalypse dans l'Islam* (Paris: Fayard, 2008), 125–45.
3. Interview with Jamal al-Murakibi, *Majallat al-Bayan*, no. 256 (December 2008); 'Abd al-Mun'im al-Shahhat, "Qanat al-rahma bayna bayanay ta'sis" (May 27, 2010), www.anasalafy.com, quoted in Mu'taz Zahir, *Min al-masjid ila-l-barlaman: dirasa hawla al-da'wa al-salafiyya wa hizb al-nur* (London: Takween, 2015), 182.
4. Wa'il Lutfi, *Zahirat al-du'a al-judud: al-da'wa, al-tharwa, al-shuhra* (Cairo: Maktabat al-usra, 2005); Patrick Haenni, *L'Islam de marché: l'autre révolution conservatrice* (Paris: Seuil, 2005), 33f.
5. See, for example, *Muhammad Hassan yuhajim 'Amr Khalid* (January 22, 2009), https://www.youtube.com/watch?v=SEbtXirq1So; *Al-shaykh al-Huwayni yuwaddih al-mushkila ma' fikr 'Amr Khalid* (June 9, 2017), https://www.youtube.com/watch?v=GkakThjUZKo.
6. For more on their cassettes and CDs, see Charles Hirschkind, *The Ethical Soundscape: Cassette Sermons and Islamic Counterpublics* (New York: Columbia University Press, 2006).
7. Moaaz Mahmoud, "Les Frères Musulmans en Égypte face à la montée du salafisme" (MA thesis, Sciences Po, Paris, 2009), 18.

4. SALAFISM'S INELUCTABLE ASCENT UNDER MUBARAK

8. This anecdote is recounted in "'Ashriyyat yanayar . . . kayfa faqad al-tayyar al-salafi fi masr hadanatahu al-sha'biyya," *Noon Post* (January 30, 2021), https://www.noonpost.com/content/39667.
9. Muhammad Yusri Ibrahim, *Al-fida'iyyat al-islamiyya: ru'ya naqdiyya* (Cairo: Dar al-yusr, 2009), 6.
10. Abu Ishaq al-Huwayni, *Tanbih al-hajid ila ma waqa' min al-nazar fi kutub al-amajid*, 1:9f, https://archive.org/details/FD61759/tnha1/page/n8/mode/2up. Also see his lecture "My Journey in Search of Knowledge" (*Rihlati fi talb al-'ilm*), https://ar.islamway.net/lesson/4116/رحلتي-في-طلب-العلم.
11. Muhammad Nasir al-Din al-Albani, *Silsilat al-ahadith al-da'ifa wa-l-mawdu'a* (Riyadh: Maktabat al-ma'arif, 1992).
12. Al-Albani seemed to deny having made such a pronouncement: https://www.youtube.com/watch?time_continue=24&v=1pTWy_TI-H4.
13. Two of his books are about al-Albani: *Al-thamr al-dani fi-l-dabb 'an al-Albani* and *Nab' al-amani fi tarjamat al-shaykh al-Albani*. Some consider al-Huwayni as having been a de facto member of the organization, at least for a time. See Ahad talabat al-'ilm, *Hiwar hadi hawla kitab qira'a naqdiyya wa ma hawluhu min i'taradat* (N.p.: 2008), 12.
14. "Al-Huwayni: al-lihya wa-l-niqab li-inqadh al-umma," *Ruz al-Yusuf* (2007).
15. Jacquelene G. Brinton, *Preaching Islamic Renewal: Religious Authority and Media in Contemporary Egypt* (Oakland: University of California Press, 2016).
16. "Nubdha mukhtasara 'an al-sira al-dhatiyya li fadilat al-shaykh Muhammad Husayn Ya'qub hafazahu Allah," http://www.saaid.net/Warathah/1/m7amad.htm.
17. These biographical details are mostly drawn from his appearance on the show *Safahat min hayati*, broadcast on Qanat al-Majd, https://www.youtube.com/watch?v=37TOAXmsNOs.
18. He says that it was Sheikh Safwat Nur al-Din of Ansar al-Sunna who brought him for the first time to hear Ibn Baz speak in Riyadh (*Safahat min hayati* on the Qanat al-Majd channel). Stéphane Lacroix, *Awakening Islam: The Politics of Religious Dissent in Contemporary Saudi Arabia*, trans. George Holoch (Cambridge, MA: Harvard University Press, 2011), 169–70.
19. For an analysis of one of Hassan's sermons and its accompanying stagecraft, see Hirschkind, *The Ethical Soundscape*, 169.
20. Asef Bayat, *Life as Politics: How Ordinary People Change the Middle East* (Stanford, CA: Stanford University Press, 2009), 14, 20.
21. Bayat, 78f; Carrie Rosefsky Wickham, *Mobilizing Islam: Religion, Activism and Political Change in Egypt* (New York: Columbia University Press, 2002), 104.
22. Lacroix, *Awakening Islam*, 42f.
23. Lacroix, 22–29.
24. Gilles Kepel, *Jihad: The Trail of Political Islam* (Cambridge, MA: Harvard University Press, 2002), 71.
25. Samuli Schielke, *Migrant Dreams: Egyptian Workers in the Gulf States* (Cairo: AUC Press, 2020), 57.
26. "Tanzim al-wa'd al-jadid fi masr," *Al-Sharq al-Awsat* (October 19, 2001), http://archive.aawsat.com/details.asp?section=4&article=62385&issueno=8361#.WYC4axjpP-Y.

27. Lucile Gruntz, "L'Amérique des Arabes, aller-retour. Les migrants cairotes au centre de la controverse religieuse," presentation at the colloquium "Migrations: nouvelles pratiques, approches plurielles" held at the EHESS in Paris (October 8-10, 2008): 4. Malika Zeghal similarly tries not to jump to conclusions regarding the al-Azhar ulema who taught in the Gulf region. See, for example, Malika Zeghal, *Gardiens de l'islam: les oulémas d'al-Azhar dans l'Égypte contemporaine* (Paris: Presses de Sciences Po, 1996), 198.
28. For example, this truism is also found in the books of Alaa al-Aswany.
29. Jalal [pronounced Galal] Amin, *Masr wa-l-masriyyun fi 'ahd Mubarak 1981-2008* (Cairo: Dar Merit, 2009), 172.
30. See, for example, the following fatwa: "Mada mashru'iyyat kasb man ya'mal bi-majal al-siyaha" (June 23, 2008), https://www.islamweb.net/ar/fatwa/109513 /مدى-مشروعية-كسب-من-يعمل-في-مجال-السياحة.
31. Carrie Wickham offers a fairly detailed picture of the various elements that make up the parallel Islamic sector. See Wickham, *Mobilizing Islam*, 97-102.
32. Wickham, 96, 100.
33. Zeghal, *Gardiens de l'islam*, 225-26.
34. The tabloids included *Al-Fajr, Sawt al-Umma, Ruz al-Yusuf, Al-Sabah*, etc. See, for example, "Rihlat milyunirat al-salafiyyin min al-faqr ila-l-qasr," *Al-Sabah*, https://www.elsaba7.com/details/153960; "Biznis al-qanawat al-salafiyya: Muhammad Hassan 10 alaf dollar shahriyyan wa Ya'qub 50 alf jinih shahriyyan" (December 11, 2011), https://www.christian-dogma.com/t50007.
35. "Nakshaf bi-l-arqam mughamarat kibar al-mashayikh ma' qafs al-zawajiyya," *Al-Nahar* (April 22, 2014), https://www.alnaharegypt.com/200753.
36. 'Amr 'Izzat, *Li-man al-manabir al-yawm? Tahlil siyasat al-dawla fi idarat al-masajid* (Cairo: Al-mubadara al-masriyya li-l-huquq al-fardiyya, 2014), 17-21; see also Zeghal, *Gardiens de l'islam*, 174-75.
37. Law 238 of 1996. See 'Izzat, *Li-man al-manabir al-yawm?*, 21.
38. Zeghal, *Gardiens de l'islam*, 183-84.
39. Patrick D. Gaffney, *The Prophet's Pulpit: Islamic Preaching in Contemporary Egypt* (Berkeley: University of California Press, 1994), 15; *Al-jam'iyyat al-ahliyya al-islamiyya fi masr*, ed. 'Abd al-Ghaffar Shukr (Cairo: Dar al-amin, 2001), 58. The first source mentions 34,000 mosques in 1979, while the second notes 28,000 in 1980.
40. Shukr, *Al-jam'iyyat al-ahliyya al-islamiyya fi masr*, 58; interview with Salim 'Abd al-Jalil.
41. Regarding Nash'at Ahmad and Fawzi al-Sa'id, see Ahmad Mawlana, *Qira'a naqdiyya fi kitab ikhtilaf al-islamiyyin*," https://gabhasalafia.com/wp-content/uploads /2014/09/قراءة-نقدية-في-كتاب-اختلاف-الاسلاميين-احمد-مولانا.pdf, 53; "Al-shaykh al-Sa'id: min muwazzaf fi sharika duwa'iyya ila qiyadat tanzim al-wa'd al-usuli fi masr," *Al-Sharq al-Awsat* (November 20, 2001).
42. The mosque website containing the course catalog is no longer available.
43. Shukr, *Al-jam'iyyat al-ahliyya al-islamiyya*, http://www.ikhwanwiki.com/index.php ?title=الجمعيات_الأهلية_الإسلامية_في_مصر#3-_.D8.AC.D9.85.D8.A7.D8.B9.D8.A9_ .D8.AF.D8.B9.D9.88.D8.A9_.D8.A7.D9.84.D8.AD.D9.82.
44. Sarah Ben Néfissa, "Citoyenneté morale en Égypte: une association entre État et Frères musulmans," in *ONG et gouvernance dans le monde arabe*, ed. Sarah Ben

Néfissa et al. (Paris/Cairo: Karthala-CEDEJ, 2004); Shukr, *Al-jam'iyyat al-ahliyya al-islamiyya fi masr*.
45. Shukr, *Al-jam'iyyat al-ahliyya al-islamiyya fi masr*.
46. Richard Gauvain, *Salafi Ritual Purity: In the Presence of God* (London: Routledge, 2013), 35.
47. "'Al-Amn al-watani'... ightiyalat tahmil alam al-tas'iniyyat," *Al-Shuruq* (November 18, 2013).
48. Reports seized from State Security. Some of these documents were published after the revolution at http://www.25leaks.com (which went dark a few months after the summer 2013 coup d'état); others were shown to me by protestors. See also Ahmad Mawlana, *Al-'aqliyya al-amniyya fi-l-ta'amul ma' al-tayyarat al-islamiyya* (Cairo: Isdarat al-jabha al-salafiyya, 2012).
49. I confirmed this with members of the Call and the Brotherhood, often on condition of anonymity due to the sensitive nature of the question.
50. For the categories used to "classify" the Islamists, also see Mawlana, *Al-'aqliyya al-amniyya*, 38f.
51. Reports seized from State Security.
52. Some Call leaders, including Ahmad Farid, were nonetheless detained in 1987. See Ahmad Farid, *Hadith al-dhikrayat* (Alexandria: Dar Ibn al-Jawzi, 2012), 57.
53. Interview with Ahmad Mawlana.
54. Egyptian author Salih al-Wardani offers a thorough analysis of these. See Salih al-Wardani, *Al-haraka al-islamiyya fi masr: al-waqi' wa-l-tahaddiyat* (Cairo: Maktabat dar al-kalima, 2000), 414.
55. Zeghal, *Gardiens de l'islam*, 243.
56. Tamir Moustafa, "Conflict and Cooperation Between the State and Religious Institutions in Contemporary Egypt," *International Journal of Middle East Studies* 32, no. 1 (February 2000): 11-12.
57. Interview with Nagih Ibrahim; Munir Adib, *'Anabir al-mawt: qisas waqi'iyya min dakhil al-sujun al-masriyya* (Cairo: Dar awraq, 2012).
58. For more on the attempt in 1993, see Zeghal, *Gardiens de l'islam*, 358-59.
59. 'Abd al-'Al, "Nash'at al-da'wa al-salafiyya."
60. Interview with Hasan Bughdadi.
61. Ahmad Zaghlul Shalata, *Al-da'wa al-salafiyya al-sakandariyya: masarat al-tanzim wa malat al-siyasa* (Beirut: Markaz dirasat al-wahda al-'arabiyya, 2016), 93.
62. Interview with Ashraf Thabit.
63. Zaghlul Shalata, *Al-da'wa al-salafiyya al-sakandariyya*, 115.
64. Interview with Ahmad Mawlana.
65. Wahid 'Abd al-Majid, *"Al-ikhwan al-muslimun" bayn al-tarikh wa-l-mustaqbal* (Cairo: Al-Ahram, 2010), 136.
66. Amr Elshobaki, *Les Frères musulmans des origines à nos jours* (Paris: Karthala, 2009), 193-98.
67. For a list of his fatwas that were "complacent" vis-à-vis the regime, see Hani al-Siba'i, *Al-hasad al-murr li-shaykh al-Azhar Tantawi* (January 9, 2004), https://archive.org/details/al_nokbah_20150920_2034.
68. Hilmi al-Namnam, *Al-Azhar: al-shaykh wa-l-mashyakha* (Cairo: Madbuli, 2012), 246.

4. SALAFISM'S INELUCTABLE ASCENT UNDER MUBARAK

69. 'Adil Ghunaym, *Azmat al-dawla al-masriyya al-mu'asira* (Cairo: Dar al-'alam al-thalith, 2005), 213.
70. Zaghlul Shalata, *Al-da'wa al-salafiyya al-sakandariyya*, 94.
71. Mu'taz Zahir, *Min al-masjid ila al-barlaman: dirasa hawla al-da'wa al-salafiyya wa hizb al-nur* (London: Takween, 2015), 217.
72. For the official narrative, see https://www.albawaba.com/ar/القصة-الكاملة/ساخرون-لتنظيم-الوعد-المصري-تورط-رجال-أعمال-في-تمويل-التنظيم. For the rebuttal by those accused, see http://alarabnews.com/alshaab/GIF/02-11-2001/Waad.htm.
73. Interview with Ahmad Mawlana. Hisham Al 'Uqda was arrested in 2005 and released in 2008.
74. Interview with 'Ali 'Abd al-'Al. This episode is also described in *al-Manar al-Jadid*, no. 3 (Summer 1998): 114. This is the continuation of a longstanding debate within the institution, which Malika Zeghal alludes to when discussing the decision in 1983 to forbid access to al-Azhar for those who hadn't been accepted into the mainstream educational system. See Zeghal, *Gardiens de l'islam*, 290. The rule would later be loosened once again before the tougher enforcement of the late 1990s.
75. As mentioned in his interview with the website of the Jama'a Islamiyya. See http://www.salafvoice.com/article.aspx?a=2489.
76. Interview with Anas Sultan.
77. For example, this was the case in the tribal regions of al-'Amiriyya and Marsa Matruh.
78. Muhammad Yusri Salama, "Al-salafiyyun wa-l-aqbat fi masr—ru'ya fi-l-judhur wa-l-ishkaliyyat wa-l-tahaddiyat," in Al-Misbar, *Al-aqbat fi Masr ba'd al-thawra* (Dubai: Markaz al-Misbar, 2012), 214.
79. There was a surge in anti-Shia writings by Salafis during 2006. See, for example, the book by Shahata Saqr, a member of the Salafi Call entitled *Al-shi'a hum al-'adu fa-uhdhiruhum* [The Shia are the enemy, so be wary of them] (Giza: Maktabat dar al-'ulum, 2006).
80. Interview with 'Amr Magdi.
81. Observation by 'Abd al-Rahman 'Ayyash, quoted in Mahmoud, *Les Frères musulmans en Égypte*, 27.
82. Mahmoud, 26.
83. Mabahith Amn al-Dawla, "Al-Idara al-'Amma li-Mukafahat al-Nashat al-Mutatarrif" (2007), n. 6.
84. "Wathiqa musarraba min amn al-dawla: al-qiyadi al-salafi alladhi ahdara dam al-Barada'i ya'mal li-salih al-amn," *Al-Masri al-Yawm* (March 7, 2011), http://www.almasryalyoum.com/news/details/117630.
85. 'Adil al-Sayyid would spark a controversy in the late 2000s when he published a book defending the association's "loyalist" approach. See 'Adil al-Sayyid, *Al-hakimiyya wa-l-siyasa al-shar'iyya 'inda shuyukh jama'at Ansar al-Sunna al-muhammadiyya* (Cairo: Dar al-Ibana, 2009).
86. Nathan Field, Ahmed Hamam, "Salafi Satellite TV in Egypt," *Arab Media and Society*, no. 8 (Spring 2009).
87. Mohamed El-Sayed, "Screens to Heaven," *Al-Ahram Weekly*, no. 988 (March 4-10, 2010), https://web.archive.org/web/20120917034857/http://weekly.ahram.org.eg/2010/988/feature.htm.

4. SALAFISM'S INELUCTABLE ASCENT UNDER MUBARAK

88. Husam Tammam, "Al-fada'iyyat al-salafiyya ... hal tuqawim al-salafiyya 'ilmanat al-fada'iyyat li-l-tadayyun," *Islamonline* (2009), quoted in Mahmoud, *Les Frères musulmans en Égypte*, 17.
89. "Masr ... I'tiqal al-da'iya Ahmad Farid bi-l-iskandariyya," *Al-Islam al-Yawm* (June 10, 2010), http://www.islamtoday.net/albasheer/artshow-12-134440.htm. According to an interview with Ahmad Mawlana, Ashraf 'Abd al-Mun'im was also threatened with arrest for appearing on Al-Khalijiyya without approval.
90. El-Sayed, "Screens to Heaven."
91. *Al-salafiyyun fi masr ma ba'd al-thawra*, ed. Mustafa Zahran, 'Umar Ghazi, et al. (Riyadh: Markaz al-din wa-l-siyasa/Beirut: Al-intishar al-'arabi, 2012), 25.
92. Personal observations from the event, March 19, 2010. Muhammad Yusri Ibrahim criticizes this summit, which alarmed Egyptian Salafis, in one of his books. See Muhammad Yusri Ibrahim, *Fiqh al-ulawiyyat fi-l-khitab al-salafi al-mu'asir ba'd al-thawra*, 2nd ed. (Cairo: Dar al-yusr, 2012), 36–37.
93. "Li-l-usbu' al-thalith mudiriyyat amn al-dawla tughliq 'adad min masajid masr" (June 14, 2010), https://www.paldf.net/forum/showthread.php?t=636052.
94. *Al-Masriyyun* (October 21, 2010).
95. "Ex-minister Suspected Behind Alex Church Bombing," *Al-'Arabiyya* (February 7, 2011), http://www.alarabiya.net/articles/2011/02/07/136723.html.
96. Salama, "Al-salafiyyun wa-l-aqbat fi masr," in Al-Misbar, *Al-aqbat fi Masr ba'd al-thawra*, 220–21.
97. "Akhtar rajul didd Masr," *Ruz al-Yusuf* (January 15, 2011).
98. Dave F. Eickelman and James Piscatori, *Muslim Politics* (Princeton, NJ: Princeton University Press, 2004), 131.
99. Zeghal, *Gardiens de l'islam*, 146.
100. Interview with Anas Sultan. Sheikh Muhammad al-Ghazali had already offered a similar criticism when he denounced "ulema-bureaucrats." See Zeghal, 85.
101. That said, his cassettes would continue to circulate. Some still listen to his recordings, but to a much lesser extent.
102. For al-Jundi's version of his own curriculum vitae: http://www.khaledalgendy.com/السيرة-الذاتية. And for the rebuttal by a group of al-Azhar ulema: "150 ustadhan bi-jami'at al-Azhar yutalibun bi ighlaq azhari," http://www.hurras.org/vb/archive/index.php/t-27099.html.
103. Interview with Sheikh Ahmad al-Tayyib.
104. Richard P. Mitchell, *The Society of the Muslim Brothers*, 2nd ed. (Oxford: Oxford University Press, 1993), 212.
105. Zeghal, *Gardiens de l'islam*, 119.
106. See, for example, "Al-ikhwan yusaytirun 'ala intikhabat tullab jami'at al-Azhar," *Al-'Arabiyya* (March 14, 2013), https://www.alarabiya.net/arab-and-world/egypt/الإخوان-يسيطرون-على-انتخابات-طلاب-جامعة-الأزهر/2013/03/14.
107. Zeghal, *Gardiens de l'islam*, 85. See also Husam Tammam, *Al-Qaradawi wa-l-ikhwan ... qira'a fi jadaliyyat al-shaykh wa-l-haraka*, http://tammam.org/دراسات 4058-11-09-02-2010-230-.html.
108. Interview with a Brotherhood official.
109. 'Isam Talima, *Al-kharijun 'an al-ikhwan: kayfa wa li-madha?*, http://www.ikhwanwiki.com/index.php?title=الخارجون_عن_الإخوان_..متى_وكيف_ولماذا؟.
110. Zeghal, *Gardiens de l'islam*, 89.

111. Mitchell, *The Society of the Muslim Brothers*, 124; Talima, *Al-kharijun 'an al-ikhwan*.
112. Emmanuel Sivan, *Radical Islam: Medieval Theology and Modern Politics*, enl. ed. (New Haven, CT: Yale University Press, 1990), 50.
113. Talima, *Al-kharijun 'an al-ikhwan*; Bettina Graf and Jakob Skovgaard-Petersen, eds., *Global Mufti: The Phenomenon of Yusuf al-Qaradawi* (London: Hurst, 2008).
114. Al-Sayyid 'Abd al-Sattar, *Tajrubati ma' al-Ikhwan: min al-da'wa ila al-tanzim al-sirri* (Cairo: Al-zahra' li-l-i'lam al-'arabi, 2009), 253-54.
115. On Salah Abu Isma'il, see Zeghal, *Gardiens de l'islam*, 253-56.
116. "Jama'at al-ikhwan al-muslimin tan'i al-shaykh 'Abdallah bin Muhammad al-Khatib" (November 3, 2015), http://islamion.com/news/م-الشيخ-تنعي-الإخوان-جماعة/; حمد-عبدالله-الخطيب-الذي-وافته-المنية-اليوم; interview with Khalid Hamza.
117. Mahmoud, *Les Frères musulmans en Égypte*, 13.
118. Waël Lotfy, "Prêches, médias et fortune: le cas de Amr Khalid," *Les Cahiers de l'IFPO*, no. 5, Beirut: Presses de l'IFPO (2010): 13-25.
119. Haenni, *L'Islam de marché*, 9.
120. Mahmoud, *Les Frères musulmans en Égypte*, 15; "'Amr Khalid . . . wa mashru' sunna' al-hayat," *Al-Jazeera* (October 3, 2004), http://www.aljazeera.net/programs/today-interview/2004/10/3/الحياة-صناع-مشروع-خالد-عمرو.
121. Yasmin Moll, "Islamic Televangelism: Religion, Media, and Visuality in Contemporary Egypt," *Arab Media and Society*, no. 10 (Spring 2010), 13.
122. Interview with Mu'adh 'Abd al-Karim, a former Brotherhood member who belonged to the coalition of young revolutionaries. This plan is also mentioned in 'Amr Faruq, *Dawlat al-khilafa al-ikhwaniyya* (Cairo: Al-Jazira li-l-nashr wa-l-tawzi', 2010), 197-98.
123. Elshobaki, *Les Frères musulmans*, 167, 178, 248.
124. Khalil al-Anani, *Inside the Muslim Brotherhood: Religion, Identity and Politics* (Oxford: Oxford University Press, 2016), 118f.
125. Lacroix, *Awakening Islam*, 38-40.
126. Husam Tammam, *'Abd al-Mun'im Abu al-Futuh: shahid 'ala tarikh al-haraka al-islamiyya fi masr 1970–1984* (Cairo: Dar al-Shuruq, 2010), 132. For biographical details on 'Abd al-Sattar Fath Allah, see http://www.ikhwanwiki.com/index.php?title=عبد_الستار_فتح_الله.
127. Husam Tammam, *Al-Qaradawi wa-l-ikhwan . . . qira'a fi jadaliyyat al-shaykh wa-l-haraka*.
128. Husam Tammam, *Tasalluf al-ikhwan: takul al-utruha al-ikhwaniyya wa su'ud al-salafiyya fi jama'at al-ikhwan al-muslimin* (Alexandria: Maktabat al-iskandariyya/ wahdat al-dirasat al-mustaqbaliyya, 2010), 36, n. 60.
129. Tammam, *Tasalluf al-ikhwan*, 18. This was the Wahba bookstore (*Maktabat wahba*), which also served as a publishing house.
130. Wajdi Ghunaym yukaffir al-Sibsi (August 24, 2017), https://www.youtube.com/watch?v=FW92qde52CY.
131. Tammam, *Tasalluf al-ikhwan*, 23. He described his background and journey in a three-part interview on the Jama'a Islamiyya website, *min dhikrayat d. Safwat Higazi* (now offline).
132. Tammam, *Tasalluf al-ikhwan*, 23.

4. SALAFISM'S INELUCTABLE ASCENT UNDER MUBARAK

133. Raghib al-Sirjani, *Qissat al-imam Muhammad bin 'Abd al-Wahhab rahamahu Allah* (Cairo: Mu'assasat iqra', 2011).
134. Interview with 'Ammar al-Baltagi.
135. Observations of and interviews with a focus group of around ten young Brotherhood members, October 2010.
136. Mahmoud, *Les Frères musulmans en Égypte*, 45, 53.
137. Interview with Khalid Hamza.
138. Mahmoud, *Les Frères musulmans en Égypte*, 47-48.
139. Interview with Ahmad, a young Brotherhood member, October 2010.
140. Muhammad Husayn 'Isa, *Al-lama' fi tajliyat al-bida'*, 2006, 3, 47-52, 81-85, 77-81, 70-77, 52-56. Document in my possession. *Dhikr* refers here to the Sufi practice of religious repetition, usually of the names of God.
141. Shahata Saqr, *Kashf al-bida' wa-l-radd 'ala al-lama'*, publisher unknown.
142. 'Abd al-Rahman al-Barr, *Al-intikhabat ... ru'ya shar'iyya* (in four parts), September 27, 2010, https://old.egyptwindow.net/news_Details.aspx?News_ID=9719.
143. Interview with 'Ali 'Abd al-'Al; 'Abd al-Rahman al-Barr, *Hiwar ma' al-ta'liqat hawla al-ru'ya al-shar'iyya li-l-intikhabat*, https://www.paldf.net/forum/showthread.php?t=684219.
144. Husam Tammam, *As'ila fi-l-zaman al-salafi*, https://tammam.org/201283-/مقالات0106-14-09-02-0-.html.
145. 'Isam Talima, *Hasan al-Banna wa tajrubat al-fann* (Cairo: Maktabat wahba, 2008), 85.
146. Interview with Khalid Hamza.
147. Carrie Rosefsky Wickham, *The Muslim Brotherhood: Evolution of an Islamist Movement* (Princeton, NJ: Princeton University Press, 2013), 58f.
148. Wickham, 139-40.
149. Interview with Khalid Dawud.
150. Regarding Khayrat al-Shatir, see Stéphane Lacroix, "Khayrat al-Shater," in *Egypt's Revolutions: Politics, Religion, and Social Movements*, ed. Bernard Rougier and Stéphane Lacroix (London: Palgrave Macmillan, 2016), 265-67.
151. Interview with Khalid Hamza. Regarding this power grab, see Wickham, *The Muslim Brotherhood*, 127f; al-Anani, *Inside the Muslim Brotherhood*, 152-54.
152. Tammam, *Tasalluf al-ikhwan*, 28.
153. Quoted in al-Sayyid Zayid, "Mudhakkarat Amin tahsim mawqif al-ikhwan min al-shi'a," *Islamonline* (September 22, 2009), republished at http://alrased.net/main/articles.aspx?selected_article_no=4247.
154. According to Moaaz Mahmoud, Brotherhood women were even discouraged from wearing the color black. See Mahmoud, *Les Frères musulmans en Égypte*, 45.
155. 'Abd al-Sattar, *Tajrubati ma' al-ikhwan*, 269; "D. Mahmud Ghuzlan 'adu maktab al-irshad yaktub: risala maftuha ila al-duktur Yusuf al-Qaradawi," *Al-Masri al-Yawm* (November 1, 2009), http://www.almasryalyoum.com/news/details/73072.
156. Tammam, *Tasalluf al-ikhwan*, 28.
157. *Dustur al-ikhwan 'am 1952*, http://www.ikhwanwiki.com/index.php?title=دستور_الاخوان_عام_1952م.
158. See, for example, Muhammad Yusri Ibrahim, ed., *Bayan li-l-nas min al-Azhar al-sharif hawla ba'd al-firaq al-munharifa* (Cairo: Dar al-yusr, 2008); *Fatawa*

4. SALAFISM'S INELUCTABLE ASCENT UNDER MUBARAK

kibar 'ulama' al-Azhar al-sharif fi-l-shi'a wa firaqiha (Cairo: Dar al-yusr, 2007); *Fatawa kibar 'ulama' al-Azhar al-sharif hawla al-niqab*, 3rd ed. (Cairo: Dar al-yusr, 2010); *Fatawa kibar 'ulama' al-Azhar al-sharif hawla khitan al-banat* (Cairo: Dar al-yusr, 2010); and *Fatawa kibar 'ulama' al-Azhar hawla al-adriha wa-l-qubur wa-l-mawlid wa-l-nudhur*, 5th ed. (Cairo: Dar al-yusr, 2010). Behind all these were, once again, Muhammad Yusri Ibrahim and his Dar al-yusr publishing house.

5. SALAFISM FACES REVOLUTION

Epigraphs: Lecture by Abu Ishaq al-Huwayni at Menoufia University (May 18, 2011), https://www.youtube.com/watch?v=jUmaK7t6yZI (quote begins at minute 38). Muhammad Isma'il al-Muqaddim, *Mu'tamar nusrat al-thawra: kalimat al-duktur Muhammad Isma'il al-Muqaddim bi-tarikh 8 fabrayar 2011* (Alexandria: Dar al-salaf al-salih, 2011), 26.

1. Michel Dobry, *Sociologie des crises politiques* (Paris: Presses de la FNSP, 1986), 140f.
2. See, for example, Neil Ketchley, *Egypt in a Time of Revolution: Contentious Politics and the Arab Spring* (Cambridge: Cambridge University Press, 2017); 'Azmi Bishara, *Thawrat Masr*, 2 vols. (Doha: Arab Center for Research and Policy Studies, 2016).
3. Youssef El Chazli, "Devenir révolutionnaire à Alexandrie: contribution à une sociologie historique du surgissement révolutionnaire en Égypte" (PhD dissertation, Paris 1/University of Lausanne, 2018).
4. For a fairly complete list of Salafi fatwas against demonstrations as a mode of action, see Ahmad Salim and 'Amr Basyuni, *Ma ba'd al-salafiyya* (Beirut: Markaz Nama' li-l-buhuth wa-l-dirasat, 2015), 550–55.
5. "Hukm al-musharaka fi thawrat yawm 25 Yanayir" (January 21, 2011), http://www.anasalafy.com/play.php?catsmktba=23685.
6. For the transcribed text in Arabic, see http://www.alsalafway.com/cms/multimedia.php?action=text&id=5620.
7. "Al-bayan al-awwal li-l-da'wa al-salafiyya al-sakandariyya bi-sha'n al-ahdath al-jariyya" (January 29, 2011), http://www.anasalafy.com/play.php?catsmktba=23935.
8. He may not have directly belonged to the Call, but he had ties to the organization and its members, who turned out en masse for his funeral. He is sometimes said to have had more affinity with jihadism, as Hasan Bughdadi, who knew him indirectly, remarked in an interview; also Ahmad Zaghlul Shalata, *Al-da'wa al-salafiyya al-sakandariyya: masarat al-tanzim wa malat al-siyasa* (Beirut: Markaz dirasat al-wahda al-'arabiyya, 2015), 120.
9. Interview with 'Ali 'Abd al-'Al.
10. Zaghlul Shalata, *Al-da'wa al-salafiyya al-sakandariyya*, 120.
11. 'Ali 'Abd al-'Al, "Al-salafiyyun wa-l-mawqif min al-tas'id amam al-dawla" (January 10, 2011), http://www.almothaqaf.com/freepens/freepens-09/42460.
12. "Hukm al-musharaka fi thawrat yawm 25 Yanayir" (January 21, 2011), http://www.anasalafy.com/play.php?catsmktba=23685.

5. SALAFISM FACES REVOLUTION

13. They wrote: "We cannot continue driving the country toward more chaos" (*Bayan al-daʻwa al-salafiyya hawla muʻalajat al-mawqif al-rahin*), February 1, 2011, https://ar.islamway.net/article/7004/3-بيان-الدعوة-السلفية-حول-معالجة-الموقف-الراهن-في-مصر.
14. "Bayan min al-hayʼa al-sharʻiyya li-himayat al-huquq wa-l-hurriyat bi shaʼn al-ahdath" (February 5, 2011), http://salafvoice.com/article.php?a=51429.
15. Al-Muqaddim, *Muʼtamar nusrat al-thawra*, 7.
16. "Hawla al-iʻtiradat ʻala bayan al-hayʼa al-sharʻiyya li-l-difaʻ ʻan al-huquq wa-l-hurriyat al-mashruʻa" (February 7, 2011), http://www.anasalafy.com/play.php?catsmktba=23999.
17. "Hawla ma fahamuhu al-baʻd min kalam al-shaykh Muhammad Ismaʻil" (February 10, 2011), http://www.anasalafy.com/play.php?catsmktba=24027.
18. Photos of these events were posted daily on the Call's websites.
19. "Hamm wa ʻajil: takwin lijan shaʻbiyya min abnaʼ al-daʻwa al-salafiyya 29-1-2011," http://www.alsalafway.com/Sisters/showthread.php?t=11885.
20. The videos, in my possession, are no longer available online.
21. The first written mention of this theme appeared in "Bayan al-daʻwa al-salafiyya hawla muʻalajat al-mawqif al-rahin" (February 1, 2011), https://ar.islamway.net/article/7004/3-بيان-الدعوة-السلفية-حول-معالجة-الموقف-الراهن-في-مصر.
22. "Hamlat al-difaʻ ʻan huwiyat masr al-islamiyya," http://anasalafy11.blogspot.com/2011/02/blog-post_14.html.
23. "Bayan min al-daʻwa al-salafiyya bi-shaʼn al-istiftaʼ ʻala al-taʻdilat al-dusturiyya" (March 7,2011),https://anasalafy.com/ar/24581-بيان-من-الدعوة-السلفية-بشأن-الاستفتاء-على.
24. The most over-the-top declaration came from Muhammad Husayn Yaʻqub, who caused a controversy when he called the victory a "razzia at the ballot box" (*ghazwat al-sanadiq*). See *Ghazwat al-sanadiq fi-l-istiftaʼ li-l-shaykh Muhammad Husayn Yaʻqub* (March 21, 2011), https://www.youtube.com/watch?v=mqO3X1hTJUc.
25. "Bayan min al-daʻwa al-salafiyya bi-shaʼn iʻadat tashkil majlis idaratiha," http://www.anasalafy.com/play.php?catsmktba=24712.30.
26. "Abu Idris raʼisan ʻamman wa Burhami naʼiban li-l-daʻwa al-salafiyya," *Al-Shuruq* (July 1, 2011).
27. "Al-ijtimaʻ al-awwal li-majlis al-shura al-ʻamm li-l-daʻwa al-salafiyya" (June 30, 2011), https://anasalafy.com/ar/27328-الاجتماع-الأول-لمجلس-الشورى-العام-للدعوة-السلفية.
28. "Muʼassasat bayt al-aʻmal . . . al-dhiraʻ al-iqtisadi li-l-daʻwa al-salafiyya fi masr," http://islamion.com/news/مؤسسة-بيت-الأعمال-الذراع-الإقتصادية-للدعوة-السلفية-في-مصر/.
29. Abu Idris explains that they were forced to use this name because the Ministry of Social Affairs refused to register them as the "Salafi Call." See "Al-shaykh Abu Idris: ikhtalafna maʻ al-ikhwan fi masʼalat al-bayʻa," *Al-Watan* (May 27, 2012), https://www.elwatannews.com/news/details/9584.
30. See, for example, Muhammad Saʻid Raslan, *Haqiqat ma yahduth fi masr* (Al-Fayyoum: Dar al-furqan, 2011).
31. For an early approach, see the writings of Salah al-Sawi, a Sururi. For example: Salah al-Sawi, *Al-thawabit wa-l-mutaghayyirat fi masirat al-ʻamal al-islami al-muʻasir* (N.p.: Akadimiyyat al-shariʻa bi-Amrika, 2009). See Ahmad Zaghlul Shalata, *Al-hala al-salafiyya al-muʻasira fi masr* (Cairo: Madbuli, 2011), 295-97.
32. "Awwal mashruʻ siyasi salafi fi masr al-thawra," *Al-Masriyyun* (March 24, 2011).

33. "Ra'is hizb al-fadila al-salafi yanshaqq wa yu'assis hizb al-asala," *Al-Yawm al-Sabi'* (July 11, 2011), https://www.youm7.com/story/2011/7/11/452334/الف-حزب-رئيس. ويؤسس-ينشق-السلفى-الفضيلة حزب-الأصالة
34. Interview with Khalid Mansur, the party's spokesman.
35. Interview with Kamal Habib.
36. "Al-nur awwal hizb salafi yatamm ta'sisuhu fi masr yadamm masihiyyin," *Al-Sharq al-Awsat* (June 13, 2011).
37. "Bayan min al-da'wa al-salafiyya bi-sha'n al-musharaka al-siyasiyya" (March 22, 2011), https://anasalafy.com/ar/24951-السياسية-المشاركة-بشأن-السلفية-الدعوة-من-بيان.
38. Interview with 'Abd al-Mun'im al-Shahhat, *Al-Sharq al-Awsat* (April 18, 2011).
39. Ahmad Zaghlul Shalata, "Hiwar ma' Yasir Burhami: al-da'wa laha ru'ya shamila bima fiha al-musharaka al-siyasiyya," islamiyun.net (April 13, 2011).
40. Nadwat "al-da'wa al-salafiyya wa-l-'amal al-siyasi" (June 3, 2011), http://www.anasalafy.com/play.php?catsmktba=26898.
41. 'Abd al-'Azim, *Al-dimuqratiyya wa nazariyyat al-islah fi-l-mizan*.
42. This talking point appeared repeatedly in my interviews with 'Imad 'Abd al-Ghaffur, Ashraf Thabit, and Nadir Bakkar. Yasir Burhami discussed it at length in Yasir Burhami, *Thawrat 25 Yanayar: basa'ir wa basha'ir wa makhatir* (N.p.: Markaz usus, 2011), 32f.
43. 'Ali 'Abd al-'Al, "Al-da'wa al-salafiyya: sa-nad'am hizb al-nur fi-l-intikhabat al-qadima," http://elbashayeronline.com/news-141680.html.
44. See, for example, Muhammad Yusri Salama's book, *Mu'jam ma tubi'a min musannafat shaykh al-islam Ibn Taymiyya* (Alexandria: Dar al-tawhid li-l-turath, 2010).
45. "'Abd al-Ghaffur wa-l-Zarqa wa-'Alam al-din . . . min manabir al-salafiyya ila salun al-ri'asa," *Al-Shuruq* (August 28, 2012), http://www.shorouknews.com/news/view.aspx?cdate=28082012&id=0f678981-0256-4536-b4e0-ffe7065d4d0f.
46. Interviews with Muhammad Yusri Salama and 'Imad 'Abd al-Ghaffur.
47. Interview with 'Imad 'Abd al-Ghaffur. He suggests that he first presented the idea to Muhammad Isma'il al-Muqaddim on February 10.
48. Zaghlul Shalata, *Al-da'wa al-salafiyya al-sakandariyya*, 149f, notes 'Abd al-Ghaffur's leadership.
49. Biography of Yusri Hammad, https://www.facebook.com/elwatanparty/posts/385430511556230/الاس-لفضيلة-الذاتية-السيرة%BD%BF%EF.
50. Interview with Muhammad Yusri Salama.
51. Interview with Muhammad Nur.
52. Mu'taz Zahir, *Min al-masjid ila al-barlaman: dirasa hawla al-da'wa al-salafiyya wa hizb al-nur* (London: Takween, 2015), 85; interview with Mahmud 'Abbas.
53. Interviews with 'Imad 'Abd al-Ghaffur and Mahmud 'Abbas. Al-Mursi Higazi would become minister of finance under Morsi.
54. Program of the Nour Party, paper document in my possession.
55. Interview with Bassam al-Zarqa.
56. Interview with 'Imad 'Abd al-Ghaffur.
57. Salama, "Al-salafiyyun wa-l-aqbat fi masr," in *Al-Misbar, Al-aqbat fi Masr ba'd al-thawra* (Dubai: Markaz al-Misbar, 2012), 222.
58. Interview with Mahmud 'Abbas.

59. "Mu'tamar jamahiri li hizb al-nur al-salafi bi-l-thaghr" (June 24, 2011), https://alexnews.wordpress.com/2011/06/24/مؤتمر-جماهيري-لـحزب-النور-السلفي-بالثغ/.
60. Interview with Mahmud 'Abbas.
61. Samuel Tadros, *Mapping Egyptian Islamism*, research report (Washington, DC: Hudson Institute, 2014), 64.
62. Interview with 'Imad 'Abd al-Ghaffur.
63. Interview with Mahmud 'Abbas.
64. Interview with Jamal al-Sa'idi, a Nour candidate in Usim (Giza).
65. Interview with Muhammad al-Mislawi.
66. Numbers drawn from my detailed analysis based on nearly five hundred biographies presented in 'Amr Hisham Rabi', ed., *Dalil al-nukhab al-barlamaniyya al-masriyya 2012* (Cairo: Markaz al-ahram, 2012).
67. "Al-tahaluf yanhar: al-jama'a al-islamiyya tansahib," *Al-Masri al-Yawm* (October 16, 2011).
68. Interview with Nadir Bakkar, the only spokesman whose vision aligned with that of Burhami.
69. The expression for "good morning" translates literally to "morning of light." The *nashid* "Good morning Egypt" thus evokes Nour, the "party of light."
70. Interview with Mahmud 'Abbas.
71. Observations and interviews in Shubra al-Khayma, November 2011.
72. Interview with Muhammad al-'Adli.
73. Zahir, *Min al-masjid ila-l-barlaman*, 98-99.
74. "Hawla ta'assuf ra'is hizb al-nur 'ala 'adam tarashshuh nasrani fi qawa'im al-hizb," *Sawt al-Salaf* (January 1, 2012), http://www.salafvoice.com/article.php?a=5914.
75. *Al-Fath* (official journal of the Salafi Call) (January 4, 2012). See also Stéphane Lacroix, "Sheikhs and Politicians: Inside the New Egyptian Salafism" (Doha: Brookings Institution, 2012), 6-7.
76. "Iqaf al-ustadh Muhammad Nur 'an al-tahadduth bi-ism al-hizb bi sabab hudurihi hifl al-safara al-iraniyya" (February 24, 2012), http://www.forsanhaq.com/archive/index.php/t-298047.html.
77. "Khilafat dakhil al-da'wa al-salafiyya bi-sabab al-ihtifal bi-zikra ta'sis al-dawla al-turkiyya," *Al-Sharq Al-Awsat* (November 6, 2012).
78. Interview with Muhammad Nur.
79. Interview with Mahmud 'Abbas.
80. For example, "Al-mujaz takshif tafasil al-harb al-maktuma bayna Burhami wa 'Abd al-Ghaffur," *Al-Mujaz* (November 22, 2012), https://www.elmogaz.com/56148.
81. On this subject, see Ashraf al-Sharif, "'An azmat hizb al-nur wa tahaddiyat al-haraka al-salafiyya fi masr" (October 2, 2012), https://www.jadaliyya.com/Details/27143.
82. Interview with Mahmud 'Abbas.
83. My observations during the Call's rally in support of Abu al-Futuh's candidacy, Alexandria, May 18, 2012.
84. Zahir, *Min al-masjid ila-l-barlaman*, 138-40.
85. "Al-shaykh Abu Idris: ikhtalafna ma' al-ikhwan fi mas'alat al-bay'a," *Al-Watan* (May 27, 2012), https://www.elwatannews.com/news/details/9584.
86. Interview with Ashraf Thabit.

87. Benjamin Beit-Hallahmi, "Israel's Ultra-Orthodox: A Jewish Ghetto Within the Zionist State," *MERIP* 179 (1992).
88. "Khilafat 'Abd al-Ghaffur tush'il al-hariq fi-l-bayt al-salafi," *Al-Tahrir* (August 29, 2012).
89. "A'da' al-nur ya'taridun 'ala ikhtibarat al-tathqif al-siyasi," *Al-Yawm al-Sabi'* (September 2, 2012), https://www.youm7.com/story/2012/9/2/773581/أعضاء-النور-يعتر ضون-على-اختبارات-التثقيف-السياسى.
90. "'Imad 'Abd al-Ghaffur li-l-shuruq: wallah al-'azim intikhabat al-nur muzawwara," *Al-Shuruq* (October 3, 2012), https://www.shorouknews.com/news/view.aspx?cdate=03102012&id=434a8764-8faf-4290-855c-8a3e544fb7f8.
91. Interview with several founders of the al-Watan Party, including Yusri Hammad and Mahmud 'Abbas.
92. "Qiyadat bi-l-da'wa al-salafiyya yastaqilun min hizb al-nur fi-l-fayyum wa yandammun l-hizb al-watan," *Al-Ahram* (February 12, 2013), https://gate.ahram.org.eg/News/308020.aspx; "Qiyadi bi-l-kunisa yu'akkid istaqalat a'da' al-nur bi-l-jiza," *Masrawi* (January 31, 2013), https://www.masrawy.com/news/news_egypt/details/2013/1/31/90666/قيادي-ب-الكونيسة-يؤكد-استقالات-أعضاء-النور-بالجيزة-والحزب-ينفي.
93. See, for example, Tariq 'Uthman, *Al-ikhwan al-muslimun wa-l-salafiyyun fi masr* (Beirut: Markaz Nama,' 2012).
94. 'Abd al-Mun'im al-Shahhat, "Tasa'ulat hawla qirar "al-da'wa al-salafiyya" bi da'm al-duktur 'Abd al-Mun'im Abu al-Futuh" (April 30, 2012), https://www.anasalafy.com/play.php?catsmktba=33917.
95. *Burhami: al-ikhwan ramuni kharij al-masjid wa lan ansaha lahum*, https://www.youtube.com/watch?v=hPpk8_B691g.
96. Including, for example, Rabab al-Mahdi, a professor at the American University in Cairo.
97. Of the 150 members on the Call's advisory board, 126 voted for Abu al-Futuh, while 23 chose Morsi; on its executive council, 8 members voted for Abu al-Futuh and 3 for Morsi; and of the Nour Party's parliamentary delegation, 74 members chose Abu al-Futuh and 30 chose Morsi. At all levels, then, Abu al-Futuh won with an overwhelming majority (source: Salafi Call).
98. Muhammad Isma'il al-Muqaddim had initially expressed a preference for Abu Isma'il, while Sa'id 'Abd al-'Azim had done likewise for Morsi.
99. Interview with Sa'id 'Abd al-'Azim.
100. Interview with Sa'id 'Abd al-'Azim; Mahmud Ghuzlan, "Risala ila ikhwanina fi-l-da'wa al-salafiyya" (May 6, 2012), https://ikhwanonline.com/article/107902
101. "Yasir Burhami ya'tarif bi liqa'ihi bi-l-fariq Ahmad Shafiq," *Al-Yawm al-Sabi'* (September 27, 2012), http://www.youm7.com/story/0000/0/0/-/798790; interview with Mahmud 'Abbas, who recounts having heard talk within the party about details of this meeting.
102. "'Abd al-Ghaffur wa-l-Zarqa wa 'Alam al-Din . . . min manabir al-da'wa ila salun al-ri'asa," *Al-Shuruq* (August 28, 2013), http://www.shorouknews.com/news/view.aspx?cdate=28082012&id=0f678981-0256-4536-b4e0-ffe7065d4d0f.
103. Carrie Rosefsky Wickham, *The Muslim Brotherhood: Evolution of an Islamist Movement* (Princeton, NJ: Princeton University Press, 2013), 271.

5. SALAFISM FACES REVOLUTION

104. "Taswit 'ala al-dustur wa Mursi yarfud ilgha' i'lanihi," *Al-Jazeera* (November 29, 2012), https://www.aljazeera.net/news/arabic/2012/11/29/تصويت-على-الدستور-ومرس ي-يرفض-إلغاء.
105. Yussef Auf, "Islam and Sharia Law: Historical, Constitutional, and Political Context in Egypt," Atlantic Council, 2016, 5, http://www.jstor.org/stable/resrepo 3458.
106. "Fidyu musarrab yakshaf mukhattat al-salafiyyin li-'azl shaykh al-Azhar," *Al-'Arabiyya* (December 24, 2012), https://www.alarabiya.net/articles/2012/12/24 /256864.html.
107. "Hizb al-nur al-salafi: muhawalat akhwanat al-dawla al-masriyya ghayr maqbula," *Al-'Arabiyya* (January 29, 2013), https://www.alarabiya.net/ar/arab-and-world/egypt /2013/01/29/حزب-النور-السلفي-محاولات-أخونة-الدولة-المصرية-غير-مقبولة.
108. "Hizb al-nur yuhaddid bi-kashf tasafil malaff akhwanat al-dawla," *Al-Watan* (February 28, 2013), http://www.elwatannews.com/news/details/139133.
109. "Hizb al-nur yatahaffaz 'ala ziyarat Nijad li masr: Iran ra'iya li-madhabih ahl al-sunna," *Al-Masri al-Yawm* (February 5, 2013), http://www.almasryalyoum.com /news/details/281836.
110. "Harb kalamiyya bayna Burhami wa Hishmat," *Al-Yawm al-Sabi'* (April 12, 2013), https://www.masress.com/youm7/1016252.
111. "Burhami: fawa'id al-qard al-duwali "laysat riban muharamman" li-annaha la tatajawaz nisbat 2%," *Al-Masri al-Yawm* (August 27, 2012), www.almasryalyoum .com/news/details/159541.
112. "Hukm qard sunduq al-naqd ba'd taghyir kalam al-mas'ulin" (September 20, 2012), https://anasalafy.com/ar/35952-حكم-قرض-صندوق-النقد-بعد-تغير-كلام. Declarations by Nour and the Call sheikhs would continue to vary according to their relationship with the Brotherhood until the loan was obtained in April 2013 (which they opposed).
113. My observations of a meeting held at the French Institute of International Relations (IFRI) with the members of the Nour delegation during its visit to France, March 2013.
114. Each of these "talking points" is found in Muhammad bin Ibrahim al-Mansur, *Mawaqif hizb al-nur—waqa'i' wa kawalis* (Alexandria: Dar al-khulafa' al-rashidin, 2014). The book was published by Nour after the coup d'état in order to justify its political choices between 2011 and 2013.
115. Zahir, *Min al-masjid ila-l-barlaman*, 125-26; "Bawwabat al-Ahram tanshur bunud ittifaq jabhat al-inqadh wa hizb al-nur li-l-khuruj min al-azma al-haliyya," *Al-Ahram* (January 30, 2013), http://gate.ahram.org.eg/News/302717.aspx; "'Abd al-Mun'im al-Shahhat: mubadarat hizb al-nur—muhawala li-haqn al-dima'" (January 31, 2013), https://anasalafy.com/ar/38114-مبادرة-حزب-النور-محاولة-لحقن-الدماء.
116. Patrick Haenni, "The Reasons for the Muslim Brotherhood's Failure in Power," in *Egypt's Revolutions: Politics, Religion, and Social Movements*, ed. Bernard Rougier and Stéphane Lacroix (London: Palgrave Macmillan, 2016), 29-30.
117. "Al-da'wa al-salafiyya: qanun al-du'at yahdaf li-akhwanat al-manabir," *Al-Masriyyun* (May 13, 2013).
118. "Bayan ri'asi hawla iqalat mustashar Mursi," *Al-Jazeera* (February 19, 2013), https:// www.aljazeera.net/news/arabic/2013/2/19/بيان-رئاسي-حول-إقالة-مستشار-مرسي.

5. SALAFISM FACES REVOLUTION

119. "Al-Zarqa yu'lin istiqalatahu ba'd rafd al-ri'asa al-i'tidhar li-'Alam al-Din," *Al-Masri al-Yawm* (February 18, 2013), https://www.almasryalyoum.com/news/details/288538; "'Alam al-Din: iqalati min al-ri'asa ghadr . . . sa-ataqaddim bi-balagh li-l-na'ib al-'amm li-l-tahqiq ma'i," *Al-Masri al-Yawm* (February 18, 2013), https://www.almasryalyoum.com/news/details/288575.
120. "Ihtijaz Burhami bi-matar Burj al-'Arab wa Bakkar: kull wasa'il al-tas'id mutaha," *Rassd* (May 30, 2013), http://rassd.com/62952.htm.
121. Post by Sheikh Ibrahim Zakariyya Muhammad on his Facebook page (May 10, 2013).
122. Ketchley, *Egypt in a Time of Revolution*, 103f.
123. "Yasir Burhami: idha kjaraja al-malayin fi 30 yunyu sa-atlub Mursi bi-l-istaqala," *Al-Masri al-Yawm* (June 5, 2013), http://www.almasryalyoum.com/news/details/215693.
124. "Hal yantabiq wasf al-khalifa wali al-amr al-shar'i 'ala ra'is al-jumhuriyya?" (March 22, 2013), http://www.anasalafy.com/play.php?catsmktba=39090.
125. "Wathiqa sirriyya musarraba li-hizb al-nur 'an al-ra'is al-maz'ul Mursi," *Al-'Arabiyya* (July 20, 2013), http://www.alarabiya.net/ar/arab-and-world/egypt/2013/07/20/وثيقة-سرية-مسربة-لحزب-النور-عن-الرئيس-المعزول-مرسي.html.
126. Zahir, *Min al-masjid ila-l-barlaman*, 137–38.
127. According to an internal survey, 60 percent of Nour members disagreed with the party's stance regarding both the coup d'état that removed Morsi and the events that followed. See Ashraf El-Sherif, *Egypt's Salafists at a Crossroads* (Washington, DC: Carnegie Endowment for International Peace, 2015), 18.
128. "Wathiqa sirriyya musarraba li-hizb al-nur."
129. Zahir, *Min al-masjid ila-l-barlaman*, 131; "Al-nur yuhajim al-ra'is wa yutalib bi-ijra' tahqiq muhayid fi ahdath fadd i'tisam Rabi'a," *ONA News* (September 4, 2013), http://onaeg.com/?p=1145997.
130. The party published a lengthy study justifying its shift: Ahmad al-Shahhat, "Al-mar'a wa-l-nasara fi-l-barlaman al-qadim: ru'ya shar'iyya" (February 12, 2015), http://www.anasalafy.com/play.php?catsmktba=54010.
131. "Al-aqbat yuwasilun intifadatahum didd Yunis Makhyun ba'd tasrihatihi hawla tarashshuhihim bi-l-intikhabat," *Al-Yawm al-Sabi'* (October 13, 2015), http://www.youm7.com/story/2015/10/13/2386006/الأقباط-يواصلون-انتفاضتهم-ضد-يونس-مخ يون-بعد-تصريحاته-حول-ترش.
132. Interview with a former Call member who remained close to the organization, October 2017. Articles frequently appeared in the press accusing the group of "complicity with the Brotherhood" and reminding it of this threat. See "Al-amn al-watani yufajjir mufaja'a 'an dawr al-da'wa al-salafiyya fi musanadat khalaya al-ikhwan," *Al-Yawm al-Sabi'* (October 26, 2015), https://www.youm7.com/story/2015/10/26/2409041/الأمن-الوطني-يفجر-مفاجأة-عن-دور-الدعوة-السلفية-فى-مساندة. This is not to mention the repeated calls for Nour's dissolution, which, while unsuccessful, kept the party under pressure. See, for example, "Ba'd rafd al-idara al-'ulya hall al-nur . . . narsud 4 da'awi qada'iyya quddimat didd al-hizb al-salafi mundhu 'azl Mursi," *Al-Yawm al-Sabi'* (July 6, 2015), http://www.youm7.com/story/2015/7/6/2253936/بعد-رفض-الإدارية-العليا-حل-النور-نرصد-4دعاوى-قضائية-قدمت-ضد.
133. "Masr . . . al-da'wa al-salafiyya tastab'id Sa'id 'Abd al-'Azim wa-l-Muqaddim," *Islam Memo* (July 26, 2015), http://islammemo.cc/akhbar/locals-egypt/2015/07/26/256200.html.

134. "Al-da'wa al-salafiyya bi-matruh tu'lin i'tizal al-siyasa wa-l-'awda li-l-'amal al-da'wi," *Al-Yawm al-Sabi'* (July 1, 2014), http://www.youm7.com/story/2014/7/1/1754163/الدعوة_السلفية_بمطروح_تعلن_اعتزال_السياسة_والعودة_للعمل_الدع.
135. Despite attempts by the Nour Salafis to prove the contrary via questionable arguments. See Zahir, *Min al-masjid ila al-barlaman*, 225f.
136. Stéphane Lacroix and Ahmed Zaghloul Shalata, "Le maréchal et les cheikhs: les stratégies religieuses du régime et leurs complications dans l'Égypte d'al-Sisi," *Critique internationale* 1, no. 78 (2018): 35; Georges Fahmi, *The Egyptian State and the Religious Sphere* (Beirut: Carnegie Middle East Center, 2014), http://carnegie-mec.org/2014/09/17/egyptian-state-and-religious-sphere-pub-56619.
137. Lacroix and Zaghloul Shalata, "Le maréchal et les cheikhs," 35, 37.
138. 'Amr 'Izzat, *Li-man al-manabir al-yawm? Tahlil siyasat al-dawla fi idarat al-masajid* (Cairo: Al-mubadara al-masriyya li-l-huquq al-fardiyya, 2014), 63–64. One could legitimately question whether the Ministry of Awqaf truly had the ability to exercise such control, given its staff shortage. Only time will tell.
139. "Al-Shaykh 'Abd al-Rahman 'Abd al-Khaliq mu'assis al-salafiyya li-Burhami: kunta min junud Iblis fa-artaqa bik al-shirr wa sirta ustadhahu," *Al-Sha'b* (December 1, 2013).
140. "Bayan hawla al-mawaqif al-siyasiyya li-hizb al-nur" (January 12, 2014), http://www.almoslim.net/ node/198580.
141. "Milad hizb al-nur al-salafi al-filastini fi ghazza," *Al-'Arabiyya* (October 8, 2012), https://www .alarabiya .net /articles /2012%2F10%2F08%2F242556; Sanaa Karim, "Party Politics for Morocco's Salafis" (October 2, 2012), https://carnegieen dow ment.org/sada/49544; Ahmad Zaghlul Shalata, "Kayfa haffaza hizb al-nur salafi-yyi al-duwal-al-'arabiyya 'ala al-'amal al-hizbi" (May 16, 2019), http://hafryat.com /ar/blog/؟كيف-حفّز-حزب-النور-سلفيي-الدول-العربية-على-العمل-الحزبي.
142. Muhammad Yusri Ibrahim, *Al-musharaka al-siyasiyya al-mu'asira fi daw' al-siyasa al-shar'iyya* (Cairo: Dar al-yusr, 2011), 6.
143. Ibrahim, *Al-musharaka al-siyasiyya al-mu'asira*; Hisham Al Barghish, *Dirasat hawla al-ta'addudiyya al-hizbiyya wa al-tahaluf ma' al-ahzab al-'ilmaniyya* (Cairo: Dar al-yusr, 2011).
144. Mounia Bennani-Chraïbi, "Parcours, cercles et médiations à Casablanca. Tous les chemins mènent à l'action associative de quartier," in *Résistances et protestations dans les sociétés musulmanes*, ed. Mounia Bennani-Chraïbi and Olivier Fillieule (Paris: Presses de Sciences Po, 2003), 351.
145. See the list of members as it appears in Muhammad Yusri Ibrahim, *Mithaq al-hay'a al-shar'iyya li-l-huquq wa-l-islah* (Cairo: Dar al-yusr, 2012).
146. 'Adil Ghunaym, *Azmat al-dawla al-masriyya al-mu'asira* (Cairo: Dar al-'alam al-thalith, 2005), 214.
147. Nasr Farid Wasil had actually belonged to a group of insubordinate ulema within al-Azhar, the al-Azhar Ulema Front (*jabhat 'ulama' al-Azhar*). See Ghunaym, *Azmat al-dawla al-masriyya al-mu'asira*, 214.
148. "Ayad khafiyya tuthir al-shiqaq bayna al-shaykh Wasil wa-l-hay'a al-shar'iyya" (July 8, 2011), https://demo.islamstory.com/الشقاق-بين-الشيخ-واصل-والهيئة-الشرعية-; "Nasr Farid Wasil yastaqil min ri'asat al-hay'a al-shar'iyya li-l-huquq wa-l-islah, 7/7/2011," *Al-Yawm al-Sabi'* (July 7, 2011), https://www.youm7.com/story/2011/7/7/450187/نصر-فريد-واصل-يستقيل-من-رئاسة-الهيئة-الشرعية-للحقوق-والإصلاح.

5. SALAFISM FACES REVOLUTION

149. "Al-hay'a al-shar'iyya tu'lin ikhtiyar Mursi bi-aghlabiyyat thulthay al-a'da'," *Al-Yawm al-Sabi'* (April 25, 2012), https://www.youm7.com/story/2012/4/25/662508/الهيئة-الشرعية-تعلن-اختيار-مرسى-بأغلبية-ثلثى-الأعضاء.
150. My observations from the rally held in Cairo's Abdeen district on May 20, 2012.
151. "Al-Qaradawi yakhtub al-jum'a bi-l-tahrir," *Al-Jazeera* (February 17, 2011), https://www.aljazeera.net/news/arabic/2011/2/17/القرضاوي-يخطب-الجمعة-بالتحرير.
152. Al-Sayyid 'Abd al-Sattar, *Tajrubati ma' al-Ikhwan: min al-da'wa ila al-tanzim al-sirri* (Cairo: Al-zahra' li-l-i'lam al-'arabi, 2009), 269.
153. "Al-Qaradawi yad'am Abu al-Futuh li-l-ri'asa," *Al-Akhbar* (February 16, 2012), https://al-akhbar.com/Arab/65420.
154. "Ghadab azhari min tarshih Muhammad Yusri li-haqibat al-awqaf," *Al-Yawm al-Sabi'* (July 29, 2012), https://www.youm7.com/story/2012/7/29/743803/غضب-أزهرى-من-ترشيح-محمد-يسرى-لحقيبة-الأوقاف-نقابة-الأئمة.
155. "'Afifi... wazir awqaf sabahan wa mudhi' fi 'al-nas' laylan," *Al-Masri al-Yawm* (August 22, 2012), https://www.almasryalyoum.com/news/details/158592.
156. This sermon was transcribed in *Egypt Through the Eyes of al-'Arifi (Masr fi 'uyun al-'Arifi)* (Cairo: Sama, 2013).
157. "Khilafat al-nur wa ikhwan masr tasil al-hay'a al-shar'iyya," *Anadolu Agency* (February 26, 2013), https://www.aa.com.tr/ar/archive/271012/خلافات-النور-وإخوان-مصر-تصل-الهيئة-الشرعية.
158. "Hizb al-nur: mawqif Mursi mun surya mukhalif li tasrihatihi al-sabiqa," *Al-'Arabiyya* (June 16, 2013), https://www.alarabiya.net/ar/arab-and-world/egypt/2013/06/16/حزب-النور-السلفي-المصري-يقاطع-مؤتمر-نصرة-سوريا.html.
159. "Bi mubarakat Mursi...'Abd al-Maqsud yad'u 'ala mutamarridi 30 yunyu," *Al-Mujaz* (June 15, 2013), http://almogaz.com/news/politics/2013/06/15/957873.
160. See, for example, "Mursi Role at Syria Rally Seen as Tipping Point for Egypt Army," *Reuters* (July 2, 2013), https://www.reuters.com/article/us-egypt-protests-army-mursi/mursi-role-at-syria-rally-seen-as-tipping-point-for-egypt-army-idUSBRE9610YX20130702.
161. Regarding this question, see Haenni, "The Reasons for the Muslim Brotherhood's Failure in Power," 19–39.

6. THE POPULIST ROUTE

Epigraph: Al-Miqdad Gamal al-Din, *Yaqazat al-Imam: maqalat fi-l-fikr al-islami al-thawri* (October 24, 2013), http://www.islamrevo.com/2013/10/1.html.
1. Jayson Casper, "Salafyo Costa: Egyptian Inclusivity," *Middle East Institute* (December 9, 2013), https://www.mei.edu/publications/salafyo-costa-egyptian-inclusivity.
2. Some elements of this chapter draw from work conducted with the independent Egyptian researcher Ahmed Zaghloul Shalata, previously published as a coauthored article. See Stéphane Lacroix and Ahmed Zaghloul Shalata, "Shari'a et révolution: émergence et mutations du salafisme révolutionnaire dans l'Égypte post-Moubarak," *Archives de sciences sociales des religions* no. 181 (January–March 2018): 201-8.

3. "Thalatha qatla wa 80 jarihan fi muzaharat kanisat al-iskandariyya," *Al-Jazeera* (October 22, 2005), https://www.aljazeera.net/news/arabic/2005/10/22/ثلاثة-قتلى-و-80جريحا-في-مظاهرات-كنيسة-الإسكندرية.
4. Ahmad Zaghlul Shalata, *Al-daʿwa al-salafiyya al-sakandariyya: masarat al-tanzim wa malat al-siyasa* (Beirut: Markaz dirasat al-wahda al-ʿarabiyya, 2016), 126; Muhammad Yusri Salama, "Al-salafiyyun wa-l-aqbat fi masr—ruʾya fi-l-judhur wa-l-ishkaliyyat wa-l-tahaddiyat," in Al-Misbar, *Al-aqbat fi Masr baʿd al-thawra* (Dubai: Markaz al-Misbar, 2012), 215.
5. See, for example, this interview with Safwat Nur al-Din, who led Ansar al-Sunna: "I hate the infidel for his beliefs; that is to say, I hate his beliefs, but if he converts, I will love him with all my heart. But there is a difference between hatred and oppression. . . . Hating does not mean oppressing, and opponents of Islam have been treated fairly throughout its history." See Safwat Nur al-Din's interview in *Majallat al-Furqan*, no. 116, https://www.saaid.net/leqa/22.htm.
6. Salama, "Al-salafiyyun wa-l-aqbat fi masr."
7. To support this assertion, Salafis often pointed to a speech by Sadat from May 1981 where he suggested that this was what Pope Shenouda III planned to do. See "Saʿid al-Shahhat yakutb . . . dhati yawm 14 Mayu 1981," *Al-Yawm al-Sabiʿ* (May 14, 2020), https://www.youm7.com/story/2020/5/14/4773486/سعيد-الشحات-يكتب-ذات-يوم--14مايو-1981-السادات-يخطب.
8. Gaëtan du Roy, "Copts and the Egyptian Revolution: Christian Identity in the Public Sphere," in *Egypt's Revolutions: Politics, Religion, and Social Movements*, ed. Bernard Rougier and Stéphane Lacroix (London: Palgrave Macmillan, 2016), 214-15.
9. Laure Guirgis, ed., *Conversions religieuses et mutations politiques en Égypte. Tares et avatars du communautarisme égyptien* (Paris: Éditions Non-Lieu, 2008).
10. "Comments on Quran Misunderstood, Says Bishop Bishoy," *Daily News Egypt* (September 27, 2010), https://dailynewsegypt.com/2010/09/27/comments-on-quran-misunderstood-says-bishop-bishoy/.
11. Salama, "Al-salafiyyun wa-l-aqbat fi masr," in Al-Misbar, *Al-aqbat fi Masr baʿd al-thawra*, 219.
12. Interview with Ahmad Mawlana.
13. Interview with Yahya Rifaʿi Surur.
14. This is the central argument of his book *The Political Vision of the Islamist Movement*. See Rifaʿi Surur, *Al-tasawwur al-siyasi li-l-haraka al-islamiyya*, 3rd ed. (Cairo: Dar hadif, 2012).
15. Surur, 13-14.
16. Interview with Ahmad Mawlana.
17. Regarding the connection between the "defense of new Muslims" and the defense of those "oppressed" by the regime, see this video where Husam Abu al-Bukhari explains that the "oppressed" must be defended, be they Muslim or not. See Husam Abu al-Bukhari (starting at minute 2), https://www.youtube.com/watch?v=BbaoRDLo_oY.
18. Interview with Hisham Kamal. The website, https://www.camlya.com, is no longer online.
19. "Muzahara dakhma wasat al-Qahira yaquduha al-shaykh Hafiz Salama," *Taqrib News* (October 2, 2010), http://www.taghribnews.com/ar/news/27222/مظاهرة-ضخمة-بوسط-القاهرة-يقودها-الشيخ-حافظ-سلامة.

6. THE POPULIST ROUTE

20. "Hawla al-waqafat al-ihtijajiyya li-nusrat al-muslimat al-asirat wa al-dawabit al-shar'iyya laha" (September 23, 2010), http://www.anasalafy.com/play.php?catsmktba=36420; "Tujad waqfa ihtijajiyya amam masjid al-qa'id al-ibrahim min ajli Kamilia Shahata fa-ma al-mawqif minha?" (September 2, 2010), http://www.anasalafy.com/play.php?catsmktba=36422.
21. "Muzahara fi-l-Iskandariyya tutalib bi zuhur Kamilya," *Al-Masri al-Yawm* (September 24, 2010).
22. Mamduh Jabir, the critical Salafi from the Cairo School, would even write a book offering a detailed religious argument that justified the protests and the revolution against Mubarak. See Mamduh Jabir 'Abd al-Salam, *Thawrat al-khamis wa-l-'ishrin min yanayar—ru'ya shar'iyya* (Giza: Dar tahrir al-watan, 2011); interview with Mamduh Jabir.
23. 'Ali al-Rajjal, "Harakat Hazimun al-islamiyya," Arab Reform Initiative, paper presented at the workshop "Al-muhtajjun wa kharitat harakat al-ihtijaj fi masr ba'd al-thawra," March 21–22, 2014.
24. Hazim Abu Isma'il's website, https://hazemsalahnet.wordpress.com/السيرة-الذاتية/.
25. "Al-qissa al-kamila li-l-shaykh Abu Isma'il," *Sada al-balad* (December 26, 2012), https://www.elbalad.news/341642; he mentions this during a program on the CBC (March 13, 2012), https://www.youtube.com/watch?v=1RYZUwcMVjs.
26. Interview with Hisham Kamal.
27. Interview with Khalid Harbi.
28. Al-Rajjal, "Harakat Hazimun al-islamiyya."
29. "Nushata' wa muhamun yudashshinun i'tilafan ahliyyan li-da'm al-muslimin al-judud," *Al-Masriyyun* (March 22, 2011); *Kalimat haqq* (Speaking the truth), the Salafi Front's first statement (undated), distributed on Tahrir Square in early February of 2011.
30. Rifa'i Surur died in February 2012, and his funeral took place before a packed crowd that included a number of elite jihadi and critical Salafi figures; Ayman al-Zawahiri sent a personal message with his condolences. Video available at https://www.youtube.com/watch?v=h_9RBxWd8do.
31. Mahmud Tarshubi, "Tarikh al-salafiyya al-jihadiyya fi masr," in *Al-salafiyyun fi masr ma ba'd al-thawra*, ed. Mustafa Zahran, 'Umar Ghazi, et al. (Riyadh: Markaz al-din wa-l-siyasa/Beirut: Al-intishar al-'arabi, 2012), 214–21.
32. *Ra'y al-duktur Ayman al-Zawahiri fi istib'ad al-Shaykh Hazim*, https://www.youtube.com/watch?v=NplGSJoJpPA.
33. *Al-Zawahiri yahuththu Abu Isma'il 'ala nusrat al-islam*, https://www.youtube.com/watch?v=VxXnnZMOjsU.
34. Interview with Yahya Rifa'i Surur.
35. In May 2012 *Al-Shuruq* even ran a piece on a former al-Baradei sympathizer, Ahmad "Prost," who joined Abu Isma'il out of revolutionary fervor. See 'Abd al-Rahman Mustafa, "Rihla fi 'aql Ansar Abu Isma'il," *Al-Shuruq* (May 17, 2012), https://www.shorouknews.com/news/view.aspx?cdate=17052012&id=45b05759-3fca-4f83-a76e-421f29b9e7c3.
36. Khalil el-Anani, "The Sheikh President," *Al-Ahram Hebdo* (April–May 2012), https://web.archive.org/web/20130424002217/http://weekly.ahram.org.eg/2012/1095/sc5.htm.
37. Lacroix and Zaghloul Shalata, "*Shari'a* et révolution," 204.

6. THE POPULIST ROUTE

38. And the fairly brief political platform published by candidate Abu Isma'il in the spring of 2012 doesn't offer much more clarity: https://hazemsalahnet.wordpress.com/ملامح-البرنامج-الانتخابي/.
39. Video available at https://www.facebook.com/HazemSalahFB/videos/895807840913253/.
40. "New Salafi Party Has Curious Policy Mix," *Egypt Independent* (October 23, 2012), https://egyptindependent.com/new-salafi-party-has-curious-policy-mix/.
41. Interview with Ahmad Mawlana.
42. Al-Rajjal, "Harakat Hazimun al-islamiyya."
43. Hazim Abu Isma'il's followers would be quick to point out that he was one of the first leaders who asked youth to remain on Tahrir Square until the "revolution's objectives" had been completely brought to fruition.
44. Lacroix and Zaghloul Shalata, "*Shari'a et révolution*," 204.
45. "Abu Isma'il: U'adi mu'ahadat al-salam," *Al-Ahram* (September 13, 2011), http://gate.ahram.org.eg/News/115129.aspx.
46. 'Abdallah 'Azzam (1941–1989) was the foremost propagandist for jihad in Afghanistan during the 1980s. Ahmed Yassine (1937–2004) founded Palestinian Hamas. Video available at https://www.youtube.com/watch?v=9zsl3JXcSMQ.
47. Muhammad Ilhami, "Al-rajul al-wadih" (January 12, 2012), http://melhamy.blogspot.com/2012/01/.
48. Regarding this demonstration, see, for example, Carrie Rosefsky Wickham, *The Muslim Brotherhood: Evolution of an Islamist Movement* (Princeton, NJ: Princeton University Press, 2013), 194.
49. Muhammad al-Dib, "Al-ikhwa al-a'da': al-ikhwan wa-l-da'wa al-salafiyya taht hukm al-majlis al-'askari," *Ida'at* (August 4, 2015), https://www.ida2at.com/الإخوة-الأعداء--1الإخوان-والدعوة-السل/; for the narrative of a flabbergasted liberal, see Majdi Khalil, "Jum'at aslamat al-thawra al-masriyya fi sutur," *Al-Hiwar al-Mutamaddin* (August 5, 2011), http://www.ahewar.org/debat/show.art.asp?aid=270045.
50. Interview with Midhat al-Haddad.
51. My observations during the tumult of late November 2011.
52. My interviews on Tahrir Square during the tumult.
53. Muhammad Yusri Salama, "'An al-shaykh Hazim atahaddath" (January 14, 2012), https://www.egyptiantalks.org/invb/topic/131613-عيكتب-سلامة-يسري-محمدن-الشيخ-حازم-أتحدث
54. Lacroix and Zaghloul Shalata, "*Shari'a et révolution*," 204.
55. "Istiqalat na'ib bi-hizb al-nur bi-masr li-kadhbihi," *Al-Jazeera* (March 5, 2012), http://www.aljazeera.net/news/arabic/2012/3/5/لكذبه-بمصر-النور-بحزب-نائب-استقالة.
56. "Bi-l-fidyu . . . al-na'ib al-salafi 'Ali Wannis yarwi haqiqat al-fa'l al-fadih," *Al-Yawm al-Sabi'* (June 9, 2012), https://www.youm7.com/story/2012/6/9/700153/بالفيديو-النائب-السلفى-على-ونيس-يروى-حقيقة-الفعل-الفاضح-ونيابة.
57. Lacroix and Zaghloul Shalata, "*Shari'a et révolution*," 209.
58. Cas Mudde and Cristóbal Rovira Kaltwasser, *Populism: A Very Short Introduction* (Oxford: Oxford University Press, 2017), 6.
59. Regarding the Call, see, for example, "Hazimun tuhajim hizb al-nur: la siyasa wa la shari'a . . . wa tudallil al-nas bi-l-shi'arat," *Al-Masri al-Yawm* (May 14, 2012), https://www.almasryalyoum.com/news/details/178789.

6. THE POPULIST ROUTE

60. "Yasir Burhami ila shabab al-tayyar al-salafi: inna Hazim Abu Isma'il min abna' al-ikhwan" (April 17, 2012), http://www.muslm.org/vb/showthread.php?477996 !‫-الشيخ-ياسر-برهامي-الى-شباب-التيار-السلفي-ان-حازم-ابو-اسماعيل-من-ابناء-جماعة-الاخوان-‬
61. On his show *Al-Barnamij*. See, for example, https://www.youtube.com/watch?v=wr73csrK3eg.
62. 'Abd al-Warith would turn against Abu Isma'il after he was eliminated from the presidential race and would also criticize his own actions: "Wisam 'Abd al-Warith: Abu Isma'il tarak ansarahu farisa sahla wa kan bi-maqdurihi himayatuhum," *Al-Yawm al-Sabi'* (May 20, 2012), https://www.youm7.com/story/2012/5/20 /682890/‫وسام-عبدالوارث-"أبوإسماعيل"-ترك-أنصاره-فريسة-سهلة-وكان-بمقدوره-حمايتهم‬.
63. "Abu Isma'il al-murashshah raqm 7 rasmiyyan bi-151 alf tawkil wa 50 tawqi'an min nuwwab," *Al-Shuruq* (March 30, 2012), http://www.shorouknews.com/news/view.aspx?cdate=30032012&id=6171ac37-4f5c-43be-bdaa-c78670df32d3; "Masirat Abu Isma'il tamtadd min al-'abbasiyya ila Salah Salim," *Al-Yawm al-Sabi'* (March 30, 2012), https://www.youm7.com/story/2012/3/30/640620/‫مسيرة-أبو-إسماع‬ ‫يل-تمتد-من-العباسية-حتى-صلاح-سالم‬.
64. "Istifa' bawwabat al-Shuruq: Abu Isma'il yatasaddir...," *Al-Shuruq* (February 21, 2012), https://www.shorouknews.com/news/view.aspx?cdate=21022012&id=5c29b204-2eb2-4dae-bd15-d71e002de475; "Abu Isma'il yatasaddir istifta' "Kulluna Khalid Sa'id" li-l-ri'asa," *Sada al-balad* (February 1, 2012), https://www.elbalad.news/67884/abo-esmaayl-ytsdr-astfta.aspx.
65. "7 nuwwab bi-l-nur yukhalifun qirar al-'ulya li-l-hizb wa yu'ayyidun Abu Isma'il," *Al-Yawm al-Sabi'* (March 7, 2012).
66. "Nanshur bayan majlis shura al-'ulama' li-ta'yid Abu Isma'il murashshahan li-l-ri'asa," *Al-Yawm al-Sabi'* (March 24, 2012), https://www.youm7.com/story/2012/3/24/635555/‫ننشر-بيان-مجلس-شورى-العلماء-لتأييد-أبوإسماعيل-مرشحاً-للرئاسة-المجلس‬.
67. See, for example, the press conference held by Abu Isma'il on May 13, 2012, https://www.youtube.com/watch?v=Hx-NQSPZ4KQ.
68. *Ansar Abu Isma'il yuhasirun majlis al-dawla* (April 11, 2012), https://www.youtube.com/watch?v=gg8BDKSudic.
69. *Ishtibakat bi-l-'abbasiyya wa-l-jaysh yafudd al-i'tisam* (May 4, 2012), https://www.youtube.com/watch?v=WY-RQIwjelo.
70. Lacroix and Zaghloul Shalata, "Shari'a et révolution," 205-6.
71. Like other Islamist-oriented pages, the 2012 page was deleted after the overthrow of Mohamed Morsi on July 3, 2013.
72. For a blog article describing the website before it was deleted, see http://ehaborabi5.blogspot.fr/2012/12/blog-post_22.html.
73. Lacroix and Zaghloul Shalata, "Shari'a et révolution," 205.
74. My observations during the sit-in, December 11, 2012. Media Production City hosted the studios for several of Egypt's largest private channels.
75. Al-Rajjal, "Harakat Hazimun al-islamiyya"; "Mu'tasimu madinat al-intaj yadhbahun 3 khuraf atlaqu 'alayha asma' 'Sabbahi wa Musa wa al-Barada'i,'" *Al-Masri al-Yawm* (December 12, 2012), https://www.almasryalyoum.com/news/details/262475.
76. Mudde and Kaltwasser, *Populism*, 43.
77. From the first post, dated September 28, 2011, on the Harakat Hazimun Facebook page, which had been created the day before. See https://www.facebook.com/Hazemon.

6. THE POPULIST ROUTE

78. "Hazimun . . . wa maʿrakat al-umma al-qadima" (April 2, 2012), https://www.facebook.com/Hazemon.
79. See https://www.facebook.com/AwladAboIsmail; https://www.facebook.com/pages/%D9%84%D8%A7%D8%B2%D9%85-%D8%AD%D8%A7%D8%B2%D9%85/268383156581609.
80. Ahmed Zaghloul Shalata's interview of Walid al-Haggag, founder of Tullab al-Shariʿa.
81. Mudde and Kaltwasser, *Populism*, 51–52.
82. "Al-shaykh ʿAbd al-Khaliq yadʿu ansar Abu Ismaʿil li-taʾsis hizb jadid," *Islam Memo* (April 10, 2012), http://www.islammemo.cc/akhbar/arab/2012/04/10/147630.html.
83. "Itlaq hizb "al-umma al-masriyya" bi-riʿayat al-Huwayni wa Abu Ismaʿil," *ONA News* (April 16, 2012), http://onaeg.com/?p=61528.
84. See, for example, his book *This Is Most Definitely a War on Islam*, subtitled *The Third World War . . . Has Already Begun*. Muhammad ʿAbbas, *Bal hiya harb ʿala al-islam*, 2nd ed. (Cairo: Dar Ibn al-Jawzi, 2012).
85. Lacroix and Zaghloul Shalata, "*Shariʿa et révolution*," 210.
86. "Abu Ismaʿil yuʿlin ʿan akbar tahaluf salafi," *Al-Masriyyun* (March 8, 2013).
87. *Abu Ismaʿil yuʿlin al-nuzul li-l-shariʿ wa maydan al-Tahrir* (March 15, 2013), https://www.youtube.com/watch?time_continue=69&v=aTPjef__WuI.
88. Lacroix and Zaghloul Shalata, "*Shariʿa et révolution*," 211.
89. Lacroix and Zaghloul Shalata, 211.
90. Interviews with intellectuals from the revolutionary Salafi movement, winter 2012.
91. Interview with Yahya Rifaʿi Surur.
92. Interview with Khalid Harbi.
93. Mustafa, "Rihla fi ʿaql Ansar Abu Ismaʿil."
94. "Abu Ismaʿil: hizb al-raya sayakun juzʾ min haraka akbar hadafuha dawlat al-shariʿa," http://islamion.com/news/أبو-إسماعيل-حزب-الراية-سيكون-جزء-من-حركة-أكبر/هدفها-دولة-الشريعة.
95. Lacroix and Zaghloul Shalata, "*Shariʿa et révolution*," 211.
96. Lacroix and Zaghloul Shalata, 211.
97. Lacroix, Zaghloul Shalata, "*Shariʿa et révolution*," 212. Regarding Ahrar, see, for example, Mokhtar Awad, "Revolutionary Salafism: The Case of the Ahrar Movement," *Hudson Institute* (April 29, 2016), https://www.hudson.org/research/12310-revolutionary-salafism-the-case-of-ahrar-movement; "Lughz harakat Ahrar," *Al-Ahram* (September 3, 2013), http://shabab.ahram.org.eg/News/14187.aspx; "Ahrar tadʿu li-l-taharrur min mabdaʾ al-taʿa al-ʿumya,'" *Al-Shuruq* (December 21, 2012), http://www.shorouknews.com/news/view.aspx?cdate=21122012&id=1d5db963-c5c4-48ed-8f16-690176279a4b.
98. "Mabadiʾ harakat al-ahrar fi ʿamaliha" (October 11, 2012), https://www.facebook.com/AhrarMov.
99. Regarding al-Hawali, see Stéphane Lacroix, *Awakening Islam: The Politics of Religious Dissent in Contemporary Saudi Arabia*, trans. George Holoch (Cambridge, MA: Harvard University Press, 2011), 147–49.
100. Ahmad Samir, *Maʿrakat al-ahrar*, https://ia800300.us.archive.org/24/items/M3RkT-ElAhrar/معركة%20الأحرار.pdf. See also the lecture given by Ahrar members

6. THE POPULIST ROUTE

at Cairo University on April 21, 2013: https://www.youtube.com/watch?v=_jxOe9komtk.
101. Awad, "Revolutionary Salafism."
102. "Mabadi' harakat al-ahrar fi 'amaliha."
103. "Al-irhabi alladhi yaqud mudarrajat al-Zamalik," *Eurosport* (July 9, 2013), https://arabia.eurosport.com/article/كرة-القدم/كرة-القدم/الإرهابي-الذي-يقود-مدرجات-الزمالك.
104. Before it was suppressed, the page was at https://www.facebook.com/AhrarMov.
105. Lacroix and Zaghloul Shalata, "*Shariʿa* et révolution," 212.
106. Lacroix and Zaghloul Shalata, 212.
107. Lacroix and Zaghloul Shalata, 211.
108. Interview with Yahya Rifaʿi Surur.
109. Program on CBC, July 6, 2012.
110. Lacroix and Zaghloul Shalata, "*Shariʿa* et révolution," 213.
111. Lacroix and Zaghloul Shalata, 213.
112. The opposition to the constitution can be seen in "Miswaddat al-dustur jinaya fi haqq al-shariʿa," a text posted to the Ahrar Facebook page (December 2, 2012), https://www.facebook.com/AhrarMov.
113. *Khanu* (June 29, 2013), https://www.youtube.com/watch?v=rZe2DF43DpI.
114. "Mutazahiru harakat Ahrar li-l-ikhwan: biʿtu al-thawra wa biʿtu al-din," *Al-Yawm al-Sabiʿ* (April 11, 2013), http://videoyoum7.com/2013/04/11/متظاهرو-حركة-أح-رار-لـالإخوان-بعتوا-ا/.
115. "Lahzat al-qabd ʿala Abu Ismaʿil," *Al-Masri al-Yawm* (July 6, 2013), https://www.almasryalyoum.com/news/details/231774.
116. See the official video of the event at https://www.youtube.com/watch?v=Vc1-Rkd5VkA. An Ultras-style anthem called "Pharaoh's Still on the Throne" (*Farʿun lessa byahkum*) was written for the occasion. See https://www.youtube.com/watch?v=36DvxPVlkU4.
117. "Al-ikhwan tadaʿ dawabit li-l-musharaka fi muzaharat 28/11" (November 27, 2014), http://www.fj-p.com/headline_Details.aspx?News_ID=57418.
118. Lacroix and Zaghloul Shalata, "*Shariʿa* et révolution," 214.
119. See, for example, the demonstration held at Cairo University on December 5, 2013, https://www.youtube.com/watch?v=mTI9gT7mRpE. Chants included "We are the youth of January 25," "We are youth who love our religion," "We are the brothers of those in jail," etc.
120. Lacroix and Zaghloul Shalata, "*Shariʿa* et révolution," 214.
121. Mahir Farghali and Salah al-Din Hasan, *Dimaʾ ʿala rimal Saynaʾ: al-qissa al-kamila li-l-tanzimat al-jihadiyya al-jadida fi masr* (N.p.: Muʾminun bila hudud, 2017), 224–30.
122. This is the opinion of Khalid al-Zaʿfarani, for example, who is more credible than many proregime sources. See https://www.youtube.com/watch?v=gHdH73I20As.
123. Georges Fahmi, "Why Aren't More Muslim Brothers Turning to Violence," *Chatham House* (April 27, 2017), https://www.chathamhouse.org/expert/comment/why-aren-t-more-muslim-brothers-turning-violence.
124. ʿAshush wrote a book intended for Abu Ismaʿil: *Guiding the Confused toward the Prohibition on Following the Path of Constitutions and Parliaments* (*hidayat al-hiran ila hurmat suluk tariq al-dustur wa-l-barlaman*), https://ketabpedia.com/تحميل/هداية-الحيران-إلى-حرمة-سلوك-طريق-الدست/. See also the debate over Abu

Isma'il on a jihadi forum, https://shamukh.net/forum/منتدى-الأ/العامة-المنتديات-قسم
/إسماعيل-أبو-صلاح-حازم-إلى-عشوش-أحمد-من-الأخير-النداء162778/-الأمة-وقضايا-خبار/
page3.

125. "From a Private School in Cairo to ISIS Killing Fields in Syria," *New York Times* (February 19, 2015), https://www.nytimes.com/2015/02/19/world/middleeast/from-a-private-school-in-cairo-to-isis-killing-fields-in-syria-video.html; "Mufaja'a: Islam Yakin fatat 'Da'ish' sharak Hazimun fi hisar madinat al-intaj," *Al-Yawm al-Sabi'* (February 20, 2016).

126. "Al-amn al-masri yusaffi munassiq hamlat Hazim Abu Isma'il bi manzilihi," *Al-'Arabi al-Jadid* (November 15, 2015), https://www.alaraby.co.uk/يُصف-المصري-الأمن; بمنزله-إسماعيل-أبو-حازم-حملة-منسق-ي "Muhammad Nasr . . . min ustadh jami'i ila mu'assis tanzim kata'ib al-Furqan al-takfiri" (November 28, 2017), https://24.ae/article/400036/.

127. See, for example, "Li-madha baya' awlad Abu Isma'il Da'ish wa-l-Qa'ida?," *Sawt al-Umma* (October 17, 2018), http://www.soutalomma.com/Article/837137/باي-لماذا. أعضاء-انضمام-قصة-والقاعدة-داعش-إسماعيل-أبو-أولاد-ع.

128. This is what Samuel Tadros seems to suggest when he describes how Abu Isma'il's campaign slogan, "We will live dignified," was appropriated by the Soldiers of Egypt. Samuel Tadros, *Mapping Egyptian Islamism* (Research Report for the Hudson Institute), 83.

129. Interview with 'Abdallah al-Fakharani.

130. The journals were called *The Guardians of the Shari'a* (*Hurras al-shari'a*), published from April 2013 to January 2014, and *Speaking the Truth* (*Kalimat haqq*), published from August 2017 to June 2020, whose editor-in-chief was Muhammad Ilhami. They are available at https://archive.org/details/horras_chareeah and https://klmtuhaq.blogspot.com/2019/01/blog-post.html.

131. Al-Miqdad Gamal al-Din, "Akhta' al-tajruba al-hazimiyya (maqalat fi-l-fikr al-islami al-thawri 2)," http://www.islamrevo.com/2013/10/2.html.

132. Olivier Roy, "Révolutions post-islamistes," *Le Monde* (February 12, 2011).

CONCLUSION

1. Khalil al-Anani, "The UAE's Manipulative Utilization of Religion" (September 29, 2020), http://arabcenterdc.org/policy_analyses/the-uaes-manipulative-utilization-of-religion/.

2. Ahmad Salim, 'Amr Basyuni, *Ma ba'd al-salafiyya* (Beirut: Markaz Nama' li-l-buhuth wa-l-dirasat, 2015).

BIBLIOGRAPHY

SOURCES IN ARABIC

'Abbas, Mahmud. *Mudhakkarat salafi fi hizb al-nur*. N.p.: Maqam li-l-nashr wal-l-tawzi', 2016.
'Abbas, Muhammad. *Bal hiya harb 'ala al-islam*. 2nd ed. Cairo: Dar Ibn al-Jawzi, 2012.
'Abd al-'Azim, Sa'id. *Al-dimuqratiyya wa nazariyyat al-islah fi-l-mizan*. Alexandria: Dar al-fath al-islami, 2009.
'Abd al-'Aziz, Hisham Mustafa. *Nahdat umma*. Alexandria: Dar al-huda, 2008.
'Abd al-Fattah, Nabil. *Al-nukhab wa-l-thawra: al-dawla wa-l-islam al-siyasi wa-l-qawmiyya wa-l-libaraliyya*. Cairo: Dar al-'ayn, 2013.
'Abd al-Ghani, Muhammad bin 'Awad (Ibn). *Lamahat 'an da'wat al-ikhwan al-muslimin*. Cairo: Dar sabil al-mu'minin, 2010.
'Abd al-Halim, Mahmud. *Al-ikhwan al-muslimun—Ahdath sana'at al-tarikh: ru'ya min al-dakhil—al-juz' al-thalith 1952–1971*. 3rd ed. Alexandria: Dar al-da'wa, 1994.
'Abd al-Halim, Tariq. *Al-Jawab al-mufid fi hukm jahil al-tawhid*. N.p.: 1978. http://www.almeshkat.net/book/1357.
'Abd al-Khaliq, 'Abd al-Rahman. *Al-usul al-'ilmiyya li-l-da'wa al-salafiyya*. 2nd ed. Kuwait: Al-dar al-salafiyya, 1977. https://shamela.ws/index.php/book/12826.
'Abd al-Latif, Umayma. *Al-salafiyyun fi masr wa-l-siyasa*. Doha: Arab Center for Research and Policy Studies, 2011.
'Abd al-Majid, Ahmad. *Al-ikhwan wa 'Abd al-Nasir: al-qissa al-kamila li tanzim 1965*. Cairo: Al-zahra' li-l-i'lam al-'arabi, 1991.
'Abd al-Majid, Sharif. *Al-ikhwan al-muslimun wa-l-sira' 'ala tarkat Hasan al-Banna*. Cairo: Al-jazira li-l-nashr wa-l-tawzi', 2010.
'Abd al-Rahman, 'Umar. *Kalimat haqq: murafa'at al-shaykh 'Umar 'Abd al-Rahman fi qadiyyat al-jihad*. https://www.tawhed.ws.

BIBLIOGRAPHY

'Abd al-Salam, Mamduh Jabir. *Thawrat al-khamis wa-l-'ishrin min yanayar—ru'ya shar'iyya*. Giza: Dar tahrir al-watan, 2011.

'Abd al-Sattar, Al-Sayyid. *Tajrubati ma' al-ikhwan min al-da'wa ila-l-tanzim al-sirri*. Cairo: Al-zahra' li-l-i'lam al-'arabi, 2009.

'Abduh, Muhammad. *Al-islam bayna al-'ilm wa-l-madaniyya*. Giza: Wikalat al-sahafa al-'arabiyya, 2019.

Abu Hashima, Tariq. *Masr fi 'uyun al-'Arifi*. Cairo: Sama, 2013.

Abu Khalil, Haytham. *Ikhwan islahiyyun*. Cairo: Dar dawwin, 2012.

Abu Rumman, Muhammad. *Al-sira' 'ala al-salafiyya: qira'a fi-l-idyulujiyya wa-l-khilafat wa kharitat al-intishar*. Beirut: Al-shabaka al-'arabiyya li-l-abhath wa-l-nashr, 2016.

Abu Zuhra, Muhammad. *Tarikh al-madhahib al-islamiyya fi-l-siyasa wa-l-'aqa'id wa tarikh al-madhahib al-fiqhiyya*. Cairo: Dar al-fikr al-'arabi, 1971.

Adib, Munir. *'Anabir al-mawt: qisas waqi'iyya min dakhil al-sujun al-masriyya*. Cairo: Dar awraq, 2012.

'Afifi, Ahmad al-. "Abu al-Wafa' Muhammad Darwish wa juhuduhu li-dirasat al-'aqida al-islamiyya." MA thesis, Cairo University, 2009.

Ahad talabat al-'ilm (pseudonym of Haytham Tawfiq). *Hiwar hadi hawla kitab qira'a naqdiyya wa ma hawluhu min i'taradat*. N.p., 2008.

Ahmad, Rifa'at Sayyid. *Al-nabi al-musallah (1)—al-rafidun*. London: Riad El-Rayyes Books, 1991.

Ahmad, Rifa'at Sayyid. *Al-nabi al-musallah (2)—al-tha'irun*. London: Riad El-Rayyes Books, 1991.

Albani, Muhammad Nasir al-Din al-. *Al-tasfiya wa-l-tarbiya wa hajat al-muslimin ilayha*. Riyadh: Maktabat al-ma'arif li-l-nashr wa-l-tawzi', 2007.

Albani, Muhammad Nasir al-Din al-. *Hukm tarik al-salat*. Riyadh: Dar al-jalalayn, 1992.

Albani, Muhammad Nasir al-Din al-. *Sifat salat al-nabi—salla Allah 'alayhi wa sallam—min al-takbir ila-l-taslim ka-annak taraha*. Riyadh: Maktabat al-ma'arif li-l-nashr wa-l-tawzi', n.d.

Albani, Muhammad Nasir al-Din al-. *Silsilat al-ahadith al-da'ifa wa-l-mawdu'a*. Riyadh: Maktabat al-ma'arif, 1992.

Al-wahhabiyya wa-l-salafiyya: awraq bahthiyya. Beirut: Al-shabaka al-'arabiyya li-l-abhath wa-l-nashr, 2016.

Amin, Jalal. *Masr wa-l-masriyyun fi 'ahd Mubarak 1981–2008*. Cairo: Dar Merit, 2009.

'Amir, Mahmud Lutfi. *Tanbih al-ghafilin bi haqiqat fikr al-ikhwan al-muslimin*. 4th ed. Damanhur: Dar al-mahja al-bayda', 2006.

'Anani, Khalil al-. *Al-ikhwan al-muslimun fi masr: shaykhukha tusari' al-zaman?* Cairo: Maktabat al-shuruq al-duwaliyya, 2007.

Ansari, Talal al-. *Safahat majhula min tarikh al-haraka al-islamiyya al-mu'asira: min al-naksa ila-l-mashnaqa*. Cairo: Markaz al-mahrusa li-nashr wa-l-khadamat al-sahafiyya wa-l-ma'lumat, 2006.

'Aql, 'Abd al-Rahman al-. *Jamharat maqalat al-'allama al-shaykh Ahmad Muhammad Shakir*. Riyadh: Dar al-Riyadh, 2005.

'Ashush, Ahmad Fu'ad. *Hidayat al-hiran ila hurmat suluk tariq al-dustur wa-l-barlaman*. N.p.: n.d. https://ketabpedia.com/تحميل/هداية-الحيران-إلى-حرمة-سلوك-طريق-الدست/.

BIBLIOGRAPHY

'Awwa, Salwa Muhammad al-. *Al-jama'a al-islamiyya al-musallaha fi masr 1974–2004*. Cairo: Maktabat al-shuruq al-duwaliyya, 2006.
Badr, Badr Muhammad. *Al-jama'a al-islamiyya fi jami'at masr: haqa'iq wa watha'iq*. N.p.: 1989.
Bakr, 'Ala'. *Al-sahwa al-islamiyya fi masr fi al-sab'iniyyat*. Alexandria: Dar al-khulafa' al-rashidin, 2013.
Bakr, 'Ala'. *Thatlathu qurun hijriyya 'ala da'wat al-shaykh Muhammad bin 'Abd al-Wahhab al-salafiyya*. Alexandria: Dar al-khulafa' al-rashidin, 2007.
Bakr, 'Ala', and Yasir Burhami. *Madhahib fikriyya fi-l-mizan: muhadarat fi-l-ghazu al-fikri*. Mansoura: Maktabat fayyad, 2011.
Banna, Hasan al-. *Mudhakkarat al-da'wa wa-l-da'iya*. N.p.: n.d. http://www.daawa-info.net/books1.php?parts=135&au=البنا%20حسن
Banna, Jamal al-. *Al-sayyid Rashid Rida: Munshi' al-Manar wa ra'id al-salafiyya al-haditha*. Cairo: Dar al-fikr al-islami, 2006.
Banna, Jamal al-. *Min watha'iq al-ikhwan al-muslimin al-majhula*. 7 vols. Cairo: Dar al-fikr al-islami, n.d.
Barghish, Hisham Al. *Dirasat hawla al-ta'addudiyya al-hizbiyya wa al-tahaluf ma' al-ahzab al-'ilmaniyya*. Cairo: Dar al-yusr, 2011.
Bassam, 'Abdallah al-. *'Ulama' Najd khilal thamaniyat qurun*. 6 vols. Riyadh: Dar al-'asima, 1998.
Bayyumi, Muhammad Rajab al-. *Al-nahda al-islamiyya fi siyar a'lamiha al-mu'asirin*. 2 vols. Beirut: Al-dar al-shamiyya, 1995.
Bayyumi, Zakariyya. *Al-ikhwan al-muslimun wa-l-jama'at al-islamiyya fi-l-haya al-siyasiyya al-masriyya 1928–1948*. 2nd ed. Cairo: Maktabat wahba, 1991.
Bayyumi, Zakariyya. *Al-sufiyya wa lu'bat al-siyasa fi masr al-haditha wa-l-mu'asira: dirasa tarikhiyya watha'iqiyya*. Dasuq: al-'ilm wa-l-iman li-l-nashr wa-l-tawzi', 2009.
Birsh, Walid Yusuf al-. *Alihat al-'unf: min manassat al-Sadat ila manassat Rabi'a*. Cairo: Kunuz li-l-nashr wa-l-tawzi', 2015.
Bishara, 'Azmi. *Fi-l-ijaba 'an su'al: ma hiya al-salafiyya?* Doha: Arab Center for Research and Policy Studies, 2018.
Bishara, 'Azmi. *Thawrat Masr*. 2 vols. Doha: Arab Center for Research and Policy Studies, 2016.
Bishri, Tariq al-. *Al-haraka al-siyasiyya fi masr 1935–1945*. 2nd ed. Cairo: Dar al-shuruq, 2002.
Burhami, Yasir. *Al-'amal al-jama'i bayna al-ifrat wa-l-tafrit*, textbook of the Salafi Call (personal photocopy).
Burhami, Yasir. *Fadl al-ghani al-hamid fi sharh kitab al-tawhid*. Alexandria: Dar al-khulafa' al-rashidin, 2009.
Burhami, Yasir. *Fiqh al-khilaf bayn al-muslimin*. 2nd ed. Alexandria: Dar al-'aqida, 2000.
Burhami, Yasir. *Qira'a naqdiyya li ba'd ma warada fi kitab "zahirat al-irja'" wa-l-radd 'alayha*. Alexandria: Al-dar al-salafiyya li-l-nashr wa-l-tawzi', 2004.
Burhami, Yasir. *Sharh fiqh al-amr bi-l-ma'ruf wa-l-nahi 'an al-munkar*, textbook of the Salafi Call (personal photocopy).
Burhami, Yasir. *Sharh masa'il al-jahiliyya—al-juz' al-awwal*. Alexandria; Dar al-khulafa' al-rashidin, 2013.

BIBLIOGRAPHY

Burhami, Yasir. *Tahqiq madhhab shaykh al-islam Ibn Taymiyya fi tarik al-salat*. 2nd ed. Alexandria: Dar al-khulafa' al-rashidin, 2011.

Burhami, Yasir. *Thawrat 25 Yanayar: basa'ir wa basha'ir wa makhatir*. N.p.: Markaz usus, 2011.

Darbala, 'Isam, and 'Asim 'Abd al-Majid. *Al-qawl al-qati' fi man imtana' 'an al-shara'i'*. N.p.: n.d.

Darwish, Abu al-Wafa'. *Sihat al-haqq*. 6th ed. Beirut: al-Maktab al-Islami, n.d.

Dasuqi, 'Abduh Mustafa, and al-Sa'id Ramadan al-'Ubadi. *Tarikh al-haraka al-tullabiyya bi jama'at al-ikhwan al-muslimin (1933–2011)*. https://www.ikhwanwiki.com.

Dawud, Muhammad 'Abd al-'Aziz. *Al-jam'iyyat al-islamiyya fi masr wa dawruha fi nashr al-da'wa al-islamiyya*. http://www.ikhwanwiki.com/index.php?title=الجمعيات_الاسلامية_فى_مصر#.D8.A7.D9.84.D9.81.D8.B5.D9.84_.D8.A7.D9.84.D8.B1.D8.A7.D8.A8.D8.B9_.D8.A7.D9.86.D8.AA.D8.B4.D8.A7.D8.B1_.D8.A7.D9.84.D8.A8.D8.AF.D8.B9_.D9.88.D8.A7.D9.84.D8.AE.D8.B1.D8.A7.D9.81.D8.A7.D8.AA.

Dijwi, Yusuf al-. *Maqalat wa fatawa al-shaykh al-Dijwi*. Cairo: Dar al-kitab al-sufi, 2011.

Dimashqi, Muhammad Munir 'Abduh Agha al-. *Namudhaj min al-a'mal al-khayriyya fi idarat al-tiba'a al-muniryya*. Riyadh: Maktabat al-imam al-shafi'i, 1930.

Farghali, Mahir. *Al-khuruj min bawwabat al-jahim: al-jama'a al-islamiyya fi Masr min al-'unf ila al-muraja'at*. Beirut: Al-intishar al-'arabi, 2012.

Farghali, Mahir, and Salah al-Din Hasan. *Dima' 'ala rimal Sayna': al-qissa al-kamila li-l-tanzimat al-jihadiyya al-jadida fi masr*. N.p.: Mu'mimun bila hudud, 2017.

Farid, Ahmad. *Al-'udhr bi-l-jahl wa-l-radd 'ala bid'at al-takfir*. Giza: Maktabat al-taw'iyya al-islamiyya, 4th ed., 2002.

Farid, Ahmad. *Hadith al-Dhikrayat*. Alexandria: Dar al-majd, n.d.

Faruq, 'Amr. *Dawlat al-khilafa al-ikhwaniyya*. Cairo: Al-Jazira li-l-nashr wa-l-tawzi' 2010.

Fawzi, Ibrahim. *Fatawa wa aqwal al-'ulama' fi jama'at al-ikhwan al-muslimin*. Alexandria: Dar al-khulafa' al-rashidin, 2009.

Fiqi, Muhammad Hamid al-. *Athr al-da'wa al-wahhabiyya fi-l-islah al-dini wa-l-'umrani fi jazirat al-'arab wa ghayriha*. Cairo: Matba'at al-nahda, 1935.

Fiqi, Muhammad Hamid al-. *Azhar min Riyadh: sirat al-imam al-'adil 'Abd al-'Aziz bin 'Abd al-Rahman Al Faysal Al Sa'ud*. Cairo: Dar 'ilm al-salaf, 2008.

Fiqi, Muhammad Hamid al-, ed. *Radd al-Imam al-Darimi 'Uthman bin Sa'id 'ala Bishr al-Marisi al-'anid*. Beirut: Dar al-kutub al-'ilmiyya, n.d.

Ghanim, Ibrahim al-Bayyumi. *Al-fikr al-siyasi li-l-imam Hasan al-Banna*. Cairo: Markaz madarat li-l-abhath wa-l-nashr, 2012.

Ghazali, Muhammad al-. *Al-sunna al-nabawiyya bayna ahl al-fiqh . . . wa ahl al-hadith*. 6th ed. Cairo: Dar al-shuruq, 2007.

Ghazali, Muhammad al-. *Humum da'iya*. 6th ed. Cairo: Nahdat masr, 2006.

Ghazi, 'Isam al-. *'Umar al-Tilmisani—min al-tanju fi 'Imad al-Din ila za'amat al-ikhwan al-muslimin*. Giza: Hala, 2008.

Ghazi, Muhammad Jamil. *Al-sufiyya—al-wajh al-akhar*. Alexandria: Dar al-iman, 2007.

Ghubashi, Sayyid al-. *Iblagh al-haqq ila-l-khalq—risala fi hukm al-musharaka fi majlis al-sha'b al-masri*. N.p.: n.d. https://www.tawhed.ws.

Ghumari, 'Abdallah al-. *Qat' al-'uruq al-wardiyya min sahib al-buruq al-najdiyya*. Leiden, Netherlands: Dar al-mustafa, 2007.

BIBLIOGRAPHY

Ghunaym, 'Adil. *Azmat al-dawla al-masriyya al-mu'asira*. Cairo: Dar al-'alam al-thalith, 2005.

Habib, Muhammad. *Dhikrayat al-duktur Muhammad Habib 'an al-haya wa-l-da'wa wa-l-siyasa wa-l-fikr*. Cairo: Dar al-shuruq, 2012.

Hamdan, Abi 'Abdallah. *Kashf al-haqa'iq al-khafiyya 'an salafiyyat al-iskandariyya*. Al-mahalla al-kubra: Dar ibn Zayid, 2009.

Hamuda, 'Adil. *Qanabil wa masahif*. 3rd ed. Cairo: Sina li-l-nashr, 1989.

Harras, Muhammad Khalil. *Al-haraka al-wahhabiyya: radd 'ala maqal Muhammad al-Bahi fi naqd al-wahhabiyya*. Beirut: Dar al-kitab al-'arabi, 1985.

Hasan, 'Ammar 'Ali. *Al-tanshi'a al-siyasiyya li-l-turuq al-sufiyya fi masr: thaqafa dimuqratiyya wa masar al-tahdith lada tayyar dini taqlidi*. Cairo: Dar al-'ayn li-l-nashr, 2011.

Hasan, Salah al-Din. *Al-salafiyyun fi masr*. Giza: Dar awraq, 2012.

Hawali, Safar bin 'Abd al-Rahman al-. *Zahirat al-irja' fi-l-fikr al-islami*. Rosmalen, Netherlands: Dar al-kalima, 1999..

Hilali, Taqi al-Din al-. *Kitab al-da'wa ila-llah fi aqtar mukhtalifa*. N.p.: n.d. http://www.alhilali.net/المكتبة/-10719كتاب-الدعوة-إلى-الله-في-أقطار-مختلفة/.

Hilmi, Mustafa. *Qawa'id al-manhaj al-salafi fi-l-fikr al-islami*. Beirut: Dar al-kutub al-'ilmiyya, 2005.

Hindawi, 'Abd al-Hamid al-. *Dirasat hawla al-jama'a wa-l-jama'at... kayf al-amr idha lam takun jama'a*. 3 vols. 2nd ed. Cairo: Maktabat al-tabi'in, 1995.

Huwayni, Abu Ishaq al-. *Tanbih al-hajid ila ma waqa' min al-nazar fi kutub al-amajid*. 6 vols. N.p.: Al-mahajja, n.d. https://archive.org/details/FD61759/tnha1/page/n8/mode/2up.

Ibrahim, Muhammad Yusri. *Al-fida'iyyat al-islamiyya: ru'ya naqdiyya*. Cairo: Dar al-yusr, 2009.

Ibrahim, Muhammad Yusri. *Al-musharaka al-siyasiyya al-mu'asira fi daw' al-siyasa al-shar'iyya*. Cairo: Dar al-yusr, 2011.

Ibrahim, Muhammad Yusri. *Fiqh al-ulawiyyat fi-l-khitab al-salafi al-mu'asir ba'd al-thawra*. 2nd ed. Cairo: Dar al-yusr, 2012.

Ibrahim, Muhammad Yusri. *Mithaq al-hay'a al-shar'iyya li-l-huquq wa-l-islah*. Cairo: Dar al-yusr, 2012.

'Imara, Muhammad. *Rawa'i' Ibn Taymiyya*. Cairo: Nur li-l-nashr wa-l-tawzi', 2017.

'Isa, Muhammad Husayn. *Al-lama' fi tajliyat al-bida'*. 2006. Electronic copy in possession of author.

'Izzat, 'Amr. *Li-man al-manabir al-yawm? Tahlil siyasat al-dawla fi idarat al-masajid*. Cairo: Al-mubadara al-masriyya li-l-huquq al-fardiyya, 2014.

Jami', Mahmud. *Wa 'araft al-ikhwan*. Cairo: Dar al-tawzi' wa-l-nashr al-islamiyya, 2003.

Kharashi, Sulayman bin Salih al-. *'Abdallah al-Qasimi... wijhat nazar ukhra!* Beirut: Rawafid li-l-tiba'a wa-l-nashr wa-l-tawzi', 2008.

Khatib, Muhibb al-Din al-. *Al-khutut al-'arida li-l-usus allati qam 'alayha din al-shi'a al-imamiyya al-ithna 'ashariyya*. Cairo: Al-maktaba al-salafiyya, 1959. https://waqfeya.com/book.php?bid=5085.

Lutfi, Wa'il. *Zahirat al-du'a al-judud: al-da'wa, al-tharwa, al-shuhra*. Cairo: Maktabat al-usra, 2005.

Madi, Abu al-'Ala'. "Dawr al-Qaradawi fi tarshid al-sahwa al-islamiyya fi awsat jil al-sab'inat fi masr." Unpublished manuscript.

BIBLIOGRAPHY

Mahdi, Islam Anwar Al-. *Du'a 'ala abwab jahannim*. N.p.: n.d. https://dawa.center/file/2050.

Majdhub, Muhammad Al-. *'Ulama' wa mufakkirun 'araftuhum*. 3 vols. Riyadh: Dar al-shawwaf li-l-nashr wa-l-tawzi', 1992.

Mansur, Muhammad bin Ibrahim. *Mawaqif hizb al-nur—waqa'i' wa kawalis*. Alexandria: Dar al-khulafa' al-rashidin, 2014.

Mawlana, Ahmad. *Al-'aqliyya al-amniyya fi-l-ta'amul ma' al-tayyarat al-islamiyya*. Cairo: Isdarat al-jabha al-salafiyya, 2012.

Mawlana, Ahmad. *Qira'a naqdiyya fi kitab "Ikhtilaf al-islamiyyin."* N.p.: n.d. https://gabhasalafia.com/wp-content/uploads/2014/09/قراءة-نقدية-في-كتاب-اختلاف-الاسلاميين-احمد-مولانا.pdf.

Milligi, Al-Sayyid 'Abd al-Sattar Al-. *Tarikh al-haraka al-islamiyya fi sahat al-ta'lim 1933–1993*. Cairo: Maktabat Wahba, 1994.

Misbar, al-. *Al-aqbat fi Masr ba'd al-thawra*. Dubai: Markaz al-Misbar, 2012.

Misbar, al-. *Al-fitna al-gha'iba: jama'at al-jihad fi masr*. Dubai: Markaz al-Misbar, 2012.

Misbar, al-. *Suwwah min ajl al-da'wa: jama'at al-tabligh*. Dubai: Markaz al-Misbar, 2012.

Muhammad, Mahmud al-Sayyid. *Da'wat Ansar al-Sunna al-muhammadiyya wa sanawat min al-'ata'*. Cairo: Editions of Ansar al-Sunna's Public Center, n.d.

Munib, 'Abd al-Mun'im. *Dalil al-harakat al-islamiyya*. Cairo: Maktabat Madbuli, 2010.

Muqaddim, Muhammad Isma'il al-. *Adillat tahrim musafahat al-mar'a al-ajnabiyya*. 14th ed. Cairo: Dar al-khulafa' al-rashidin, 1993.

Muqaddim, Muhammad Isma'il al-. *Al-mahdi haqiqa la khurafa*. 11th ed. Alexandria: Al-dar al-'alamiyya li-l-nashr wa-l-tawzi', 2008.

Muqaddim, Muhammad Isma'il al-. *'Awdat al-hijab*. 3 vols. 20th ed. Alexandria: Dar al-khulafa' al-rashidun, 2011.

Muqaddim, Muhammad Isma'il al-. *Hurmat ahl al-'ilm*. Cairo: Dar Ibn al-Jawzi, 2005.

Muqaddim, Muhammad Isma'il al-. *Khawatir hawla al-wahhabiyya*. Alexandria: Dar al-tawhid li-l-turath, 2008.

Muqaddim, Muhammad Isma'il al-. *Mu'tamar nusrat al-thawra: kalimat al-duktur Muhammad Isma'il al-Muqaddim bi-tarikh 8 fabrayar 2011*. Alexandria: Dar al-salaf al-salih, 2011.

Muru, Muhammad. *Tanzim al-Jihad: afkaruhu, judhuruhu, siyasatuhu*. Cairo: Al-sharika al-'arabiyya al-duwaliyya li-l-nashr wa-l-i'lam, 1990.

Nafisi, 'Abdallah al-, and Hamid al-Quwaysi. *Al-naqd al-dhati li-l-haraka al-islamiyya: ru'a mustaqbaliyya*. Cairo: Maktabat al-shuruq al-duwaliyya, 2009.

Namnam, Hilmi al-. *Al-Azhar: al-shaykh wa-l-mashyakha*. Cairo: Madbuli, 2012.

Nuh, Mukhtar. *Man qatala al-shaykh al-Dhahabi? qira'a fi-l-watha'iq al-sirriyya li-tanzim al-takfir wa-l-hijra*. Cairo: Al-mahrusa, 2008.

Nuh, Mukhtar. *Mawsu'at al-'unf fi-l-harakat al-islamiyya al-musallaha*. Cairo: Sama li-l-nashr wa-l-tawzi', 2014.

Nuh, Mukhtar. *Qadiyyat al-fanniyya al-'askariyya: awwal muhawalat inqilab islami 'askari fi-l-qarn al-'ishrin*. Cairo: Al-mahrusa, 2006.

BIBLIOGRAPHY

Nusayr, 'Ai'da Ibrahim. *Al-kutub al-'arabiyya allati nushirat fi masr bayna 'amay 1900–1925.* Cairo: American University of Cairo Press, 1983.

Nusayr, 'Ai'da Ibrahim. *Al-kutub al-'arabiyya allati nushirat fi masr bayna 'amay 1926–1940.* Cairo: American University of Cairo Press, 1980.

Nusayr, 'Ai'da Ibrahim. *Al-kutub al-'arabiyya allati nushirat fi masr fi-l-qarn al-tasi' 'ashar.* Cairo: American University of Cairo Press, 1990.

Qaradawi, Yusuf al-. *Al-ikhwan al-muslimun: 80 'aman fi-l-da'wa wa-l-tarbiya wa-l-jihad.* Cairo: Maktabat wahba, 1999.

Qasimi, 'Abdallah al-. *Al-buruq al-najdiyya fi iktisah al-zalamat al-dijwiyya.* Cairo: Matba'at al-Manar, 1931.

Qasimi, 'Abdallah al-. *Al-fasl al-hasim bayna al-wahhabiyyin wa mukhalifihim.* Cairo: Matba'at al-tadamun al-akhawi, 1934.

Qasimi, 'Abdallah al-. *Al-thawra al-wahhabiyya.* Cairo: Matba'at masr, 1936.

Qasimi, 'Abdallah al-. *Shuyukh al-azhar wa-l-ziyada fi-l-islam.* 2nd ed. Beirut: Al-intishar al-'arabi, 2007.

Qutb, Muhammad. *Waqi'una al-mu'asir.* Cairo: Dar al-shuruq, 1997.

Qutb, Sayyid. *Ma'alim fi-l-tariq.* Beirut: Dar al-shuruq, 1979.

Rabi', 'Amr Hisham, ed. *Dalil al-nukhab al-barlamaniyya al-masriyya 2012.* Cairo: Markaz al-ahram, 2012.

Radwan, Tala'at. *Al-thaqafa al-masriyya wa-l-usuliyya al-masriyya qabl wa ba'd thawrat yulyu 1952.* Cairo: Al-dar li-l-nashr wa-l-tawzi', 2010.

Ra'if, Ahmad. *Al-bawwaba al-suda'.* Cairo: Al-zahra' li-l-i'lam al-'arabi, 1985.

Rajjal, 'Ali al-. *Harakat Hazimun al-Islamiyya.* Paper presented at Arab Reform Initiative workshop entitled " Al-muhtajjun wa kharitat harakat al-ihtijaj fi masr ba'd al-thawra," March 21–22, 2014.

Raslan, Muhammad Sa'id. *Haqiqat ma yahduth fi masr.* Al-Fayyum: Dar al-furqan, 2011.

Rida, Muhammad Rashid. *Al-sunna wa-l-shi'a aw al-wahhabiyya wa-l-rafida.* Cairo: Dar al-nashr li-l-jami'at, 2010.

Rida, Muhammad Rashid. *Al-wahhabiyyun wa-l-hijaz.* Cairo: Manar Masr, 1926.

Salama, Muhammad Yusri. *Mu'jam ma tubi'a min musannafat shaykh al-islam Ibn Taymiyya.* Alexandria: Dar al-tawhid li-l-turath, 2010.

Salim, Ahmad. *Ikhtilaf al-islamiyyin: al-khilaf al-islami—al-islami (halat masr namudhajan).* Beirut: Markaz Nama' li-l-buhuth wa-l-dirasat, 2013.

Salim, Ahmad, and 'Amr Basyuni. *Ma ba'd al-salafiyya.* Beirut: Markaz Nama' li-l-buhuth wa-l-dirasat, 2015.

Salim, Muhammad Rashad. *Muqarana bayna al-Ghazali wa Ibn Taymiyya.* Kuwait: Dar al-qalam, 1992.

Samannudi, Ibrahim al-. *Sa'adat al-darayn fi al-radd 'ala al-firqatayn al-wahhabiyya wa muqallidat al-zahiriyya.* 2 vols. Cairo: Dar al-khulud li-l-turath, 2008.

Samhan, Faysal bin 'Abd al-'Aziz al-. *Al-Imam al-sayyid Rashid Rida fi mayadin al-muwajaha.* Kuwait: Maktabat ahl al-athar, 2011.

Samir, Ahmad. *Ma'rakat al-ahrar.* N.p.: n.d. https://ia800300.us.archive.org/24/items/M3RkT-ElAhrar/الأحرار20%معركة.pdf.

Sanadbisi, Muhammad Abu 'Atiyya al-. *Al-inqilab al-fikri li-l-jama'a al-islamiyya.* Giza: Dar awraq, 2012.

Saqr, Shahata. *Al-shi'a hum al-'adu fa-uhdhiruhum*. Giza: Maktabat dar al-'ulum, 2006.

Saqr, Shahata. *Kashf al-bida' wa-l-radd 'ala al-lama'*. Electronic copy in possession of author.

Sarwi, Muhammad al-. *Tanzim 65—al-zalzal... wa-l-sahwa (1955-1975)*. N.p.: n.d. http://www.ikhwanwiki.com/index.php?title=الجزء_الأول_:_الواقع_المصري_بين_عامي_(1954)_-_(1965)_ونشأة_تنظيم_1965).&direction=next&oldid=29364.

Sawi, Salah al-. *Al-ta'addudiyya al-siyasiyya fi al-dawla al-islamiyya*. N.p.: Dar al-i'lam al-duwali, 1992.

Sawi, Salah al-. *Al-thawabit wa-l-mutaghayyirat fi masirat al-'amal al-islami al-mu'asir*. N.p.: Akadimiyyat al-shari'a bi-Amrika, 2009.

Sayyid, 'Adil al-. *Al-hakimiyya wa-l-siyasa al-shar'iyya 'inda shuyukh jama'at Ansar al-Sunna al-muhammadiyya*. Cairo: Dar al-Ibana, 2009.

Sayyid, Husayn Ahmad Muhammad al-. "Al-'ilaqa bayna al-Azhar al-Sharif wa quwa wa jama'at al-tayyar al-islami fi masr min 1919 ila 1936." MA thesis, Al-Azhar University, Cairo, 2008.

Shahada, Usama. *Min tarikh al-harakat al-islamiyya ma' al-shi'a wa Iran—Kitab al-rasid 7*. N.p.: n.d. https://osamashahade.com/الكتب/من-تاريخ-الحركات-الإسلامية-مع-إيران-والشيعة.

Shaykh, 'Abd al-'Aziz bin 'Abd al-Latif bin 'Abdallah, Al al-. *Mashahir 'ulama' Najd wa ghayruhum*. Riyadh: Dar al-yamama li-l-bahth wa-l-tarjama wa-l-nashr, 1974.

Shaykh, 'Abd al-Rahman bin Hasan, Al al-. *Fath al-majid sharh kitab al-tawhid*. 7th ed. Cairo: Matba'at al-sunna al-nabawiyya, 1957.

Shazli, 'Abd al-Majid al-. *Hadd al-islam wa haqiqat al-iman*. Mecca: Umm al-Qura University Press, n.d.

Shukr, 'Abd al-Ghaffar, ed. *Al-jam'iyyat al-ahliyya al-islamiyya fi masr*. Cairo: Dar al-amin li-l-nashr wa-l-tawzi', 2001.

Sirjani, Raghib al-. *Aslak Sha'ika*. Cairo: Aqlam, 2011.

Sirjani, Raghib al-. *Qissat al-imam Muhammad bin 'Abd al-Wahhab*. Cairo: Mu'assasat iqra', 2011.

Sisi, 'Abbas al-. *Fi qafilat al-ikhwan al-muslimin*. 4 vols. N.p.: n.d. https://www.ikhwanwiki.com/index.php?title=في_قافلة_الإخوان_المسلمين.

Subki, Mahmud Khattab al-. *Al-'ahd al-wathiq li-man arada suluk ahsan tariq*. Cairo: Matba'at Hassan, 1980.

Subki, Mahmud Khattab al-. *Al-din al-khalis aw irshad al-khalq ila-l-din al-haqq*. 9 vols. 4th ed. Cairo: Al-maktaba al-mahmudiyya al-subkiyya, 1977.

Subki, Mahmud Khattab al-. *Al-maqamat al-'aliyya fi-l-nash'a al-fakhima al-muhammadiyya*. Cairo: Matba'at al-sa'ada, n.d.

Subki, Mahmud Khattab al-. *Fatawa al-'ulama' al-muslimin bi-qat' lisan al-mubtadi'in*. Cairo: Al-matba'a al-husayniyya bi kafr al-tama'in, n.d.

Subki, Mahmud Khattab al-. *Ithaf al-ka'inat bi bayan madhhab al-salaf wa-l-khalaf fi-l-mutashabihat*. 2nd ed. Cairo: n.p., 1974.

Surur, Rifa'i. *Al-tasawwur al-siyasi li-l-haraka al-islamiyya*. 3rd ed. Cairo: Dar hadif, 2012.

Surur, Rifa'i. *Ashab al-ukhdud*. New ed. N.p.: Hadif li-l-nashr wa-l-tawzi', 2012.

Tahir, Ahmad Muhammad al-. *Jama'at Ansar al-Sunna al-muhammadiyya: Nash'atuha, ahdafuha, manhajuha, juhuduha*. Riyadh: Dar al-fadila/Dar al-hadi al-nabawi, 2004.

Talima, 'Isam. *Hasan al-Banna wa tajrubat al-fann*. Cairo: Maktabat wahba, 2008.

Tammam, Husam. *'Abd al-Mun'im Abu al-Futuh: shahid 'ala tarikh al-haraka al-islamiyya fi masr 1970–1984*. 2nd ed. Cairo: Dar al-shuruq, 2012.
Tammam, Husam. *Tahawwulat al-ikhwan al-muslimin—tafakkuk al-idyulujya wa nihayat al-tanzim*. Cairo: Madbuli, 2010.
Tammam, Husam. *Tasalluf al-ikhwan: takul al-utruha al-ikhwaniyya wa su'ud al-salafiyya fi jama'at al-ikhwan al-muslimin*. Alexandria: Maktabat al-iskandariyya/ wahdat al-dirasat al-mustaqbaliyya, 2010.
Tawfiq, Haytham. *Al-irja' taht al-majhar*. Alexandria: Dar al-khulafa' al-rashidin, 2011.
Tawfiq, Muhammad. *Al-naqd al-dhati 'inda al-islamiyyin (1): al-tayyarat al-qitaliyya*. Beirut: Markaz Nama', 2015.
Tawfiq, Muhammad. *Al-naqd al-dhati 'inda al-islamiyyin (2): al-islam al-siyasi*. Beirut: Markaz Nama', 2016.
Taymiyya, Ahmad (Ibn). *Iqtida' al-sirat al-mustaqim li mukhalafat ashab al-jahim*. Riyadh: Maktabat al-rushd, n.d.
'Uqda, Hisham Al. *Al-ijabat*. Cairo: Dar al-safwa, 2008.
'Uthman, Tariq. *Al-ikhwan al-muslimun wa-l-salafiyyun fi masr*. Beirut: Markaz Nama', 2012.
'Uthman, Wa'il. *Asrar al-haraka al-tullabiyya—handasat al-Qahira 1968–1975*. 2nd ed. N.p.: 2006.
Wakil, 'Abd al-Rahman al-. *Hadhihi hiya al-sufiyya*. 4th ed. Beirut: Dar al-kutub al-'ilmiyya, 1984.
Wardani, Salih al-. *Al-haraka al-islamiyya fi masr: al-waqi' wa-l-tahaddiyat*. Cairo: Maktabat dar al-kalima, 2000.
Zaghlul Shalata, Ahmad. *Al-da'wa al-salafiyya al-sakandariyya: masarat al-tanzim wa malat al-siyasa*. Beirut: Markaz dirasat al-wahda al-'arabiyya, 2015.
Zaghlul Shalata, Ahmad. *Al-hala al-salafiyya al-mu'asira fi masr*. Cairo: Madbuli, 2011.
Zaghlul Shalata, Ahmad. *Al-islamiyyun fi-l-sulta: tajrubat al-ikhwan al-muslimin fi masr*. Beirut: Markaz dirasat al-wahda al-'arabiyya, 2017.
Zahir, Mu'taz. *Min al-masjid ila al-barlaman: dirasa hawla al-da'wa al-salafiyya wa hizb al-nur*. London: Takween, 2015.
Zahran, Mustafa, 'Umar Ghazi, et al. *Al-salafiyyun fi masr ma ba'd al-thawra*. Riyadh: Markaz al-din wa-l-siyasa / Beirut: Al-intishar al-'arabi, 2012.
Zawahiri, Ayman al-. *Al-tabri'a: tabri'at ummat al-qalam wa-l-sayf min manqasat tuhmat al-khawr wa-l-da'f*. N.p.: n.d.
Zayyat, Muntasir al-. *Al-jama'at al-islamiyya: ru'ya min al-dakhil*. Cairo: Dar masr al-mahrusa, 2005.
Zumay', 'Ali Fahd al-. *Fi-l-nazariyya al-siyasiyya al-islamiyya*. Kuwait: Waqf nuhud, 2018.

SOURCES IN ENGLISH, FRENCH, AND GERMAN

Abdalla, Ahmed. *The Student Movement and National Politics in Egypt 1923–1973*. London: al Saqi Books, 1985.
Abou Lahoud, Carine. *Islam et politique au Koweït*. Paris: PUF, 2011.

BIBLIOGRAPHY

Al-Anani, Khalil. *Inside the Muslim Brotherhood: Religion, Identity and Politics.* Oxford: Oxford University Press, 2016.

Al-Anani, Khalil, and Malik Maszlee. "Pious Way to Politics: The Rise of Political Salafism in post-Mubarak Egypt." *Digest of Middle East Studies* 22, no. 1 (2013): 57–73.

Al-Arian, Abdullah. *Answering the Call: Popular Islamic Activism in Sadat's Egypt.* Oxford: Oxford University Press, 2014.

Al-Berry, Khaled. *La terre est plus belle que le paradis.* Paris: JC Lattès, 2002.

Amghar, Samir. "Les salafistes français: une nouvelle aristocratie religieuse?" *Maghreb Machrek* 183 (2005): 13–32.

Amin, Galal. *Whatever Happened to the Egyptians?* Cairo: AUC Press, 2000.

Asad, Talal. *The Idea of an Anthropology of Islam.* Washington, DC: Center for Contemporary Arab Studies, 1986.

Awad, Mokhtar. "Revolutionary Salafism: The Case of Ahrar Movement." Hudson Institute, April 19, 2016. https://www.hudson.org/research/12310-revolutionary-salafism-the-case-of-ahrar-movement.

Awad, Mokhtar. "The Salafi Dawa of Alexandria: The Politics of a Religious Movement." Hudson Institute, August 14, 2014. https://www.hudson.org/research/10463-the-salafi-dawa-of-alexandria-the-politics-of-a-religious-movement-.

Ayalon, Ami. *The Arabic Print Revolution: Cultural Production and Mass Readership.* Cambridge: Cambridge University Press, 2016.

Baker, Raymond William. *Islam Without Fear: Egypt and the New Islamists.* Cambridge, MA: Harvard University Press, 2003.

Baron, Beth. *The Orphan Scandal: Christian Missionaries and the Rise of the Muslim Brotherhood.* Stanford, CA: Stanford University Press, 2014.

Bayat, Asef. *Life as Politics: How Ordinary People Change the Middle East.* Stanford, CA: Stanford University Press, 2009.

Becker, Howard S. "The Life History and the Scientific Mosaic." In *Sociological Work: Method and Substance—Essays by Howard S. Becker,* 63–73. New York: Routledge, 2017.

Becker, Howard S. *Outsiders: Studies in the Sociology of Deviance.* New York: Free Press / London: Collier-Macmillan, 1966.

Ben Néfissa, Sarah. "Citoyenneté morale en Égypte: une association entre État et Frères musulmans." In *ONG et Gouvernance dans le monde arabe,* ed. Sarah Ben Néfissa et al., 213–71. Paris: Karthala-CEDEJ, 2004.

Bennani-Chraïbi, Mounia, and Olivier Fillieule, ed. *Résistances et protestations dans les sociétés musulmanes.* Paris: Presses de Sciences Po, 2003.

Boudon, Raymond. *The Unintended Consequences of Social Action.* London: Palgrave Macmillan, 1977.

Bouras, Naïma. "Émergence d'un discours salafiste féminin en Égypte." *Afrique(s) en mouvement* 1, no. 2 (2020): 25–31.

Bourdieu, Pierre. "The Biographical Illusion," trans. Yves Winkin and Wendy Leeds-Hurwitz. In *Biography in Theory,* ed. Wilhelm Hemecker and Edward Saunders, 210–16. Berlin: De Gruyter, 2017.

Bourdieu, Pierre. *Language and Symbolic Power,* trans. Gino Raymond and Matthew Adamson. Cambridge: Polity Press, 1991.

Bourdieu, Pierre. *Sociology in Question,* trans. Richard Nice. London: SAGE, 1993.

BIBLIOGRAPHY

Bozarslan, Hamit. *Révolution et état de violence. Moyen-Orient 2011–2015*. Paris: CNRS Éditions, 2015.

Brinton, Jacquelene G. *Preaching Islamic Renewal: Religious Authority and Media in Contemporary Egypt*. Oakland: University of California Press, 2016.

Brown, Jonathan A. C. *Hadith: Muhammad's Legacy in the Medieval and Modern World*. Oxford: Oneworld Publications, 2009.

Brunner, Rainer. *Islamic Ecumenism in the Twentieth Century: The Azhar and Shiism Between Rapprochement and Restraint*. Leiden: Brill, 2004.

Bunzel, Cole M. "Manifest Enmity: The Origins, Development and Persistence of Classical Wahhabism (1153–1351/1741–1932)." PhD dissertation, Princeton University, 2018.

Burgat, François. *L'islamisme en face*. Paris: La Découverte, 2007.

Burgat, François. *Understanding Political Islam*. Manchester, UK: Manchester University Press, 2020.

Calvert, John *Sayyid Qutb and the Origins of Radical Islamism*. London: Hurst, 2010.

Carré, Olivier. *Mystique et politique: Lecture révolutionnaire du Coran par Sayyid Qutb, Frère musulman radical*. Paris: Presses de Sciences Po, 1984.

Cavatorta, Francesco, and Fabio Merone, eds. *Salafism After the Arab Uprising: Contending with People's Power*. London: Oxford University Press, 2017.

Chih, Rachida. " La célébration de la naissance du prophète (al-Mawlid al-nabawi): Aperçus d'une fête musulmane non canonique." *Archives de Sciences Sociales des Religions* 178, no. 2 (2017): 177–94.

Commins, David. *Islamic Reform: Politics and Social Change in Late Ottoman Syria*. New York: Oxford University Press, 1990.

Commins, David. *The Wahhabi Mission and Saudi Arabia*. London: Tauris, 2006.

Cook, Michael. *Forbidding Wrong in Islam*. Cambridge: Cambridge University Press, 2003.

Cook, Michael. "The Origins of Wahhabism." *Journal of the Royal Asiatic Society* 2, 3rd series, no. 2 (July 1992): 191–202.

Crawford, Michael. *Ibn 'Abd al-Wahhab*. London: Oneworld Publications, 2014.

Crecelius, Daniel. "Sa'udi-Egyptian Relations." *International Studies* 4, no. 4 (1975): 563–85.

De Jong, Frederick, and Bernd Radtke, eds. *Islamic Mysticism Contested: Thirteen Centuries of Controversies and Polemics*. Leiden: Brill, 1999.

Della Porta, Donatella, and Mario Diani. *Social Movements: An Introduction*. 2nd ed. Oxford: Blackwell, 2006 [1999].

Dobry, Michel. *Sociologie des crises politiques*. Paris: Presses de la FNSP, 1986.

Drevon, Jérôme. *Institutionalizing Violence: Strategies of Jihad in Egypt*. Oxford: Oxford University Press, 2022.

Eickelman, Dave F., and James Piscatori. *Muslim Politics*. Princeton, NJ: Princeton University Press, 2004.

El Chazli, Youssef. "Devenir révolutionnaire à Alexandrie: Contribution à une sociologie historique du surgissement révolutionnaire en Égypte." PhD dissertation, Paris 1/Université de Lausanne, 2018.

El-Rouayheb, Khaled. *Islamic Intellectual History in the Seventeenth History*. Cambridge: Cambridge University Press, 2015.

El Shamsy, Ahmed. *Rediscovering the Islamic Classics: How Editors and Print Culture Transformed an Intellectual Tradition*. Princeton, NJ: Princeton University Press, 2020.

El-Sherif, Ashraf. *Egypt's Salafists at a Crossroads*. Washington, DC: Carnegie Endowment for International Peace, 2015.

Elissa-Mondeguer, Nadia. "Al-Manâr de 1925 à 1935: La dernière décennie d'un engagement intellectuel." *Revue des Mondes Musulmans et de la Méditerranée* 95–98 (2002): 205–26.

Encyclopedia of Islam. Leiden: Brill.

Escovitz, Joseph H. "'He Was the Muhammad 'Abduh of Syria'—a Study of Tahir al-Jaza'iri and His Influence." *International Journal of Middle East Studies* 18, no. 3 (1986): 293–310.

Fahmi, Georges. *The Egyptian State and the Religious Sphere*. Beirut: Carnegie Middle East Center, 2014. https://carnegie-mec.org/2014/09/18/egyptian-state-and-religious-sphere-pub-56619.

Field, Nathan, and Ahmed Hamam. "Salafi Satellite TV in Egypt." *Arab Media and Society* 8 (2009). https://www.arabmediasociety.com/salafi-satellite-tv-in-egypt/.

Filiu, Jean-Pierre. *L'apocalypse dans l'Islam*. Paris: Fayard, 2008.

Foucault, Michel. *Dits et Ecrits (III)*. Paris: Gallimard, 1994.

Foucault, Michel. "The Political Function of the Intellectual." *Radical Philosophy* 017 (1977). https://www.radicalphilosophy.com/article/the-political-function-of-the-intellectual.

Gaborieau, Marc. "Tablīghī djamā 'at." In *Encyclopaedia of Islam*, ed. P. Bearman et al., 38–39. 2nd ed. Leiden: Brill, 1998.

Gaffney, Patrick D. *The Prophet's Pulpit: Islamic Preaching in Contemporary Egypt*. Berkeley: University of California Press, 1994.

Gardet, Louis. "Les noms et les statuts. Le problème de la foi et des œuvres en Islam." *Studia Islamica*, no. 5 (1956): 61–123.

Gauvain, Richard. *Salafi Ritual Purity: In the Presence of God*. London: Routledge, 2013.

Gilsenan, Michael. *Recognizing Islam*. London: Tauris, 1993.

Gilsenan, Michael. *Saint and Sufi in Modern Egypt: An Essay in the Sociology of Religion*. Oxford: Clarendon Press, 1973.

Gilsenan, Michael. "Some Factors in the Decline of the Sufi Orders in Modern Egypt." *Muslim World* 67 (1967): 11–18.

Goldziher, Ignaz. *Die Richtungen der Islamischen Koranauslegung*. Leiden: Brill, 1920.

Gramsci, Antonio. *Guerre de mouvement et guerre de position*. Paris: La Fabrique, 2012.

Gruntz, Lucile. "L'Amérique des Arabes, aller-retour. Les migrants cairotes au centre de la controverse religieuse." Text presented at the seminar on Migrations: nouvelles pratiques, approches plurielles, organized by EHESS, Paris, October 9–10, 2008.

Guirguis, Laure, ed. *Conversion religieuses et mutations politiques en Égypte. Tares et avatars du communautarisme égyptien*. Paris: Éditions Non Lieu, 2008.

Habermas, Jürgen. " The Public Sphere: An Encyclopedia Article (1964)." *New German Critique*, no. 3 (Fall 1974): 49–55.

Halverson, Jeffry R. *Theology and Creed in Sunni Islam: The Muslim Brotherhood, Ash'arism and Political Sunnism*. London: Palgrave Macmillan, 2010.

Hegghammer, Thomas, and Stéphane Lacroix. "Rejectionist Islamism in Saudi Arabia: The Story of Juhayman al-'Utaybi revisited." *International Journal of Middle East Studies* 39, no. 1 (2007): 103–22.

Heyworth-Dunne, James. *Religious and Political Trends in Modern Egypt*. Washington, DC: Self-published, 1950.

Hirschkind, Charles. *The Ethical Soundscape: Cassette Sermons and Islamic Counterpublics*. New York: Columbia University Press, 2006.

Ibrahim, Saad Eddin. "Anatomy of Egypt's Militant Islamic Groups: Methodological Note and Preliminary Findings." *International Journal of Middle East Studies* 12, no. 4 (1980): 423–53.

Jansen, J. J. G. *The Interpretation of the Koran in Modern Egypt*. 2nd ed. Leiden: Brill, 1980.

Kendall, Elisabeth, and Ahmad Khan, eds. *Reclaiming Islamic Tradition: Modern Interpretations of the Classical Heritage*. Edinburgh: Edinburgh University Press, 2016.

Kepel, Gilles. *Muslim Extremism in Egypt: The Prophet and Pharaoh*. Berkeley: University of California Press, 1985.

Kepel, Gilles. *Jihad: The Trail of Political Islam*. Cambridge, MA: Harvard University Press, 2002.

Kerr, Malcolm H. *Islamic Reform: The Political and Legal Theories of Muhammad 'Abduh and Rashid Rida*. Berkeley: University of California Press, 1966.

Ketchley, Neil. *Egypt in a Time of Revolution: Contentious Politics and the Arab Spring*. Cambridge: Cambridge University Press, 2017.

Lacroix, Stéphane. *Awakening Islam: The Politics of Religious Dissent in Contemporary Saudi Arabia*. Cambridge, MA: Harvard University Press, 2011.

Lacroix, Stéphane. *Egypt's Pragmatic Salafis: The Politics of Hizb al-Nour*. Washington, DC: Carnegie Endowment for International Peace, 2016.

Lacroix, Stéphane. "Ḥākimiyya." In *Encyclopaedia of Islam*, 3rd ed., ed. Kate Fleet et al., 30–32. Leiden: Brill, 2017.

Lacroix, Stéphane. "Sheikhs and Politicians: Inside the New Egyptian Salafism." Doha: Brookings Institution, 2012.

Lacroix, Stéphane, and Ahmed Zaghloul Shalata. "Le maréchal et les cheikhs: Les stratégies religieuses du régime et leurs complications dans l'Égypte d 'al-Sisi." *Critique Internationale* 78, no. 1, (2018): 21–39.

Lacroix, Stéphane, and Ahmed Zaghloul Shalata. "*Sharī'a* et révolution: Émergence et mutations du salafisme du salafisme révolutionnaire dans l'Égypte post-Moubarak." *Archives de Sciences Sociales des Religions* 181 (2018): 201–18.

Lagroye, Jacques. *La vérité dans l'Église catholique: Contestations et restauration d'un régime d'autorité*. Paris: Belin, 2006.

Laoust, Henri. *Essai sur les doctrines sociales et politiques de Taqi ed Din Ahmad b. Taimiya*. Cairo: IFAO, 1939.

Laoust, Henri, "Le réformisme d'Ibn Taymiyya." *Islamic Studies* 1, no. 3 (September 1962): 27–47.

Laoust, Henri. "Le réformisme orthodoxe des 'salafiya' et les caractères généraux de son orientation actuelle." *Revue des Études Islamiques* (1932): 175–224.

Laoust, Henri. *Le traité de Droit Public d'Ibn Taymiya*. Beirut: Institut Français de Damas, 1948.

Lauzière, Henri. "The Construction of *Salafiyya*: Reconsidering Salafism from the Perspective of Conceptual History." *International Journal of Middle East Studies* 42, no. 3 (2010): 369-89.

Lauzière, Henri. *The Making of Salafism: Islamic Reform in the Twentieth Century*. New York: Columbia University Press, 2015.

Lav, Daniel. *Radical Islam and the Revival of Medieval Theology*. Cambridge: Cambridge University Press, 2012.

Lazar, Marc. " Le parti et le don de soi." *Vingtième siècle. Revue d'histoire* 60 (1998): 35-42.

Lemieux, Cyril. *La sociologie pragmatique*. Paris, La Découverte, 2018.

Lemieux, Cyril. *Le devoir et la grâce*. Paris: Economica, 2009.

Lotfy, Waël. "Prêches, médias et fortune: Le cas de Amr Khalid." *Les Cahiers de l'IFPO* 5 (2010): 13-25.

Mahmood, Saba. *Politics of Piety: The Islamic Revival and the Feminist Subject*. Princeton, NJ: Princeton University Press, 2005.

Mahmoud, Moaaz. "Les Frères Musulmans en Égypte face à la montée du salafisme." MA thesis, Sciences Po, Paris, 2010.

Mannheim, Karl. "The Problem of Generations." In *Essays on the Sociology of Knowledge*, ed. P. Kecskemeti, 276-320. London: Routledge and Kegan Paul, 1952.

Makdisi, George. *L'islam hanbalisant*. Paris: Geuthner, 1983.

Mayeur-Jaouen, Catherine. " 'À la poursuite de la réforme': Renouveaux et débats historiographiques de l'histoire religieuse et intellectuelle de l'islam, xve-xxie siècle." *Annales* 73, no. 2 (2018): 317-58.

Mayeur-Jaouen, Catherine. *Histoire d'un pèlerinage légendaire en islam. Le mouled de Tantâ du XIIIe siècle à nos jours*. Paris: Aubier, 2004.

Mayeur-Jaouen, Catherine. "Les débuts d'une revue néo-salafiste: Muhibb al-Dîn al-Khatîb et Al-Fath de 1926 à 1928." *Revue des Mondes Musulmans et de la Méditerranée* 95-98 (2002). http://remmm.revues.org/234.

McCarthy, John D., and Mayer N. Zald. "Resource Mobilization and Social Movements: A Partial Theory." *American Journal of Sociology* 82, no. 6 (1982): 1212-41.

McPherson, J.W. *The Moulids of Egypt*. Cairo: Ptd. N. M. Press, 1941.

Meijer, Roel, ed. *Global Salafism: Islam's New Religious Movement*. London: Hurst, 2009.

Metcalf, Barbara. *Islamic Revival in British India: Deoband 1860-1900*. Princeton, NJ: Princeton University Press, 1982.

Meyer, David S., and Debra C. Minkoff. "Conceptualizing Political Opportunity." *Social Forces* 82, no. 4 (2004): 1457-92.

Mitchell, Richard P. *The Society of the Muslim Brothers*. 2nd ed. Oxford: Oxford University Press, 1993.

Moll, Yasmin. "Islamic Televangelism: Religion, Media, and Visuality in Contemporary Egypt." *Arab Media and Society* 10 (2010): 1-27.

Mouline, Nabil. *Les clercs de l'islam: Autorité religieuse et pouvoir politique en Arabie saoudite XVIII-XXIe siècle*. Paris: PUF, 2011.

Moustafa, Tamir. "Conflict and Cooperation Between the State and Religious Institutions in Contemporary Egypt." *International Journal of Middle East Studies* 32, no. 1 (2000): 3-22.

BIBLIOGRAPHY

Mudde, Cas, and Cristobal Rovira Kaltwasser. *Populism: A Very Short Introduction*. Oxford: Oxford University Press, 2017.

Nada, Youssef (with Douglas Thompson). *Inside the Muslim Brotherhood: The Truth About the World's Most Powerful Political Movement*. London: Metro Publishing, 2012.

Olidort, Jacob. "The Politics of 'Quietist' Salafism." Washington, DC: Brookings Institution, 2015. https://www.brookings.edu/wp-content/uploads/2016/06/Olidort-Final-Web-Version.pdf.

Pall, Zoltan. *Kuwaiti Salafism and Its Growing Influence in the Levant*. Washington, DC: Carnegie Endowment for International Peace, 2014.

Rapoport, Yossef, and Shahab Ahmed, eds. *Ibn Taymiyya and His Times*. Oxford: Oxford University Press, 2010.

Ridgeon, Lloyd, ed. *Sufis and Salafis in the Contemporary Age*. London: Bloomsbury, 2015.

Rock-Singer, Aaron. *In the Shade of the Sunna: Salafi Piety in the Twentieth Century Middle East*. Oakland: University of California Press, 2022.

Rock-Singer, Aaron. *Practicing Islam in Egypt: Print Media and Islamic Revival*. Cambridge: Cambridge University Press, 2019.

Rock-Singer, Aaron. "The Salafi Mystique: The Rise of Gender Segregation in 1970s Egypt." *Islamic Law and Society* 23 (2016): 279–305.

Rougier, Bernard, ed. *Qu'est-ce que le salafisme?* Paris: PUF, 2008.

Rougier, Bernard, and Stéphane Lacroix, eds. *Egypt's Revolutions: Politics, Religion, Social Movements*. London: Palgrave Macmillan, 2016.

Roy, Olivier. *The Failure of Political Islam*. Cambridge, MA: Harvard University Press, 1998.

Ryzova, Lucie. *L'effendiyya ou la modernité contestée*. Cairo: Éditions du CEDEJ, 2013. https://books.openedition.org/cedej/923.

Saleh, Walid. "Preliminary Remarks on the Historiography of Tafsir in Arabic: A History of the Book Approach." *Journal of Qur'anic Studies* 12 (2010): 6–40.

Salvatore, Armando. *The Public Sphere: Liberal Modernity, Catholicism, Islam*. London: Palgrave Macmillan, 2007.

Scharbrodt, Olivier. "The Salafiyya and Sufism: Muhammad 'Abduh and His Risalat al-Waridat (Treatise on Mystical Inspirations)." *Bulletin of SOAS* 70, no. 1 (2007): 89–115.

Schielke, Samuli. "Hegemonic Encounters: Criticism of Saints-Day Festivals and the Formation of Modern Islam in Late 19th and Early 20th-Century Egypt." *Die Welt des Islams* 47, no. 3–4 (2007): 319–55.

Schielke, Samuli. *Migrant Dreams: Egyptian Workers in the Gulf States*. Cairo: AUC Press, 2020.

Schielke, Samuli. *The Perils of Joy: Contesting Mulid Festivals in Contemporary Egypt*. Syracuse, NY: Syracuse University Press, 2012.

Sivan, Emmanuel, *Radical Islam: Medieval Theology and Modern Politics*. New Haven, CT: Yale University Press, 1990.

Skovgaard-Petersen, Jakob. *Defining Islam for the State: Muftis and Fatwas of Dar al-Ifta*. Leiden: Brill, 1997.

Steinberg, Guido. *Religion und Staat in Saudi-Arabien*. Würzburg: Ergon, 2002.

Steuer, Clément. "Les salafistes dans le champ politique égyptien." *Politique étrangère*, no. 4 (2013): 133–43.
Tadros, Samuel. *Mapping Egyptian Islamism*. Washington, DC: Hudson Institute, 2014.
Tilly, Charles. "Contentious Repertoires in Great Britain, 1758–1834." *Social Science History* 17, no. 2 (Summer 1993): 253–80.
Vassiliev, Alexei. *The History of Saudi Arabia*. London: Saqi Books, 2000.
Wagemakers, Joas. "Revisiting Wiktorowicz: Categorising and Defining the Branches of Salafism." In *Salafism After the Arab Uprising: Contending with People's Power*, ed. Francesco Cavatorta, and Fabio Merone, 7–24. London: Oxford University Press, 2017.
Wagemakers, Joas. *Salafism in Jordan: Political Islam in a Quietist Community*. Cambridge: Cambridge University Press, 2016.
Wasella, Jurgen. *Vom Fundamentalisten zum Atheisten: Die dissidentenkarriere des Abdallah al-Qasimi, 1907–1996*. Gotha, Ger.: J. Perthes, 1997.
Weber, Max. *The Vocation Lectures*. Indianapolis: Hackett, 2004.
Wickham, Carrie Rosefsky. *Mobilizing Islam: Religion, Activism and Political Change in Egypt*. New York: Columbia University Press, 2002.
Wickham, Carrie Rosefsky. *The Muslim Brotherhood: Evolution of an Islamist Movement*. Princeton, NJ: Princeton University Press, 2013.
Wiktorowicz, Quintan. "Anatomy of the Salafi Movement." *Studies in Conflict and Terrorism* 29, no. 3 (2006): 207–39.
Wiktorowicz, Quintan, ed. *Islamic Activism: A Social Movement Theory Approach*. Bloomington: Indiana University Press, 2004.
Zaman, Muhammad Qasim. *The Ulama in Contemporary Islam: Custodians of Change*. Princeton, NJ: Princeton University Press, 2002.
Zeghal, Malika. *Gardiens de l'islam: Les oulémas d'al-Azhar dans l'Egypte contemporaine*. Paris: Presses de Sciences Po, 1996.
Zollner, Barbara H. E. *The Muslim Brotherhood: Hasan al-Hudaybi and Ideology*. London: Routledge, 2009.

INTERVIEWS

Formal interviews I conducted and that appear in the notes are listed here. They were supplemented by dozens of other, informal interviews. When an interview took place on a single day, I specify the date. When it was a more extended process, I specify the period of time.

Mahmud 'Abbas (October 2012)
Muhammad al-'Adli (November 5, 2011)
Muhammad 'Affan (2010–2020)
Rif'at Sayyid Ahmad (December 12, 2010)
'Ali 'Abd al-'Al (September–December 2010)
'Isam al-'Aryan (March 22, 2011)

BIBLIOGRAPHY

'Abd al-Rahman 'Ayyash (2010–2013)
Usama al-Azhari (December 10, 2010)
Sa'id 'Abd al-'Azim (December 28, 2012)
Nadir Bakkar (June 2, 2012)
'Ammar al-Baltagi (2010–2017)
Jamal al-Banna (November 22, 2010)
Zakariyya Bayyumi (December 15, 2010)
Hasan Bughdadi (October–December 2011)
Khalid Dawud (January 12, 2013)
'Abdallah al-Fakharani (2010–2015)
Nabil 'Abd al-Fattah (2010–2013)
'Ammar Fayid (October 29, 2011; November 15, 2016)
'Abd al-Mun'im Abu al-Futuh (January 15, 2013; November 20, 2015)
'Imad 'Abd al-Ghaffur (December 1, 2011)
Kamal al-Sa'id Habib (September 25, 2010)
Midhat al-Haddad (January 14, 2012)
Ahmad Hamdi (November 12, 2010)
Yusri Hammad (January 13, 2013)
Khalid Hamza (2010–2013)
Khalid Harbi (January 20, 2013)
Ahmad Harqan (October 10, 2014
'Ammar 'Ali Hasan (September 29, 2010)
Salah al-Din Hasan (May 5, 2011)
Najih Ibrahim (December 2, 2011)
Mamduh Isma'il (June 15, 2011)
'Amr 'Izzat (2010–2020)
Mamduh Jabir (November 15, 2012)
Salim 'Abd al-Jalil (September 20, 2010)
Hisham Kamal (December 19, 2012)
Mu'adh 'Abd al-Karim (May 12, 2012)
Haytham Abu Khalil (October 28, 2011
Islam Lutfi (July 2, 2012)
'Abd al-Fattah Madi (June 1, 2012)
Abu al-'Ala' Madi (June 25, 2011)
'Amr Magdi (2010–2020)
'Abd al-Rahman Mansur (October 2010–January 2011)
Khalid Mansur (October 14, 2011)

Ahmad Mawlana (December 2012–January 2013)
Muhammad al-Mislawi (November 5, 2011)
Hisham Mustafa (October 11, 2012)
Ahmad Naji (October 10, 2012)
Muhammad Nur (June–December 2011)
Ayman ʻAbd al-Rahim (2010–2013)
Khalid Saʻid (July 5, 2012)
Jamal al-Saʻidi (November 18, 2011)
Muhammad Yusri Salama (January 5, 2012)
Subhi Salih (January 15, 2012)
ʻAbd al-Munʻim al-Shahhat (May 10, 2011)
Ihab Shiha (October 12, 2011)
Anas Sultan (May 2, 2012)
Yahya Rifaʻi Surur (January 20, 2013)
Muhammad Tawfiq (2012–2020)
Ahmad al-Tayyib (March 20, October 1, and November 11, 2010)
Ashraf Thabit (January 9, 2012)
Tariq ʻUthman (2010–2013)
Muhammad Yaqut (October 1, 2010)
Khalid al-Zaʻfarani (November 13, 2010; September 1, 2012)
Muhammad Hamdi Zaqzuq (November 1, 2010)
Bassam al-Zarqa (January 8, 2012)
Muntasir al-Zayyat (September 30, 2010)

INDEX

'Abbas, Mahmud, 191, 192, 195
'Abd al-'Azim, Sa'id, 108, 112–113, 124, 160, 185, 187, 207, 210, 229
'Abd al-'Azim, Usama, 95, 100, 103, 119, 139
'Abd al-Ghaffur, 'Imad, 108, 110, 112, 120, 188–91, 193–98, 200–201, 204
'Abd al-Hadi, Gamal, 173–74
'Abd al-Hamid, Mahmud, 113, 187–88, 275n4
'Abd al-Khaliq, 'Abd al-Rahman, 95, 96, 113, 119, 126–28, 208, 229, 233
'Abd al-Maqsud, Muhammad, 113, 134–35, 159, 186, 189, 210–12, 218, 282n172
'Abd al-Rahman, 'Umar, 84–85, 103, 131
'Abd al-Wahhab, Muhammad (Ibn), 9–13, 31, 33, 35, 39, 48, 80, 86, 89, 92, 110, 112, 114, 136, 138, 173, 252n13, 257n42
'Abduh, Muhammad, 6, 18, 32, 34–35, 41, 57, 113, 255n14, 256n20
Abu al-Bukhari, Husam, 219, 222, 301n17
Abu al-Futuh, 'Abd al-Mun'im, 172, 173, 177, 199–201, 211, 213, 228–29, 239

Abu Idris, 'Abd al-Fattah, 106, 108, 110, 116, 185, 196
Abu Isma'il, Hazim, 4, 28, 169, 174, 199–200, 211, 215–16, 220–35, 237–41, 246–47
Abu Isma'il, Salah, 169, 174, 221
Abu al-Samh, 'Abd al-Zahir, 36–37, 45, 47, 54
'Afifi, 'Abd al-Razzaq, 47, 54–55, 112–13, 138
'Afifi, Tal'at, 210, 212
Afghanistan, 96, 161, 188
Ahmad, Nash'at, 135, 153, 157, 162, 210
Ahmadinejad, Mahmoud, 162, 203
Ahrar (movement), 235–39
'Alam al-Din, Khalid, 201, 204
Albani, Muhammad Nasir al-Din al-, 13, 62, 72, 88, 90, 95, 109–15, 128, 135, 143, 149–51, 285n12, 285n13
'Ali, Muhammad (viceroy of Egypt), 33, 77
Al Jazeera, 169
Al-Qaeda (organization), 133, 161, 222, 240
Alusi, Nu'man al-, 11, 35
'Amir, Mahmud Lutfi, 140, 163

INDEX

Ansar al-Sunna (organization), 7, 14–15, 18, 20, 28, 36, 43–63, 68–74, 77, 79–80, 85–86, 89–90, 92, 94, 101, 107–9, 112–13, 117, 119, 126, 127, 130, 138, 140, 151–53, 155–57, 163, 168, 208, 210, 229, 243, 260n83,
Ansari, Talal al-, 85–88, 90,
'Aryan, 'Isam al-, 99–100
Asala, al- (party), 186, 192–93, 211
Ash'ari, Abu al-Hasan al-, 8, 165
Ash'arism, 1, 3, 8, 10–11, 30–32, 34, 43–44, 51–52, 56, 60, 64, 69–72, 78–79, 85–86, 88, 101, 165, 248, 268n69
'Awda, Salman al-, 136
Azhar, al- (mosque-university), 3, 26, 30–33, 37, 41–43, 45–47, 50–52, 54–60, 62–63, 67–68, 70, 78, 84, 89, 103, 120, 136–37, 139, 147, 149, 155, 157, 159, 161–62, 165–172, 174–78, 202–5, 208–12, 221, 229, 244–45, 247–48
'Aziz billah, al- (mosque), 71, 157, 165

Badawi, al-Sayyid al- (mausoleum), 32, 68, 83, 180
Badi', Muhammad, 177
Bakkar, Nadir, 200, 203
Banna, Hasan al-, 18, 59–62, 74, 76–77, 80, 95, 97–98, 116, 118, 167–168, 172, 263n166
Baradei, Mohamed el-, 140, 205
Barr, 'Abd al-Rahman al-, 169, 176
Baz, 'Abd al-'Aziz (Ibn), 111–112, 136, 138, 150–151, 276n30
Bilal, Sayyid, 166, 183
Bin Laden, Osama, 222, 224
Bina' wa-l-Tanmiya (al-) (party), 186, 192–93
Burhami, Yasir, 75, 106, 108, 110–12, 114, 116–17, 119, 122–23, 128, 141, 144, 160–62, 166, 183–85, 187–88, 191–201, 202–8, 228, 276n30

Christians/Copts, 10, 49, 61, 71, 102–3, 120, 165, 174–75, 178, 190–91, 194, 202–3, 206, 216–220, 245
Coalition of Support for New Muslims (organization), 219, 222

Darwish, Abu al-Wafa', 30, 37
Da'wat al-Haqq (organization), 155, 157
Dawud, Khalid, 86, 100, 177
Dijwi, Yusuf al-, 41, 46, 56–57
Dubaysi, Muhammad al-, 103, 139

El-Sisi, Abdel Fattah. *See* Sisi, Abdel Fattah El-

Fadila (al-) (party), 186, 233
Faraj, 'Abd al-Salam, 91, 103, 112, 271n164
Farid, Ahmad, 96–97, 106, 108, 110–12, 143, 164, 185, 229, 277n40
Fath Allah, 'Abd al-Sattar, 172, 210
Fiqi, Muhammad Hamid al-, 31, 36–37, 42, 45–47, 49–50, 52–59, 61–62, 117
Freedom and Justice (party), 186, 193
Furqan (al-) (institute), 122, 124, 160, 185, 189

Gamal al-Din, al-Miqdad, 215, 231–32, 234–35, 24
Ghazali, Abu Hamid al-, 8, 32, 51, 60, 71, 88
Ghazali, Muhammad al-, 94, 101, 168–69, 172
Ghazali, Zaynab al-, 87
Ghazi, Muhammad Jamil, 70, 85, 94, 266n28
Ghunaym, Wagdi, 86, 173
Ghuzlan, Mahmud, 95, 176–77

Habib, Kamal, 89–90, 187
Habib, Muhammad, 177, 268n75
Hadi al-Nabawi (al-) (journal), 48, 50–52, 58, 61, 68–70
Hakami al-, Hafiz, 75, 84, 122
Halawi, Hasan al-, 82, 90
Hammad, Yusri, 126, 189
Hanbal, Ahmad (Ibn), 8, 12, 48, 57, 252n13
Hanbalism, 6, 8–9, 11–13, 33–35, 40–43, 56, 63, 75, 101, 110, 165, 203
Haqq, Gad al-, 159–161, 167
Harbi, Khalid, 219, 221–22, 234
Harras, Muhammad Khalil, 53, 89, 113
Hashim, Yahya, 85, 88–89, 91

INDEX

Hassan, Muhammad, 151, 153, 157–58, 163–64, 175, 210, 212, 229
Hawali, Safar al-, 136, 143–44, 236
Hazimun (movement), 231–32, 235, 241
Higazi, Safwat, 170, 173–74, 210–11
Hilali, Taqi al-Din al-, 20, 37, 45
Hilmi, Mustafa, 71–72, 127–128, 173
Hudaybi, Hasan al-, 78, 87, 98
Hutayba, Ahmad, 106, 108, 110, 117, 120, 122, 185, 207
Huwayni, Abu Ishaq al-, 113, 149–150, 157–58, 164, 180, 229

Ibrahim, Muhammad Yusri, 136–137, 148, 185, 209–11
Iran, 60, 97, 116, 159, 162, 194, 203
'Isa, Muhammad Husayn, 175
Islamic Jihad (organization), 131–33, 140–42, 161
Islamic State (organization), 1, 240, 248
Israel, 65, 84, 93, 97, 162, 197, 221, 224, 227
Istiqama, al- (mosque), 44, 157
I'tisam, al- (journal), 68–69, 157
'Izzat, Ibrahim, 72–73, 94

Jama'at islamiyya (student organizations), 21, 65, 92–103, 106–7, 109, 111–12, 115–16, 144, 172–73
Jama'a Islamiyya (armed group), 102–4, 116, 124, 131–33, 140–42, 158–160, 186, 192, 210, 217, 231
Jam'iyya Shar'iyya, 14, 33, 42–44, 47, 68–70, 73, 79–81, 90, 92, 101, 126, 152, 155, 157, 208
Jawzi, Ibn al-, 12, 110, 257n37
Jaza'iri, Abu Bakr al-, 94–95, 112
Jazeera, Al, 169
jihadism, 1, 19, 21, 26, 76, 80, 85–91, 93, 103–4, 106–7, 114, 120, 131–134, 137, 139, 144, 158, 161–62, 186–87, 216, 218, 220, 222–23, 225, 239–40, 248–49
Jum'a, 'Ali, 212

Kathir (Ibn), 11–12, 38, 40, 48, 64, 74, 77, 82–83, 88, 171, 175, 244
Khalid, 'Amr, 148, 163, 170
Khatib, Muhibb al-Din al-, 40, 89

Khomeini, Ruhollah, 60, 116, 241
Kishk, 'Abd al-Hamid, 84, 148–49, 168
Kuwait, 55, 95, 115, 119, 126–27, 152

Madkhali, Rabi' al-, 139
Mahawalli, Ahmad al-, 72, 84, 94
Makhyun, Yunis, 203, 206
Manar, al- (journal and press), 34, 36–40, 45–46, 61
Maraghi, Mustafa al-, 58
Mashhur, Mustafa, 94, 98–100, 176
Maturidism, 3, 72, 215
Maududi, Abul A'la, 76–78, 86, 91–92, 95, 129
Mawlana, Ahmad, 219, 224
Ministry of Awqaf, 67, 82, 84, 117, 155–57, 161, 165, 167–68, 199, 204, 208, 211, 299n138
modernizing reformism, 7, 12, 32, 34, 38, 57–58, 69
Mongols, 9, 11, 91
Morsi, Mohamed, 22, 199–206, 208, 211–214, 216, 228, 234, 237–39
Mubarak, Hosni, 2, 27, 87, 128–29, 133–34, 140, 146–47, 155, 157, 161–62, 164–65, 169, 178–79, 180–81, 183–85, 189, 194, 201, 208, 211, 213, 216–18, 221, 224, 245–46
Muqaddim, Muhammad Isma'il al-, 86, 95–96, 106–117, 120, 128, 143, 180, 182–85, 188, 210, 229
Muslim Brotherhood (organization), 2, 16, 18–23, 26, 41, 49, 59–63, 66–69, 71–78, 80–81, 84, 86–90, 94–105, 106–7, 109, 111–12, 115–121, 123, 125–131, 134–136, 139, 141, 144, 148, 152, 154, 157–59, 161–179, 181–82, 185, 190, 192–94, 198–204, 206–213, 219, 221–223, 225–228, 230, 232, 234, 237–241, 244, 246–248, 253n51,
Mustafa, 'Alawi, 89
Mustafa, Hisham, 137, 144, 186
Mustafa, Shukri, 81–83, 268n86
Mu'tazilism, 8, 34, 64, 85, 215

Nada, Youssef, 177
Nasif, Muhammad, 53–54

INDEX

Nasser, Gamal Abdel, 65–71, 73, 75, 78–80, 84–86, 90, 92, 98, 100, 138, 154, 166, 168, 172, 174
Nour (party), 2, 4, 21–22, 108, 121, 124, 126, 180–181, 186–209, 211–213, 226–27, 229–230, 233–34, 246–47
Nur, Muhammad, 121, 189, 194–95
Nur al-Din, Safwat, 47–48, 70, 301n5

Ottoman Empire, 9–11, 33, 59, 68

Palestine, 88, 94, 96, 134, 162

Qanat al-Hikma (satellite TV channel), 163, 228
Qanat al-Nas (satellite TV channel), 148, 163–64, 173–74
Qaradawi, Yusuf al-, 95, 101, 168–69, 172, 176–78, 211
Qasimi, 'Abdallah al-, 46–47, 56–57, 63
Qatar, 55, 96, 152, 169
Qawsi, Usama al-, 83, 140
Qayyim al-Jawziyya, Ibn, 11–12, 34, 38, 40, 48, 50, 56, 65, 75, 77, 86, 91–92, 95, 109–110, 138, 149, 244
Qutb, Muhammad, 135–139, 143
Qutb, Sayyid, 19, 65–66, 75–78, 80–88, 90–92, 95–96, 98–99, 101–2, 104, 129–130, 135, 138, 143, 171, 177, 246
qutbiyyun (movement), 137–139, 142, 218, 223

Rabaa al-Adawiya (massacre), 206, 238–240
Raya, al- (party), 233–34
Religious Council for Rights and Reform (organization), 209–212
Rida, Rashid, 34–42, 45–46, 48, 52–53, 56, 59, 61, 72, 113
Rimali, Muhammad al-, 37, 47, 56

Sabiq, Sayyid, 75, 94, 149, 168–69
Sadat, Anwar, 28, 65, 79, 83–85, 91, 97–98, 102–3, 112, 116, 120, 131, 138, 155, 159, 184
Sahwa (Saudi movement), 115, 125, 135, 137, 140, 143–44, 151, 188, 208

Sa'id, Fawzi al-, 135, 157, 162, 218, 229
Salafi bookstore, 40–41, 45, 89
Salafi Call (organization), 4, 15, 21–22, 25, 27, 95–97, 103–5, 106–45, 146–48, 150–51, 154, 156–161, 164–166, 181–189, 191–213, 217, 219–220, 225–229, 231–32, 243, 245–47
Salafi Front (organization), 137, 186, 219, 222–24, 238, 241
Salafi Press, 40, 46, 68
Salafi School (organization), 103, 107, 109, 115, 117, 119–120
Salama, Hafiz, 84, 94, 103, 220, 222–23, 230
Salama, Muhammad Yusri, 188–89, 226
Samawi, 'Abdallah al-, 81–83, 95
Sarwi, Muhammad al-, 73–74
Sa'ud, 'Abd al-'Aziz Al, 13, 35, 39–40, 53, 257n45
Saudi Arabia, 1–2, 10–13, 15, 22, 24, 30–31, 33, 35–36, 39–41, 43–44, 46–49, 52–55, 63, 66–67, 69, 71–72, 76–77, 85, 91, 95–96, 103–104, 107–108, 111–115, 122, 125–26, 135–140, 142–44, 147, 150–55, 163, 172–74, 177–78, 204, 208, 210, 212, 225, 236, 243, 248
Sawi, Salah al-, 136–37
Sawiris, Naguib, 194, 217
Sawt al-Da'wa (journal), 122, 160
Shafiq, Ahmad, 201
Shahhat, 'Abd al-Mun'im al-, 187, 192, 199
Shakir, Ahmad, 45, 47–48, 53, 62, 68, 74
Shaltut, Mahmud, 41, 58, 69, 263n159
Sha'rawi, Muhammad Mitwalli al-, 94–95, 150, 167
Shatir, Khayrat al-, 170, 177, 199, 207, 210, 228
Shawkani, Muhammad al-, 12, 83, 91, 110
Shaykh, 'Abd al-Rahman bin Hasan (Al al-), 12, 33, 48
Shazli, 'Abd al-Majid al-, 138–39, 142–43, 218, 223
Shehata, Kamilia, 165, 218–220
Sahman, Sulayman (Ibn), 12, 39–40
Sirjani, Raghib al-, 173
Sirriyeh, Salih, 87–88, 90–91, 96

INDEX

Sisi, Abdel Fattah El-, 28, 205–6, 213, 247
6 April (movement), 218, 226, 230
Society for the Revival of Islamic Heritage, 55, 119, 126
Society of Muslims (organization, also called *al-takfir wa-l-hijra*), 81–82
State Security, 27, 120, 129, 136, 140, 157–160, 162–164, 221
Subki, Mahmud Khattab al-, 33, 42–45, 69, 79
Sufism, 2–4, 9, 19, 25, 30–32, 34, 36–37, 42–43, 50–52, 56–57, 59–63, 68–72, 77–80, 83, 87, 92, 95, 99, 101–2, 114, 117, 132, 139, 174, 178, 180, 248
Supreme Council of Armed Forces (SCAF), 205, 224–27, 230
Surur, Rifa'i, 85–86, 88–89, 103, 132, 138, 218–19, 222–23, 234, 302n30
Sururism, 135–139, 144, 185–86, 209
Syria, 35, 39–41, 212, 240

Tabligh (organization), 72–73, 79, 92, 94, 122, 155, 210
Tamarod (campaign), 204–5
Tammam, Husam, 24, 60, 72, 94, 98, 146, 164, 171, 176
Tantawi, Isma'il, 89–90
Tantawi, Muhammad, 161, 165, 177
Taymiyya, Ahmad Taqi al-Din (Ibn), 9–13, 34–35, 38, 40–41, 48, 50, 64–66, 71–72, 74–75, 77–80, 84, 89–92, 110–13, 118, 138, 141–42, 150, 171, 175–76, 188, 244, 247
Tayyib, Ahmad al-, 165, 203, 212, 248
Thabit, Ashraf, 160, 191, 197
Tilmisani, 'Umar al-, 172, 176, 273n193
Tullab al-Shari'a, 235
Tunisia, 173, 213, 246
Turkey, 188–89
Two Saints Church (bombing), 165, 183

'Umar, Nasir al-, 136–37
Umm al-Qura (university), 135, 137–38, 142–43, 172, 174
'Uqda, Hisham (Al), 134, 136–37, 160, 162, 186, 210, 288n73
'Uthaymin, Muhammad (Ibn), 111–12, 115, 136, 151

Wadi'i, Muqbil al-, 113, 139
Wafd (party), 58, 61, 63, 159, 170
Wahhabism, 11–13, 31, 33, 35–36, 39–40, 42, 46–47, 49–50, 52–54, 56–57, 63, 77, 96, 101, 135
Wakil, 'Abd al-Rahman al-, 51–52, 54–55, 62, 72
Watan, al- (party), 198, 204, 233

Ya'qub, Muhammad Husayn, 150, 153, 164, 229
Yemen, 12, 108, 113, 139

Za'farani, Khalid al-, 82
Za'farani, Ibrahim al-, 99–100, 112
Zarqa, Bassam al-, 114–115, 120, 189–90, 201, 204
Zawahiri, al-Ahmadi al-, 56
Zawahiri, Ayman al-, 89, 131, 133, 161, 222–23
Zawahiri, Muhammad al-, 223
Zayni, 'Abd al-Fattah, 90, 124–25

GPSR Authorized Representative: Easy Access System Europe, Mustamäe tee
50, 10621 Tallinn, Estonia, gpsr.requests@easproject.com

www.ingramcontent.com/pod-product-compliance
Lightning Source LLC
Jackson TN
JSHW020254140825
89344JS00007B/199